Contested Frontiers in Amazonia

STUDY AREA
*showing location in Brazilian
Amazonia*

⊙   National Capital
──   State Boundaries
─ · ─   International Boundaries

EMW 1991

CONTESTED FRONTIERS IN AMAZONIA

Marianne Schmink and
Charles H. Wood

COLUMBIA UNIVERSITY PRESS
NEW YORK

COLUMBIA UNIVERSITY PRESS
NEW YORK   OXFORD

Library of Congress Cataloging-in-Publication Data
Schmink, Marianne.
    Contested frontiers in Amazonia / Marianne Schmink and Charles H. Wood.
        p.   cm.
    Includes bibliographical references and index.
    ISBN 0-231-07660-6
    1. Man—Influence on nature—Amazon River Region. 2. Economic
development—Environmental aspects—Amazon River Region. 3. Land
settlement—Environmental aspects—Amazon River Region. 4. Frontier and
pioneer life—Amazon River Region. 5 Kayapó Indians—Land tenure. 6. Kayapó
Indians—Social conditions. 7. Pará (Brazil: State)—Social conditions. 8. Pará
(Brazil: State)—Economic conditions. I. Wood, Charles H. II. Title.
GF532.A4S36   1992
33.73'0981'1—dc20   91-44979

 ∞   CIP
Casebound editions of Columbia University Press
books are Smyth-sewn and printed on permanent
and durable acid-free paper

Printed in the United States of America
c   10   9   8   7   6   5   4   3   2   1

To Samantha

CONTENTS

MAPS

TABLES

GLOSSARY OF ACRONYMS

ABA	Associação Brasileira de Antropología Brazilian Anthropological Association
ACISO	Ação Cívico Social (Civic Social Action)
ACTUC	Associação Cultural de Tucumã (Cultural Association of Tucumã)
AEA	Associacão dos Empresários da Amazônia (Association of Amazonian Entrepreneurs)
AO	Autorizaçao de Ocupação (Land Occupation Authorization)
APGAM	Associação Profissional de Geólogos da Amazônia (Professional Association of Geologists of Amazonia)
ARENA	Aliança para Renovação Nacional (Alliance for National Renovation)
BASA	Banco da Amazônia (Amazon Bank)
BBC	British Broadcasting Corporation
BCB	Banco de Crédito da Borracha (Rubber Credit Bank)
CAG	Colonizadora Andrade Gutierrez (Andrade Gutierrez Colonization Company)
CAPEMI	Caixa de Pecúlio dos Militares (Military Pension Fund)
CCPY	Comissão para a Criação do Parque Yanomami (Commission for the Creation of the Yanomami Park)

INPS	Instituto Nacional de Previdência Social (National Institute for Social Welfare)
ISEA	Instituto Superior de Estudos de Amazônia (Institute for Advanced Amazon Studies)
ITERPA	Instituto de Terras do Pará (Pará State Land Institute)
IUM	Imposto Único sobre Minérios (Unitary Mineral Tax)
LANDSAT	U.S. Satellite Mapping Agency
LO	Licença de Ocupação (Land Occupation License)
MDB	Movimento Democrático Brasileiro (Brazilian Democratic Movement); also, Multilateral Development Bank
MEAF	Ministério Extraordinário de Assuntos Fundiários (Special Ministry for Land Affairs)
MEC	Ministério de Educação e Cultura (Ministry of Education and Culture)
MIRAD	Ministério da Reforma e do Desenvolvimento Agrário (Ministry of Agrarian Reform and Development)
MLAP	Movimento para a Libertação dos Presos do Araguaia (Movement for the Liberation of the Araguaia Prisoners)
MME	Ministério de Minas e Energia (Ministry of Mines and Energy)
OAB	Organização dos Advogados do Brasil (Brazilian Lawyers Organization)
PC do B	Partido Comunista do Brasil (Communist Party of Brasil)
PDA	Plano de Desenvolvimiento da Amazônia (Amazon Development Plan)
PDS	Partido Democrático Social (Social Democratic Party)
PDT	Partido Democrático dos Trabalhadores (Democratic Workers' Party)
PIN	Programa de Integração Nacional (National Integration Program)

PMACI	Projeto de Proteção do Meio Ambiente e das Comunidades Indígenas (Environment and Indigenous Communities Protection Project)
PMDB	Partido do Movimento Democrático Brasileiro (Brazilian Democratic Movement Party)
PNRA	Plano Nacional de Reforma Agrária (National Agrarian Reform Plan)
PNPF	Programa Nacional de Política Fundiária (National Program for Land Policy)
POLAMAZONIA	Programa de Polos Agropecuários e Agrominerais da Amazônia (Program of Agricultural and Mineral Poles in the Amazon)
POLONOROESTE	Northwest Brazil Integrated Development Program
PROMIX	Produtora de Minérios Xingu (Xingu Mineral Producers)
PT	Partido dos Trabalhadores (Workers' Party)
PTB	Partido Trabalhista Brasileira (Brazilian Workers' Party)
RADAMBRASIL	National Radar Mapping Program
RDC	Rubber Development Corporation
SAE	Secretaria para Assuntos Estratégicos (Secretariat for Strategic Affairs)
SAGRI	Secretaria de Agricultura (State Secretariat of Agriculture)
SEMA	Secretaria Especial do Meio Ambiente (Special Secretariat for the Environment)
SEPLAN	Secretaria de Planejamento (Planning Secretariat)
SESP	Serviço Especial de Saúde Pública (Special Public Health Service)
SNI	Serviço Nacional de Informação (National Intelligence Service)
SPI	Serviço de Proteção aos Índios (Indian Protection Service)

SPVEA	Superintendência do Plano de Valorização Econômica da Amazônia (Superintendency for the Amazon Economic Valorization Plan)
SUCAM	Superintendência do Combate da Malária (Superintendency to Combat Malaria)
SUDAM	Superintendência de Desenvolvimento da Amazônia (Superintendency for Development of Amazonia)
SUDENE	Superintendência de Desenvolvimento do Nordeste (Superintendency for Development of the Northeast)
UDR	União Democrático Rural (Rural Democratic Union)
UNI	União das Nações Indígenas (Union of Indigenous Nations)

GLOSSARY OF PORTUGUESE TERMS

abertura	political liberalization
aforamento (perpétuo)	lease from the state for forest extraction
aldeia, aldeiamento	mission settlement for Indians
alimentador	miner who operates mechanical crushers
alqueire	land measure (approximately five hectares)
alvará de pesquisa	mineral research permit
amontoeira	pile of discarded material at Serra Pelada mining site
apontador	record keeper
apuração	purification
apurado	purified
arrecadação	collection of fees or taxes
aviador	creditor/supplier in *aviamento* system
aviado	worker in *aviamento* system
aviamento	supply and credit system for extractive activities
balseiro	owner of mining dredge
bamburrado	miner who has struck it rich
barracão	trading post
barreira	barrier
batedor	miner who manipulates the *bateia* to purify gold
bateia	pan for washing ore-bearing sand or gravel

blefado	a bankrupt miner
Cabanagem	Nineteenth-century popular revolt in Pará
cabano	rebel involved in the Cabanagem
cabeça de caixa	miner who controls the flow of ore thorugh the sluice box
caboclo	Amazonian peasant of mixed ethnic descent
cachaça	cane liquor
capanga	henchman
capitalista	investor in Serra Pelada mining site
cascalho	sand or gravel bearing valuable minerals
castanhal (plural: *castanhais*)	Brazil nut grove
castanheira	Brazil nut tree (*Bertoletti excelsa*)
castanheiro	Brazil nut collector
caucho	rubber from *Castilla ulei* tree
cavador	digger; miner who digs a work pit
comissário volante	river trader
controlador	miner who operates sluice box
coronel do barracão	rubber baron
corrutela	settlement alongside airstrip in jungle mining areas
cuia	small bowl or gourd used for panning gold
despescagem	cleaning of machinery and collection of gold
diarista	day worker
discriminatória branca	land assessment without survey of occupants
dono da pista	builder of airstirp in mining area
dono de seringal	owner or leaseholder of rubber tapping area
dono do garimpo	owner of mining claim
embarcador	miner who guides water through sluice box
empate	nonviolent protest against forest clearing

empreitada	contract for temporary labor
empreiteiro	temporary labor contractor
estrada de seringa	rubber trail
explorador	woodsman
fiscal	inspector
fofoca	rumor or gossip, referring to news of gold strikes
foreiro	leaseholder of *aforamento*
formigas	ants; miners who carry bags of dirt at Serra Pelada mining site
fornecedor	supplier in *aviamento* or *garimpo* system
gaiola	small steam-powered boat
garimpagem	small-scale surface mining
garimpeiro-entrepreneur	upwardly-mobile mining claim owner
garimpeiro	small-scale surface miner
garimpo	small-scale surface mining site
gateiro	hunter of large wild cats
gato	slang for *empreiteiro*
gleba	block of state or federal land
grilagem	land grabbing
grileiro	fraudulent land speculator
guarita	border guard gate station
indústria da posse	land claims resale business
jaborandi	*Pilocarpus jaborandi*, a medicinal plant whose leaves are extracted for glaucoma treatment
jagunço	henchman
jangada	log raft
jateiro	miner who handles hydraulic hose
latifúndio	large landholding
limpar a terra	to clear the land of occupants
lingua geral	*lingua franca* introduced in Amazonia by Jesuits
machadinho	rubber tapper
maracajá	small wild cat, *Felis pardalis*
mariscador	hunter

maroqueiro	miner who feeds rocks and gravel into a hydraulic suction tube
mateiro	woodsman
meia-praça	share-worker in small-scale mining; also the relationship between share-worker and supplier
melexete	slippery mud at hydraulic mining sites
município	municipality
paleador	miner who fills bags of ore at Serra Pelada mining site
peão	peon; worker
pistoleiro	gunslinger; also, miner who handles hydraulic hose
plano de lavra	mining production plan
porcentista	percentage worker in a mining area
pornochanchada	soft-porn movie
posse	de facto land rights
posseiro	homesteader with de facto land rights
puxada	a day's washing of gold in the sluice box
rádio peão	the "grapevine"; informal communication network
raleiro	miner who removes rocks from the sieve of the sluice box
rapadura	block of brown sugar
recorte	subdivision of land for distribution
regatão	river trader
reque	bonus payment in small-scale mining system
requerimento	formal land petition
seringa	rubber from *Hevea brasiliensis* tree
seringueiro	rubber tapper
tapuio	deculturated native Amazonian
terra firme	upland
terra roxa	rich red soil
turma	work crew

PREFACE

This book is the result of a fifteen-year longitudinal study that began in 1976. It is the joint product of an anthropologist and a sociologist-demographer who drew on the theory and methods of their respective disciplines to document and interpret the process of frontier change in one region of the Brazilian Amazon.

The story told in this volume is about an unlikely cast of characters who in the short span of a decade or two set in motion a sequence of events that forever changed the social and physical landscape of Amazonia. Leading figures in the drama included peasants, ranchers, loggers, Indians, and gold miners. They were joined in one fashion or another by businessmen and politicians, bureaucrats and planners as well as by soldiers, judges, and priests. By virtue of their greater economic, political, and ideological power, certain groups, such as ranchers and large-scale investors, usually came out ahead in the intense and often violent competition for land, gold, and timber that followed the construction of new roads into Amazonia.

Yet, as it turned out, frontier change in Brazil was not a relentless chronicle of the powerful prevailing over the weak. There were also numerous and significant instances when peasants defended their land against ranchers and speculators, when Indians prodded lethargic bureaucracies to recognize their territories, and when miners fended off the companies that tried to take possession of the gold fields the miners had discovered. Marshaling their respective sources of economic, political, and ideological power and drawing on alliances with other interests both inside and outside of the country, each group devised its own means to combat the expropriation, displacement, and violence wrought by the massive development projects and by the incursion of private capital, profiteers, and land speculators. Over time the experience gained in the art of resistance led these groups to redefine their collective self-concept and to adopt new and different rationales to legitimate their claims to valued resources. The result was the emergence of new political actors on the regional political stage and a reshaping of the terms and premises of the national debate over the fate of the Amazon.

Our analysis of these changes was predicated on the idea that the phenomena we observed and documented in the field—for example, deforestation, land use and settlement patterns, the rise and decline of different economic activities—were the net outcomes of the contest for resources among social groups capable of mobilizing varying degrees of power. The perspective we endorsed further recognized that the initiatives taken by the participants in a given conflict as well as the power hierarchies that prevailed were heavily contingent upon the changing alignment of influencing factors. Many of these factors operated within economic and political spheres far afield from the site of the contest in question. National and international factors thus comprised a matrix of shaping influences that propelled the story of frontier change in different and unexpected directions at decisive moments in the plot.

This book is, first and foremost, a blow-by-blow account of events in the southern region of the state of Pará and of the policy decisions made in Belém and Brasília that promoted them. If nothing else, we hope that the factual record alone will be of value to future researchers who pick up the story where this volume leaves off.

Second, this book is a statement about the nature of history and the problems of writing it. At every turn in the analysis we faced the challenge of linking events we witnessed in the field to the economic, political, and ideological trends simultaneously underway in regional, national, and global arenas. Similarly, at every point in the text we confronted the inevitable tension between a strict chronology on the one hand and the need to sort our observations into thematic categories on the other. If the former appealed to the ethnographer's predilection for rich detail, the latter played on the theorist's penchant for generalization. It is our hope that the compromise we struck between the two strategies—achieved after lengthy, often impassioned debates between us—yields a more effective analysis than either alone.

The third aim of this volume is a plea for a broader and more nuanced vision of Amazonia than that which characterizes the contemporary policy and academic debate. As the recent spate of books on Amazonia attests, the complexity of what happened in this vast region of the world and the urgency many people feel to do *something* about it invite hyperbole, oversimplification, and time-bound generalizations. If we too have committed these errors, we sought to minimize them by resting our case not on a priori generalizations but rather on the details of this astonishing saga. We do so on the assumption that no better tactic serves the cause of in-depth understanding than does the illustration of general principles by well-chosen particulars. Ridden with subplots and implausible turns and lacking a happy ending, it is an inelegant tale that we set out to tell in the pages that follow. But then the very complexity of the story captures the reality of Amazonia far better than any abstraction can.

ACKNOWLEDGMENTS

In 1984 we approached a modest house on a back street of São Felix do Xingu to interview the people who lived there. It was the third household survey our various field work teams had carried out in the small town since 1978. But going to each new house, and carrying out the hour-long interview about their lives, work, and eating habits didn't seem to get any easier. Gratefully, we accepted the invitation to duck inside the front door to escape the sun. Once inside, we explained that we were studying how the lives of people in São Felix had changed during the past few years. We requested their permission to ask a few questions and mentioned that they might remember us from past years. After a pause, an elderly woman seated on a stool responded that she did, indeed, remember us coming to her house a few years before. "You said you would ask just a few questions", she teased with a smile, "but you went on forever." We explained that this was the last time we would impose on their patience. With that promise, the woman consented to be interviewed.

After eleven years of research and another five years of analysis and writing, a study of this magnitude is bound to try the patience of countless people, many more than we can possibly thank in these few pages. We are grateful to the townspeople of São Felix do Xingu, like that woman, who graciously accepted our intrusions from year to year. We can only hope that, in return, our motley research teams provided some diversion from the routine of a small town.

We are grateful to the municipality of São Felix do Xingu for providing us with access to housing in public buildings during our fieldwork in 1978, 1981, and 1984, and we wish to thank prefects Raimundo Pinto de Mesquita and Filomeno de Souza Reis for extending the city's hospitality to us. Luís Otávio Montenegro Jorge was also extremely helpful to us during all our visits to São Felix. Local authorities, church people, and union representatives in Tucumã, Ourilândia, Agua Azul, Xinguara, Rio Maria, Redenção, Conceição do Araguaia, Marabá, and Itupiranga received us time and again and provided us with information and assistance in many forms. José Candido dos Santos in Ourilândia was especially generous with his time. In Tucumã, Apolo Gazel, Suely, and Bel provided a home away from home and help with every aspect of our work. Personnel of the Construtora Andrade Gutierrez not only consented to many interviews but also provided us with invaluable support with transportation, including vehicles and space on their aircraft. We are especially indebted to Marília Andrade for her unfailing friendship and assistance.

During our years of research we talked with many people from governmental and nongovernmental agencies in São Paulo, Rio de Janeiro, Belo Horizonte, Brasília, Belém, and in southern Pará. We can only acknowledge the institutions whose personnel opened their doors to us: Associação Brasileira de Reforma Agrária (ABRA); Associação dos Empresários da Amazônia (AEA); Câmara dos Deputados; Centro Ecuménico de Documentação e Informação (CEDI); Comissão Pastoral da Terra (CPT); Conselho Nacional de Pesquisa (CNPq); CONTERPA construction company; Departamento de Estradas e Rodagem (DER); Departamento Nacional de Pesquisa Mineral (DNPM); DOCEGEO, of the Companhia Vale do Rio Doce (CVRD); Empresa de Assistência Técnica Rural (EMATER); Empresa Brasileira de Pesquisa Agropecuária (EMBRAPA); Fundação Nacional do Índio (FUNAI); Grupo Executivo de Terras do Araguaia-Tocantins (GETAT); Instituto Brasileiro de Desenvolvimento Florestal (IBDF); Instituto de Desenvolvimento Econômico e Social do Pará (IDESP); Instituto Nacional de Colonização e Reforma Agrária (INCRA); Instituto de Pesquisa Econômica e Administrativa (IPEA); Instituto de Terras do Pará (ITERPA); Mamoré mining company; Mineração Taboca; Ministério da Agricultura; Ministério do Interior; Ministério da Reforma Agrária (MIRAD); Organization of American States (OAS); Programa de Proteção ao Meio-Ambiente e às Comunidades Indígenas (PMACI); PROMIX mining company; Receita Federal; Secretaria de Agricultura (SAGRI); Secretaria de Planejamento (SEPLAN); and Superintendência do Desenvolvimento da Amazônia (SUDAM). Some individuals gave us help year after year, such as Ricardo Rezende and Emmanuel Wambergue of CPT, Luís Antônio Bandeira of DOCEGEO, and Violeta Loureiro of IDESP.

SUDAM provided financial support for the 1975–1977 research, which was carried out by the Centro de Desenvolvimento e Planejamento Regional (CEDEPLAR) of the Federal University of Minas Gerais (UFMG). At the time, Wood was a Visiting Professor and Schmink was a Research Associate with CEDEPLAR. We have been privileged to work closely with CEDEPLAR throughout the research that led to this book. Fellow members of the field research team in 1976 included José Alberto Magno de Carvalho, José Henriques Maia Filho, Morvan de Mello Moreira, Antônio Carlos Casulari Rôxo de Motta, Fernando Antônio Oliva Perpétuo, Malory Pompermayer, Maria do Carmo Fonseca do Vale, and Teresa Simões of SUDAM. We are especially grateful to these individuals and to members of subsequent field research teams for their company and intellectual stimulation and for sharing the information and analysis gathered during our travels.

During 1978 and subsequent years we were fortunate to be accepted as Research Associates with the Núcleo de Altos Estudos Amazônicos (NAEA) of the Federal University of Pará (UFPa). NAEA's sponsorship was invaluable in helping to open doors and in providing an opportunity to dialogue about our research with colleagues in the Amazon region. Field research team members in 1978 included Raquel Lopes and Fernando Perpétuo. In 1981 fellow fieldworkers included John Butler, Apolo Gazel, Carmen Macedo, Cid Moreira, Sílvia Pinheiro, Diana Sawyer, and Donald Sawyer. Our fieldwork companions in 1984 were Benedito Caravalho and Christine Horak.

The 1978 and 1981 field research was financed by grants to CEDEPLAR from the International Development Research Centre (IDRC). With support from CEDEPLAR and a grant from the Tinker Foundation, Schmink was able to return to the field in 1980 for a brief visit in the company of Fernando Perpétuo. Fieldwork in 1983, 1984, and 1987 was supported by the University of Florida through the Division of Sponsored Research and the Amazon Research and Training Program. A final return trip to the region in 1989 was made possible by Christopher Uhl's invitation to Schmink to travel as a consultant with his Projeto Madeira team.

Over the years many colleagues provided advice and consultation about our ongoing research. Charles Wagley's extraordinary scholarship and humanism were a source of constant inspiration. Diana and Donald Sawyer were close advisers and coworkers. Lúcio Flávio Pinto befriended us early on, provided invaluable information and advice, and encouraged us to see the project through to its completion. Leslie Lieberman provided advice on nutritional research, and John Dixon helped with the computer work. Conversations with Neide Esterci, Jean Hébette, Otávio Ianni, José de Souza Martins, Octávio Velho, and Alfredo Wagner were often as useful as reading their own valuable writings on topics related to our research. Many people also read various versions of this book: Harley Browning, Stephen Bunker, John Butler, Joe Foweraker, Richard Graham, Peggy Lovell, Elizabeth Lowe, Terry McCoy, Steven McCracken, Anthony Oliver-Smith, Darrell Posey, Pamela Richards, Samuel Sá, Steven Sanderson, and Verena Stolcke. We are grateful for their generosity in sharing their ideas and criticisms and retain responsibility for the analysis as it stands.

Gay Biery-Hamilton and Margarita Gandía provided competent assistance in putting together the final manuscript. We are grateful to the World Bank for permission to use Map 5, a figure that originally appeared in a publication authored by Dennis Mahar. We especially appreciate the care taken by E. Michael Whittington in producing the maps for the book.

Much of the book was written in Cedar Key, Florida during leave periods, several summers, and countless weekends. We are grateful to the human and wildlife inhabitants of that seaside village for providing the peace of mind required to finish this book.

Contested Frontiers in Amazonia

ONE

Contested Frontiers in
Amazonia: Introduction

In contrast to the cheerless mood of today's headlines, the early 1970s was a time of effusive optimism in the Brazilian Amazon. The military regime, then in power for nearly a decade, set out to populate the region and exploit its natural resources through a series of widely publicized development schemes. The federal government promoted credit and tax incentives to attract private capital to the region and financed the construction of the Transamazon highway—an unpaved road that extended some five thousand kilometers from Maranhão and Pará in the east across the uncharted Amazon basin to the westernmost state of Acre on the border with Bolivia. The cornerstone of the effort to modernize Amazonia was the National Integration Plan that called for the colonization of small farmers on one-hundred hectare plots along both sides of the highway. Like the Homestead Act in the United States a century before, the settlement project sought to create a prosperous small-farmer class by freely distributing agricultural land in sparsely populated territories. Colonists were drawn from the ranks of poor farmers and from the rural landless in the overpopulated northeastern region of the country.[1] According to the official propaganda of the day, the Transamazon would connect "people with no land to a land with no people."

The initial euphoria soon gave way to a more sober appreciation of the difficulties entailed in agricultural projects in lowland tropical areas. Colonists settled by the Institute of Colonization and Agrarian Reform (INCRA) in Marabá, Altamira, and Itaituba faced numerous problems, especially getting crops to market. The colonization projects nonetheless continued to attract migrants from all parts of Brazil who arrived in Pará in numbers that far exceeded INCRA's capacity to absorb in the planned communities. With few alternatives available, small farmers staked out whatever land was accessible, laboring under the mistaken assumption that state lands not being cultivated were theirs for the taking.

The north-south road (PA-150) that connected the towns of Marabá and Conceição do Araguaia to the Transamazon and the Belém-Brasília highways provided a corridor through which settlers entered and spontaneously occupied small plots of land in southern Pará. In the meantime, well-financed investors, mostly from central and southern Brazil, took advantage of profitable tax and credit programs offered through SUDAM (Superintendency for the Development of the Amazon).[2] They converted huge tracts of land to pasture or bought land to hold in investment portfolios as a hedge against future inflation. Violence became commonplace when cattle ranchers, land grabbers, and peasant farmers competed for control of the newly accessible territories. Newcomers clashed among themselves and with natives of the region who resolved to defend their way of life against the onslaught. The furious confrontations that ensued claimed the lives of thousands of people and bestowed on Pará its unfortunate notoriety as the "Wild West" of Amazonia.[3]

By the middle of the 1970s many of the small farmers who informally claimed untitled land (called *posseiros*) had been driven off the plots they had cleared. The dispossessed faced a difficult and uncertain future. Many moved on down the road. Others ventured farther back into the bush, only to fall victim again to expropriation. Thousands of families drifted from one work site to another, temporarily employed by labor recruiters

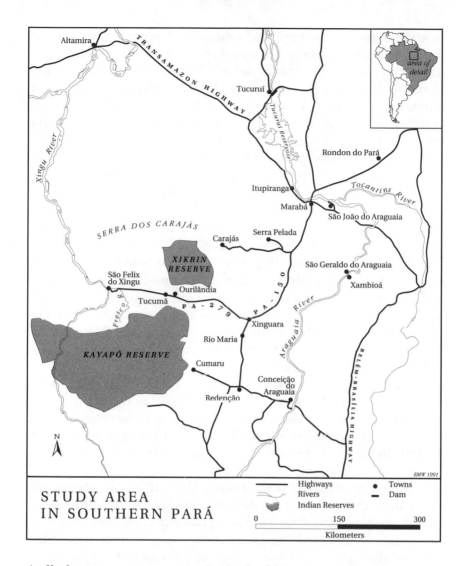

Altamira

TRANSAMAZON HIGHWAY

Tucuruí

Xingu River

Tucuruí Reservoir

Rondon do Pará

Itupiranga

Tocantins River

Marabá

São João do Araguaia

SERRA DOS CARAJÁS

Carajás

Serra Pelada

XIKRIN
RESERVE

São Geraldo do Araguaia

São Felix
do Xingu

Ourilândia

Xambioá

Fresco R.

Tucumã

PA-279

PA-150

Araguaia River

Xinguara

KAYAPÓ RESERVE

Rio Maria

Cumaru

Conceição
do
Araguaia

Redenção

BELÉM-BRASÍLIA HIGHWAY

N

EMW 1991

STUDY AREA
IN SOUTHERN PARÁ

— Highways   ● Towns
Rivers   — Dam
Indian Reserves

0   150   300
Kilometers

(called *gatos* or *empreiteiros*) who had been contracted by ranchers to clear land for pasture during the dry season. Those with
enough money to do so packed their belongings and went back
to their home states. Many more lost their land but were too poor
to return. They sought refuge in the new villages that sprang up
along the roads or in the shantytowns on the outskirts of established cities like Marabá. In as little as two or three years places
that once held only a handful of people suddenly exploded into
makeshift towns of fifteen to twenty thousand. Most urban centers

Introduction

lacked sanitation, medical, and educational services and offered displaced peasants and new migrants neither regular employment nor the means to support themselves.[4] The growing apprehension in the mid-1970s was captured in a caustic remark made by an attendant working at a gas station located along the first few kilometers of the crimson, dust-choked Transamazon highway. "You are embarking on the Great Transamargura ('Transbitterness'),'' he said as he refueled our vehicle. "It's a poor man's road. It links nothing but poverty in the Northeast to misery in Amazonia."

The deadly conflict between ranchers and peasant farmers in southern Pará was often cast in Cold War terms by military authorities. In the early 1970s the armed forces confronted and eventually defeated a small but well-organized leftist guerrilla group. Using Vietnam-style tactics, the Brazilian army units swept through the countryside rounding up anyone found in the area, including peasant farmers, many of whom had only the vaguest notion of what was happening to them.[5] As a consequence of the "Araguaia War," the federal authorities classified the Marabá area as a national security zone. The new designation meant a heavy military presence and gave the federal government the right to appoint people to local political posts. In the countryside, individuals who helped peasants resist expropriation by cattle ranchers were regarded by the military and police authorities as communist instigators. Community leaders, including a number of activists in the Catholic church, were jailed for "subversive" behavior.

By equating criticism with treason, the military's national security doctrine made it both difficult and dangerous to find fault with the way colonization was taking place in Amazonia. Military authorities interpreted the international outcry over deforestation and the threat to Indian groups as an imperialist plot. They saw evidence of communist infiltration in the violent confrontations between ranchers and peasants. In this way legitimate ecological and social concerns as well as localized struggles between different groups were elevated to an importance on a par with the international competition between North and South and between East and West. It was a posture that permitted the military and the police to act with impunity in frontier areas.[6]

The heavy influx of population and the front-page publicity

given to the violent confrontations between ranchers and peasants served to undermine support for the INCRA program at a time when the colonization program came under growing criticism for being expensive and failing to live up to its objectives. In the tradition of blaming the victim, the colonists themselves were faulted for their presumed lack of managerial skills even though many of the problems they confronted were hardly of their own making.[7] Business interests seized the opportunity to wage a campaign in support of the view that a more "rational" and less "predatory" process of occupation could be achieved by backing the private sector.[8] By the mid-1970s pressure from the business lobby had succeeded. Public colonization, the only relatively safe haven for the small farmer, was virtually abandoned in favor of privately owned and operated colonization schemes. Large-scale, government-administered colonization projects continued only in the northwestern state of Rondônia, where they suffered their own difficulties.

Development policies for the Amazon turned from an initial emphasis on absorbing excess population in other regions of Brazil to favoring the expansion of large-scale capitalist ventures. Official documents published after 1974 called on the government to halt the influx of peasant migrants and to adopt a different strategy by which to settle the region. The new approach was reflected in the second National Development Plan, which set forth a regional agenda called POLAMAZONIA. As the acronym implied, the objective was to create growth poles by redirecting public and private investment into areas with economic potential: cattle raising and large-scale farming and mining operations.

POLAMAZONIA emphasized a set of familiar assumptions. Since the 1950s politicians and planners in Brazil had been thoroughly wedded to the "developmentalist" paradigm. This perspective saw capital accumulation, foreign investment, and big economic projects as a means of achieving high rates of growth. Embedded in such a view was a preference for large, capital-intensive investments rather than for small, labor-oriented projects. The approach invoked a firm belief in advanced technology as a means to promote the general welfare and to resolve external difficulties associated with economic growth, such as environmental degradation or the displacement of people.[9] In retrospect, official Amazonian policy in the early 1970s, with its emphasis on small farmers, was clearly out of step with the main direction of this development policy. The change in priorities in the mid-1970s away from the National Integration Plan's concern for the mass of poor people in the Northeast did not represent a new agenda so much as a return to the long-standing priority given to private capital and to massive development schemes.

Implicit in the developmentalist paradigm were a host of negative conclusions: Small producers were regarded as inefficient and peasants as culturally retrograde. Extractive activities practiced by Indians and native Amazonians were seen as backward traits of an undesirable form of existence, and traditional knowledge systems were believed to be worthless. The tropical forest was considered as having little economic or biological worth beyond the monetary value of a limited number of hardwoods. And communal property rights, typical of Indian and some peasant communities, were seen as antithetical to private property, an institution deemed essential to the expansion of a modern, capitalist economy.[10]

Given the hegemony of the developmentalist worldview within the authoritarian regime, it was hardly surprising that attempts to protect the environment, to preserve the boundaries of Indian lands, or to defend the rights of small farmers—indeed, any idea that ran counter to development or to the interests of the major players in Amazonia—were notions that, at best, received little attention in the halls of political power and within the administrative agencies of the state. At worst, such views were labeled "subversive," and their proponents silenced by murder, imprisonment, and torture.[11]

Nowhere was the impact of the policy shift more keenly felt than in southern Pará. In 1976 INCRA increased the maximum size of land purchases. A private colonization company purchased an immense area of fertile soils near São Felix do Xingu that had been earmarked for a public settlement project. And the federal government pushed ahead with major construction projects, such as the Tucuruí hydroelectric dam along the Tocantins River and the huge iron ore mining operation in the Serra dos Carajás.

Violent confrontations between the various social groups on the frontier persisted and multiplied. In 1980 the federal government created GETAT (Executive Group for the Araguaia-Tocantins Lands), a powerful agency that answered directly to the National Security Council. Armed with the power to cut through red tape, GETAT's primary objective was to defuse tension by resolving the most threatening cases of land conflict. The agency relied on streamlined bureaucratic authority to accomplish its purpose via a kind of "crisis colonization" program that provided titled land to migrants in areas where land disputes threatened to erupt into a major conflagration. Although the interventions were designed to cultivate political support, more often than not GETAT's activities undermined rather than strengthened the military regime's already declining political legitimacy.

In the 1980s the military faced a host of new challenges, including the discovery of rich deposits of gold in southern Pará. The gold rush set in motion a new wave of migrants to Amazonia and thoroughly transformed the regional economy. Once a promising claim was discovered, it was only a matter of days before thousands of people converged on the site. Landless workers turned to mining activities as a source of livelihood. Investors who supplied the food and equipment to the mining camps reaped handsome profits, which they invested in other enterprises. The prospecting and sale of gold and other valued metals soon became the financial mainstay of towns and cities across southern Pará.[12]

The spread of small-scale mining led to new forms of violence. Miners confronted Kayapó Indians over access to reservation lands and competed with mining companies that held rights to gold deposits on state lands. Unlike in the confrontation between peasants and ranchers, even the most powerful mining companies generally found themselves on the losing end of battles with *garimpeiros*, whose growing political and economic power added a formidable new voice on the frontier. In 1980 tens of thousands of miners invaded an area controlled by the powerful state-controlled Vale do Rio Doce company and refused to abandon the rich deposit known as Serra Pelada. Perceiving an opportunity to cultivate the miners as a local political constituency, the federal government decided against the company's claim and allowed the *garimpeiros* to stay on under the supervision of military authorities. But the strategy was to no avail. Following a dramatic showdown between miners and the Brazilian army in 1984, the *gar-*

impeiros abandoned their commitment to the regime and took Serra Pelada into their own hands.

By the mid-1980s the military's plan to develop and control the Amazon region was in disarray. In the countryside, claims to land and minerals by large investors were effectively contested by peasants, miners, Indians, and rubber tappers. Successive interventions on the part of the military to resolve these disputes only exacerbated the very tensions they were intended to defuse. Indeed, it was partly as a consequence of the militarization of Amazonia that sporadic incidents grew into well-organized efforts by previously "invisible" populations to resist threats to their livelihood. In local and state elections people cast their votes for opposition candidates. And in Brasília—once the political climate leading to the New Republic allowed open debate—activists and politicians mounted a vocal campaign condemning the environmental and social consequences of the regime's development policies.

The criticism of Amazonian development that began in Brazil in the late 1970s soon dovetailed with the growing worldwide concern about deforestation and its effects on native peoples and global climate change. Sharing a new vocabulary and a similar set of goals, conservation and environmental activists in Brazil and in developed countries participated in a new discourse that lent both visibility and legitimacy to the alternatives proposed by small producers in the Amazon. By the end of the 1980s the direct links established with international lobbyists and the alliances forged with opposition political parties within the country empowered local groups with resources and credibility that they had never before enjoyed. These changes altered the character of the confrontations on the frontier and introduced new ideas into the debate over Amazonian development policy.

If the battles fought in the late 1960s and throughout most of the 1970s were almost always one-sided in favor of large-scale investors who benefited most from the regional development policies, the balance of political power began to shift by the end of the decade. In the course of defending themselves, rubber tappers, miners, small farmers, Indians, and *caboclos* of mixed descent became better organized and learned to protect their interests more effectively against the threats posed by ranchers, mining companies, land speculators, and bureaucrats. The odds remained against them; yet they showed with greater frequency that they could win major contests against their adversaries. Victories in Amazonia were facilitated by the political opening in Brazil and by the declining power of the military regime. In some instances the outcome of local conflicts affected economic and political trends on the national level, thus changing the conditions under which subsequent regional contests took place.

The case of Chico Mendes, a rubber tapper in the remote state of Acre, illustrates this new feature of the resistance in Amazonia. Chico, who began his career on the rubber trails at age 9 and learned to read only at age 24, led a successful attempt to prevent the deforestation that threatened the livelihood of rubber gatherers who had lived in the jungle for generations. From 1985, when he was the leading figure in the first national meeting of the rubber tappers union, until his murder at age 44 at the hands of cattle ranchers, his importance and visibility soared. By the time of his death Chico had expressed his views before the World Bank, the Inter-American Development Bank, United States legislators, and other world leaders. His efforts were recognized by awards from the United Nations and the Better World Society and by posthumous honors granted by numerous organizations in the United States and Europe. That a backwoodsman such as Mendes could emerge as an international figure capable of forcing both the Brazilian government and international lending agencies to modify their plans for Amazonian development was a phenomenon that no one, including us, had anticipated.

By 1990 the terms of the Amazonian debate had shifted. The environmental and human rights consequences of the development policy became the target of headline stories in Brazil and across the world. The expansion of cattle ranching in the Amazon, once the mainstay of the modernization program, was condemned in favor of extractive activities that would leave the forest intact. Other questions arose about the equity and the sustainability of the developmentalist model, prompting a new appreciation of traditional Amazonia. Analysts reassessed the economic value of lesser-known forest products, which found their way into specialty items marketed in the United States and Europe. Indigenous cultures came to be viewed as repositories of practical knowledge, and the management systems of Indians and peasants, especially those based on forest extraction, were treated as credible alternatives in the search for new policy directions. Innovative proposals included forms of collective property systems called "reserves." Like many other initiatives proposed by peasants, rubber tappers, and Indian groups, the notion of extractive reserves arose not from a planning office or from the handiwork of a particular individual but from more than a decade of struggle in a changing political environment.

Conceptualizing Frontier Change

The contemporary movement of people into Amazonia is the most recent, and presumably the last, of three more or less distinct phases of frontier expansion that took place in Brazil after World War II.[13] The first occurred in Paraná and involved the southward spread of coffee that began in the 1940s and continued through the mid-1960s.[14] The second frontier movement took place in Goiás and Mato Grosso in the 1950s and 1960s when the rise in the internal demand for beef led to the expansion of cattle ranches into the vast plains of western Brazil. Moving the country's capital inland from Rio de Janeiro provided further stimulus to the westward movement of population. So did the construction of new roads, the most important of which was the paved link between Brasília and Belém, capital of the northern state of Pará.[15] The Belém-Brasília highway, completed in the 1960s, made new lands accessible to wealthy investors and reduced transportation costs.

The occupation of new agricultural lands manifested the general tendency inherent in growth-oriented capitalism to absorb excess capital and labor through geographical displacement.[16] In Brazil, the spatial displacement that occurred during the three periods of frontier expansion was an integral feature of the far-reaching transformations that took place in the country in the postwar period.[17] Brazil's capital-intensive and uneven style of industrial growth meant that far too few jobs were created in the urban and rural economies.[18] The result was a surplus population that migrated to frontier areas in search of agricultural plots to cultivate. At the same time, entrepreneurs channeled surplus capital to the countryside in search of productive investments and to purchase cheap land as a hedge against future inflation. As a consequence, an increase in agricultural production in Brazil, as in many other countries in Latin America, largely occurred as a result of the expansion into new lands rather than because of yield increases. Between 1950–54 and 1970–74, horizontal expansion alone explained 89 percent of the growth in grain production in Brazil.[19]

In Paraná and Goiás-Mato Grosso, the expansion of agrarian capitalism occurred at the expense of pioneer smallholders. The process occurred in stages.[20] When markets for land and labor penetrated into areas previously isolated from the national economy and the political system, settlers and long-time residents were dispossessed, and land became concentrated in large holdings. Small farmers either found employment as wage earners or moved on to the next frontier.[21] Over time, the tendency (although not fully realized) was for private property to replace informal means of land tenure and for the wage relationship to become the dominant means of labor recruitment and remuneration.

The third phase of expansion occurred in northern Brazil during the 1970s and 1980s. It was driven by many of the same underlying forces and exhibited many of the same outcomes as those that appeared earlier in the south and in the west. The Amazon frontier nonetheless had a number of specific features, the most important of which was the prominent role played by state agencies. Earlier periods of expansion had been relatively spontaneous. In the 1970s the exploitation of Amazonia was enthusiastically promoted by the federal government, then under the control of a centralized and repressive military regime.

The decision to develop Amazonia in part represented a solution to political dilemmas that confronted the authoritarian regime at the time. In the years immediately following the coup in 1964, military authorities and civilian technocrats embraced orthodox development policies that favored foreign capital and promoted a drastic restructuring of the economy. To their chagrin, various factions of the national bourgeoisie, many of whom had supported the military takeover in the first place, soon discovered that they were not among the beneficiaries of—and, in some cases, were directly threatened by—the development plans initially put into effect. Because the authoritarian regime could not long remain impervious to the demands of domestic capital, development planning in the late 1960s and early 1970s became less orthodox in philosophy and more nationalistic in rhetoric.[22]

Through the Operation Amazonia project and related development initiatives, federal agencies encouraged Brazilian investors to avail themselves of the tax and credit advantages presented to them. Amazonian development policy thus became one way by which the military regime sought to rebuild the broad political alliance that had brought it to power. Similarly, to counter the accusation of selling out to foreign capital, geopolitical concerns provided the overarching rationale for the extraordinary development plan. With its appeal to long-standing nationalist themes and its invitation to domestic capital to participate in a great and profitable venture, the "conquest of Amazonia" became a kind of exalted mission linked to the grandeur of the nation itself.

Against this background, it is unsurprising that the proposed initiatives were on a scale never before attempted in the region or, for that matter, anywhere else in the country. State-financed investments favored a wide range of economic interests and heavily promoted capital-intensive development projects. As a consequence of massive public spending, the Amazonian frontier was from the outset more heterogeneous and far more urbanized compared to what took place in Paraná and in Goiás-Mato Grosso.[23]

The settlement of northern Brazil also occurred within an economic and political setting quite different from the one that had obtained before. The interplay of international and domestic events in the 1970s and 1980s established a context that affected the outcome of local struggles in ways that were often as unforeseen as they were improbable. In addition, capital and labor in Amazonia were displaced into a cultural and ecological environment markedly different from that in any other part of the country. Rather than being destroyed or pushed aside, tenacious elements of traditional Amazonian extractivism merged with modern systems of production to bring about novel forms of socioeconomic and political organization. The variations of preexisting mechanisms of labor recruitment that developed and the evolution of differentiated systems of subcontracting bore little relationship to the anticipated movement toward a thoroughly proletarianized labor market observed in other contexts.

The frontier conflicts associated with these changes were correspondingly complex. Contested claims to land, gold, and timber existed simultaneously across the landscape, as did competing forms of labor control and political authority. In addition, the actions of regional elites and the grassroots mobilization of peasants, Indians, rubber tappers, and independent miners repeatedly subverted the military's agenda and the institutions that large capital attempted to impose on the region. The result was not a single process of linear change but instead a diversity of contested frontiers with highly varied outcomes. To account for these events, the framework we constructed gave priority to the conflict between the various social groups involved in the making of Amazonian history.

Conflict and Power

By *social group* we mean collectivities of people defined by common forms of access to productive resources and by their participation in similar social relations in the process of making a living. The patterned behavior of individuals within a particular group derives from their shared material circumstances and their common position within the social structure. Intrinsic to these positions is a more or less shared sense of the problems to be solved, the goals to be sought, and the means to achieve desired objectives. These commonalities shape the cultural, ideological, and political perspectives people invoke in their daily lives. Such commonalities form the basis of the concerted action that transforms individual actors into a politically mobilized collective.

We can sort the legion of social groups operating on the frontier setting into dominant or subordinate strata based on their relative degrees of power—the capacity of an actor to impose his or her will successfully on another. The dominant stratum encompasses owners of large ranches and sawmills and the managers and directors of mining companies as well as independent merchants and representatives of corporate capital. Members of the subor-

ficiency and the dignity of fulfilling God's mandate to make the earth produce as a means to vindicate their informal appropriation of land.

More recently, Indians and rubber tappers, in their attempt to protect themselves from encroaching ranchers and gold miners, have extolled the wisdom of traditional culture and the virtues of conserving the forest. By so doing, they established an affinity with—and to some degree were prompted by—the worldwide environmental movement. Indeed, the ascendance of environmental criteria within Brazil and across the world has profoundly altered the content of the debate over the fate of Amazonia and over the merits of "development" in general. The result has been what we call the "greening of the discourse," a process by which nearly all social actors on the frontier—including unlikely groups such as ranchers, loggers, and military geopoliticians—have recast the justifications for their respective interests in environmental terms.

A dramatic example of the greening of the discourse—and the problems it raised for a particular group—was the way rubber tappers in the state of Acre, in defending their territories against encroaching ranchers bent on replacing the forest with pasture, came to define themselves as conservationists and ecologists, labels that emerged from the alliances they had forged with national and international activists whose mission was to defend the forest. As Chico Mendes had put it in an interview just before his death, "until recently, the word 'environment' didn't even exist in our vocabulary." Several years later, Osmarino Amâncio Rodriques, Chico's successor, questioned the political usefulness of the environmental discourse that the rubber tappers had endorsed. He feared that an exclusive emphasis on ecological themes ran the risk of drawing attention away from what he regarded as the priority issue—land reform. If the defense of the environment is divorced from social justice, Osmarino claimed, the rubber tappers union ran the risk of endorsing what he called an "empty environmentalism" (ambientalismo vazio).[27]

Ideological positions (and repositioning) such as these are not mere reflections of material interests. Nor are they static features of people's consciousness. To the contrary, we treat ideologies as part of the arsenal of weapons the contestants actively forge and mobilize in the contest over the boundaries and the content of accepted discourse. In the process, they alter the definitions of themselves and their understanding of the world around them. Social action therefore has a *constitutive* property. By this we mean that the preferences, interests, and ideas that define individuals—and that become the basis for collective action—are formed or constituted in the process of actions that engage participants in a dispute.[28] From this perspective, people act not merely to meet preexisting ends but also to constitute themselves as persons and as groups with particular and desired attributes. Because the interests that characterize different social groups are as much formed as they are revealed in the contests in which people are engaged, they are mutable and subject to continual redefinition.[29]

In this light, we can identify contradictory interests—and therefore the potential for social conflict—between, say, peasants who staked their livelihood on the use value of land and ranchers and speculators whose interests were based on the concept of private property and of land as a marketable commodity. Even if peasants and ranchers had different interests, the latter were not construed as constant or a priori features of either group. To the contrary, the constitutive aspect of social process stresses the idea that both peasants and ranchers, in negotiating the contests that involved them and in the process of mobilizing the various sources of power at their disposal, continually reconstructed their respective interests, amending their strategies, bonds, and alliances accordingly.

The multidimensional bases of power—physical, economic, political, ideological—meant that a particular group might be well-endowed in one domain but less so in another. Compared to peasant farmers, gold miners commanded greater coercive capability but less ideological currency. Indians benefited from alliances with domestic and international human rights and environmental lobbies, but peasants and miners did not. Large-scale ranchers, for their part, brought considerable economic resources into play and possessed the means and credibility—at least early on—to promote their interests within planning agencies and courts of law. As these examples illustrate, the strategies adopted by participants in a particular conflict largely depended on the type and the effectiveness of power available to actors at a given point in time.

The Matrix of Contested Frontiers

"Winning" a contest is further conditioned by the alignment of opportunities and constraints defined by the social context within which the contest is embedded. By *context* we mean the configuration of economic, political, and ideological factors—within global, national, and regional arenas—that structure local outcomes by shifting power balances and by altering the incentives and disincentives for alternative courses of action, constraining some options while enabling others.

The significance of context is revealed by comparing the same action at two different points in time. Take, as an example, an attempt by peasant farmers to resist dispossession by ranchers. In 1973 the outcome was contingent on such factors as the strength of the military regime and its readiness to use force to silence opposition, a booming national economy, the undisputed acceptance within planning agencies of cattle raising as a modernizing economic activity, and a small and poorly organized peasantry in Amazonia. By 1984 the matrix of shaping influences was altogether different. The discredited military regime was engaged in a policy of crisis colonization; a severe economic crisis had weakened the power of the federal government and the private sector; ranchers were under intense criticism by environmentalists; and by then a far more articulate peasantry, aware of its strength in numbers, had emerged on the frontier. Ranchers held the stronger hand in both contexts; yet the configuration in the second instance permitted a wider range of outcomes, including the outright victory of peasant resistance.[30]

At times, the consequences of a particularly significant local contest alter economic-political structures and ideological discourses at regional and national levels. This in turn constructs a new context within which subsequent local conflicts play themselves out. If we expand the above example of ranchers and peasants to include the many other contests simultaneously underway in Amazonia, it is possible to see the mosaic of victories and defeats across the landscape. Together, these outcomes propel the evolution of the plot in unexpected directions, each iteration creating a new stage upon which another round of events is contingent.[31]

The result is social change, evidenced by transformations in the structure of the regional economy, the constitution of new social actors, the demise of others, and the reconfiguration of the economic, political, and ideological arrangements that defined critical periods in frontier history. Observable changes—such as deforestation, the geography of land use and human settlement, and the rise and decline of different economic activities—are therefore understood as net outcomes of multiple determinations, operating within different spheres of the social organization and influenced by the contest for resources among groups capable of mobilizing varying degrees of power.

Such conflicts were not limited to the question of direct access to land or gold. They also took place over the way in which resources were to be exploited (wage work versus other social relations of production) and, more abstractly, over the very definition of what constituted a "resource" in the first place. The latter was reflected by competing assessments of the value of the forest (versus pasture), the utility of Indian culture (versus modern technology), and the legitimacy of alternative forms of land tenure (private property versus collective ownership or informal possession). As these examples suggest, a "frontier" can refer to the physical edge of a settled area and to the battle lines that marked the confrontation between competing claims. It can also refer, metaphorically, to the uneasy boundary between alternative definitions of what resources are to be appropriated how and by whom. What we witnessed in Amazonia, therefore, was not a unitary process of change defined solely by the physical occupation of space and exploitation of resources but rather, as the title of this book indicates, a multiplicity of simultaneous and overlapping contested frontiers, both palpable and abstract.

The perspective we used to analyze and interpret events in Amazonia thus places the notion of social conflict at the center of our vision of frontier change. Our account gives importance to historical time and to the way participants in a dispute mobilize their respective power bases. In the process, they come to new understandings of themselves and of the world around them and alter their strategies accordingly. This perspective recognizes that the political initiatives invoked by the participants as well as the power hierarchies that prevail within a given context are heavily contingent upon the changing alignment of influencing factors, many of which operate within economic and political arenas far afield from the site of the contest in question. Finally, this approach attends to the interplay of social action and structural context and takes temporal sequence to heart in accounting for both intended and unintended outcomes.[32]

The Study

Our work in the Brazilian Amazon first began in 1976 when we participated in a study of the sociodemographic impact of migration and colonization in and around the town of Marabá in southern Pará.[33] The project, which involved two months of intensive fieldwork, generated useful information on one of the most conflict-ridden frontier areas in Brazil. But that introduction to southern Pará left too many incomplete stories and too many unanswered questions for us not to go back again. What started out as a one-time analysis grew into a longitudinal study to track the evolution of frontier events. We returned to the same region in 1978 and made six additional visits between 1980 and 1989.

The initial study in 1976 was burdened by the paucity of secondary sources and by our lack of firsthand knowledge of the history of the Marabá area.[34] These limitations forced us to rely heavily on a retrospective construction of the events that had taken place before our arrival. Although the method is commonly used by historians and social scientists, the strategy was especially problematic in a place like southern Pará where the vast majority of our informants were themselves newcomers to the region.

In our later work we sought to redress this problem by collecting systematic "before" and "after" data in one community. A research design of this kind, sometimes referred to as a "natural experiment," required a research site that met two criteria. To ensure that the initial data reflected as closely as possible the characteristics of a traditional Amazonian community, we first had to find an isolated place that was relatively untouched by the massive transformations already underway by 1976. It also had to be a place that would not remain isolated indefinitely but would be significantly affected by the expanding frontier within a reasonable period of time. The site that most closely approximated these special conditions was the town of São Felix do Xingu.

Like countless other backwater villages, São Felix was founded during the rubber boom early in this century. In 1976 it could only be reached by boat or plane. There were no motor vehicles on the unpaved streets save a rusty yellow tractor that was the property of the municipal government and a late model jeep that the mayor had barged upstream from Altamira. Although more recent in origin, São Felix appeared to resemble the old-style Amazonian community Charles Wagley described in his classic book, *Amazon Town* (1964).

We came upon São Felix quite by accident. Toward the end of the field work in 1976 we boarded a single-engine plane to take us to a mining community located about two hundred kilometers northwest of Marabá. On the return flight, the pilot changed course in order to attend to a mechanical problem. We landed on a newly built runway just outside of São Felix do Xingu, a small riverine community at the confluence of two wide and beautiful rivers, the crystal blue Xingu and the slightly murky Rio Fresco, which joins the Xingu from the east. Several long-time residents were gathered by a stand-up bar on main street, and they drew us into their conversation. Did we know, they asked, about the PA-279, the state road then under construction, scheduled to reach São Felix in two or three years?

As it happened, we had traveled the initial stretch of the PA-279 only a few days before. At the time it amounted to little more than twenty kilometers of dirt trail jutting westward from the PA-150, which connected Marabá to Conceição do Araguaia. The desirability of the road and of the changes that it would bring to São Felix were the topic of debate that afternoon. The store owner readily endorsed the virtues of *desenvolvimento* (development) but not without some reservation. "The road will enable us to reach the rest of Brazil," he said enthusiastically. Then, in a more somber tone, he added: "It will also bring the rest of Brazil to us."

were chosen for the strategic positions they held within various agencies and economic activities located in the research site and in the state and federal capitals.

In the course of this study we collected survey data on over four hundred households, recording the occupations, the living conditions, and the sociodemographic characteristics of the approximately twenty-five hundred people living in them. Together with other members of the various research teams, we carried out another six hundred or so in-depth interviews with respondents in southern Pará, Belém, and Brasília. Except where it is explicitly noted in the text, the material presented in this book is based on information from our own observations, surveys, and field reports.

In the initial stages of research, the first task was simply to identify the principal economic activities in the area. Traditional means of sustenance included Brazil nut collecting, rubber tapping, hunting, and fishing. The newer activities that began to penetrate the study area in the 1960s and 1970s included land clearing and ranching, logging and sawmills, farming, mining, and a host of parallel or support activities, such as transportation, banking, and service provision, as well as public and private colonization schemes. The prevalence and the spatial distribution of people and activities changed dramatically in response to a wide range of factors, the causes and consequences of which we set out to understand.

We were especially concerned with how the type and the intensity of social conflict between different groups varied over time and space. Conflicts that involved acts of resistance were methodologically valuable for several reasons. Changes in the pattern of outcomes over time revealed important shifts in the relative power of different social groups and provided insights into the role played by the contextual factors that distinguished one historical period from another. Similarly, local confrontations—because they were nearly always linked to broader economic, political, and ideological contests—drew attention to numerous properties of the social structure that we might otherwise have overlooked or understood only partially. Confrontations that resulted in violence further revealed the state's role in mediating social conflict, evidenced by the responses of the military, the courts, and by the actions and inaction of responsible administrative agencies.

Conflicts among social groups were only part of the larger picture of the social organization that included also the functional interdependence of various economic activities. For example, ranchers frequently employed small farmers on a seasonal basis to clear land for pasture and often purchased food crops sold by peasant producers. Such arrangements provided ranchers with a source of cheap labor and commodities while small farmers earned much-needed cash. Similarly, logging and farming were related activities. Sawmills purchased tree trunks from the peasant farmers who were in need of supplemental income. The makeshift roads that loggers built also made new areas of land accessible and thus affected the process by which land was occupied and cleared by small farmers.

We interviewed individuals who occupied key positions within strategically important agencies and activities. In the case of ranching, for example, we interviewed ranch owners and their administrators (if any), the people permanently employed on the ranch as well as the labor recruiter and the men he temporarily hired to clear land for pastures. Additional interviews were carried out with respondents several steps removed from the ranch itself, such as people involved in banking and credit institutions, public servants in land offices, nearby small farmers who provided occasional labor to the rancher, loggers who purchased mahogany trunks as land was being cleared, and so on. Local authorities and old-timers who knew the area well were a further source of information. We posed the same questions to a variety of informants until we were satisfied that we had obtained an understanding of the characteristics of each of the economic activities, of the perspectives of the various social groups involved, and of how and why these characteristics varied over time and space.

A consistent theme in our interviews concerned the migratory history of the individuals with whom we spoke. Where did they come from? How long had they been at the frontier? Why did they migrate to the frontier? Did they expect to return, or did they intend to stay? These and other questions addressed the issue of labor absorption by the various economic activities and provided crucial insights into the factors that stimulated the flow of people into the region. In responding to these questions, informants shared their personal experiences with us. Some were stories of victory over astonishing adversity and of high risk gambles that paid off handsomely. Many others were tragic tales of plans gone awry, of illness, violence, and death. Whole families who had staked everything on a new beginning in Amazonia found themselves on the roadside in an alien environment with no roof over their heads and with no land or job. Whatever the informants' particular story, virtually everyone provided moving accounts of the profound human drama that lay at the heart of the process of frontier change.

Several steps removed from the site-specific events were a host of economic and institutional processes at the regional, national, and international levels that affected the course of frontier change in one way or another. We were thus compelled to collect further information at a variety of levels of economic and bureaucratic organization. This included a sustained attempt to track the evolution of Amazonian development policy within the planning bureaucracies of the state and federal governments. It was an avenue of research that took us from the small and understaffed office on a dusty roadside in southern Pará to the air-conditioned buildings that housed administrators and planners in Belém and Brasília and back again. This trajectory impressed upon us the divergence of opinions, perspectives, and expertise at the various levels. It also gave us an appreciation for the sharply different constellations of economic and political pressures that came to bear on the policy-making apparatus within the federal and state government and at the local level. Indeed, many of the factors that determined the content and the execution of development policies had little at all to do with what was going on in the frontier towns.

Beginning in 1976 and upon our return to southern Pará in 1978 as well as on six different occasions in the 1980s, we were able to keep a more or less running account of the changes that took place in the area. On the basis of the information collected at each point in time, we then reconstructed events that had occurred between our visits. In the later stages of fieldwork, the research assumed the quality of a detective story, with all the excitement and challenge of finding the clues to a complex, even

Byzantine, plot that constantly evolved in new and unforeseen directions.

In field interviews it was usually impossible to track the same individuals over time. But we were often able to contact the same person over and over again in the various government agencies. Through repeated contacts we came to know the people involved, and that made it easier to assess and account for each informant's level of expertise and for the political persuasions that were sure to affect his or her perspective. The method also established an important degree of rapport as many of our principal informants came to appreciate our long-term commitment to understanding the same issues that were central to their own lives and careers. The technique of keeping track of individuals had yet another advantage associated with the rapid movement of people from one institution to another. An informant within SUDAM in 1976 might be employed by INCRA in 1978, only to be found in private business in 1984. Each post made the individual privy to different types of information, and the movement itself provided a valuable comparative perspective on events and institutions.

Secondary sources of information on these topics were difficult to come by. Nearly all of the conventional materials, such as census data on population or official statistics on production and prices, were either out of date, inaccurate, or reported information in a fashion rarely useful to our purposes. We therefore turned to newspaper accounts, planning reports, statements by the Catholic church, transcriptions of legislative hearings, and so on. These sources of information, many of which are known only to specialists in the field, are compiled in the reference list at the end of this volume. Throughout our analysis and interpretation, we sought to remain true to the voices of the people involved and to the specifics of local histories that comprised the wider panorama of social change in Amazonia.

What began in 1976 as a relatively limited before-and-after study of a particular site in southern Pará thus evolved during fifteen years of research into a project that was wider in scope and different in emphasis than the study we first had in mind. Over time we increasingly came to appreciate the importance of local diversity in shaping what took place in the Amazon and to recognize the capacity of resistance movements to alter the course of history, often in unexpected ways. In many cases, the outcomes we documented in the countryside ran counter to the predictions that dominated the social sciences a decade ago, just as our interpretation of events often involved concerns that remained peripheral to main theoretical perspectives in development studies at the time. These dilemmas compelled us to abandon or amend some of the theoretical assumptions we were initially committed to, notably the tendency implicit in our earlier work to emphasize structural constraints at the expense of a keener appreciation for the capacity of local groups to defend themselves. The conceptual framework that emerged in the course of this study thus attempts to account for the contingencies associated with acts of resistance without losing sight of the structural factors that led to patterned and more or less predictable outcomes.[35] The perspective we adopted is reflected in the way we present the material in this volume.

Organization of the Book

This book is divided into three main sections. Each section represents a different level of analytical specificity. Part one concerns Amazonia as a whole. Parts two and three successively narrow the focus to the region of southern Pará and then to the town of São Felix do Xingu and its surroundings.

The opening chapter in part one (chapter 2) summarizes the history of the region from the colonial period through the early 1960s. Chapter 3 analyzes the development initiatives of the military regime after 1964, focusing mainly on the parallel evolution of the policies that governed access to land and minerals. Chapter 4 concerns the end of the military rule and the early years of the civilian New Republic, a period that saw the growing strength of resistance movements in Amazonia and a profound shift in the terms of the policy discourse favoring environmental and human rights concerns.

The chapters in part two show how the local battles that took place in southern Pará were associated with and contributed to the evolution of the regional policies described in part one. Chapter 5 provides a history of the towns of Marabá and Conceição ter 5 provides a history of the towns of Marabá and Conceição do Araguaia and the economic and political changes brought on by the roadbuilding programs of the 1960s and 1970s. The tortuous story of the PA-279 highway to São Felix do Xingu provides a detailed example of the multiple forces that impinged on the planning and execution of development policies. Chapters 6, 7, and 8 follow the road as it pushed westward across the state. Each chapter highlights a different aspect of the frontier change: the intense conflict over public lands (the town of Xinguara, chapter 6); private colonization in Amazonia (Tucumã, chapter 7); and the massive gold rush that profoundly transformed the character of the regional economy and the urban ecology of towns and cities in the area (Serra Pelada, Cuca, and Ourilândia, chapter 8).

The way the various themes presented in the first two parts of the book play themselves out in São Felix do Xingu is the topic of part three. Chapter 9 recounts the struggle by the Kayapó Indians to secure their land and the cultural and political transformation they experienced in the process. Chapter 10 reviews the recent history of São Felix do Xingu and the changes set in motion by the road and other development initiatives in the 1970s and 1980s. Finally, chapter 11 draws on the social survey data we collected in 1978, 1981, and 1984 to measure the changes in employment, housing, and other quality of life indicators among migrants and old-timers in the town of São Felix.

Our conclusions about the process and impact of frontier expansion (chapter 12) are not encouraging to those who wish to find the solution to rural poverty in Brazil in clearing the tropical forest and settling people in Amazonia. Nor will our findings provide much solace to those analysts who cling to the idea that the patterns of settlement and land use on the Brazilian frontier can be significantly influenced by simply passing enlightened legislation or by urging new regulatory procedures within the administrative bureaucracy. New development priorities and new policies to meet such goals are clearly in order. But to be effective, future initiatives must be formulated in light of the socioeconomic, political, and ideological factors that motivate the process of frontier expansion in Amazonia.

NOTES

1. Analyses of the colonization projects introduced in the 1970s can be found in Fearnside (1986b), Moran (1981), and Smith (1982).

2. See Hecht (1985) and Mahar (1979).

3. See Branford and Glock (1985).

4. The urbanization of Amazonia is discussed by Becker (1982). See also Godfrey (1990).

5. The story of the guerrilla movement in southern Pará is recounted in Doria et al. (1979), Moura (1979), and the collection of documents entitled *Araguaia: O Partido e a Guerrilha. Documentos Inéditos* (São Paulo: Brasil Debates, 1980).

6. José de Souza Martins (1984) provides an account of the militarization of frontier areas in Amazonia during the 1970s.

7. Wood and Schmink (1979).

8. See Pompermayer (1984) and Horak (1984).

9. In keeping with the precepts of modernization theory, poverty and underemployment are understood to be transitory phenomena, the solution to which will come about automatically through the "trickle-down" effect as the benefits of high rates of aggregate economic output diffuse from the rich to the poor, leading in the long run to a more affluent and egalitarian society.

10. In the developmentalist view, the dismantling of traditional cultural traits and socioeconomic arrangements occurs through a process of "creative destruction," in which the unproductive is replaced by the efficient and the traditional gives way to the modern. As the term implies, such transformation is not without its costs. Yet, in the neorealist worldview common to the higher military ranks and to aggressive proponents of industrial capitalism, the social and ecological costs are to be stoically borne until the transition to modernism is completed. Our review in Chapter 3 amply documents the extent to which these and similar assumptions found concrete expression among ranchers and mining companies on the frontier and in the numerous projects and incentive programs that have defined Amazonian development policies since the 1960s.

11. Ideas, as Eric Wolf (1982:390) put it, form an "ecology" of collective representations that is created through a process of selection among alternatives. "This process of inclusion and exclusion is not only cognitive; it also involves the exercise of power. To sustain ideological hegemony, the defenders of orthodoxy must carry their message into an ever larger number of instrumental domains, while curtailing the ability of subaltern groups to advance viable alternatives. Where redundancy falters and ideology-making fails, the deficit may be made up by force."

12. John Butler (1985) and David Cleary (1990) show the important role that gold came to play in local economies.

13. The history of Brazil's export cycles and the associated changes in population distribution are recounted by numerous authors: Baer (1965), Burns (1970), Furtado (1963), Caio Prado Junior (1971), Simonsen (1969), Merrick and Graham (1979).

14. For a history of the moving frontier in Paraná, see Foweraker (1981) and Margolis (1973 and 1979).

15. Merrick and Graham (1979).

16. David Harvey (1989:183) labeled the geographical displacement of capital and labor the "spatial fix" to the accumulation problem under capitalism.

17. The relationship between the agricultural frontier and the structure of post-World War II development in Brazil is discussed by Foweraker (1981).

18. Wood and Carvalho (1988:237–245) provide estimates of the rate of population growth and the rate of job creation in Brazil.

19. De Janvry (1981:61–93).

20. Analyses of frontiers in Brazil can be found in Monbeig (1952), Roche (1959), and Margolis (1973). Discussions of the meaning of a "frontier" and the stages of frontier expansion are presented by Katzman (1978), Martins (1975), Foweraker (1981:27–57), and Sawyer (1984).

21. Beginning in the 1940s and through the 1960s, Paraná was a major recipient of population. The rate of net migration suddenly turned negative in the 1970s. Between 1960 and 1970 Paraná experienced a heavy outflow of people from the rural area (Wood and Carvalho 1988). This turnaround was caused by the closing of the agricultural frontier and by the expulsion of population due to changes in agricultural production, especially the replacement of coffee by laborsaving soybean cultivation. Many of those who left Paraná found their way to Amazonia as agricultural colonists or adapted their skills as pine loggers and sawmill operators to exploit mahogany and other hardwoods on the new frontier.

22. See O'Donnell (1978).

23. See Becker (1982, 1990).

24. Tilly (1978) and Skocpol (1979) draw an important distinction between conflict and violence, treating the former as an inherent property of a class-divided society and the latter as a specific manifestation of social antagonisms. Our analysis pays attention to both conflict and violence, including the everyday forms of nonviolent resistance by subordinate groups, such as those discussed by James Scott (1985) in his book, *Weapons of the Weak.*

25. The dominant thrust of state policy favors the interests of capital inasmuch as the actors within the realms of legal-political organization are hardly neutral arbiters in the tug and pull of competing agendas. Powerful economic groups have a stronger grip on the levers of state power and a louder voice in planning agencies compared to members of the subordinate class. More generally, the very stability and the legitimacy of the state itself depends heavily on the performance of the economic sector (Soares 1978). Nonetheless, by seeking a path through the thicket of conflicting pressures and by attempting to maintain its own legitimacy, state action displays a certain autonomy between the economic and the political realms. Such partial autonomy explains instances when state policy serves the interests of subordinate groups without losing sight of the greater power that dominant economic interests wield within the state apparatus. Treatments of the conceptual issues involved in the study of the relationship between the state and civil society can be found in Benton (1984), Carnoy (1984), O'Donnell (1973), Offe (1985), and Skocpol (1979). With regard to Amazonia, see Bunker (1985) and Foweraker (1981), from whom we have taken many insights.

26. See Bunker (1985).

27. Rodriques (1990).

28. Our understanding of constituent properties of social action owes much to Bowles and Gintis (1987) and to Giddens (1984).

Introduction

29. An important issue that arises here is the question of the kinds of action that are the focus of data collection and interpretation. In this regard, we find Ortner's (1984:150) review of anthropological theory to be insightful. In the section devoted to "practice" theory, she makes the following point: "Everyone seems to agree in opposing a Parsonian or Saussurian view in which action is seen as sheer enactment or execution of rules and norms (Bourdieu 1978; Sahlins 1981; Giddens 1979). Moreover, everyone seems also to agree that a kind of romantic or heroic 'volutarism,' emphasizing the freedom and relatively unrestricted inventiveness of actions, will not do either (e.g., Thompson 1978). What is left, then, is a view of action largely in terms of pragmatic choice and decision making and/or active calculating and strategizing." Indeed, it is this kind of action that is analytically central to the approach we use in this book.

30. The example brings home the point that frontier change was not a process controlled by any one class or group, no matter how central the group may have been. "The evident importance of the actors in a drama, " Eric Hobsbaum wrote in reference to another time and place, "does not mean that they are also dramatist, producer, and stage designer" (Hobsbaum 1975, cited in Skocpol 1979).

31. If society can be likened to a theatrical performance, it is one inspired by Pirandello's *Six Characters in Search of an Author*, a production in which the struggle between the various actors takes place over, not within, the plot (see Bowles and Gintis 1987:118).

32. The problem of agency and the constraints that structural contexts impose on it is a matter of considerable complexity. The issues at hand are brought into relief by critical exchanges between Thompson (1978) and Anderson (1980), usefully summarized by Giddens (1987). See also Gouldner's (1980) book, *The Two Marxisms: Contradictions and Anomalies in the Development of Theory.*

33. At that time we were members of a twelve-person team of researchers from the Center for Development and Regional Planning (CEDEPLAR) at the Federal University of Minas Gerais in Belo Horizonte. The group included a regional economist, several demographers, two sociologists, a social worker, a political scientist, and an anthropologist. Names of these and subsequent research team members who participated in the collection of data analyzed in this book are listed in the acknowledgements.

34. The study by Velho (1972) was the exception. See also Emmi (1988).

35. A conceptual framework does not comprise a theory (a system of interrelated propositions capable of being empirically tested). Rather, it is properly understood as a "map" of the terms and relationships that organize the research agenda. The framework provides guidelines for data collection and for shaping the welter of information into explanations that are logically situated within a general conception of social organization and change.

1

❖

Amazonia

Our account of contested frontiers in Amazonia begins with the region's pre-Colombian inhabitants and the devastation wrought by the Portuguese presence in northern Brazil. Chapter 2 traces the early formation of the uniquely Amazonian socioeconomic system that the rubber barons later drew on at the turn of the twentieth century to exploit the area's abundant supply of natural latex. The review of Amazonian history underscores the particular features of social organization that shaped the regional society long before the Brazilian military set in motion its ambitious modernization plan in the 1970s. Chapter 3 shows how the national security doctrine that infused the military agenda prompted direct federal interventions in land and mining policy. The widespread social and ecological turmoil that ensued stimulated a public debate that steadily gained importance and visibility with the gradual political liberalization that took place in Brasília in the late 1970s and 1980s. Chapter 4 traces the origins and evolution of the collective strategies Amazonian peoples devised to defend themselves against the mounting threats to their land and livelihood. The analysis documents the confluence of national and international events that enhanced the salience of environmental concerns, thereby transforming the terms and the premises of the development debate. The three chapters in part one introduce the more detailed examination of the contested frontiers in southern Pará in part two.

TWO

Remaking Amazonia, 1500–1964

Anthropologists who wrote in the 1950s extrapolated from the modern ethnographic record to describe precolonial Amazonia in terms of small bands of Indians who lived in temporary settlements and subsisted by fishing, hunting, and shifting cultivation.[1] In contrast to this familiar image, current reconstructions of the preconquest era vindicate the chronicles written by Carvajal and other explorers who registered the existence of permanent settlements that held from several thousand to tens of thousands of individuals, possibly more.[2] Recent findings point to a range of culturally diverse communities of varying sizes that lived throughout the basin, connected by trade networks and warfare. The sedentary chiefdoms once found in Amazonia—apparently characterized by stratified hierarchies of nobles, commoners, servants, and slaves—bore little resemblance to the small groups that predominate there today.

The five centuries that have passed since the Europeans first arrived in the New World witnessed the thorough remaking of Amazonia. Accounts of the transformation properly emphasize the devastation the colonial experience visited upon unwilling Amerindian peoples and the extensive consequences that were later brought on by the rubber boom. But the weight analysts have given to those turning points marking discontinuities between periods has frequently led to giving less attention to the interim years, which saw the gradual evolution of enduring features of Amazonian society that persist to this day.[3] Similarly, the modern record concerning the subtle changes that occurred between World Wars I and II and during the 1950s is spotty. Inconspicuous and overlooked as they often have been, the modifications in economic and political structure that took place during those forgotten years added important dimensions to the small towns and villages that dot the riversides across the region. Later chapters will show how the colonial legacy and the more recent changes in social structure affected the course of frontier change in Amazonia after 1970.

The Destruction of Amerindian Society, 1500–1750

The Portuguese sighted the eastern seaboard of the South American continent on 22 April, 1500; yet it took more than a century before they established permanent settlements in Amazonia. In the early seventeenth century, the Portuguese gradually pushed westward along the Amazon river and its major tributaries in search of clove, sarsaparilla, cacao, cinnamon, aromatic roots, and palm oils. Other sought-after items included hardwoods, fruits, and game, particularly manatees, giant river turtles, and spotted cats. The expeditions depended on Amerindians as rowers, collectors, and guides. Forays into the hinterland, which frequently turned into slaving expeditions, carried European diseases and death far into the interior.[4]

Missionaries from the newly created Society of Jesus, who arrived in Brazil in 1549 with the first Portuguese governor, Tomé de Souza, became both the Amerindian's defenders as well as the instruments of the wholesale transformation of indigenous material and cultural life. In 1645 Jesuits under the leadership of Antonio Vieira began establishing missions along the major Amazonian tributaries. Amerindian groups were relocated into large settlements, called *aldeias*, where their daily activities could be closely supervised, their souls could be saved, and their labor could be put to new tasks, such as raising cattle. In the *aldeias*, natives were deprived of their tribal identity under the homogenizing influence of the missionaries. Compelled to communicate with whites and other natives in the *lingua geral*, tribal Amerindians were gradually transformed into "generic Indians" or *tapuios*.[5]

For a time at least, the missions provided a measure of protection from the slavers who made annual expeditions into the interior. Yet the *aldeia* system and the twin assault on the mental and material bases of Amerindian culture forever changed the way of life that had existed before the Portuguese came to Amazonia. Although nominally free, mission Amerindians were obliged to provide labor to royal authorities and to colonists, a practice that frequently deteriorated into forced work hardly distinguishable from outright slavery. Moreover, by concentrating people in high density settlements, *the aldeias* greatly facilitated the spread of European diseases, such as whooping cough, influenza, and smallpox, against which native populations had no immunity. By the end of the seventeenth century successive epidemics had killed tens of thousands of Amerindians. The dense populations once the marvel of early explorers had been destroyed or had retreated into less accessible reaches of Amazonia.[6]

Reform and Rebellion, 1750–1850

The catastrophe that befell native groups reduced the already short supply of colonial labor, leading to conflicts between the colonists and the missionaries in the intense competition for workers. In 1751 the capital of the northern colony, then called Grão Pará and Maranhão, was moved to Belém under the command of a new governor, Francisco Xavier de Mendonça Furtado. The governor's stepbrother, the powerful Sebastião José de Carvalho e Melo—better known as the Marquis de Pombal—enlisted Furtado's aid in overthrowing the powerful Jesuits who by then were a formidable presence in the region, controlling some twelve thousand Amerindians in sixty-three Amazonian missions.[7] A series of laws passed in 1755 took the *aldeias* out of the hands of the Jesuits, who were expelled altogether from Brazil in 1759.

Pombal's Directorate, as it came to be known, was the first state-imposed attempt to "modernize" Amazonia.[8] Under the new regulations, larger consolidated settlements were ruled by appointed lay directors responsible for allocating Amerindian labor to colonists and to colonial authorities. The revised system gave rise to new tyrants whose unrelenting demand for Amerindian labor thwarted the Crown's officially humanitarian policies.[9] Elites with larger holdings and more capital were able to monopolize most of the available indigenous labor. Small settlers without the resources or influence to secure access to labor became *comissários volantes*, or river traders, later known as *regatões*.[10]

Expeditions organized by colonial authorities, landowners, and merchants now took the place of the previous "rescue" missions to bring Amerindians into the mixed-race towns.[11] During the forty years of Directorate rule, Old World diseases killed perhaps one-third of the remaining Amerindians, causing the population in the *aldeias* to fall from thirty thousand in 1757 to about nineteen thousand in 1798.[12] Before Pombal, the Amazonian population was mainly indigenous except in the urban centers of Belém, Cametá, Viseu, Santarém, and Gurupá. By the middle of the eighteenth century, except for native groups that fled to remote refuge areas, the region's population consisted mostly of detribalized, subjugated *tapuios*.[13]

Pombal fell from power in 1777. The failure of his Directorate to transform detribalized mission Indians into a docile labor force capable of supporting the regional economy was evident in a succession of revolts.[14] Attempts to maintain control resulted in harsher legislation, especially after the Portuguese Crown relocated to Brazil in 1808. Remaining mission villages were destroyed, their resources seized, and inhabitants pressed into forced labor. Better communications and transportation and the growing size of the white population led to a new wave of military action against remaining tribal groups.

After the Directorate was abolished in 1798, the populations once congregated into settlements became scattered along the rivers, streams, and lakes of the Amazon basin where they lived primarily in small family groups. Their dispersal and isolation contrasted with the dense settlement patterns of precolonial flood plain dwellers. The sustenance strategies *tapuios* developed drew heavily from the indigenous groups from whom they were descended. Yet unlike their predecessors, *tapuios* were distinguished by an enduring, if tenuous, link to the market. Whereas preconquest Amerindian populations labored only for subsistence and occasional trade with neighboring tribes, the Jesuits taught the *tapuios* to produce commodities, with the priests serving as the middlemen in commercial exchanges.[15]

When the Jesuits were replaced by the Directorate system, the change brought Amerindians into direct contact with the *regatões* who supplied even the most remote settlements that dotted the riversides.[16] The river traders provided the lifeline between the dispersed collectors of forest products and the exporters who would deliver the goods to distant world markets. Other traders set up posts at key river junctions or in small towns where they became part of an extensive system of credit and trade middlemen. Much of the sugar produced in the colony was diverted to the making of cane liquor, or *cachaça*, which served (along with cacao seeds and cotton spools) as exchange medium along the rivers where cash was scarce.[17] The dispersed population of *tapuio* producers and the complex network of small traders on whom they depended formed patterns of sociocultural and economic organization that would be mobilized with the onset of the rubber boom.

In early colonial times Amazonia was linked directly to the king in Lisbon, not to Brazil's governor. Not until 1823, a year after Brazil's independence was proclaimed, did the northern colony of Grão Pará declare its allegiance to the new nation, and Amazonia for the first time was formally integrated into Brazil. The "Brazilianization" of the government led to heated political tensions that erupted into rebellions in several regions of the new nation, including Amazonia. The most extensive uprising was the *Cabanagem* revolt in Pará that began as a dispute between rival elites following Brazil's independence.[18] In 1835 and 1836 the revolt spread from urban centers into the interior, where rebels (known as *cabanos*) turned with a vengeance on their landlords and patrons. An estimated thirty thousand people died in the ensuing violence. The death toll represented nearly one-quarter of the population of Pará.

The region's labor force was devastated by the violence and by the spread of diseases that soon followed. *Tapuios*, black slaves, and other workers fled because they were *cabanos* or to escape forced labor.[19] Agrarian legislation passed just prior to independence in 1822 had abrogated the land grant system and, for the first time, recognized rights accrued by primary occupation, or *posse*.[20] Small producers could establish their independent claims to land through the *posse* system, which remained the dominant form of land appropriation until new legislation was passed in 1850. The loss of control over their work force and the destruction of agricultural fields and sugar mills undermined the dominance of the plantation and ranch owners. The *Cabanagem* left an economic and political power vacuum in Amazonia soon occupied by a new elite: the merchants, traders, and exporters who rose to prominence with the rubber boom.[21]

The Rubber Boom, 1850–1920

Amerindians had long found uses for the latex drawn from various species of trees dispersed throughout the Amazon basin. In the nineteenth century technological innovation stimulated the industrial demand for rubber. In 1839 Goodyear discovered how to treat the natural latex so that it would maintain its consistency despite changes in temperature. Known as vulcanization (because, like the god Vulcan, it relied on heat and brimstone, or sulfur), the process turned rubber from a novelty item into a valued commodity on the world market. The rubber trade further expanded with the introduction of steamships in 1853, an innovation that reduced the time it took to transport rubber from forest to port, and with the invention of the pneumatic tire by John Dunlop in 1888. Balloon tires found their first use on bicycles whose soaring popularity in Europe and the United States in the late nineteenth century became known as the "bicycle craze." Later, the demand for natural latex came from automobile manufacturers who used the material for tires and accessories.

The *regatão* transportation system of supply and collection, long established for marketing other forest products, permitted the intensified extraction of latex beginning in the middle of the nineteenth century. From 1825 to 1850 production was mainly concentrated around Belém and in the nearby island districts. In contrast to the arrangements that developed later, in this early period independent rubber tappers (seringueiros) collected the latex on unclaimed sites while their wives and children cultivated subsistence crops on the flood plain. When the demand for rubber increased in the period between 1850 and 1870, the preexisting network of itinerant traders and riverside merchants evolved into a hierarchy of middlemen dominated by the rubber export houses of Belém and Manaus.[22] Suppliers spread their network of tappers and traders westward to the Madeira and Purus rivers.[23] Recruits typically migrated without their families and were often prohibited by their patrons from engaging in any subsistence activities that would distract from their rubber tapping. The arrangement made them far more dependent on the trading post owners than the autonomous rubber tappers near Belém.[24]

Because the rubber tapper's allotment of tools, firearms, and food was minimal and since most trade relations were elaborations of the preestablished credit and regatão transport system, the collection of rubber required little investment of capital. In effect, what the rubber boom did was to organize and link together much of what already existed, adding new institutional layers to the way the extraction of forest products was financed. The result became known as the aviamento system of supply, credit, and labor control.

The extraction and marketing of natural latex became so elaborate that even the simplest transaction could span six levels of middlemen from producer to manufacturer.[25] At the bottom of the hierarchy were the rubber tappers (seringueiros) who trekked through their rubber trails (estradas), making a gash in the tree and leaving a cup to collect the milky sap, then returning to collect the latex, and finally smoking it into large balls. Tappers exchanged the smoked rubber at the trading post (barracão) operated either by the local landowner (dono de seringal) or by an individual who paid the owner a commission. Trading post operators paid the tappers in kind, providing them with basic necessities at inflated prices. Such were the terms of exchange between tapper and trading post that nearly all of the *seringueiros* were in debt to the *barracão*. The owner of the trading post was indebted to a local supplier (*aviador*) in the nearest town. The latter collected rubber and shipped it to the *aviador* house in Belém, the central figure in the rubber system. The great merchant houses that rose to power and prominence during the rubber boom were responsible for receiving rubber from the remote *estradas*, financing the vast supply network, recruiting labor, and expanding rubber collecting activities into new areas to keep up with demand. The *aviador* houses then sold the rubber to Belém-based export houses, usually controlled by foreigners, who worked on behalf of rubber buyers. Finally, the overseas purchasing houses sold the rubber to manufacturers across the world.

Social relations under the *aviamento* system depended on debt, on personalized forms of patron-client relations, and, in some cases, on violent coercion.[26] Wages were all but unknown in this exchange-dominated economy in which money itself was of little importance. Until the middle of the eighteenth century, there was no metal currency in use at all in Pará.[27] Even after the declaration of the Republic in 1889, a succession of different currencies, some of them fraudulent, reinforced the traditional Amazonian distrust for money. Under the *aviamento* system, security came not from the amount of earnings but from the continuing relationship, based on debt and obligation, that ensured survival and indirect contact with the monetized world economy. While the *aviamento* patrons wielded significant control over the far-flung rubber tappers, the latter nevertheless resorted to numerous forms of resistance to this domination, including outright desertion.[28]

By the end of the nineteenth century several hundred thousand migrants from Brazil's Northeast had ventured into remote regions of the Amazon basin in response to the incentives of the rubber traders. The recruitment of migrants from the Northeast to Amazonia was facilitated by the coincidence of two economic factors. One was the rising price of rubber; the other, a devastating drought that struck the Northeast between 1877 and 1900. The drought brought an end to the cotton boom that had sustained the colony since the 1820s, leaving thousands of people without a livelihood. With few other options open to them and inspired by rumors of fabulous wealth to be had in the forest, northeasterners were easily enticed to migrate westward.

In 1910 the Amazon rubber boom peaked and then suffered a crash from which it never fully recovered. By then the expanding international demand for industrial rubber far outstripped the supply capacity of the *aviamento* system.[29] The deficit of rubber on the world market caused prices to soar to as much as seven dollars per kilo in early 1910, the year that marked the beginning of major harvests from the first successful rubber plantations in Asia. Almost overnight the lower price of Asian rubber stole the world rubber market from Brazil.[30]

Though the foreign currency generated from the rubber trade helped underwrite the costs of industrialization in southern Brazil, the same did not apply to Amazonia.[31] The limited effect of the rubber boom on the remote settlements in the region owed much to the peculiar characteristics of the extractive economy. Most of the accumulated assets consisted of uncollected debts or real estate whose inflated value quickly vanished with the economic downturn.[32] Between 1910 and 1920 migrants from the Northeast returned to their homeland, causing a decline in the size of Pará's population.[33] Foreigners who controlled the export of rubber departed the country, and the Belém *aviadores* reduced the scale of their commercial operations. Moreover, the economic power of the *coroneis do barracão*—which derived from their monopoly over transportation, communications, and commerce through the *aviamento* system[34]—provided little incentive to invest in extractive technology, and few profits made their way to direct producers. When the price of rubber increased, merchants charged more for the goods sold to their clients and purchased latex from them at rates set months previously. The *aviamento* system thus worked against the accumulation of capital and the creation of an internal market that could stimulate in Amazonia the kind of development that took place in southern Brazil.

Circumstances changed least for the *seringueiros* themselves. By the time the rubber trade collapsed, the vast majority of tappers who survived the ordeal were little better off than when they had started. Those who remained in Amazonia directed their efforts to subsistence activities, such as hunting, fishing, flood plain agriculture, and the extraction of other forest products. The rubber tappers added a northeastern flavor to Amazonian culture and mixed with the *tapuio* population to produce the Amazonian peasant called the *caboclo*.[35]

Economic Diversification and State Expansion, 1920–1964

Examining the historical record of most of Amazonia from the 1920s through the 1960s, one comes away with the impression of a region in the doldrums, languishing in unrelenting economic stagnation.[36] The image is only partly true. Appearances to the contrary, a number of significant changes took place during this period.[37] The most important included the growing demand for raw materials in Brazil's industrializing south, the effects of development initiatives adopted by the federal government, and the diversification of the region's economy.

In the aftermath of the rubber boom, the *caboclo* population responded to the demand for new extractive commodities while continuing to garden, hunt, and fish. The export market for animal pelts expanded in the 1920s to include capybara, jaguar, iguana, boa, anaconda, and caiman.[38] In areas endowed with dense stands of the *castanheira* tree (*Bertholletia excelsa*), Brazil nuts became an especially important export item. These included locations along the Solimões and Madeira tributaries, the communities of Faro and Oriximiná in middle Amazonas, and the southern Pará region centered around Marabá, described in chapter 5.[39] Food production and local diets improved in areas where subsistence activities previously had been prohibited.[40] The *aviamento* system was adapted to support these new extractive activities, and the economy became more monetized. The rubber barons lost the absolute power they once wielded, affording *caboclos* a degree of autonomy they had rarely enjoyed before.

When Asian plantations took over the world rubber market in 1912, U.S. industrialists sought a supply of rubber that was closer to home and under their own control. The 1920s and 1930s witnessed several unsuccessful attempts to establish rubber plantations in the Amazon, the most famous of which was Henry Ford's ill-fated "Fordlândia," which was later moved to the nearby site of Belterra.[41] Tapping of natural rubber nonetheless continued in Brazil. Indeed, production increased in the late 1930s when world prices edged upward and Brazil's automobile tire industry generated a growing internal demand for rubber.[42]

Under President Getúlio Vargas the Brazilian economy expanded its industrial base in the 1930s. Industrialization brought sweeping changes in social structure and redefined the role the frontier came to play in the national setting.[43] The ascendance of economic and political groups whose fortunes were bound to urban-based manufacturing shifted the balance of national political power away from the once dominant agricultural elite into the hands of the rising urban bourgeoisie. The change brought into prominence a host of new ideas about the nature of "modern" society and about the role public policy could play in achieving that goal of progress. Under Vargas, who saw the road to progress in expanded industrial production, the federal government became a dominant actor in the economic arena. The premises of the "developmentalist" paradigm forged during this period would again play a dominant role in the 1970s when the federal government launched various initiatives to populate and exploit Amazonia.

Following the Second World War, import substitution industrialization became the explicit goal of Brazilian development policy. Rapid urbanization was accompanied by equally significant changes in the countryside as new lands continued to be brought into the production of coffee, cattle, and food crops. Unlike previous frontiers that were driven by international demand for specific export commodities, the westward expansion of ranching and agriculture into Goiás and Mato Grosso that began in the late 1950s occurred in response to changes in Brazil's national economy.[44]

World War II resuscitated the rubber trade, if only briefly. In the 1930s Germany stockpiled Brazilian rubber in anticipation of the war effort. By the end of the decade the United States worried that Brazil would side with the Axis powers, thereby closing off access to rubber as well as strategic supply lanes that crisscrossed the South Atlantic.[45] The shortage of rubber became especially critical after Japan took control of rubber plantations in southeast Asia.[46] In March of 1942 the U.S. and Brazilian governments signed a five-year agreement, known as the Washington Accords.[47] A crucial provision of the agreement was a bilateral effort to boost rubber production in the Amazon to as much as one hundred thousand tons per year. The United States financed the revamping of credit, production, transportation, and public health systems and paid the costs of a massive labor transfer from the Northeast of Brazil to Amazonia.

The wartime effort, known as the "rubber battle," was fought by as many as fifty-five thousand migrants from northeastern Brazil, recruited and shipped to remote corners of Amazonia during the five-year period covered by the Accords.[48] About a third of them died from poor health and working conditions in the jungle. The recruitment effort mobilized one-third of the Amazonian shipping fleet to carry workers to Belém and from there to distant tapping areas.[49] The Rubber Development Corporation (RDC) coordinated the recruitment effort and other measures to reactivate the rubber-producing system. New agencies were created to handle transportation, supply, sanitation, public health, and credit. Probably the most important of these were the Special Public Health Service (SESP) and the Rubber Credit Bank. Both organizations became lasting features of Amazonia's institutional landscape.[50]

Formidable problems beset the execution of the program, notably the active resistance by merchants to attempts to modernize rubber extraction and to circumvent the traditional *aviamento* system. Unable to fully overcome the opposition, the Accords only reinforced the position of the rubber elites without significantly improving the conditions of the producers themselves.[51]

Once the war ended, the United States expressed little interest in continuing its support for Amazonian rubber extraction beyond 1947, the year the Accords expired. By then the demand for rubber from Brazil's own industrial sector outstripped the volume of exports anyway. Goodyear, Firestone, and Pirelli had opened the first tire factories in 1926 and 1937, and by 1946 there were 138 factories.[52] With a growing stake in ensuring a stable supply of rubber, São Paulo industrialists forged alliances with Amazonian elites to pressure the Brazilian government to extend price supports and credit lines provided by the Rubber Credit Bank.[53] In 1950 the institution was renamed the Amazonian Credit Bank, and after that price supports were continued as part of Vargas' proposed Plan for Valorization of the Amazon, but the new emphasis was on diversification away from rubber.

In 1953 President Vargas created the Superintendency for the Valorization of the Amazon (SPVEA) to implement development programs financed by a special fund designated in the 1946 constitution. Under Vargas and his successor, Juscelino Kubitschek, SPVEA achieved only some of its goals.[54] The most important was the construction of the Belém-Brasília Highway (1956–1960) that provided the first ground link between Pará's capital city and the rest of southern Brazil. Other SPVEA-financed roads connected communities within the region, such as the road completed in 1965 that links Itacoatiara to the city of Manaus.[55]

Though SPVEA was generally ineffectual, the agency nonetheless stimulated a change in the general policy climate—a shift that began to have an effect even in remote Amazonian communities. Chief among these changes was the promise of new credit lines through the Amazon Credit Bank. The incentives enabled local elites to appropriate land and to invest in new agricultural and ranching activities that in some places began to compete with extractive activities. Merchants working the rivers between Santarém and Manaus profited from the demand of southern Brazil's textile industries for jute, a flood plain crop cultivated by small producers.[56] Growing populations in the northern capital cities of Belém and Manaus also increased the need for basic food items.[57] To the benefit of regional elites, SPVEA sponsored industrial investments in Belém, which absorbed the lion's share of the available funds.[58] New sources of credit led to economic diversification and transformations of the local patron-client relationships. In a series of moves that signaled a fundamental change in the socioeconomic and political organization of traditional Amazonia, merchants began to call in outstanding debts from clients, seizing control over land in lieu of payment and then charging rent to the producer for the continued use of the land or its products.[59]

The creation of new *municípios* in 1961 added yet another dimension to the transformations underway. In southern Pará, a portion of the *município* of Conceição do Araguaia became Santana do Araguaia, and São Felix do Xingu was separated from

Altamira. The process of dismembering old *municípios* into several smaller ones was important because the creation of new municipal bureaucracies and budgets meant that new resources were available for political patronage, including the distribution of urban jobs that provided a modest but steady monetary wage.[60] Services and jobs in the fledgling municipal seats such as Gurupá, Limoeiro do Ajurú, Itacoatiara, and São Felix do Xingu attracted people from the surrounding rural areas (see chapter 10).[61] Local elites took advantage of the resources provided by federal intervention in the region to consolidate their control over land and labor.

The rural-to-urban migration flow received further impetus from the high inflation rates in the late 1950s and 1960s that finally put an end to many trading post owners who had managed to survive the earlier fluctuations in the price of rubber. The introduction of consumer goods into the interior gradually stimulated the use of cash, especially in the younger generation. Although there were exceptions to the trend—particularly in areas where Brazil nut gathering, the skin trade, or mining remained profitable—these economic and political changes undermined the *aviamento* system and laid the basis for a market in land and labor that began to function in the 1970s.

The post-World War II period also witnessed the slow but steady migration of people into the eastern and southern Amazonian states of Maranhão, Goiás, and Pará.[62] These precursors of the massive influx that took place in the 1970s produced subsistence goods and most agricultural surpluses, especially rice, that supplied the growing size of the low-income populations living in urban areas. The small farmers who populated the lower rim of the Amazon basin together with *caboclos* who began to shift to agricultural pursuits constituted an expanding peasantry that was increasingly linked to Brazil's national economy.[63]

The Mining Boom, 1950–1964

A salient but often overlooked facet of postwar Amazonia was the progressive expansion of the mining sector. The first large-scale mining operation in the region was ICOMI, a consortium of Brazilian companies and Bethlehem Steel that began to exploit manganese deposits in Amapá in the early 1950s. On a smaller scale, *garimpeiros* had begun to prospect in Amazonia as early as the 1930s. By the 1940s and 1950s there were an estimated 160,000 freelance miners in Brazil. The tin rush in Rondônia, beginning in 1952, attracted an estimated forty-five thousand *garimpeiros*, many of them former rubber collectors from Rondônia and neighboring Acre and Amazonas.[64] The placer mines (*garimpos*) were accessible by water or by air from the towns of Porto Velho and Ariquemes, which experienced a boom during this period.[65] But it was mainly in the Tapajós region that the traditional *garimpo* system developed most fully, portending the massive gold rush that would play such an important role in Amazonia in the 1980s (see chapter 8).[66]

During the 1960s the Tapajós gold fields were "closed" or "wild" *garimpos*, meaning that access to the area was controlled by the owner, usually a buyer, merchant, supplier, or pilot. The mine owner (*dono do garimpo*) might invite others to set up business in the *garimpo* or to build and control the landing strip. The builder of the airstrip, known as the *dono da pista*, would then charge a landing fee for its use. Dozens of landing strips were built in the early 1960s, lined on either side by a *corrutela*, a row of shacks that served as supply stores and residences. Given the rudimentary technology, lack of infrastructure, and low price of labor, air transportation was the main production cost of mining in the region.[67] As a consequence, pilots assumed an important role, not just as transporters but also as bosses in their own right, as well as gold buyers, airstrip builders, and advisors to the *garimpeiros*.

Merchants and gold buyers in the towns of Santarém and Itaituba who serviced the *garimpos* made up a new class of wealthy people. This was especially true in Itaituba, the "nerve center" of the *garimpo* where the population grew rapidly after 1960.[68] Nilson Pinheiro, who discovered the gold fields, was later elected a state deputy in Pará in 1982. Similarly, the legendary Zé Arara, who began as a Tapajós *garimpeiro*, had become Brazil's wealthiest *garimpo* entrepreneur by the 1980s, with fleets of private planes, chains of gold-buying and retailing shops, and other investments.[69] As these examples illustrate, the *garimpo* brought into prominence a group of new social actors whose economic activities were based on elaborate, and in some ways quite novel, variants of the traditional *aviamento* system.

The central axis of the *garimpo* was the relationship between the *fornecedor* (supplier) and the *garimpeiros*. The former provided the capital, the latter provided the labor (and occasionally some tools) to extract gold, cassiterite, and other valued minerals. The supplier furnished basic food rations and a place for workers to hang their hammocks during the time in the field. By tradition, the supplier was responsible for the miners' needs, such as caring for a *garimpeiro* if he fell ill.[70] In exchange for their respective contributions, supplier and *garimpeiro* divided between them whatever returns accrued from their association. The supplier had the right to half the product. The other half was equally divided among all the *garimpeiros* in the *turma*, or work crew. The term *meia-praça* initially referred to this relationship between the supplier and the *garimpeiro*. The term was also applied to the miner himself under this system.[71] In more recent years *fornecedor* and *meia-praça* have been replaced by the terms *dono* (owner) and *peão* (peon), a change indicative of the transformation in work relations described in the next chapter.[72]

The *meia-praça* system had several features in common with the traditional *aviamento* system. Both involved a supplier, who advanced capital and labor, and a producer. Under the *aviamento* system, suppliers were themselves provisioned by larger-scale merchants, who in turn were tied to a monopoly of exporters. Products moved "up" the system to buyers and financiers as supplies moved "down" to producers. In the *garimpo*, the *fornecedor* generally received credit and supplies from a merchant who was, in turn, tied to one or more mineral buyers. As in the *aviamento*, merchants in the *garimpo* were able to capture a portion of the miners' surplus production by manipulating the price of gold and provisions. And, like the rubber tapper, the *garimpeiros* worked under adverse conditions, had no guarantee of medical assistance or other benefits, and were subject to summary dismissal by his supplier at any moment.

The *garimpo* system nevertheless differed in important ways from *aviamento*. What held the *aviamento* system together during the rubber boom were the debts the tapper owed to the owner of the trading post, who in turn owed money to others up the line. But the debt trap that held tappers and merchants under the control of the rubber barons did not develop in the mining fields. Here the *garimpeiro* received his sustenance from, say, a pilot or merchant and would work the claim under the latter's control. If the effort produced no profit, the *garimpeiro* lost the time and energy he invested, but incurred no obligation to his suppliers. This arrangement constituted a pivotal difference between the rubber and the mining boom, allowing the *garimpeiro* to operate in a far more independent fashion compared to his predecessor on the rubber trails. Furthermore, the element of luck inherent in the mining activity held the possibility of sudden wealth. Such a prospect did not exist for the traditional forest gatherer under the *aviamento* system.[73] These properties of small-scale mining meant that *garimpagem* became one of the few activities in the region that offered the promise—and in rare cases the reality—of upward mobility.[74]

The adaptation of the *aviamento* system to the prospecting and exploitation of minerals and the increasing size of the small-scale mining sector in the 1950s and 1960s paved the way for the massive gold rush that took place several decades later. Moreover, the associated network of economic and political groups on the frontier as well as the miners themselves became powerful forces to reckon with when the military regime set in motion its plans to modernize Amazonia in the 1970s.

NOTES

1. Steward (1946–1950); Steward and Fanon (1959). On the basis of these observations, Meggers developed her influential theories about environmental limitations on cultural development (Meggers 1954, 1971). For a critique and opposing theory, see Lathrap (1970).

2. See Balée (forthcoming); Bush, Piperno, and Colinvaux (1989); Denevan (1976); Gibbon (1990); Moran (1981:32–34, 41–57; 1989); Oliveira (1988); Roosevelt (1987); Ross (1978). There is growing evidence that current forms of indigenous adaptation are the result of de-evolutionary change due to the depopulation and wholesale disruption wrought by the European conquest.

3. This observation is elaborated by Oliveira Filho (1978).

4. This account of the colonial period draws primarily on Hemming (1978); Moreira Neto (1988); Oliveira (1983, 1988); and Parker (1985a).

5. See Moreira Neto (1988:23–25). The term *tapuio* originally meant "slave"; later, like *caboclo*, the term came to refer to detribalized Indians. The concept of "generic Indians" was first discussed by Ribeiro (1970).

6. See Hemming (1978) and Oliveira (1983).

7. Hemming (1978:455–476).

8. Hecht and Cockburn (1989:58–59).

9. Hemming (1987:40) and Parker (1985a:27–28).

10. Hecht and Cockburn (1989:59).

11. Oliveira (1983:214).

12. Hemming (1987:57).

13. Moreira Neto (1988:43). Following Veríssimo, Moreira Neto refers to the *tapuio* as a biological descendant of indigenous people, not a mixed race group.

14. Moreira Neto (1988:26–33).

15. Ross (1978).

16. Parker (1985b:33–34).

17. Parker (1985b:31).

18. Anderson (1985).

19. Santos (1980:34–35).

20. Monteiro (1980:149–150); Moreira Neto (1988:86); Santos (1984).

21. Anderson (1985:79).

22. Independent traders represented an inconvenience to the export houses in Belém and Manaus as their own operations expanded. Anti-*regatão* sentiment, which sometimes took on anti-Semitic and xenophobic overtones due to the prominence of Jews and Arabs among the *regatão* population, led to the imposition of crushing taxes on river traders beginning in 1842 (Pinto 1977:262; Hemming 1987:253). Despite the *regatão*'s indispensable role in reaching remote settlements, the view of them as an outlaw element in Amazonian society lingers to the present.

23. Oliveira Filho (1979) and Santos (1980:72).

24. Oliveira Filho (1979) and Weinstein (1983, 1985). Migrants from Ceará who settled in remote areas of western Amazonia, such as the Juruá river, had health problems due to diets limited to manioc flour, dried meat, and fish (Whitesell 1988:15).

25. Weinstein (1983:16–21). See also Wagley's (1964) classic description of social relations in rubber tapping.

26. Because African slaves did not participate in this activity, the abolition of slavery in 1888 did not have much impact in the Amazon where the rubber trade was dominated by *tapuios* and Amerindians.

27. Santos (1980:155–157).

28. Oliveira Filho (1979) and Weinstein (1983, 1985).

29. Weinstein (1983:165–167).

30. Under plantation conditions, the cost per unit of rubber production declined with increases in scale. The opposite was true of the extraction of native rubber, which implied higher costs per unit as rising demand pushed the collection of latex into more and more remote areas that were increasingly expensive to reach. For a discussion of the implications of extractive systems of production, see Bunker (1985).

In Amazonia, investments had gone into the marketing and supply network rather than into production, and the merchants themselves had only indirect and imperfect control over the extraction of latex. Attempts at planting rubber were restricted by capital and labor shortages and, most importantly, by biological problems planters were unable to overcome. Chief among these was the South American leaf blight, a fungus that spreads rapidly once trees are planted in close proximity. For different versions of the reasons for the failure of plantation rubber schemes in Amazonia, see Bunker (1985), Dean (1987), and Weinstein (1983).

31. See Santos (1980:260).

32. Weinstein (1983:232–238).

33. Santos (1980:261).

34. Emmi (1985:35–36), Weinstein (1983:132–133), and Whitesell (1988:29,36).

35. The term *caboclo*, widely used in Brazil to refer to rural peoples, had a special meaning in Amazonia. According to Parker (1985a), the term first referred to Amerindians. It was later applied to the offspring of mixed unions between Europeans and Amerindians. Eventually the term came to designate the rural population of mixed racial and cultural origins that shared the peculiarly Amazonian sustenance strategies based on a mixture of hunting, fishing, forest collecting, and subsistence agriculture. Unlike *tapuios*, as used by Moreira Neto (1988), *caboclo* culture is dominated by the Portuguese language and culture. See also Moran (1974, 1981:98–113), Parker (1985a), and Wagley (1964, 1985).

36. Martinello (1988:14) comments that there is a gap in the literature on the Amazon during the period from 1920–1940 "as if the melancholy and necrosis that had devastated the whole valley with economic stagnation were also reflected in peoples' minds" (authors' translation).

37. See also Oliveira (1985:25–28).

38. McGrath (1986:5).

39. Martinello (1988:58–59).

40. Whitesell (1988:38).

41. See Schmink (1988), Dean (1987:67–86). The rubber boom swept Amazonia into the world market during the period of vast expansion of foreign trade and investment after 1850 that "changed the map of domination of the world's spaces" beyond recognition (Harvey 1989:260–264). Many famous American capitalists became involved in Amazonian ventures during the early twentieth century, including Henry Ford after he had just set up the first assembly line in his automobile factory a few years earlier. See also Hecht and Cockburn (1989:69–85).

42. Martinello (1988:127).

43. Foweraker (1981) pays close attention to the relationship between frontier expansion and the changing structure of the Brazilian economy in the twentieth century.

44. Becker (1982:111), Foweraker (1981), and Bunker (1985:81–82).

45. Martinello (1988:65–68, 127).

46. The scarcity of rubber posed so serious a threat to the war effort that the United States government began rationing rubber along with gasoline and other vital materials.

47. Promising to reequip Brazil's armed forces and to finance the state-sponsored steel industry at Volta Redonda near Rio de Janeiro, the United States succeeded in winning over the Brazilians who until then had been undecided

about which side to back (Martinello 1988:16; see also Dean 1987:87–107; Mahar 1979:3–6).

48. Dean (1987:94) and Mahar (1979:5) suggest a lower figure of thirty-two thousand migrants. Reliable measures of migration during this period are lacking.

49. Martinello (1988:220).

50. Anthropologist Charles Wagley, who worked with SESP in the Amazon in the 1940s, described the impact of many of these changes on local Amazonian communities in his classic study *Amazon Town* (1964).

51. Initial plans included model contracts for workers that sought to avoid the worst abuses of the rubber boom period and provisioning through the RDC and the Superintendency for Provisioning of the Amazon Valley (SAVA). Exclusive buying and selling of rubber by the Rubber Credit Bank disrupted the power of merchants in the *aviamento* chain and provided rubber tappers with access to a cash income for the first time. However, protective measures for the workers were not enforced, and the RDC's usurpation of provisioning led to an uproar in the commercial associations of Manaus and Belém. The merchant elites revolted against the plan by creating chaos in the precarious supply system for the 1943 harvest, and by 1944 the RDC had capitulated by gradually retiring from commerce (see Martinello 1988:156–159, 211–260; Dean 1987:94–95).

52. Pinto (1986/1987:4).

53. Martinello (1988: 285–312; Dean 1987:108–127). Industrialists lobbied to impose a three-year limit on the price supports and argued for a gradual loosening to bring prices into line with the international market.

54. Mahar (1979:6–10).

55. Wesche (1985).

56. Bunker (1982), Wagley (1964:307), and Zimmerman (1987).

57. Sawyer (1979:109–116).

58. Pinto (1986/1987:5).

59. Pace (1987:95), Parker (1983:246–247), and Wagley (1964:300).

60. Parker (1983:304).

61. Pace (1987:99), Parker (1983:226), Wagley (1964:299–300), and Wesche (1985:126).

62. Branford and Glock (1985) and Velho (1972).

63. See Sawyer (1979) for an excellent analysis of the evolution of Amazonian peasantries in relation to capitalist development in Brazil.

64. Monte-Mór (1980:79).

65. The Rondônia tin fields would later be the site of one of the first major confrontations between *garimpeiros* and government-backed mining companies in the 1970s. See Chapter 3.

66. At first these *garimpos* were accessible only by boat. The first airstrip was built by Nilson Pinheiro at Cuiu-Cuiu in 1960. Others followed in 1961–63. Before long, the use of small planes to reach the *garimpos* stimulated a gold rush in the Tapajós in the 1960s. By the 1980s there were several hundred functioning airstrips in the region.

67. Lestra and Nardi (1982:105).

68. Miller (1985).

69. Cleary (1990).

70. Obligations depended on the personal relationships, the economic situ-

ation of the patron, and the productivity of the *garimpo*. The existence of a strong *meia-praça* system with large work crews depended primarily on the capacity of the *garimpo* to attract potential suppliers. For example, during the boom period in the 1930s and 1940s, in the *garimpos* at Poxoréo, Mato Grosso, 90 percent of the *garimpeiros* worked as *meia-praças*, commonly in teams of eighteen to twenty men. By the mid-1970s, when mining was in decline there, it was difficult to find a patron; while 63 percent of the *garimpeiros* worked as *meia-praças*, only 8 percent worked in groups larger than two people, and most worked alone (Baxter 1975).

71. Sales (1955:34).

72. There were many variations of the basic *meia-praça* relationship. Some *garimpeiros* who were specialized in the final washing or *despescagem*, for example, hired out on a daily basis to other work crews. In some cases whole crews exchanged labor for particular tasks, a practice known as *troca de dias*. Technological changes in the 1970s and 1980s led to the growing importance of day laborers and created new and elaborate forms of financing and labor deployment (see Chapter 3).

The supplier was the patron most directly related to the *meia-praça*, yet other bosses often extracted a percentage of production. In *garimpos* located on private land, for example, the landowner had a customary right to collect a ten-percent share of all minerals extracted. More formalized partnerships, known as *sociedades*, also existed between suppliers. The divisions between supplier and *meia-praça* were often unmarked by noticeable differences in lifestyle. A supplier might work as part of his own crew, receiving the two shares corresponding to his two roles. There was also a degree of mobility from *meia-praça* to supplier in the *garimpo* (see Cleary 1990).

73. Salomão (1981:43).

74. Cleary (1990).

THREE

❖

Militarizing Amazonia, 1964–1985

After the armed forces took control of the Brazilian government in 1964, the military regime adopted a series of aggressive development policies designed to attract foreign investment and stimulate capital accumulation in the country's industrial sector. The goal of modernizing the economy was to be achieved via tax incentives and wage containment measures to boost economic growth and reduce regional and sectoral imbalances. The resulting increases in aggregate output that took place between 1968 and 1974, dubbed the "Brazilian miracle," were regarded a premier accomplishment of economic planning. The allusion to divine intervention notwithstanding, the "miracle" was the consequence of a more or less distinct model of development, the implementation of which relied on political repression and the centralization of power in the hands of the federal government.

The Amazon played a special role in the regime's overall development plan. The wealth of untapped resources in the lowland basin and the vast expanse of sparsely populated territories in Amazonia made the region a good place to absorb investment capital and surplus labor from other parts of the country. In addition, the geopolitical criteria that figured so prominently in the military's worldview prescribed the urgent need to inhabit vulnerable areas along northern Brazil's sensitive international borders. These objectives were to be met by promoting in-migration and colonization and by providing financial incentives to private capital to invest in the region. The military's intention, expressed by the regime's preeminent strategist, General Golbery do Couto e Silva, was to "inundate the Amazon forest with civilization."[1]

Central to the modernization plan was the need to wrest control from the traditional Amazonian elites in command of state legislatures and administrative agencies. The transfer of power and authority to the federal government was accomplished by unilateral decrees handed down from Brasília and imposed on reluctant state politicians. The changes that held the most far-reaching consequences targeted the institutions and procedures that regulated access to Amazonian resources. By increments the federal assault on state autonomy revamped the entire bureaucratic framework that governed the procurement of land and minerals on the frontier.

The substance of the new provisions—notably the contradictory goals contained within them—were a powerful stimulus to impassioned confrontations in the countryside, shaping both the character and the outcome of the conflicts that raged in rural areas. Frontier violence in turn provoked hasty and heavy-handed responses by federal authorities. The militarization of Amazonia eroded the very institutions the regime had set out to build in the first place. The deadly struggle for land intensified in the mid-1970s as a result of the policy shift away from the priority initially given to small farmers and toward an emphasis on the private sector. Bureaucratic disarray, not to mention a fractious political climate and widespread environmental devastation in Amazonia, loomed large among the dubious legacies that the military left for the civilians to resolve under the New Republic in 1985.

The Bureaucratic Framework

Operation Amazônia, introduced in 1966, featured generous fiscal incentives to be financed through the Amazon Bank, BASA. The

Superintendency for the Development of the Amazon (SUDAM) replaced SPVEA as the executing agency of federal programs. The purpose of the new policies was to make it attractive for entrepreneurs from other parts of Brazil to reinvest taxable income in the Amazon. Companies established in the region before December 1974 and those that SUDAM certified to be of regional economic interest enjoyed a ten-year tax holiday. Funds were also made available through BASA for loans or as equity for approved projects. At first, the investor had to put up one dollar for every two received through the fiscal incentive system. The equity requirement eventually dropped to twenty-five percent of the total cost of the investment.[2] In addition, a free trade zone was established in Manaus in 1967 in order to stimulate industrial and commercial growth.

Over the next decade and a half, investments of well over a billion dollars were approved for Amazonian cattle ranches, the sector that received the largest share of the direct tax credits under the new program. Producers of industrial wood together with the ranchers captured most of the SUDAM subsidies. Wood producers also benefited from separate measures designed to promote exports.[3] Both activities expanded rapidly in southern Pará during the 1970s. By contrast, credit for traditional activities like rubber extraction was de-emphasized when BASA replaced the Amazon Credit Bank. The shift further undermined the *aviamento* system and encouraged traditional elites to sell their landholdings or to diversify their own activities.

On paper SUDAM was charged with the responsibility to assess each project's economic feasibility and potential benefit to the region. Once a venture was approved, it fell to SUDAM to supervise its implementation. Projects could be canceled if the proposed investment was abandoned or if resources were wrongly used. In practice the shortage of SUDAM technicians to cover such a vast area and the fact that project accounting was generally handled by company headquarters in southern Brazil made effective supervision of the subsidies virtually impossible. A frequent result was the diversion of funds through a number of imaginative schemes that contributed far more to corporate profits than to Amazonian development. Some companies used the SUDAM subsidies to speculate on the stock market.[4] Others reformulated the same project, repeatedly submitting it to SUDAM for additional credits. So prevalent was this ploy that it became known as the "Industria da Reformulação"—the reformulation industry. It was only one of many ways to take corrupt advantage of federal development funds.

The creation of SUDAM was accompanied in the 1960s by parallel efforts of the military regime to overhaul the legal and bureaucratic agencies and regulations governing the use of land and mineral resources. In a flurry of activity, the regime produced a new Land Statute in 1964, a Forest Code in 1965, and a Mining Code in 1967. The National Indian Foundation (FUNAI) was created in 1968 to replace the discredited Indian Protection Service (SPI), and Article 198 of the constitution gave native peoples exclusive rights to ancestral territories.

The various initiatives sought to discipline the process of acquiring and exploiting land and mineral deposits. The objective was to stimulate capitalist production in agriculture and mining by fostering a stable and attractive investment climate. Yet these same bureaucratic reforms also legitimized the status of independent producers—such as Indians, *posseiros*, and *garimpeiros*—who continued to operate in their traditional fashion. The crux of the matter was the incompatibility between two opposing sets of priorities. On the one hand, there was an emphasis on private property and on incentives to capital accumulation and technological change; on the other, there were the provisions for state intervention to reduce poverty and to make land available to those who worked it. The contradiction lay at the heart of the so-called "agrarian question," which commanded the attention of institutional reformers immediately following the military takeover in 1964.

Land Rights

That the military regime should tackle the thorny question of the concentration of land ownership at the very outset of its rule was hardly surprising. It was, after all, President Goulart's Land Reform Decree of March 13, 1964, and the growing mobilization of peasant groups in northeastern Brazil who demanded the redistribution of property that had been high on the list of factors provoking the military to depose the civilian president.[5] But the actions taken by the military junta after the takeover were ironic indeed. If the generals regarded agrarian reform as sufficiently inflammatory to mobilize the troops in 1964, the main obstacle to Goulart's reform plan was removed by the postrevolution constitutional Amendment No. 10.

The new amendment superseded the reimbursement procedures spelled out in the 1946 constitution for expropriating private property, permitting the government to pay landowners in twenty-year public bonds that were indexed to keep pace with inflation.[6] Similarly, the 1964 Land Statute reaffirmed the premise that private property rights were contingent on productive use and social justice. Yet, legal provisions aside and despite the creation of new federal agencies to carry out agrarian reform—for example, the National Institute of Colonization and Agrarian Reform, INCRA—the expropriation of private property unsurprisingly met with intense political opposition. Throughout the period of military rule, and even after the return to democracy in 1985, the actual expropriation of privately held land was a rare event.

Like so many other reforms carried out during the 1960s, the intent of the land reform measures was to centralize power in the hands of technocrats in Brasília. Constitutional Amendment No. 1 was consistent with this objective inasmuch as it usurped the state's administrative control of public lands by extending federal authority to public territories deemed essential to national security and development. The strategy had vital consequences for the Amazon. Among other things, it established both the legal premises and institutional mechanisms that gave federal authorities unbridled power to intervene in a realm of affairs previously controlled by state-level governments.[7] The measure allowed the military regime to compel Amazonian states to endorse federal development and security objectives and to impose new standards on the state agencies that granted titles to land.

Sorting out the land situation in Pará was a daunting task that dragged on for years under successive state governors. The problems began before the armed forces took power and remained far from settled when the military stepped down. Between 1959 and 1963 alone, state agencies sold over 5.6 million hectares to private investors in a series of poorly documented and legally suspect transactions.[8] When the military appointed Jarbas Passarinho as governor of Pará in 1964, one of his first acts was to revoke all previous land legislation and turn control of state agrarian policy over to the Secretariat of Agriculture (SAGRI).[9] The measure was not implemented until 1965, after the election of his successor, Alacid Nunes, who demanded a review of all land sales back to 1954.[10]

As a consequence of the decrees by Passarinho and Nunes, thousands of title applications were stalled within the bureaucracy, many of which were of dubious legality to begin with. Meanwhile, five local notary offices, including the one in Conceição do Araguaia, were under investigation for fraud.[11] To make matters worse, employees of the state bureau destroyed the land registry in an apparent attempt to conceal past irregularities.[12]

In 1975 a new agency—the Land Institute of Pará, ITERPA—took over from SAGRI and again suspended all titling in order to attend to thousands of pending cases. Special decrees permitted the "repurchase" of land acquired irregularly prior to 1964.[13] With new titling suspended, and previous documents subject to nullification or dispute, the rare "good" title, even for a small area, was worth a fortune. Under the circumstances, the business of forging titles became increasingly widespread and reached new heights of ingenuity. In some cases, forgers perfected the art of aging the paper and imitating the ink of old documents to simulate land concessions dating as far back as the nineteenth century.[14]

Two factors added further confusion. One was the extractive nature of the Amazonian economy, which made it especially difficult to define property rights in a manner compatible with standards spelled out in the bureaucratic procedures. Legal protocols assumed neatly surveyed plots of land, but this bore little relationship to the vast expanse of territory controlled by powerful economic groups who made their income from the extraction of rubber and Brazil nuts and who thought more in terms of the distribution of trees than in acreage of land. Reflecting this tradition, the state of Pará had once granted *aforamentos* in the Marabá region, a category of land tenure that amounted to perpetual leases to exploit forest products. In effect, the arrangement meant that enormous tracts of land in southern Pará fell into a nebulous legal realm somewhere between private and public property.

The other problem had to do with the fact that, unlike the land in many of the states in southern Brazil, a large percentage of the land in the state of Pará was appropriated on the basis of provisional titles and *posse*—legal right based on de facto possession. Since the preindependence period in the nineteenth century, both small and large producers in Brazil were permitted to establish legal access to land based on "habitual occupation" and "effective cultivation."[15] In the Amazon region, "cultivation" was broadly defined to include extraction of forest products. This long tradition of land rights based on *posse* rather than on title conferred a legal status to *posseiros*.

At the end of 1974 Médici's successor, President Ernesto Geisel, announced that his land program for the Amazon region would include the auction and sale to private bidders of public lands controlled by INCRA. In 1976 new INCRA instructions raised the ceiling on public auctions from three thousand to sixty-six thousand hectares for agricultural and ranching enterprises, seventy-two thousand for forestry operations, and five hundred thousand for colonization projects or agricultural cooperatives.[16] Regardless of the widespread confusion over land titles or the proper demarcation of Indian territories, the land rush in Amazonia was on.

Under the circumstances, pragmatism prevailed over the finer points of law. Two controversial directives, known as 005 and 006, were prepared by the National Security Council and the Ministry of Agriculture and issued by INCRA in 1976 but were never published. The first explicitly recognized that some investors had occupied land illegally although, in some cases, their projects had been approved by federal agencies and supported by fiscal incentives. The text of Directive 005 unambiguously endorsed the principle that the ends justified the means. Because they "promoted the development of the region," landholdings in Amazonia would be recognized as legal "even though constituted through devious, reprehensible practices, constituting a breach of law and order." By dispensing with the need for surveys and circumventing the requirement of senate approval of transactions of over three thousand hectares, the device permitted the legalization of irregular titles held by investors.

Directive 006 provided a mechanism for recognizing the claims of long-term residents of the region by granting them title to up to three thousand hectares if they had effectively occupied the land for ten years.[17] The measure was sometimes invoked by INCRA authorities to undermine the claims of more recent migrants.[18] Small farmers who were newcomers to the region were the vast majority of parties to land conflicts, and they were least likely to be able to document their presence in Amazonia even if they had been there for the required ten-year period.[19] Both directives facilitated fraudulent land sales and further stimulated the brisk market in false titles and other bogus means of laying claim to land.

In late 1976 the death of ITERPA's president provided a further opportunity for direct federal intervention. Iris Pedro de Oliveira, an INCRA employee, was named to head ITERPA and to work with INCRA to reform the state's land procedures. Under his leadership, the prior systems of land rights like *aforamento* and *posse* became subject to increasing scrutiny. One of the provisions of an agreement signed in 1977 between INCRA and ITERPA called for a review of all existing *aforamentos*. Those that did not meet the legal requirements for payment of the lease were canceled.[20] In other cases, federal authorities resorted to an attempt to transform *aforamento* into short-term "concessions" by bringing disputed lands into the federal domain. By invoking federal authority, INCRA could legally overturn the perpetuity of use rights granted by the state to the *foreiros* (see chapter 5).[21]

The traditional leaseholders, whose economic and political dominance was based on their continuing control over land, at first sought to defend their rights in court (see chapter 5). But it was not long before they realized that the tide had turned against the political alliances that once supported the *aforamento* system. In July of 1977 the Association of Brazil Nut Exporters of Pará sent a conciliatory statement to ITERPA that recognized the anachronistic nature of *aforamento*. By offering to cooperate with authorities, *foreiros* hoped to retain control over areas of land larger than the legal three-thousand-hectare limit. But the gesture was to no avail. *Foreiros* were the first target of the special federal

strictions were exceedingly difficult to enforce. As was the case with so many other aspects of the frontier, the regulations cooked up in the centers of bureaucratic control in Belém and Brasília bore little relationship to what took place in the field.

If *garimpeiros* discovered minerals in an area where a mining firm held a research permit, the company could request exclusive rights to buy the ore. At the end of the research period, the firm could present its findings to DNPM. If approved by the agency, the firm would be qualified to submit a more detailed proposal showing a smaller area where they proposed to carry out mining activities. Once the company's production plan (*plano de lavra*) was ratified, mining operations could begin and *garimpeiros* would be forced to leave.

Mining companies devised ingenious ways to circumvent DNPM restrictions. The limit of five permits a year was easy to get around by creating "ghost companies" or by requesting permits for a whole list of different substances. Using such measures, vast areas of southern Pará were monopolized by firms including the state-controlled CVRD whose 38 subsidiaries held 1,674 research permits and 89 production concessions.[29]

In the absence of quality geological maps, it was impractical for mining companies to employ the thousands of workers and air support required to research the vast area of Amazonia. Many of the companies attracted by government subsidies for Amazon mining had little previous experience in the business. A common practice was not to carry out research at all but simply to wait for *garimpeiros* to make a find. The firm would then exercise its right to buy whatever the *garimpeiros* mined, making substantial profits by merely purchasing gold or cassiterite in the field.[30] Next, the firm would submit the production plan to DNPM. When this was approved, the company had the right to oust the *garimpeiros*. This was easier said than done. There were many instances when armed *garimpeiros* stood their ground, denying access to the deposits they had discovered (chapter 8).[31]

When the search for gold and cassiterite intensified in the late 1970s and 1980s, mining legislation and the actions (and inactions) of DNPM came to play pivotal roles in the process of frontier expansion in southern Pará. Indeed, the institutional arrangements that regulated access to minerals on the frontier produced a curious parallel to the outcome of federal attempts to regulate access to land. Among other things, it put DNPM squarely in the middle of the feud between *garimpeiros* and mining companies (see chapter 8). Just as federal land agencies were drawn into the pitched battles between ranchers and *posseiros*, so did DNPM find itself with the formidable task of mediating the tangled, often bloody, conflicts over the right to gold, cassiterite, and other minerals.

National Security Interventions and the Military Worldview

Restructuring the legal-administrative framework that governed access to land and mineral resources was only one facet of the modernization agenda. Related goals were achieved by state intervention in the economy, which to many people at the time showed every indication of being effective. During the heady years of the "economic miracle" in the late 1960s and early 1970s, few people in power questioned the government's ability to reform the country's ills through aggressive central planning—hardly a new idea in Brazil. Indeed, the strategy of using the state apparatus to promote development could be traced to the Vargas administration three decades earlier (see chapter 2). In the hands of the military regime that took power in 1964 developmentalism became firmly joined to the national security doctrine. The fusion of the two produced a distinctive perspective that informed every aspect of the military's behavior in Amazonia.

According to the military's worldview, the goal of filling the "empty spaces" in the region—never mind the two hundred thousand or so Indians who lived there—was justified in terms of the geopolitical necessity to protect Brazil's vulnerable interior from foreign encroachment. Similarly, the conflicts over land and the evidence that peasant farmers were becoming politically organized to defend themselves were interpreted as the handiwork of communist opportunists bent on taking unfair advantage of an ignorant populace. This perspective further promoted the conclusion that any interest group standing in the way of capitalist development presented a threat to the public interest and was equivalent to nothing less than treason.

It is against these background assumptions that we discuss the significance of the colonization project and the federal land takeover that occurred in the 1970s. Similarly, the military worldview makes it possible to appreciate the long-term significance of the army's counterinsurgency campaign in southern Pará and to comprehend the assumptions that justified the systematic assault on the rights of Amazonian Indians.

Colonization and the Federal Land Takeover

The National Integration Plan (PIN) was made public in 1970 during a visit President Médici made to northeast Brazil, which was then in the grips of one of the droughts that periodically afflict that poverty-stricken region. The PIN called for the construction of the Transamazon and Cuiabá-Santarém highways and for a commitment to finance and administer the colonization of lands made accessible by the new roads.

The sight of thousands of famished refugees seeking work and food along the roadside provided an appropriate backdrop to Médici's politically astute announcement. By declaring that public lands would be opened for settlement, the president addressed the conditions of the rural poor; yet, at the same time, he sidestepped what most observers considered the root of the problem: the extraordinarily high concentration of land ownership in the Northeast.[32] Moreover, the populist strategy of providing free land to the landless poor responded to critics who charged the military regime with promoting a "model of development" that favored the interests of the rich.[33]

When the colonization program was announced, there was hardly a consensus concerning the initiative. Because no prior analysis indicated that there was a critical need for the costly Transamazon Highway, conservatives attacked the PIN as a backward step in planning competence. The political left considered colonization a poor substitute for the real need—full-scale agrarian reform. Politicians in the Northeast greeted the proposal with a noticeable lack of enthusiasm because it diverted resources to other regions. Within Amazonia, SUDAM's opposition was also intense. The sudden emphasis on colonization challenged SUDAM's leading role in Amazonian development programs and threatened private sector interests who benefited from the fiscal incentives administered by the superintendency.[34] Other commentators, wary of the emphasis on mass migration, held that unless accompanied by enough capital and technological support, Brazil would find itself confronting an Amazon separatist movement of frustrated colonists.[35] As we will show later in this chapter, the political opposition of powerful economic groups caused the federal government to abandon the public settlement plan.

In the meantime, the colonization program was impressive in scope and design. A ten-kilometer strip of land on either side of the highways was set aside for small farmers who received one-hundred-hectare agricultural plots. The plan called for a hierarchy of administrative and residential centers and stipulated that colonists would receive a medical examination, a six-month wage, a modest house, guaranteed prices for agricultural goods, and education for their children. A battery of government agencies was charged with delivering these services. The responsibility for administering the colonization project fell to the newly created Brazilian Institute for Colonization and Agrarian Reform (INCRA). To finance these activities, 30 percent of all fiscal incentives were to be transferred to the PIN for the period from 1971 to 1974. The goal was to settle a hundred thousand families between 1971 and 1974 and to provide sufficient support for the colonists to develop into a "rural middle class" rather than fall into subsistence agriculture.[36]

The highways themselves offered the pretext for federal seizure of vast areas of public land previously under state control. In 1971 Decree Law 1164 extended INCRA's authority to land lying one hundred kilometers on either side of federal roads. Citing unspecified national security needs, the decree brought approximately thirty-one million square kilometers of territory— about 70 percent of all land in the state of Pará—into the federal domain. DL-1164 also permitted federal authorities to easily expand their jurisdiction at any moment inasmuch as the decree equally applied to actual as well as to projected roads.[37] In 1976, for example, an INCRA directive unveiled a new map that rerouted the federal road BR-158 from Cuiabá to Altamira. That single stroke of the cartographer's pen removed another thirty-two million hectares from the states of Pará and Mato Grosso. The proposed road encompassed stretches of the state road PA-150 and the land along the PA-279, which was then under construction (see chapters 5 and 6). The new, semicircular trajectory allowed INCRA to take control of the most fertile lands in São Felix do Xingu and most of the Serra dos Carajás.[38]

By centralizing control in the hands of technocrats in the federal government, Decree Law 1164 freed Brasília of interference from Amazonian states and gave the military free reign to operate as it wished in much of Amazonia. By the same token, the Transamazon Highway and the colonization schemes that attracted tens of thousands of migrants to Amazonia opened the floodgates of "civilization," just as Golbery had prescribed. The results turned out to be vastly different from what the general had anticipated.

The Araguaia War

Migrants to the Amazon in the late 1960s included sixty-nine members of the Communist Party of Brazil (PC do B) who established headquarters in the area between Marabá and Conceição do Araguaia. The guerrillas were mostly urban professionals fleeing the intense military repression then underway in southern Brazil. In Amazonia they settled quietly among the peasant farmers in remote towns like São Geraldo, Xambioá, Itaipavas, São João do Araguaia, and Palestina. Members of the group sponsored literacy classes and provided medical care and other services in the political mobilization campaign they carried out in this remote rural area.

The small guerrilla operation never posed a real threat to the Brazilian state, yet the military reaction was swift and heavy-handed. In 1972 the federal government issued a decree that gave the National Security Council jurisdiction over industrial and colonization activities in Amazonia and mobilized several thousand conscripts from nearby bases in what was called Operation Presence. In the first year of the operation, the army used conventional military tactics in an unsuccessful attempt to defeat the guerrillas. In mid-1973 the army adopted a new anti-insurgency strategy—the main elements of which the United States military had perfected in Vietnam—under the leadership of Sebastião Rodrigues de Moura, better known by his childhood nickname, Curió. Over the next fifteen years or so, the young officer's checkered career would make him one of the more flamboyant personalities in Amazonian politics. His name will turn up again and again in the chapters that follow.

Under Curió's command, small groups of special forces units from the Parachute Brigade defeated the guerrillas by the middle of 1974. A campaign of terror waged against the unwitting local civilian population enabled the troops to flush out the guerrillas.[39] The army lost perhaps a dozen men in the battles that took place in the countryside. Only a handful of the guerrillas were taken alive, all during the initial phases of the military campaign that came to be known as the *guerrilha do Araguaia*.[40] In the aftermath of the operation, Curió concluded that military action was only part of the solution to the perceived "national security problem." If Brazil was to avoid further political movements of this kind, Curió and his superiors reasoned, it was necessary to follow the insurgents' example of extending needed services to the rural population.

To win over the peasantry in southern Pará, Curió created his own colonization project along a road built during the army's campaign and rewarded peasants who had served as guides with clear title to land. He also ordered mobile army units to regularly provide health and dental services in the areas the guerrillas once commanded. What developed from Curió's initiative in the years that followed was a kind of "military populism" in which the army deployed its resources and personnel in "civic action" campaigns to benefit selected target groups on the frontier. The strategy began as a series of ad hoc interventions but later became institutionalized in the form of quasi-military agencies (e.g., GETAT; see below) that perfected the kinds of activities the army had performed in southern Pará immediately following the Araguaia War. By the late 1970s and throughout the remaining years of authoritarian rule, military populism was the hallmark of federal attempts to deal with land and mining conflicts in Amazonia.

Curió became widely recognized as a troubleshooter whose charismatic leadership and persuasiveness as a public speaker were talents that could be relied upon to handle the toughest situation. As we shall see in chapter 8, Curió's unique career would lead him to the gold fields of Serra Pelada in 1980, where he took charge of some forty thousand *garimpeiros*. Drawing on the miners' political support, he later become a federal deputy in Brasília under the New Republic. Ironically, one of Curió's fellow representatives in the national Congress was none other than José Genoíno Neto, the first of the guerrillas to be taken prisoner and one of the few to survive the Araguaia War.

The Assault on Indian Rights

The military worldview, characterized by the fusion of developmentalism and national security concerns, was especially damaging to tribal groups in Amazonia.[41] The ideology of nation-building made little room for ethnically distinct societies, much less autonomous tribes who identified with their own form of political organization. Moreover, Indian subsistence strategies ranged extensively across a variety of ecological zones, constituting what development planners regarded as an unproductive monopoly over resources that could be put to better use. Groups such as the Yanomami, who moved freely across the Brazil-Venezuela border, were particularly suspect as they could not be counted on in a crisis to defend the country's territorial boundaries.

The region's primordial inhabitants, initially driven into the hinterland by European colonizers, were now treated as intruders on Brazilian turf.[42] Federal policy under the military regime therefore stressed the "integration" of the Indians into the national society. The relentless propensity to see Indians as culturally retrograde and as obstacles to progress led to the systematic erosion of Indian land rights and contributed to an attitude that implicitly tolerated violence against them. The new highways and colonization efforts affected the territories of ninety-six groups. Another sixty-five groups lived on the lands over which the federal government claimed jurisdiction.[43] Diseases, such as malaria, measles, and influenza carried by road construction workers, had disastrous effects among previously isolated tribes, such as the Parakanã (along the Transamazon), the Krenakarore (near the Cuiabá-Santarém), and the Yanomami on the northern perimeter.

The Indian Statute passed in 1973 provided broad protection and called for the demarcation of Indian lands by 1978. But the bill contained numerous loopholes. The federal government reserved the right to mineral resources, a provision that allowed the government to relocate the native population whenever the "national interest" was at stake. Moreover, top administrators of FUNAI persisted in seeing natives as unproductive obstacles that stood in the way of the exploitation of natural resources and the development of the region. The first attempt to undermine the protection provided by the Indian Statute came in 1978 when Minister of the Interior Rangel Reis proposed an "emancipation decree." The proposal would transfer ownership of Indian land to natives themselves in the form of individual land titles.[44] Like the Dawes Act passed in 1887 in the United States, the measure would have eliminated the Indians' special status under the law, leaving Indian lands vulnerable to fragmentation and loss. Indeed, the very idea of individually held land rights was incompatible with the collective ownership and diverse sustenance strategies that the natives used to exploit the whole of their territories. When FUNAI announced the decree, it created such an uproar from national and international Indian support groups that the foundation was forced to shelve the idea.

But the same proposal would reappear in other forms in later years. In 1979 Colonel João Nobre da Veiga took office as the new president of FUNAI; his first act was to purge the agency of anthropologists, replacing them with military personnel. He also closed Indian areas to access by anthropologists and journalists. Da Veiga and his advisers launched a new version of the "emancipation" proposal by creating the so-called criteria for Indianness. According to the proposed method, the ethnic purity of Indian populations and individuals could be quantified along a scale from o to 100.[45] Those who scored in the bottom half of the scale were to be classified as non-Indian, thereby falling outside the scope of FUNAI's protection.

As happened with the earlier emancipation decree, the proposed method of quantifying degrees of "Indianness" met with such intense public outcry that FUNAI was forced to retreat. These setbacks notwithstanding, the initiatives FUNAI proposed reappeared in the debates over Brazil's new constitution in 1988 and in the demarcation of Indian reserves under civilian governments (see chapter 4). Indeed, the continuing hostility to Indian rights would constitute one of the major policy showdowns between the Brazilian military and an increasingly mobilized civilian society.

Change in Development Priorities

By the time the army had defeated the Araguaia guerrillas in 1974, the main thrust of government policies in Amazonia began to shift away from those spelled out in the PIN. If the cornerstone of the National Integration Plan was the free distribution of land, it did not take long before political pressures mounted to abandon the concern for small farmers in favor of large-scale investments. The reversal amounted to a return to earlier priorities, such as the Operation Amazônia implemented by SUDAM in the 1960s.

Politicians and businessmen who pushed for a more "rational" approach to the problem of developing the Amazon built their case on a number of considerations. One argument pointed to the high cost of the publicly funded colonization project and to the many shortfalls in its implementation. The heavy and disorderly influx of population and the front-page publicity given to the violent confrontations between ranchers and squatters further undermined the rationale for the INCRA colonization program. Supporting arguments stressed ecological themes on the (dubious) assumption that cattle ranches and other large investments were kinder to the environment than small farmers.

Indeed, only a fraction of the target population had been settled along the Transamazon Highway, and there were serious administrative failures in the support of agricultural production.[46] Engineers had demarcated agricultural plots using a grid-square method that failed to account for hills, access to water, and other critical variations such as soil quality. Land erosion, difficulties in obtaining credit as well as malaria and other health problems were additional constraints. Poor technical guidance led to low yields of basic food crops during the project's first years, followed in the next year by bumper crops that created bottlenecks in storage, transportation, and marketing.[47]

Although problems of this kind were to be expected in the initial years of a settlement project of such magnitude,[48] INCRA was blamed for failing to live up to its administrative responsibilities. In the inter-ministerial competition for dominance within the federal government, the agency became an easy target of criticism. Technocrats in Brasília, especially in the Ministry of Planning, did little to hide their scorn for most INCRA officials, whom they considered woolly-headed idealists trying ineffectually to carry out an egalitarian land settlement program that ran counter to the main thrust of the country's development priorities. In the Amazon itself, INCRA became jokingly known as the *Instituto que Nada Conseguiu Realizar na Amazônia* ("the Institute that Managed to Accomplish Nothing in Amazonia").

Wholesale abandonment of the small-farmer settlement programs was further justified by blaming the migrants themselves for their presumed lack of managerial skill and rudimentary technological sophistication.[49] A well-orchestrated ideological campaign portrayed migrant farmers as environmental outlaws both ignorant and uncontrollable. Criticism of small producers surfaced within SUDAM as early as 1972 when a new administrative team took over.[50] The following year a meeting of businessmen from the Center-South foreshadowed the attitude that soon dominated the policy agenda. At that gathering, the Minister of Planning explained that the "need to avoid predatory forms of occupation . . . and to promote the maintenance of ecological equilibrium leads us to invite large enterprises to assume the task of developing the region."

The São Paulo-based Association of Amazonian Entrepreneurs (AEA) mounted a systematic campaign in support of the view that a more "rational" and less destructive occupation of the lowland tropical basin could be achieved by backing the private sector.[51] At times the arguments mustered to support their case bordered on the absurd. A controversial study published by a RADAM consultant portrayed the Amazon forest as "senile" and clogged with unproductive vegetation. The conversion to pasture, the study concluded, would increase the availability of oxygen and water. Reputable scientists regarded the findings as preposterous, but the AEA seized upon the conclusion for reasons that were not hard to see. In a twist of sophistry, the Association attempted to promote the idea that deforestation was good for the environment.[52] The cattle lobby cited other studies showing that, once the tree cover was removed, pastures actually improved soil quality.[53]

The policy shift away from small farmers and toward large-scale projects became official with a new regional development program launched in 1974 and called POLAMAZONIA. The approach designated sixteen growth poles in Amazonia that were supported by redirecting public and private investment into areas deemed to have economic potential. Poles 1 (Xingu-Araguaia) and 3 (Araguaia-Tocantins) reserved vast areas of southern Pará for SUDAM-supported cattle ranching.[54] The new development priorities found unambiguous expression in the Second Development Plan for the Amazon for the period from 1975 to 1979. According to the document, the "indiscriminant migration of poorly educated groups, without capital to invest and using rudimentary technology, only exacerbated problems that already beset the region." "Semidirected" public colonization efforts henceforth were concentrated in western Amazonia via the PO-LONOROESTE program that began in the late 1970s.[55] In other areas, notably in Mato Grosso, colonization projects were left in the hands of private companies that targeted their land development schemes to wealthier farmers from southern Brazil who could afford to purchase lots in Amazonia (see chapter 7).

Violence and the Militarization of Land Agencies

The shift in development priorities intensified the conflicts over land on the frontier. In Amazonia violent incidents most frequently arose between the *posseiros* who responded to the government's call for small farmer colonization and the investors attracted by the profits that could be made by acquiring land with subsidies from the fiscal incentive programs. The manner in which the confrontations played themselves out varied in detail, but the basic plot remained pretty much the same.

As soon as an area was made accessible by a new road, or as soon as there was even the prospect of a new road, migrant farmers would move into the area, taking de facto possession of small plots. At the same time, other more economically powerful groups, such as ranchers, land speculators, and corporate investors, purchased claims to the same land by wheeling and dealing in the various agencies in Brasília and Belém. Most of the transactions took place without proper surveys to determine the exact boundaries of the property in question. Nor was there much information about whether there were people already settled there, which was of little concern anyhow. Finding that the land was occupied, ranchers sought to *"limpar a terra"* ("clear the land"). In frontier style, conflicts of this type were often resolved outside the legal or official system. Hired guns and paid-off police resorted to a variety of violent means (burning, beatings, torture, even murder) to persuade the *posseiros* to move on.

In the early 1970s Pará became the Brazilian state with the largest number of deaths of rural workers (see chapter 6). Statistics indicate that the number of murders roughly doubled in the 1970s and doubled again in the 1980s.[56] In many cases the threat of violence was sufficient to convince *posseiros* that it was in their best interest to accept whatever offer they could get for the "improvements" they had made. As a result, it became common practice for migrants to occupy a lot, clear it of trees, and then sell out. Known as the *indústria da posse* ("land claims industry"), the procedure was one of the few avenues open to migrants to earn cash. With no way to establish legal ownership and with none of the economic or political clout necessary to hang on to the claims they so desperately wanted, small farmers found that the only way to survive was to stay on the move, clearing one plot of land and then moving on to the next.

On those occasions when land disputes were brought before government agencies, they were usually settled through an ad hoc process of mediation in which the deck was heavily stacked against the small farmer. The typical encounter would take place in the offices of a federal or state land agency. There a representative of a group of *posseiros* would plead their case by invoking their "God-given right to the Lord's bounty" and by recounting poignant stories of dire economic need. The rancher, for his part, relied on a lawyer or two as well as on documents purchased in Brasília, a file of tax receipts, and perhaps a letter from a local or federal political figure to justify his claim. For the most part the outcome was a foregone conclusion inasmuch as the criteria invoked by the rancher and his legal staff were far more compatible with the categories and the procedures established by the bureaucracy.[57]

Because normal bureaucratic procedures failed to resolve the underlying causes of land conflicts, mounting social tensions led to intervention by National Security agencies. The "military populist" approach that Curió had used after the Araguaia War initially took the form of a series of "administrative" actions targeting highly localized situations that posed a "social problem." In the vocabulary of the security forces, a "social problem" was any dispute (say, between *posseiros* and ranchers) that threatened to lead to a major conflagration. Special steps were taken on a selective basis by military authorities who had the power to invert the routine outcome of conflict mediation by at least temporarily guaranteeing the rights of *posseiros*.[58]

When direct military intervention worked in favor of small farmers, the example was hardly lost on other *posseiros* whose land was threatened by ranchers or speculators. The message was clear enough. To defend your plot it was necessary to get organized and to pose a sufficient threat so that the military would intervene on your behalf. The result was the very process of politization that the military most feared. Although a full-scale peasant movement never developed in Amazonia, there was little doubt that the sporadic character of military intervention on behalf of small farmers increased, rather than reduced, the likelihood of organized resistance, prompting the federal government to take more systematic action.

Soon after General Figueiredo assumed the presidency in 1979, he asked the National Security Council to study the necessary measures to deal with the escalating violence in the area along the Araguaia and Tocantins rivers in southern Pará. On the Council's recommendation, Figueiredo established a new agency called the Executive Group for Araguaia-Tocantins Lands (GETAT) in

February of 1980.[59] GETAT took over INCRA's personnel and resources, but it answered directly to the president and the National Security Council, bypassing the INCRA hierarchy. Iris Pedro de Oliveira, the former INCRA staff member who had overhauled ITERPA, was named president of GETAT and granted unusually independent powers. In an apparent return to the goals of the early 1970s, the agency's mandate was to improve land distribution and to regularize land rights in order to promote "social justice" and the "progress" of the region. It was also to coordinate the activities of the diverse federal, state, and municipal institutions functioning in the area of its jurisdiction.

From the beginning, GETAT's mandate extended far beyond the mere bureaucratic handling of land problems and included ideological and political objectives. A primary goal was to counter the growing political opposition to the regime's policies for the region. In August of 1982 the creation of the National Program of Land Policy (PNPF) and of the Extraordinary Ministry for Land Affairs (MEAF) strengthened military control over Amazonian land issues. With the National Security Council in charge of agrarian policy, INCRA was reduced to a weak administrative agency. Only the responsibilities for agricultural cooperatives and rural electrification were retained by the Ministry of Agriculture.[60] As Brazil moved toward civilian government, MEAF consolidated a more aggressive political campaign to counter the antigovernment sentiment not only of the progressive Catholic church but also of a growing political opposition movement.[61]

GETAT far surpassed the achievements of previous land agencies in surveying, registering, and titling lands under its jurisdiction. GETAT also created a special colonization program on the fringes of the Carajás project area and settled some fifteen hundred families to help provide a buffer for the mining operation.[62] Unlike INCRA and its criteria to select colonists along the Transamazon Highway, GETAT gave preference to *posseiros* involved in land conflicts and sometimes offered titles to land in exchange for support for government electoral candidates (see chapter 6). GETAT's efforts amounted to a kind of "crisis colonization" policy designed to defuse localized tensions and build grassroots political support for the government.

These political uses of land were reinforced by the selective distribution of medical services, road construction, and other favors provided by GETAT through its agreements with other government agencies. In effect, GETAT was a mechanism by which the federal government, through the National Security Council, monopolized the application of resources once controlled by politicians, police forces, the army, SUCAM (the malaria control agency), EMATER (the agricultural extension agency), FUNAI, ITERPA, MEC (the Ministry of Education and Culture), and municipal governments.[63]

Although it can hardly be said that GETAT resolved the land problem in southern Pará, the act of handing out thousands of legal titles significantly affected the character of social conflict in frontier areas. Violent confrontations between ranchers and small farmers continued to take place through the 1980s, but the struggle for land assumed a different form in the places where GETAT operated. Although direct and violent confrontations continued, now it was the impersonal workings of the land market that increasingly governed the continued trend toward the concentration of land ownership on the frontier.

Despite some impressive achievements, distrust of GETAT was strong among area residents who referred to the agency's takeover of INCRA as a case of "old wine in new bottles." *Posseiros* were pleased to receive titles to land, but they were dismayed to find themselves settled in remote areas with virtually no technical assistance (see chapter 6). *Posseiros* complained bitterly about the arbitrary way GETAT established boundaries around their land and especially about the *recorte*, or subdivision of plots, in order to settle more *posseiros*.[64] Neither did GETAT gain the unqualified support of the large landowners in the area. The agency imposed a *recorte* for them, too, via the controversial *"indice 3"*—a provision that limited the size of landholdings ranchers were permitted to keep to an area three times the size of that already cleared. The federal police presence that came with GETAT curbed the activities of the ranchers' hired guns. Moreover, large landholders complained that GETAT was ineffective in stemming the tide of land invasions.[65] They also accused GETAT of intimidating private landowners with veiled threats of expropriation in violation of former INCRA policies. For all the public outcry on the part of large landowners it would appear that GE-

TAT posed a significant threat to the property rights established in the federal constitution. But that was hardly the case.[66] It was not until 1982 that GETAT carried out its first three expropriations in southern Pará. Even then, the expropriation created a precedent that agency officials later regretted as it only encouraged *posseiros* to further invade lands.

In fact, GETAT's form of "military populism" ultimately worked to the advantage of the large landowners.[67] In the short run, the military government may have benefited from the popular support generated by distributing land titles to small farmers. In the long run it was hardly lost on anyone that the net effect of GETAT's actions favored large-scale investors and that the magnitude of the political disaffection in southern Pará was so great that it could not be countered by the ad hoc strategies the agencies carried out. GETAT's most concrete achievement in its areas of jurisdiction was to significantly advance the process by which public lands were converted to private property.

Technological Change and the Militarization of Mining Areas

As conflicts over land increased in southern Pará, so did the tensions between *garimpeiros* and mining companies. New *garimpos* for cassiterite and for gems such as emeralds, diamonds, and aquamarine were opened up in the frontier areas of Goiás, Maranhão, and Mato Grosso in the 1970s.[68] In contrast to the "closed" *garimpos* in the Tapajós, mining camps in these frontier areas, located along roads and with free access to commerce, were known as "open" or "tame" mining fields. Many of the *garimpeiros* were locals who had lost their land and found themselves in towns like Santa Terezinha where employment was scarce.[69] Others were farmers who supplemented their agricultural earnings with work in the mining camps, primarily as seasonal day workers.[70]

The expansion of the *garimpo* was related to a technological transformation that began in the Tapajós in the late 1970s and spread to Goiás, Maranhão, Mato Grosso, and Pará. Although the legal definition of the *garimpeiro* envisioned a single individual with a panning tray and a box of rustic digging tools, in reality semimechanized methods had been introduced gradually in mining areas throughout the twentieth century. By the 1920s and 1930s miners were using motor-driven pumps, suction hoses, mechanical panning devices, and tractors.[71] The use of the airplane was an important innovation of the 1960s, and in 1976/1977 the first suction dredges were introduced in the riverbeds of the Tapajós.[72] Other machines were also introduced, including hydraulic pumps (*chupadeiras*) and high pressure hoses (*bico-jatos*) (see chapter 8), tractors, trucks, and mechanical hammers.[73] Strictly manual operations soon became the exception in the region.

Technological change diversified work relations in the frontier *garimpos* of Goiás, Maranhão, Mato Grosso, and Pará during the 1970s and 1980s.[74] The *meia-praça* arrangement slowly gave way to the fixed percentage worker (*porcentista*) who earned a preset share of the production; thus a larger proportion of earnings was reserved for the owner of the machines. In the "open" *garimpos* located near towns and agricultural settlements, there were significant numbers of day workers who were paid a flat daily rate and who typically worked on a seasonal basis as a complement to their agricultural work. Both day workers (*diaristas*) and percentage workers received food and shelter as part of their pay, and both might receive traditional bonuses known as the *reque*.[75]

The expansion of dredge-mining stimulated a new mining boom in the Tapajós gold fields. Between 1950 and 1970 the population of Itaituba grew from 653 to 2,000 (due to the gold boom) and then to 8,000 in 1974 with the impact of the Transamazon Highway.[76] But by 1981, after the introduction of dredges, there were an estimated forty thousand residents.[77] Businesses diversified in town and in the *garimpos* with the expansion of prostitution, restaurants, and a range of associated activities.[78] People who produced equipment and the mechanics who fixed the machines benefited, as did the contraband gold buyers who were responsible for about one-third of the purchases.[79] Changes like these created a wide constituency in favor of the *garimpo* and fostered the emergence of new economic elites.

The improved productivity of the Tapajós gold fields contributed to the concentration of income and the astronomical cost of living in Itaituba and enhanced the wealth and power of local dominant groups.[80] New economic niches for *garimpo* "bosses," including those who specialized in renting equipment, expanded. Whereas the equipment needed for manual mining had been virtually free, dredge-mining required the most expensive capital investments of all the new forms of semimechanized mineral extraction. The *garimpeiro*-entrepreneur who could afford the new capital requirements to become a *balseiro*, or dredge owner, began to dominate the scene.[81]

Money for the equipment came from a complex network of investors who lived in nearby towns and in places as far away as Rio de Janeiro and São Paulo. The considerable profits that made their way from the mining fields into the pockets of an ever larger number of people won powerful allies for the *garimpeiros* in their struggles against mining companies. By 1980 DNPM had received more than four hundred requests for research and mining licenses in the Tapajós, mostly from small mining companies based in Santarém and Itaituba.[82] Some *donos* were also able to parlay their wealth and influence from the *garimpo* to become entrepreneurs in other realms of the local economy and politics. A few became important regional figures.[83]

As the manual *garimpo* lost its traditional character in the 1970s, conflicts with the legally constituted mining companies became more common. The first major contest had been fought in Rondônia a few years earlier over the right to mine the cassiterite deposits found in the state. The mining companies argued that the crude technology used by *garimpeiros* was spoiling the deposits and that mechanization was the only rational solution to the problem. In response to the companies' pressure, the Minister of Mines and Energy, Antonio Dias Leite, announced the closing of the *garimpos* in 1970. The decree created the immense six hundred thousand square kilometer Tin Province of Rondônia (including parts of Amazonas, Mato Grosso, and Acre), which would be reserved for fourteen tin companies (most of them foreign, including the French Patiño group, the world's largest tin producer) that were granted tax exemptions and other fiscal incentives.[84] Some four thousand miners were evicted in a military operation that marshalled dozens of small airplanes to fly *garimpeiros* from Rondônia to other locations.[85]

At a time when industrialists were criticizing small-scale agriculturalists for their irrational and environmentally destructive forms of production, prominent figures in the mining sector used similar arguments against the *garimpeiros*. Some companies argued that there could be no role for *garimpeiros* in a rational system of mineral production. In his testimony before a congressional inquiry committee on multinationals in 1975, ex-Minister of Mines and Energy Dias Leite contrasted the "predatory," disorderly, and diseased *garimpeiro* with the "civilizing" influence of the companies.[86]

By the late 1970s conflicts between *garimpeiros* and mining companies paralleled the growing tensions from conflicts over land in southern Pará. Mining agencies, like those charged with regulating access to land, sought ways to accommodate the small producers. The ambitious proposal for a "Transgarimpeira" highway through the Tapajós basin was the product of this concern. The highway would traverse the main *garimpo* areas and connect to the Cuiabá-Santarém Highway, with a trunk road leading to the Transamazon; thus it would end the costly dependence on air transportation. DNPM even intended to carry out a colonization program that would provide plots of land to *garimpeiros*.

By increments, DNPM thus found itself deeply embroiled in the same sort of intractable dilemmas that had defeated the best efforts of INCRA and other land agencies operating on the frontier. Indeed, intervention in Amazonia's mining sector in the 1980s was part of the same strategy that had motivated the creation of GETAT, but there were important political differences in the case of mining. The state itself had a direct stake in the struggle for Amazonian minerals—the centerpiece of which was the Carajás project, implemented by the powerful state mining company, Companhia Vale do Rio Doce (CVRD). The government also stood to benefit from the revenues generated by the unitary tax on minerals (IUM), a portion of which was returned to the state and municipal governments.

On the other hand, the growing *garimpeiro* presence and the incidence of conflicts with mining companies constituted a dilemma parallel to that of the land conflicts, but the forces allied on either side were different. The church and other progressive opposition leaders in the region had not championed the cause of the *garimpeiros*. The gold rush was a potential threat to the growing mobilization of *posseiros* since it temporarily absorbed the thousands of landless migrants who gathered in the region's towns. In effect, the *garimpeiros* represented an alternative populist political base that the regime cultivated under the leadership of Curió. Moreover, the *garimpo* question brought the government into alliance with regional elite groups who were the principal investors behind the *garimpo*, often at the risk of alienating the private mining companies.

It was in the extraordinary open-pit mine called Serra Pelada that the regime's new *garimpo* strategy emerged (see chapter 8). CVRD had a research permit for iron in the area, but the gold on that site was discovered by *garimpeiros* in December of 1979. Rumors quickly spread, triggering a rush that attracted thousands of *garimpeiros* to the site. As the richness of these concentrated deposits became known, Brazil's Amazon jungle once again became the focus of intensive international media attention. The Brazilian government immediately took steps to extend its control over the rapidly expanding gold extraction. DNPM technicians established a presence in Serra Pelada, and DOCEGEO, a branch of the CVRD, began purchasing gold. On May 21 the government took the unprecedented step of taking direct control of the *garimpo* (see chapter 8). By that time an estimated ton of gold had already been extracted.

Brazil's gold rush was part of a global response to the sudden increase of gold prices, which peaked at $850 an ounce in January of 1980 just as Serra Pelada was getting started. But the gold fields remained attractive even after the subsequent fall in world prices for gold. The *garimpos* absorbed people who otherwise would have been unemployed in poor regions like the Northeast, in urban centers like São Paulo, and in regional towns like Xinguara and Redenção.[87]

If the gold rush created new headaches for the Brazilian government, it also provided solutions—however partial and temporary—to some intractable problems. At a time when the country's billion-dollar debt was becoming international news, the discovery of new gold reserves was certainly welcome. The *garimpeiros* themselves often told visitors of their role in paying the national debt. Federal intervention in the southern Pará *garimpos* also allowed DOCEGEO, a subsidiary of the CVRD, to assert its claim to the whole Serra Pelada and surrounding areas even though private companies had originally claimed significant parts of the area.[88] Government officials and politicians defended the strong state role in the mining sector in order to protect Brazilian mineral resources from control by foreign companies.[89]

Both economic and political concerns motivated the Brazilian government to intervene directly in the rapidly expanding gold extraction. By itself, the need to control gold smuggling and to collect government taxes on gold sales would have dictated a policy banning *garimpagem* outright in favor of mechanized mining. But the persistent "social tensions" that reigned in southeastern Pará made this strategy ill-advised if not impossible. Instead, the government's strategy attempted to transform the tens of thousands of *garimpeiros* in Serra Pelada into a base of political support. In the elections of 1982 Curió was one of the most popular and successful candidates for federal deputy on the government party (PDS) ticket thanks to the *garimpeiros* of Serra Pelada. But the strategy, as we shall see in the next chapter, was ultimately to no avail.

By the end of the 1970s development policies for the Amazon were openly subverted to the cause of defending the regime's political and ideological position against growing opposition supported by the progressive church and emerging political parties. The heavy-handed strategy of "military populism" won the regime some initial political battles, such as the support of the *garimpeiros* in Serra Pelada, but these victories were short-lived. When the military relinquished control to a civilian government in early 1985, the persistent and increasingly violent conflicts over land and minerals were no closer to a solution than when the regime had confidently begun its Amazonian conquest. The legacy of federal intervention in the Amazon was a daunting bureaucratic muddle, which the newly instated administration was left to resolve. If the military, with all the arbitrary powers at its disposal, was unable to do so, it would be doubly challenging under the new conditions of open political debate in Brazil.

NOTES

1. Hecht and Cockburn (1989:102–103). Golbery was first chief of the intelligence service (SNI) and later chief of staff until 1981.

2. Katzman (1976) and Mahar (1979). For more on SUDAM policies, see also Hecht (1985).

3. Browder (1986).

4. Browder (1986) and CPI (1980:9).

5. J. Martins (1984).

6. Inspired by post-World War II liberalism, the 1946 Constitution had officially endorsed the idea that the state had the responsibility to see that land was used in a way that met social welfare objectives. It followed that the state had the right—indeed, the obligation—to expropriate idle lands, turning them over to those who would put them to productive use. In practice agrarian reform proved difficult. The main roadblock was Article 141, a provision that stipulated that indemnification for land had to be made in cash. For years the so-called golden clause effectively limited the federal government's ability to expropriate unused land. The legal obstacle that Article 141 put in the way of agrarian reform was removed by the 1964 amendment (Monteiro 1980:102) and by Article 184 of the 1988 constitution.

7. Santos (1984:454).

8. Santos (1984:453).

9. Monteiro (1980:71–93).

10. The evolution of land policy in the state of Pará during this period was influenced by the fervent political feud between two men, Jarbas Passarinho and Alacid Nunes. At first the two were allies with a friendship that dated back to their days in the same military academy in Rio de Janeiro. In the wake of the military takeover in 1964, when the new regime appointed its allies to positions of power across the country, Passarinho became governor of the state of Pará, and Nunes became mayor of Belém. In 1965 Nunes was elected to the governor's post while Passarinho moved on to Brasília as a senator. He was soon named Minister of Labor by President Castello Branco and later headed the Ministry of Education under President Médici in 1970.

The rift between the two began when Passarinho took up residence in Brasília and when his influence grew stronger within the federal government. One outcome of the rupture was the creation of two factions within the government party, ARENA. The schism between the *alacidistas* and the *jarbistas* not only contributed to the already Byzantine style of Pará politics but also came to symbolize the contest between state and federal authority. The row would dominate Pará's political arena until the end of the 1970s, and it contributed much to the victory of opposition politicians in the 1980s.

11. Pinto (1980:149–159); see also Almeida (1983:12–16).

12. When Aloysio Chaves became governor in 1974, he found more than eight thousand irregular land processes still pending with SAGRI. State authorities annulled 185 fraudulent titles issued between 1967 and 1972 (Pinto 1980:31).

13. Pinto (1980:20–21).

14. Pinto (1980:44,160).

15. Santos (1984:447–448). *Posse* rights accrued after one year and one day

controlled small farmer colonization program called POLONOROESTE (Branford and Glock 1985:28–30). This was the only "growth pole" to emphasize small producers. For more detailed discussions of the Rondônia experience see Milliken (1988), Monte-Mor (1980), and Wilson (1985).

56. Movimento dos Trabalhadores Sem Terra (1987).

57. The outcome of agency mediation, which relentlessly worked against small farmers, amounted to what J. Martins (1984:479) characterized as the "subordination of public authority to private interests."

58. The populist stance (however limited in its scope) contributed to the legitimacy of the military regime inasmuch as the army could come away from the fray as hero, having defended the rights of small farmers. On the other hand, it meant that the armed forces increasingly found themselves mediating a whole range of disputes from marital squabbles to a worker's grievance with his boss. In the mid-1970s, for example, migrants frequently took their problems to the "8th," as the Jungle Battallion based in Marabá was known. There Curió was prone to making unilateral decisions, many of which ran counter to established legal principles. In the small town of São Pedro da Agua Branca, for example, growing tensions from a 1976 dispute between *posseiros* and a would-be owner led Curió to send an army detachment to occupy the town and help the farmers to get their rice harvest to market without fear of violence. Whatever INCRA's commitment to small farmers might have been, it was action of this type by the military that infuriated civilian officials trying to establish a consistent legal framework for a more generalized solution to social conflict.

59. By 1982 the agency controlled over 65 percent of the state of Pará (Santos Filho 1984:30–31). GETAT was modelled after a similar ad hoc institution, GETSOP, established in the 1960s to resolve land problems in the earlier frontier area of southeastern Paraná. Another group called GEBAM was created to handle the area of the controversial Jari project.

60. MEAF was created in part to make a place for General Venturini, due to retire from the military the following year (Branford and Glock 1985:176; Pinto 1983:11).

61. For example, the MEAF publication "ABCs of Land," produced in comic-book format, sought to co-opt most of the opposition's demands. Even the slogan of the National Agrarian Reform Movement, "Land for Those Who Work It" was paraphrased: "Land in the Hands of Those Who Produce." Besides informing farmers about their rights and obligations under the law, the pamphlet stated that "The land problem is being resolved. The federal government is carrying out this task."

62. Becker (n.d.) and Kohlhepp (1987:337).

63. Santos Filho (1984:5).

64. Santos Filho (1984:8–10).

65. In 1981 dozens of ranchers from around Marabá signed a petition asking for the removal of GETAT's two top people and charging that the agency generated unrest in the area (*Informe Amazônico*, Belém, 15–20 June 1981, 1:12). In 1983 the São Paulo-based Association for Amazon Entrepreneurs called a meeting with Venturini to express their concern with GETAT's seeming overemphasis on smallholders and called for a more "global" application of the Land Statute—in order to avoid "ideological situations that depart from the doctrinary principles

that guided its conception." They complained about the lack of support provided to private colonization since GETAT's creation; only seven projects were approved in 1981 and one each in 1982 and 1983. The AEA further complained that GETAT did not move fast enough in disciplining the titling process, which was essential to a sound business climate. To dramatize the point, the AEA even offered to subsidize the costs of surveying Indian lands (Almeida 1985).

66. GETAT's president stressed in a 1981 interview that expropriation was not necessary since ranchers willingly cooperated by spontaneously ceding parts of their holdings for distribution. In some cases GETAT permitted landowners to exchange their disputed claims for better holdings elsewhere.

67. J. Martins (1984:25–26).

68. Baxter (1975), Cleary (1990), Garrido Filho (1984), and Lazarin and Rabelo (1984).

69. See Lisansky (1988).

70. The expansion of mining interfered with agricultural production in regions of the Center-West that had previously been important rice producers. More money reportedly could be made in three days of mining than could be earned in a month's work of farming (Procopio Filho 1984:125–126).

71. Cleary (1990).

72. The dredges consisted of a pump connected to a Volkswagen motor, mounted on a platform that floated above empty two-hundred-liter drums. The use of dredges was introduced by *garimpeiros* returning from Venezuela, where they had worked with pumps and dredges in diamond mining (Lestra and Nardi 1982:103–104,159). After 1977 dredges proliferated in the Tapajós; by 1982 there were 457 dredges functioning there, more than twice the number (203) there had been in 1981 (Guimarães 1982).

73. Cleary (1990), Salomão (1984:65–66), and Schiller (1985:318–319). The new techniques allowed *garimpeiros* to exploit some primary lode deposits as well as the alluvium, to expand into new areas, and to reduce waste by repeatedly rewashing ore. The shift from manual to semimechanized mining dramatically increased production although the new techniques still required much manual labor. A claim previously dug by ten men in twenty days now could be dug by four men in five to seven days using a hydraulic unit (Salomão 1984:65). Production rose from two square meters per worker per day to twenty square meters per worker per day, a tenfold increase. One report claimed that the gains in increased production would pay for the cost of a dredge in a week's time (DNPM 1979:48).

74. Baxter (1975), Cleary (1990), Garrido Filho (1984), and Lazarin and Rabelo (1984).

75. Cleary (1990).

76. Miller (1985:175).

77. Lestra and Nardi (1982:105–106).

78. Lestra and Nardi (1982:159–160).

79. DNPM (1979) and Guimarães (1982).

80. Martins and Pastana (1983:95) and Miller (1985).

81. Salomão (1984:65–66).

82. DNPM (1979) and Guimarães (1982).

83. Cleary (1990).

84. Becker (1982:73–74).

85. Despite government support, cassiterite production initially fell after the introduction of mechanized extraction in Rondônia. In 1974 the companies produced only 3,935 tons. It became a point of honor to surpass the production of 5,106 tons during the last year of operation of the *garimpo*. Some of the companies were inexperienced in mining and were primarily interested in their tax breaks. Several companies went too heavily into debt and found it hard to apply the technology borrowed from Bolivia and Malaysia to Rondônia (*Minérios*, September 1977:79). Rising costs led to a process of decapitalization of Brazil's tin companies during the mid-1970s. The Tin Province of Rondônia also turned out to be dotted with small pockets of rich cassiterite that could not be exploited mechanically (*Veja*, 2 April, 1975). In 1975 DNPM backed off from its original plan and permitted *garimpeiros* to return to some areas.

Cassiterite production in Rondônia began to recover in 1975. In 1983 the companies produced twelve thousand tons of cassiterite, three times the peak *garimpo* production, and employed four thousand workers—the same number who had previously worked in the *garimpo*. The recuperation rate of the ore had risen from less than 70 percent with the *garimpo* to 85 percent using mechanized techniques (Pereira 1983:19). Three firms produced 98 percent of the province's tin, the Brazilian Paranapanema and Brumadinho and the mixed BRAS-CAN/BP; the Brazilian company BEST & Co. produced the remaining 2 percent. By the 1980s Brazil was the world's sixth producer of tin.

86. See also the debate over Rondônia recorded in Santana (1972). Some, however, noted the important role *garimpeiros* could play in reducing costs during the initial stages of discovery and in the exploitation of deposits near the surface (*Minérios*, September 1977). Others argued that with minimal technological improvements the *garimpo* system could greatly increase its productivity (Dall'Agnol 1982; Salomão 1982).

Controversy over the experience in Rondônia left the government undecided about the viability of evicting *garimpeiros* en masse from frontier areas. The search for new policy directions that followed in the late 1970s caused uncertainty among both companies and *garimpeiros* (*Minérios*, September 1977). In December of 1976 a government decree prohibited *garimpo* activities in areas where legitimate companies had legal license. The following year the decree was challenged during a dispute over a cassiterite *garimpo* in Goiás. An agreement was reached by which the licensed company conceded the area to the *garimpeiros*, who henceforth sold their ore directly to the claim owners. In June of 1978 licensed companies were granted exclusive buying rights in the *garimpos* within their area. The intent was to gradually deactivate the *garimpo*.

87. The migrants took refuge in the Amazonian gold fields motivated by the same factors—unemployment, economic recession, and rising prices for gold—that led to the minor gold rush in the United States during the Great Depression. A survey of those miners found that three-quarters of them had had no experience in mining before the depression (Merrill, Henderson, and Kiessling 1937). They too were attracted to the gold fields by the low cost of living, the relative autonomy of the work process, and the dream of large profits.

88. Lestra and Nardi (1982:197).

89. Santos (1981:235–237) and *Jornal do Ouro*, January 1985.

❖

FOUR

Contesting the Military in Amazonia, 1979–1990

The late 1970s was a period of gradual political liberalization in Brazil. After a decade of military repression, President Geisel and his successor, João Figueiredo, endorsed a step-by-step plan to loosen the regime's grip on public dissent. The more relaxed political environment allowed critics to speak out on topics that once would have landed them in jail. In Amazonia, the political opening coincided with the increasing mobilization of small farmers, miners, rubber tappers, and Indians. What began as precarious and sporadic local protests evolved in the following decade into resistance movements that found allies among state and national opposition parties.

To stem the tide, the regime engaged in a kind of "military populism," a strategy institutionalized by GETAT and perfected during Curió's takeover of the Serra Pelada gold field. But the efforts were to no avail. By the mid-1980s GETAT was thoroughly discredited, *garimpeiros* in Serra Pelada had taken matters into their own hands, and opposition parties across the region enjoyed sweeping victories in county elections. The regime's modernization agenda was further disrupted by the growing sophistication

Indians displayed in their ability to manipulate the media and the national political system in defense of the lands they claimed.

When a reform-minded civilian defeated the military's hand-picked candidate for president of the Republic in 1985, the tantalizing prospect of a new era of Amazon development priorities appeared on the horizon. A far-reaching land reform program figured prominently among the host of progressive initiatives proposed under the newly instated democratic system. Yet these and other reforms were soon stalled by forceful opposition from landowners and an array of allied investors whose interests such measures threatened. As a result, the legacy of authoritarian policies and the social conflicts they engendered persisted without interruption in the first years of the New Republic, as did the military's presence in the region. Although one step removed from formal decision-making power, the military remained in command of Amazonian development policies, whose form and content changed little from the days of outright authoritarian rule. Illustrative of the postdemocratic initiatives is the Calha Norte program the military proposed along Brazil's border with Venezuela—a policy that explicitly echoed the familiar national security creed, including its profound disdain for the land rights and ethnic diversity of the Yanomami Indians who lived there.

But the troubling continuities between pre- and postdemocratic Brazil hardly meant that nothing had changed in Amazonia. By the late 1980s the interests expressed by grassroots movements in the region and by opposition groups at the national level increasingly coincided with the content of the new international debate regarding the environmental consequences of conventional development models. The result was the forging of novel alliances that established direct links between lobby groups with a global agenda and activists that operated at the local level. New sources of power—including material resources, access to information, and new bases of legitimacy—became available to native Amazonians and their supporters. For the first time, the people who lived in the region began to have an impact on the course of Amazon development policy.

The internationalization of the debate about Amazonia's future and the growing popularity of environmental concerns altered the content of the political confrontations that introduced the

1990s. The "greening of the development discourse" meant that Indians and rubber tappers—as well as ranchers, military strategists, mining companies, bankers, politicians, scientists, and citizen's groups—increasingly found it advantageous to couch their respective interests in terms of ecological principles and the conservation ethic. The interplay of these social groups, each pursuing their particular agenda via a bewildering array of alliances both inside and outside of Brazil, constituted the new matrix for the contested frontiers in Amazonia.[1]

Critique of the Military's Amazon Policies

Brazil's national Congress initiated the first comprehensive assessment of the consequences of Amazonian development policy. In 1979 federal deputy Jáder Barbalho, a member of the opposition political party, convened a parliamentary commission (CPI) "to investigate the distortions that occurred in SUDAM's execution of the Amazon Development Plan." The report, unanimously approved by the bipartisan commission, was highly critical of the regime's development strategies and of the role played by the regional planning agency.[2] The evidence was startling indeed. From 1966 to 1978 SUDAM had spent Cr$5.7 billion, an amount equivalent to double the annual budget for the entire state of Pará. Yet the massive expenditures seemed only to have worsened Amazonia's position within the national economy. Per capita income in the northern region (Acre, Amazonas, Amapá, Pará, Rondônia, and Roraima) was still only 62.7 percent of that for Brazil as a whole in 1978. Moreover, the region's trade balance—the difference in the value of exports from and imports into Amazonia—had deteriorated from a surplus of $26 million in 1964 to a deficit of $350 million in 1979.

Nor did SUDAM programs improve the internal distribution of income and resources.[3] In his deposition before the CPI, BASA President Oziel Carneiro observed that the vast majority of the fiscal incentives had gone to larger enterprises controlled by investors from outside Amazonia. Although 85 percent of the region's rural properties were in the hands of smallholders (up to one hundred hectares), only three projects in this category had received SUDAM support. Similarly, small-scale industries (those with fewer than fifty employees) represented 96.2 percent of the region's industrial sector but only 9.6 percent of the SUDAM budget. The 333 cattle projects that occupied an area of nine million hectares had created only sixteen thousand jobs, and that at a cost of over Cr$1.5 million per job. By the same token, only 14 percent of the value added in SUDAM industrial projects went to salaries. The result, Carneiro concluded, was to worsen rather than improve regional disparities in income due to the low rate of job creation. The report noted that most of the benefits of the incentive programs had flowed out of Amazonia and that within the region the incentives contributed to a greater concentration of land and income by neglecting small enterprises and native populations.[4]

SUDAM support for foreign-controlled ranching enterprises added fuel to the controversy. Although projects with foreign participation or control were a small minority of SUDAM's constituency, they were particularly visible because of their large scale. Foreign-owned projects averaged about 90,000 hectares compared to 22,500 hectares in the case of Brazilian firms.[5] Volkswagen's 135,000-hectare Rio Cristalino ranch in the *município* of Santana do Araguaia drew national attention in 1978 when the company set fire to 25,000 hectares of land. The blaze, which was the largest single burn on record, was plainly visible in weather satellite photos.[6]

The immense Jari project, owned by American shipping magnate Daniel Ludwig, was the most glaring symbol of the foreign presence in Amazonia and epitomized the preference the PO-LAMAZONIA program gave to large rather than to small projects.[7] In 1967, with the blessing of Brazil's new military government, Ludwig purchased some three million acres near the mouth of the Amazon to develop plantation forestry and pulp processing as well as mining, livestock, and irrigated rice cultivation. The regime went so far as to guarantee a $240 million loan from the Japanese Export-Import Bank to finance a pulp mill and wood-fired power plant built in Japan and towed halfway around the world to its home at the Jari River port of Munguba.[8]

The Tucuruí dam, the fourth largest in the world, was the focal point of similar criticism. The multimillion dollar project was be-

gun in 1975 as part of the government's plan to provide hydroelectric power to large-scale industries in Amazonia. Despite a
twelve-year planning period, neither the environmental and nor
the social consequences of the enterprise had been effectively
addressed.[9] Much of the flooded area was dense tropical forest,
nearly all of which was used by Indian groups, riverside dwellers,
migrants, or ranchers. Few of the estimated 2.8 million trees and
shrubs to be flooded were catalogued, and no biological inventory
was carried out. To make matters worse, CAPEMI, the military
pension fund company, was awarded the contract to extract lumber from the area of the reservoir and went bankrupt shortly after
securing a hundred million dollar loan from a French bank.[10] The
trees that remained in the basin posed a long-term threat to the
ecology of the reservoir and were a potential danger to the hydroelectric turbines that could be damaged by large debris.

Environmental and social concerns also called attention to the
array of projects that comprised the Carajás development pole
in eastern Amazonia. Between 1980 and 1985 the state-owned
Companhia Vale do Rio Doce (CVRD) invested sixty-three million
dollars in an exemplary environmental program linked to the Carajás iron ore project. Research in botany, zoology, archaeology,
climatology, and marine engineering was carried out around the
mining site. An independent scientific advisory board composed
of respected scientists monitored the project's impact on the environment. But controversies remained, especially with regard to
the activities beyond the boundaries of the well-protected mining
site.[11] In contrast to the mining area, plans for the large areas that
fell under the Carajás umbrella were never more than a series of
vague, overly ambitious initiatives that showed little concern for
the environment or the people involved.[12]

In 1986 federal authorities approved the construction of two
cement factories and nine pig iron factories in eastern Maranhão
and southwestern Pará to process iron ore from Carajás. The idea
was to stimulate local processing rather than the export of raw
minerals. To make use of the wood that would otherwise be
burned in land clearing, the factories were to be fueled by charcoal made from natural and plantation forests yet to be established. The planning document anticipated the potential threat
that a "charcoal army" might pose to the remaining trees in sur-

rounding areas, but this possibility was never adequately dealt with.[13]

By the end of the 1970s even cattle ranching, the main economic activity in southern Pará at that time, had come under fire. If earlier studies had shown pasture to be an environmentally sound land use that improved soil nutrient status,[14] the results of later research concluded that the original findings were overly optimistic. More detailed analyses showed that the initial enrichment of the soil that came from cutting and burning the biomass occurred at the expense of the total available nutrient stocks in the ecosystem, which gradually declined in subsequent years.[15] Lacking the defenses of the diverse natural system, pastures were invaded by pests and weeds, many of them highly toxic to cattle. In some places, such as Paragominas, vast areas once devoted to cattle ranching had to be abandoned altogether.

The high cost of fertilizing and of weeding meant that ranchers found it more profitable to clear new forest than to recuperate old pastures. In addition, rising inflation rates, fiscal incentives, tax holidays, and government-sponsored roadbuilding programs drove up the price of Amazonian land even as its productivity declined. These circumstances provided little incentive for ranchers to engage in long-term management strategies such as selective clearing in accordance with topography, preservation of forest corridors along watercourses and between cleared areas, and rotation of pastures.[16] By 1976 the controversy over ranching in Amazonia forced SUDAM to restrict its support for new livestock projects to scrub forest areas.[17]

Cattle ranching was correctly associated with the rapid deforestation of Amazonia.[18] By the late 1970s the topic had become a major concern although estimates of the rate of forest clearing were subject to divergent interpretations. In 1978 SUDAM used LANDSAT data to show that only 1.5 percent of the Amazon basin had been deforested at that time.[19] On the basis of these estimates, the agency dismissed as "alarmist" the concerns expressed in the media and voiced by scientists in Brazil and other countries. Critics were quick to note that the overall average SUDAM published concealed the very high deforestation rates that were underway in certain areas, such as Rondônia and southern Pará, where development activities were concentrated. In any case, the key issue in their view was not the size of the area deforested thus far but the increasing rate of deforestation, which in some states appeared to be exponential.[20] The deforestation controversy resurfaced with greater urgency in the late 1980s because of its perceived link to global climate change.

The *garimpos* that spread across southern Pará in the 1980s were of concern to both environmental activists and public health workers. The surge in the number of malaria cases in Amazonia was a particularly ominous development. Brazil had tackled its serious malaria problem with the creation of the National Malaria Service in 1941 when six million Brazilians—one-sixth of the total population—suffered from the disease.[21] Programs to spray DDT and to diagnose and treat active cases of malaria, begun in 1959, were so effective that by 1970 there were only 52,469 cases in the whole country. In 1982 the figure rose to 222,000 cases, concentrated in Amazonia's new settlements and mining areas. The number of malaria victims continued to rise in later years, reaching about half a million by 1988.[22] The incidence of malaria was heavily concentrated in a relatively few municipalities, especially in Rondônia, southern Pará, and Maranhão.

The mercury that miners used to separate gold from the sand and pebbles dredged up from the riverbeds was a particularly toxic threat to people's health and to the environment.[23] It took several years before the magnitude of the problem was recognized. Doctors were rare in the *garimpos*, and health conditions were so poor that many symptoms of mercury poisoning were attributed to other causes. It was not until 1985 that a pilot study carried out by a commission in the state of Goiás found critical levels of mercury pollution in the nearby rivers. The contamination of the rivers posed a danger to fish, soils, vegetation, and livestock and polluted the water supply for some hundred thousand downstream residents.[24] Subsequent studies confirmed the magnitude of the potential mercury contamination in the Pará *garimpos* and prompted efforts to monitor mercury toxicity and to explore alternative technologies.[25] The use of mercury was outlawed in the *garimpo* in March of 1988, but the prohibition was almost impossible to enforce.[26]

Environmental concerns led to national debate on a comprehensive new program for ecological zoning of the Amazon region.

The first proposal was prepared in 1979 by an interministerial group representing sixteen institutions at state and federal levels, and it was subsequently revised by specialists in the Ministries of Agriculture, Planning, and Interior. When the document was submitted to the congress in 1980, debate on competing versions of the proposal hardened into polarized factions. The newly formed Amazon Defense Movement along with environmental and Indian rights groups urged the state to regulate the occupation of the region as a means to protect the environment and local populations. The Amazon Defense Movement's recommendations aroused the enmity of mining and ranching interests as well as that of die-hard nationalists who saw in these proposals the clandestine work of communists, the liberal wing of the Catholic church, and the U.S. Central Intelligence Agency.[27] The unresolved controversy brought the zoning program to a halt; yet the debate foreshadowed the issues and the alignment of interests that shaped the contests over Amazonian development during the decade that followed.

Organizing Resistance in the Amazon

The climate of open political debate and the emergence of opposition groups and political parties seeking constituencies at the national level coincided with a new phase of resistance movements in the Amazon. In the late 1970s and early 1980s struggles by farmers, rubber tappers, miners, Indians, and other groups affected by the changes underway in the region began to take on a more organized form. The trend toward collective action was facilitated by improved communications between groups and was associated with the growing realization that their only chance of success lay in coordinated efforts.[28] A contributing factor was the military's ad hoc intervention to resolve cases of "social tension" (see chapters 3 and 6), a strategy that inadvertently promoted the conclusion that concerted acts of resistance were an effective way to pressure the state into granting land concessions.

Organizations linked to the Catholic church provided support for grassroots organizing in Amazonia, as they did elsewhere in Brazil during the 1970s. The Pastoral Land Commission (CPT) and the Missionary Indian Council (CIMI), linked to the Brazilian National Bishops' Council (CNBB), were created in the 1970s to coordinate the church's support activities for Indians and for people involved in land conflicts, primarily in Amazonia. Through these organizations the church publicized incidents of violence, formulated its own critique of government policies, and helped local populations defend themselves. Church-supported organizations, such as the Christian Base Communities, formed all over the country and provided the forum to develop resistance strategies.[29] The network of church groups also permitted local populations to learn from one another and, in southern Pará, to develop region-wide strategies (see chapter 6).

In the 1970s a number of native groups, including the Kayapó (see chapter 9), took direct action to expel invaders and to pressure FUNAI officials and representatives of other agencies in Brasília.[30] CIMI helped organize over a dozen meetings that brought together the dispersed groups, which had historically been divided by cultural, linguistic, and geographic distances. Improved communication among native groups laid the basis for more unified strategies to fend off encroachment of their territories.[31] The first national-level Indian organization in Brazil, the Union of Indigenous Nations (UNI), brought together thirty-two tribes in 1981. The following year, Mário Juruna, a Xavante, became the Indians' first elected federal deputy from the state of Rio de Janeiro. For the first time, Brazilians had to come to grips with the fact that Amazonian Indians were a legitimate political presence in the national and state congresses.[32]

In Acre, the rubber tappers' resistance movement emerged in the 1970s with the support of the Catholic church and the rural workers unions.[33] The tappers developed unique forms of nonviolent resistance that centered on *empates*, community organized "stand-offs" against the workers clearing forested areas for pasture. By the early 1980s the rubber tappers had established ties to national and international supporters in their effort to stop ranchers from deforesting the areas that the tappers depended on for their livelihood.

Nowhere was the military's waning political power more evident than in the confrontation that took place in Serra Pelada when miners resisted the government's attempt to turn the gold field over to the state mining company CVRD. The regime's loyal troubleshooter, Curió, was recruited to take charge of the mine and mediate the dispute. With the support of the *garimpeiros* of Serra Pelada, Curió won election to public office in 1982 just as the government had hoped. But the victory was short-lived. After the election results were in, President Figueiredo decided to turn the mine over to CVRD after all. Figueiredo's change of heart prompted the miners to take immediate action to defend themselves (see chapter 8). In the months that followed it became increasingly evident that the *garimpeiros* were going to succeed in retaining control of the mine by force. Curió, ever the pragmatist, promptly switched allegiance to his constituency in the mining fields, but that too was short-lived. By the mid-1980s the miners had grown in number and economic influence and had become a major independent force in the life and politics of southern Pará.

The resettlement of people from land flooded by the Tucuruí dam sparked its own resistance movement. Part of the Parakanã Indian reserve was inundated, as were six towns and a stretch of the Transamazon Highway populated by small farmer colonists. Resettlement arrangements were late and minimal for the estimated twenty-five thousand to thirty-five thousand people who were forced to move from the reservoir site. The woefully inadequate relocation measures led to confrontations between the expropriated populations and ELETRONORTE, the military-controlled regional electric company in charge of the dam.[34] With the support of opposition politicians and the Catholic church, expropriated populations organized demonstrations that forced concessions from ELETRONORTE.

In the explosive political climate that characterized the last years of military rule, the mobilization of peasants, rubber tappers, and miners in Amazonia became increasingly visible. Even in remote communities in the region, organized protests erupted against outside companies that attempted to exploit forest resources, such as timber and palm heart.[35] In southern Pará and northern Goiás, new strategies of organized invasion and armed collective defense by *posseiros* posed a growing threat to ranchers (see chapter 6). And across Amazonia *garimpeiros* refined the tactics they had used to frustrate police efforts to evict them.[36]

With the presidential election on the horizon, an array of political parties jockeyed for new constituencies. As a result, grass-roots organizations in Amazonia took on broader political overtones. For example, the mobilization of people dispossessed by the Tucuruí dam began with the local Associação dos Expropriados and neighborhood groups in Tucuruí. It later spread to the rural workers union and eventually to the directorate of the opposition party, PMDB.[37] Although the details varied from place to place, the same process occurred across the region. By 1984, as popular resistance movements drew strength from the alliances they had forged with opposition groups within local, state, and national political arenas, the military regime's policies for the Amazon were in thorough disarray

The New Republic

Reform was the New Republic's dominant theme. Or so it appeared during the first year or two of civilian rule after 1985 when the tenor and the content of Amazonian development policies promised to address the criticisms of earlier methods and priorities.[38] The objectives of the New Republic's First Amazon Development Plan (I PDA-NR), published in April of 1986, were to "accelerate the growth of the regional economy while maintaining ecological balance and reducing social inequalities."[39] Accordingly, the export orientation of previous policies would be reversed, and the regional and state institutions that had been weakened by past federal intervention were to be given greater power and autonomy. These and related issues were the focus of intense debate in 1987 and 1988 by the seven hundred members of Brazil's Constituent Assembly who wrote the new constitution approved in October of 1988. With respect to Amazonia, the two most controversial matters concerned agrarian reform and the rights of Indian groups.

Agrarian Reform

The agrarian sector was the initial focus of the New Republic's most sweeping reform efforts. In May of 1985 President Sarney announced that he would implement the agrarian reform that had been promised by Tancredo Neves before his untimely death. The reform bill published in October of 1985, however, contained a number of revisions that toned down the redistributive language of the original document. In a manner reminiscent of the political rhetoric just after the military coup in 1964, the revised proposal shifted the emphasis from the expropriation of large private land-holdings to the settlement of public lands. Throughout the rest of the 1980s any chance of significant agrarian reform was steadily undermined by mounting bureaucratic impediments and the increasingly well-orchestrated resistance by landowners. In the end, landowners were able to turn the reform effort to their benefit.

Already discredited, GETAT also became a target of reform. Opponents charged that the agency was too closely linked to the National Security Council and had used its power for unsavory ends not within its mandate (see chapter 6). Congressional proposals to abolish GETAT circulated as early as March of 1985, but its newly appointed civilian president, Asdrubal Bentes, successfully argued for a temporary stay.

Bentes published the first public data on GETAT's achievements during its five years of existence: over nine million hectares of land had been registered, nearly sixty thousand lots surveyed, five holdings occupying nearly four hundred thousand hectares had been expropriated, 54,570 titles been issued, and almost twenty thousand colonist families been settled. By 1986, when GETAT was brought back into INCRA's regional offices, the agency had reportedly issued 61,912 titles.[40] In southern Pará, the process of titling lands reduced the intensity of rural violence in the early 1980s somewhat, but it did not reverse the market forces that led to a greater concentration of land ownership. After two years in limbo, GETAT was finally abolished altogether in 1987. But the impasse over agrarian policy in Pará was no closer to a solution.

A new Ministry of Agrarian Reform (MIRAD), created in 1985, was administered by a series of five different ministers before it too was abolished four years later in 1989. Under the new organizational scheme, INCRA was to implement the ambitious National Agrarian Reform Program (PNRA) within MIRAD. The enormous task added to the agency's existing responsibilities for colonization, land tenure regularization, and rural taxation.[41] In

1987 the new head of MIRAD, Jáder Barbalho, the former governor of Pará, abolished INCRA altogether. During his tenure as chief administrator of MIRAD, Barbalho also increased the amount the government would pay for expropriated properties. Expropriation thus became an attractive alternative, especially to those who had invested in large projects (for example, Jari and Tucumã) and to local elites, like the *castanhal* owners in southern Pará, whose land was already occupied.[42]

The mere talk of agrarian reform caused an escalation in rural violence. The landless in Amazonia and elsewhere in Brazil interpreted the rhetoric surrounding the reform effort as license to take matters into their own hands. In southern Pará, the Tucumã private colonization project became the site of a massive land invasion (see chapter 7). Landowners across the country responded to these events by creating their own armed militias and by establishing the Rural Democratic Union (UDR), an organization founded in May of 1985 by a charismatic young rancher named Ronaldo Caiado from Mato Grosso. The UDR provided organization and financial support for the landowners' resistance to the reform effort and to the threat posed by an increasingly organized peasantry.

The first state-level agrarian reform plans were submitted to the federal government for approval in January of 1986. The Pará plan focused on 122 areas that had been the site of land conflicts. The initiative called for settling of 16,136 families on 965,192 hectares of land, including 200,000 hectares of public property in Altamira and São Felix do Xingu.[43] In order to facilitate the implementation of state-level agrarian reform, the Amazonian state governments successfully pressed for revocation of Decree Law 1164 of 1971, the provision that allowed the federal government to assume control over most of the region. But decentralization hardly solved the problems at hand, nor did it speed up the reform effort. The state-level agrarian commissions, created to "democratize" the implementation of the agrarian reform, were stalled by the continued opposition of the landed elite. In Pará, for example, the state commission met only once in 1987. In the end, the expropriations carried out in the state primarily benefited landowners seeking a federal bailout for investments that had gone sour.[44]

In Brasília, landowners were well represented among the members of the assembly that was convened to write the new constitution. In the long and heated debate over each provision of the constitution, the opponents of the progressive agenda applied their extensive resources to a concerted effort to undermine the articles dealing with the agrarian sector. The final document approved in 1988 so limited the legal basis for expropriation of land as to effectively spell the end of any hope for a significant change in land tenure. In the following year the Agrarian Reform Ministry itself was abolished. What continued in Amazonia and elsewhere in Brazil were the violent confrontations over land in the countryside.

Ironically, it was the armed forces that benefited most from the redistribution of Amazonian land under the New Republic. When President Sarney revoked Decree Law 1164, the federal government retained the power to grant land concessions to the armed forces for use as military bases and training areas. Under this provision, new decrees issued in 1988 and 1989 turned over more than six million hectares of Amazonian land to the army. Another area in Pará, called the Serra do Cachimbo, had been set aside in 1982, reportedly for nuclear testing or for disposal of nuclear wastes.[45] These concessions made the army Brazil's largest landholder. In addition to the international border areas included under the Calha Norte program, which is discussed below, the military directly controlled ten million hectares in the Amazon, seven million of which were located in the state of Pará.[46]

Indian Policy

The agrarian question was closely tied to the equally persistent and intractable problems regarding Indian lands in Amazonia. Since 1964 successive military governments had failed to implement their own policies to protect Indian rights (see chapter 3). In November of 1983 the military regime issued Decree Law 88.118, which changed the procedure for the demarcation of Indian lands. The new protocol required studies by the Ministries of Land Affairs and Interior and approval by an interministerial working group before the president could issue the official decree. This measure considerably slowed the process of demarcation, which was already far behind the 1978 deadline established by the Indian Statute.[47]

A companion decree, DL 88.985 issued in 1983, permitted state companies—and private firms in the case of strategic minerals—to carry out mining operations on Indian reserves under FUNAI's supervision. The measure was challenged as unconstitutional and generated strong opposition. Public pressure forced the Ministers of Planning and of Mines and Energy to promise that mining permits would not be issued on Indian lands.[48] The measure was opposed by FUNAI President Jurandir Marcos de Fonseca, who was promptly fired from his post when he refused to acquiesce. Thus began a period of prolonged institutional crises that continued well into the period of civilian rule.[49]

During the first years of the New Republic, there was some progress in the demarcation of Indian lands. In September of 1986 the president of FUNAI dubbed Sarney the "President of the Indians" for reportedly having signed the demarcation of nearly thirteen million hectares to benefit forty native groups. But by 1987 Indian policy under FUNAI President Romero Jucá Filho turned more hostile. In September of that year a new decree further modified the demarcation process. The National Security Council, INCRA, and other agencies were added to the FUNAI working group that decided on land demarcation. The coordination of the group was handed over to the Ministry of the Interior instead of to FUNAI.[50]

A companion decree enacted on the same day distinguished between Indian "areas" and Indian "colonies," depending on their "degree of acculturation." Precisely what the decree meant by the latter was presumably clarified in a document SUDAM published in June of 1988, which established the criteria to determine the extent to which a particular Indian group was acculturated. The distinction between Indian areas and colonies and the attempt to establish degrees of ethnic identity bore a close and disturbing resemblance to earlier attempts by the military regime to promote the "emancipation" of acculturated Indians (see chapter 3).

Those who opposed the idea of granting land to Indians seized the opportunity to express their views before the Constituent

contrary, the initiatives taken under the New Republic in Amazonia were strikingly similar to the goals and methods that had characterized past development policies.[55] Although the POLA-MAZONIA program was formally abolished in 1987, the "growth pole" emphasis continued. Similarly, even though a new ministry was created explicitly to enact an agrarian reform, nothing was accomplished in this regard, leaving the whole issue of land concentration and titling at an impasse. Finally, the content of the new Indian policies remained as openly hostile to native groups as any put forth under the military regime.

What did change was the context within which these continuities persisted. Unlike in the earlier period, a series of events in the late 1980s catapulted Amazonian issues into the center of an intense national and international debate regarding the environmental impact of economic growth and development. Grassroots organizations in Amazonia continued to mobilize their constituents, this time aided by alliances established with international lobby groups. By putting Amazonia on the front page of newspapers in Brazil and across the world, this turn of events introduced new elements into the matrix of influences that shaped the content, the form, and the outcome of the contests in the region.

International Issues and Alliances

The mid-1980s saw the beginning of a global trend that eventually brought together environmental and human rights activists in Brazil, the U.S., and Europe. The history of environmental lobby groups in the U.S. paralleled similar movements in Europe that led to the growth of the Green Party. In southern Brazil, small environmental organizations of varied political persuasions existed, including some that focused on the Amazon. A Brazilian Green Party was also formed in the 1980s under the leadership of Fernando Gabeira. But Brazil's fledgling conservation movement had relatively little impact on Amazonia. The most effective voices in defense of the environment in northern Brazil came, instead, from grassroots movements in the region itself.

It was the convergence of several events in 1988 that served to focus international attention on the Brazilian Amazon. One factor was the severe drought that occurred in the U.S. during the summer of that year. For the first time, an alarmed U.S. public began to take seriously the predictions of some scientists about global climate change as a result of the "greenhouse effect."[56] At about the same time, U.S. and Brazilian scientists released new data that documented a sharp rise in the rate of deforestation in Amazonia—a phenomenon associated with the release of CO_2, a principal "greenhouse gas."

In fact, most of the world's carbon dioxide comes from industrial pollution and burning of fossil fuels in the developed countries, especially the U.S. Brazil was nonetheless the fourth country in the world in terms of the volume of carbon dioxide emissions, contributing an estimated 5.5 percent to the total amount produced per year.[57] Excluding other sources of CO_2, about 20 percent of the carbon dioxide produced in Brazil came from forest burning.[58] As the drought in the U.S. deepened and the public became increasingly aware of these relationships, support for environmental activities assumed a legitimacy and an urgency that they had not enjoyed before.

One of the more imaginative, if controversial, proposals devised by U.S.-based environmentalists was the "debt-for-nature" swap. The arrangement would reduce the debt burden and, at the same time, finance conservation efforts.[59] In Brazil, debt-for-nature swaps were less important compared to the link between external financing and Amazon development policies.[60] Multilateral development banks (MDBs), such as the World Bank and the Inter-American Development Bank, financed projects in the region that drew the attention of U.S.-based environmental lobby groups.[61] In the 1970s they successfully pressured the U.S. Congress to pass a new Foreign Assistance Act. The Act required the U.S. Agency for International Development to address the environmental impact of bilateral assistance. The legislation also instructed the U.S. representatives to MDBs to use their influence to force the multilateral agencies to address the protection of natural resources.

Most of the MDBs had environmental policies on the books, but these were granted little more than lip service. In the meantime, there was mounting evidence of adverse environmental effects of bank-funded projects, especially in the agricultural and energy sectors. Two projects that received special scrutiny in the 1980s were the Indonesian transmigration program and the PO-LONOROESTE project in the western Amazon state of Rondônia. The campaign for public accountability of World Bank financing of the POLONOROESTE project consolidated an effective lobbying strategy by U.S.-based environmental groups and forged all-important links with nongovernmental groups and Amazonian populations in Brazil.

POLONOROESTE and Acre

The completion of the BR-364 highway from Cuiabá to Porto Velho in 1968 stimulated increased migration into Rondônia. To absorb the incoming migrants, INCRA established a series of semidirected colonization programs in the state.[62] As in Pará, the number of people seeking land soon exceeded the capacity of the official projects. Unlike Pará, where small farmer settlement was de-emphasized after 1974, Rondônia in 1981 became the site of the Northwest Brazil Integrated Development Program known as POLONOROESTE. The World Bank provided about one-third of the funding to pave the BR-364 highway and to develop sustainable farming systems for some forty-five thousand small farmer migrants. In accordance with its new environmental policies, the World Bank made the loan contingent on the implementation of measures to protect the environment and indigenous peoples in the project area.

By late 1984 it was clear that the World Bank's environmental regulations were being ignored. Ranchers and small farmers were deforesting protected areas, and other provisions were also not being met. In October, representatives of a group of thirty-two nongovernmental organizations from the U.S., Brazil, and seven other countries wrote a letter to the World Bank urging the president to take immediate action. The response was a bland and reassuring letter. Dissatisfied with the bank's attitude, the Natural Resources Defense Council, the Environmental Defense Fund, and the National Wildlife Federation took their case to the United States Congress, where hearings were held with key committees in late 1984. Gaining the support of well-placed senators and legislators was an effective strategy because Congress controlled the purse strings.[63] Congress in turn put pressure on the U.S. Treasury Department, which voted on projects proposed by the World Bank and the Inter-American Development Bank. In March mounting political pressure compelled the World Bank to halt disbursement of the POLONOROESTE loan pending compliance with the protection policies.

Wary of getting involved in another controversial project in western Amazonia, the World Bank declined a request from the Brazilian government to extend the paving of the BR-364 highway into the neighboring state of Acre. Attention then turned to the IDB, which was considering a loan for the same purpose. In January of 1985 pressure on the U.S. Treasury Department forced the U.S. Executive Director of the IDB to take the unprecedented step of abstaining on the vote related to the road project. The IDB eventually proceeded with the loan for the BR-364 extension but not without making it contingent on the creation of a companion program known as the Environment and Indigenous Communities Protection Project (PMACI).

The PMACI was formulated and administered by an intergovernmental working group coordinated by the planning ministry in collaboration with other federal, regional, and state agencies. In practice, PMACI—like so many other Amazon-related programs—was designed in Brasília with scant local participation. The preliminary PMACI program called for demarcation of Indian lands, soil surveys and zoning, forestry extension programs, and the creation of state environmental agencies. But the flurry of on-paper projects failed to deflect the attention of environmental groups who now kept a close watch on every turn of events. By August of 1987 the IDB loan was suspended due to noncompliance with the PMACI. Further negotiations stalled over the PMACI, which then came under military control in March of 1988. In July of 1989 a new agreement was reached with the IDB, and the bank finally released funds for the road.[64]

The convoluted history of the MDBs' involvement in the BR-364 loan illustrates the effectiveness of the new strategy environmentalists had devised. The new approach involved directly lobbying the donor agencies, especially those in the United States. But the method also had the effect of strengthening the ties between world environmentalist groups and grassroots organizations in the Amazon. The campaign to pressure the World Bank and the IDB, for example, required information about the ecological and social failures of specific projects—information that, for the most part, was hidden away in inaccessible documents if it existed at all. The U.S.-based conservationists therefore turned to nongovernmental church, union, and other groups in countries like Brazil to assist in providing the necessary information on what was happening on the ground.

The Ecumenical Center for Documentation and Information (CEDI), based in São Paulo and Rio de Janeiro, had developed a network of collaborators among individuals and organizations concerned with tribal peoples. The network allowed CEDI to collect and disseminate accurate and timely data about Brazil's 180 tribes living in thousands of villages, most of them in Amazonia.[65] The result was a loose coalition with grassroots organizations who became a local constituency for the U.S.-based lobbying efforts. In return for information and support, these local entities gained organizational support, access to the media, and international legitimacy that strengthened their political position in regional and national arenas.[66]

A case in point was the strong resistance movement that developed among rubber tappers in Acre and was led by Chico Mendes. By the time of his death in December of 1988, Mendes and other rubber tappers had worked for a decade and a half to devise ways to protect the forest resources on which they depended from ranchers seeking to convert the area to pasture. The movement began in local rural workers unions in Xapuri and Brasileia, south of Rio Branco, with the support of the church, nongovernmental organizations, and, later on, in alliance with the workers' party, PT. In 1985 the rubber tappers formed a national-level council and established formal ties with tribal peoples.

Using organized nonviolent tactics, their efforts to halt logging and the clearing of forest won international attention. At the invitation of U.S. environmentalists, Mendes addressed the Board of Directors of the IDB in 1987 at its annual meeting in Miami and briefed political leaders in Washington, D.C. That a native Amazonian could put face-to-face pressure on such powerful agencies was an event that symbolized the new character of the political mobilization underway. Later that year, Mendes received two international prizes in recognition of his efforts. After his murder in late 1988, Mendes' memory was celebrated in the international press, which brought his cause to the attention of the Brazilian public.[67] He was awarded several posthumous honors for his work in Amazonia.[68]

The rubber tappers' movement achieved some success in influencing both federal policies and state-level politics. While Mendes was still alive, the movement won a significant legal victory when the tappers convinced INCRA to create a new form of land settlement called the "extractive reserve." This concept for the first time permitted collective occupation of land by non-Indian groups who traditionally had exploited forest products for their livelihood. The change was significant because it established the legal basis for a type of land use that previously was unrecognized in the statutes.[69] Victories such as these introduced new elements into the content of state-level politics.

The first local elections under the civilian regime brought environmental issues into the Amazonian state arena for the first time in the late 1980s. In a daring move for the times, newly elected Acre Governor Flaviano Melo proudly called himself an "ecologist" and proposed that the state strive for "forest-based" development rather than for the wholesale forest conversion policies typical of states like Pará and Rondônia. He created new state-level environmental and forest management agencies. Under pressure from the rubber tapper organizations, Melo also decreed the first extractive reserve in Acre in early 1988. In the following months the governor created several others, including one in the contested Seringal Cachoeira, the area that was claimed by the cattle ranchers who later were responsible for Chico Mendes' murder.

The Kayapó and the Xingu dams

In eastern Amazonia, a similar drama involved the Kayapó Indians. Pacified only in the mid-1960s, the Kayapó had carried out a prolonged but successful struggle to secure the demarcation of their land in 1985 (see chapter 9). In the process, the Indians acquired valuable experience in negotiating with outsiders, be they ranchers, loggers, bureaucrats, the army, or anthropologists. An invitation to a meeting in Miami took two Kayapó chiefs, accompanied by an anthropologist who served as interpreter, on their first visit to the U.S. in January of 1988.[70] In Miami, the chiefs expressed concern about the dams the Brazilian government planned to build along the Xingu river. They later traveled to Washington where they took their cause to officials at the World Bank, the State Department, the Treasury Department, and to members of the U.S. Congress.

Planned or not, the Kayapó's trip to Washington was opportune as it coincided with the visit by a Brazilian government delegation seeking to obtain a five hundred million dollar energy sector loan from the World Bank. In September of 1988 the regional energy agency, ELETRONORTE, unveiled a plan to construct seventy-nine new dams in the Amazon by the year 2010, including several on the Xingu River. The Indians had not been consulted about the desirability of this proposal, nor were they informed about the possible threat to their lands. On their return to Brazil the two chiefs were interrogated by the police about their activities in the U.S. In August, they were charged under Brazil's "foreign sedition act" for interfering with Brazil's economic affairs abroad.[71] The Kayapó responded by intensifying their international public relations campaign (see chapter 9).

The Kayapó objections notwithstanding, the Xingu hydroelectric proposals were already controversial in Washington, where the World Bank was in the process of preparing a new policy on environmental aspects of dams and reservoirs that was completed in 1989.[72] Under pressure for financing the POLONOROESTE project, the bank went on the defensive in 1989 by publishing documents that laid the blame for Amazonian deforestation on Brazilian development policy.[73] By then the bank had decided not to finance Brazil's energy sector loan but, instead, to provide funds for energy conservation. The change infuriated Brazilian authorities, who countered with charges that Brazil's contributions to the bank far surpassed the aid the country received in return.

The Yanomami

Treatment of the Yanomami Indians in Roraima was the source of another international controversy.[74] In 1985 FUNAI officially recognized but did not definitively demarcate the nine and a half million hectares traditionally occupied by the group. Later the same year the territory was included under the jurisdiction of the Calha Norte program (described above), a designation that gave the military direct control of the area. As in the rest of the Amazon, military authorities viewed the Indians with considerable distrust and with very little sympathy. This attitude became an issue after 1987 when gold was discovered in Roraima and thousands of *garimpeiros* invaded Yanomami lands. The gold rush posed a threat to the very survival of the Yanomami, but the wealth that mining brought to Roraima generated strong support for the *garimpeiros*. The press and public officials close to the military insisted on portraying the Yanomami as a retrograde people standing in the way of progress and civilization. The more vehement denouncements saw the Indians and their supporters as agents of international mining companies bent on inhibiting Brazil's mineral development.

In late 1988 the Sarney administration in Brasília enacted two decrees that finally set aside land for the Yanomami. Much to the consternation of those who had long pressured for such action, the statutes defined nineteen scattered "islands," rather than one continuous area. As if the fragmentation were not bad enough, several Yanomami villages fell outside of the designated islands— the sum of which was an area about 13 percent smaller than what FUNAI had recognized back in 1985. Other aspects of the legislation created two national forests and one national park. In early 1989 the national forests were opened up to mining. In June, another decree announced the creation of a *garimpeiro* reserve in areas traditionally claimed by the Yanomami. The mining reserves went into effect in January and February of 1990. Taken together, these bureaucratic steps confined the Indians to a discontinuous archipelago and permitted the *garimpeiros* to expand their activities.

Opposition to these measures was immediate. In January of 1989 a coalition of priests, lawyers, journalists, scientists, teachers, and labor organizers founded Ação pela Cidadania, a citizens action group. The newly formed organization gave priority to the issue of human rights in Acre and in Roraima. In June the group sponsored a delegation to visit Roraima to collect firsthand information on the situation of the Yanomami. Their report (*Roraima: O Aviso da Morte*) verified the spread of disease and accounts of violence against the Yanomami and other Indian groups, including the Macuxi, Wapixana, Taurepang, and Ingaricó. On the grounds that these events amounted to a breach of citizen's rights as defined by the constitution, the report called for the immediate restoration of some eight million hectares to the Yanomami and the removal of the miners from the territory.

The Indians engaged in their own form of protest. Yanomami leader Davi Kopenawa, a FUNAI employee, was awarded the United Nations Global 500 prize in January of 1989. In April he traveled to Brasília where he spoke with Sarney as well as with FUNAI chief Iris de Oliveira (previously head of ITERPA and GETAT; see chapter 3), National Security representatives, and members of the Brazilian Congress. In an unprecedented show of unity, Yanomami leaders from several villages began to meet to devise coordinated ways to remove gold miners from their lands. As a result of these efforts, President Sarney was confronted with a massive anti-*garimpeiro* demonstration when he visited Roraima in August of 1989. Later that month sixty tribal groups, including the flamboyant Kayapó, assembled in Brasília to demand that the Yanomami be protected from the gold miners.

The Yanomami crisis grew into a constitutional showdown. In October of 1989 a civil suit contesting the legality of the Yanomami reserve decrees was upheld by the attorney general, who promptly issued a court order to remove the miners from the area.[75] When the federal police protested that this was an impossible task, a second court order required the armed forces to intervene. By the end of the year some airstrips had been interdicted and Congress had allocated funds to support the emergency action.

In March of 1990 Brazil's new president, Fernando Collor de Melo, inherited the Yanomami controversy. The priority that environmental and Indian rights issues had assumed at that point in time was evident by the fact that one of Collor's first acts in office was to visit Roraima accompanied by the head of the federal police and by Environmental Secretary José Lutzenberger. By the time the rainy season began in May of that year only fourteen airstrips had been destroyed, eight of which the miners put back into operation as soon as the rains had subsided. By January of 1991 the situation took on international dimensions when Brazilian miners crossed the border into Venezuela in their search for gold. In the meantime, the health conditions of the Indians in northern Brazil continued to deteriorate.[76]

Green Geopolitics

For the most part, the centuries-long struggle by Amazonian Indians, rubber tappers, and other native groups had gone unnoticed by most Brazilians living along the coast and in the developed cities in the central and southern regions of the country. The extensive coverage that the international media devoted to events in the Amazon thus came as a surprise to the Brazilian public and as an embarrassment to authorities. The burst of notoriety fostered the impression in southern Brazil that the grassroots movements that now filled the headlines had somehow been created by the foreigners who took up their cause. Adverse press coverage and the apparent success of opposition groups in stalling external financing for road building projects ignited long-standing resentment of foreign meddling in Amazonia.[77] Voices on both the right and left of the political spectrum in Brazil questioned the motivations of U.S.-based conservation organizations that were suspected of serving as fronts for foreign companies intent on exploiting Amazonian resources for their own benefit.[78]

Business groups, government officials, and military officers went on the offensive against the growing "internationalization" of the debate over the Amazon. At multinational meetings of the Amazon Treaty for Cooperation and Development in 1988 and before the United Nations General Assembly in 1989 Brazilian authorities reaffirmed their sovereign control over the region and repudiated foreign attempts to intervene in Brazil's internal affairs. The Association of Amazonian Entrepreneurs convened a meeting in 1989 to discuss international pressures, the debt swap proposal, international boycotts (such as those of tropical hard-woods), and the new government program Nossa Natureza (see below).[79] Interior Minister João Alves reiterated accusations of collusion between Indian rights groups and international mining interests seeking to restrict development of Brazil's mineral re-sources.[80] The Paranapanema mining company went so far as to hire a Swiss detective company to investigate the foreign mining interests behind the church-based indigenous rights commission CIMI. The investigation turned up no evidence.[81] A document issued by the Superior War College in March of 1990 accused international environmentalist and Indian organizations of col-luding with the governments of developed countries to use Indian areas as bridgeheads to internationalize strategic parts of Ama-zonia. In the post-Cold War era, the handy references geopoli-ticians used to make to the East-West confrontation and to com-munist infiltration in Amazonia were replaced by new concepts and concerns. The threat was serious enough in the military's view to justify the "extreme expedient of war" against smugglers, drug traffickers, and indigenous and environmental organiza-tions.[82]

Although ecological concerns had never been a military prior-ity, the regime did establish the Special Secretariat for the En-vironment (SEMA) in 1973.[83] The IBDF's Department of National Parks was also charged with implementing conservation policies. Similarly, a comprehensive National Environmental Policy was approved in 1981 to be implemented by the newly created Na-tional System for the Environment. The various agencies suc-ceeded in establishing an impressive number of protected areas, at least on paper. But the impact of these initiatives was limited by weak political support, the lack of resources, and the priority given to development even within the ministries responsible for these programs.[84]

The Brazilian Institute for Renewable Natural Resources and the Environment (IBAMA), established by Sarney in 1988, proved somewhat more effective. The agency enforced the requirement that investors produce environmental impact statements, and it levied fines for illegal deforestation. Although IBAMA did not stop deforestation in Amazonia, it did reduce the proportion of illegal land clearing in the region. Enforcement of the environmental protection policies was carried out at considerable risk to IBAMA personnel. After numerous threats, IBAMA helicopter pilots who patrolled southern Pará and Acre requested the protection of the federal police. IBAMA's regional director and the coordinator of the PMACI program were assaulted and beaten in Acre in May of 1989.[85]

In October of 1988 the Sarney administration announced a new plan for the Amazon region called *Nossa Natureza* ("Our Nature"). The objective was to restrict "predatory incursions" against the region's natural resources and to build an effective environmental protection system. Other features of Nossa Natureza were intended to promote environmental education and public awareness of the Amazon, regulate human settlement and resource use, recuperate damaged ecosystems, and protect Indian communities and other local populations engaged in the sustainable use of Amazonian natural resources. The program called for participation by federal, state, and municipal governments, the scientific community, and nongovernmental organizations. It established six interministerial working groups to propose and implement specific measures. The emphasis on open decision-making processes, environmental protection, and the rights of native groups represented a remarkable departure from previous policies.

In practice, however, only federal ministry representatives served as members of the working groups to implement the program. Meetings to define the specific goals held in March of 1989 at the Instituto Superior de Estudos da Amazônia (ISEA) in Manaus (an organization formed in 1987) were open only to the governors of the Amazonian states. Scientists at the respected Instituto Nacional de Pesquisas Amazônicas (INPA), located in the same city where the meeting was convened, protested against their exclusion from the discussions and the lack of resources to support their ongoing research programs in Amazonia. Businesspeople represented by the Association of Amazonian Entrepreneurs and state-level organizations likewise complained that they were not consulted.[86]

In fact, Nossa Natureza was firmly under military control.[87] It was coordinated by the Special Secretariat on National Defense, a newly created entity linked to the presidency and under the command of General Bayma Denis. Bayma Denis was both military chief of staff and the former general secretary of the National Security Council, which had been abolished by the constitution. The new agency was renamed the Secretariat for Strategic Affairs (SAE) in 1990 under President Collor and continued to play a central role in Indian affairs and Amazonian policy making.

The main purpose of the Nossa Natureza Working Group on Environmental Protection, Indigenous Communities, and Extractive Producers was to implement the environmental-economic planning model of the PMACI with international funding. This aspect of Nossa Natureza as well as other military policies adopted in the late 1980s relied on the concept of strategic "set asides." The zoning approach based on "ecological expropriations" permitted whole territories to be put under military control while ostensibly satisfying environmental pressure groups.[88] Executive decrees set aside zones for specific uses such as National Forests or National Parks (as in the Yanomami territory) or for direct control by the military itself (see the section "Agrarian Reform"). Companion measures then permitted these "protected areas" to be used for particular purposes.

It was this dual strategy that the federal government employed to first create Natural Forest reserves in the disputed Yanomami territories in Roraima and then open the same areas to mining companies. Other places were designated as "reserves" for indigenous groups, rubber tappers, and other petty extractors, including *garimpeiros*. Contrary to the spirit of the 1988 constitution, which legitimized the ethnic distinctiveness of Indian groups in Brazil, the guidelines for the Nossa Natureza working group set out to demarcate reserve areas in order to facilitate "total integration (of the Indians) into regional society."[89]

Some of the changes Collor implemented during his first months in office suggested an attempt to wrest control of Amazon policy from the hands of the military. The appointment of the outspoken environmentalist José Lutzenberger as Secretary of the Environment and Collor's efforts to remove *garimpeiros* from the Yanomami territory were applauded by environmentalists and human rights advocates. Likewise, Collor's decision to host the 1992 United Nations Conference on Environment and Development in Brazil signaled his determination to turn international public opinion in favor of Brazil's environmental policies. By 1990 a remarkable upsurge in environmental concern and activism had taken hold in virtually all spheres of Brazilian society. The change in public opinion and the political experience gained by Amazonian grassroots organizations are among the factors that favored the possibility of shaping new alternatives for Amazonia's future.

The New Contest over Amazonia

The internationalization of the Amazonian debate did much to legitimize and to strengthen grassroots movements in the region. But there is little doubt that the factors of major importance were internal to Brazil. Indeed, the international support could not have had the national impact that it did were it not for the profound transformations already well underway in Brazil and in the Amazon. The years between 1979 and 1990 witnessed important economic and political changes in Brazil and in Amazonia. The erosion of support for the military regime, the liberalization of the political arena in the late 1970s, and the inauguration of a civilian administration in 1985 were among the most significant events on the national horizon. Within the Amazon region, the 1970s saw the growing mobilization of peasant farmers. By the end of the decade, resistance movements had grown to include miners, rubber tappers, and Indians. In the process of defending themselves, each of the various groups constructed their own ways to make themselves better heard.

In the twilight of military rule in the early 1980s, political parties of all persuasions sought to expand their constituencies in preparation for the transition to a democracy. This was especially true in the small towns and cities across the region that had suffered the impact and the turmoil of the events set in motion by the development policies adopted a decade earlier. Peasants found support and a means to express themselves through the Catholic church. Miners were backed by local merchants and investors based in the region's boom towns. Indians and rubber tappers successfully established alliances with human rights and environmental activists both within and outside of Brazil.

Such alliances introduced a new set of actors and issues onto

9. Monosowski (1990).

10. The CAPEMI scandal came to light through a dossier left by Alexander von Baumgarten, a journalist linked to the National Intelligence Service (SNI), who was mysteriously murdered in October of 1982. The information showed that CAPEMI was awarded the contract in return for the agreement to contribute part of the profits to the presidential campaign fund of General Medeiros, head of the SNI. It was one of the first cases of corruption by the military government to come to public attention.

11. On the basis of an agreement signed in 1982 between CVRD and FUNAI, anthropologists and environmental experts were hired to monitor the effects of the project on Indian communities. There were over thirteen thousand Indians living in forty-some settlements in the project area. In 1983/1984 the anthropologists represented by the Brazilian Anthropological Association (ABA) criticized the two agencies for failing to implement the recommendations (Treece 1987:6,37–39).

12. Bunker (1990) and Fearnside (1986a).

13. Most species of Amazonian hardwoods are not of the appropriate density for manufacturing charcoal. Nonetheless, incentives to small producers of charcoal began in 1987, and the pig iron factories began to come on line in 1988. Demand was projected to rise to more than a million tons of charcoal per year by 1991, an elevenfold increase over current levels of production. Half of the charcoal was to come from fast-growing plantation trees, an overly optimistic projection given the dismal history of plantation forestry experiments in Amazonia.

Smoke pollution led public health authorities to close down some of the charcoal furnaces based near Marabá. In October of 1988 a group of nongovernmental organizations linked to environmentalist, labor, and indigenous groups as well as to lawyers and the media took advantage of a provision in the new constitution to open an unprecedented civil investigation into the environmental impact of the Greater Carajás Program. Among other things, the group requested access to government documents on the charcoal-using pig-iron projects. The dossier prepared by the group presented evidence by several scientists to demonstrate that the charcoal projects were not viable and suggested alternatives for the development of the local iron and steel economy (Inquérito Civil Programa Grande Carajás. Rio: Instituto Apoio Jurídico Popular, Informativo No. 1, January 1989). See also Shaeff (1990).

14. For example, Falesi (1976).

15. Hecht (1985).

16. Hecht (1985), Hecht, Norgaard, and Possio (1988), Binswanger (1989), Mahar (1979:118–134, 1989), and Yokomizo (1989).

17. However, SUDAM did not always comply with the ban (Pandolfo 1989:21). Ranching enterprises continued to expand because of the availability of other sources of credit, opportunities for speculation, and opportunities to take advantage of mineral and timber resources.

18. Browder (1988). Later research showed that selective logging also contributed to the burning of forests adjacent to pasturelands by opening corridors for the penetration of fire (Uhl and Buschbacher 1985).

19. Tardin et al. (1980).

20. Fearnside (1982). These predictions were supported by information published by the World Bank that revealed that by 1988 nearly six hundred thousand square kilometers, or 12 percent, of the Legal Amazon region had been cleared of forest (Mahar 1989:6). The controversy over measures of deforestation continued into 1989; see, for example, *Estado de São Paulo* and *Jornal do Brasil*, 7 March; *Folha de São Paulo*, 14 March.

21. Sawyer and Sawyer (1987).

22. *Jornal do Ouro*, October 1984 and World Bank (1989).

23. Mercury was used in the cloth lining of the wash boxes and again in the final burning of the mercury-gold combination, which was usually carried out over the cookstove in the miners' hut or even in the stores in local towns while others gathered around to see how much the gold was worth. The mercury used in the wash boxes escaped into the soils and waters at the work site, and the burning released highly toxic vapors. Once present in the rivers and streams, inorganic mercury could be transformed by micro-organisms into methylmercury and enter the food chain as food for carnivorous and bottom-dwelling fish, or through animals who drank the water. Inorganic mercury could also be absorbed directly through the lungs in the burning process; less than half a gram could be a lethal dose. Acute and chronic forms of toxicity from mercury contamination attacked the digestive and nervous systems, potentially leading to death (Mallas and Benedicto 1986).

24. Bittar et al. (1985). The commission found that for each kilo of gold extracted, about 1.7 kilos of mercury were used. Calculations based on official production figures (which underestimate by one-half to one-third due to contraband) suggested that seven tons of mercury (as well as unmeasured amounts of oil, grease, and detergents) had been released into the environment in the Goiás *garimpos'* three years of activity. The study urged the prohibition of the use of mercury in favor of alternative distillation techniques.

25. In 1986 preliminary research on mercury contamination financed by DNPM and the CVRD in Serra Pelada found 5.8 times the maximum tolerance level among workers in the cooperative who were responsible for the burning process (*O Liberal*, 10 March, 1987). Similarly, a 1988 DNPM study found that 37 percent of the Tapajós miners had excessive blood mercury levels (Silva, Souza, and Bezerra 1988, cited in Hecht and Cockburn 1989:143–144). A 1989 study by DNPM and the Federal University of Pará estimated that eighteen hundred tons of mercury had been released into Amazonian rivers between 1980 and 1988, nine times more than in the famous Minimata disaster in Japan (Pinto, *Jornal Pessoal* 2 (63) (June 1990):7–8.

26. Cleary (1989). In 1989 new legislation required the registration of mercury importers, producers, and users. Brazil imports all of its mercury, 183 tons in 1984, at a cost of over two million dollars (*O Liberal*, 10 March 1987).

27. A government-party congressman from São Paulo, Sérgio Cardoso de Almeida, articulated this position: "If the police discover and invade a communist apparatus, they won't find arms, bombs, or any object for the practice of violence. They will find only an abundant literature involving three issues: Indians, Amazonia, and the Jari project" (*Estado de São Paulo*, 23 March 1980). A series of front-page articles published by the same influential newspaper in 1987 argued that environmental and indigenous defense groups were representing the inter-

ests of multinational mining companies concerned about competition from Brazilian producers. These accusations by government officials continued into 1989.

28. Becker (1990:39–40), Branford and Glock (1985:123), and Hébette (1986), cited in Hecht and Cockburn (1989:179). Hecht and Cockburn (1989:162) point out that the history of resistance movements in Amazonia and the Northeast (such as the *Cabanagem*, the Acre revolution, and the Canudos revolt) left an "insurgent memory" that contributed to contemporary resistance.

29. See Mainwaring (1986).

30. See, for example, the description of Xavante resistance in Branford and Glock (1985:197–199).

31. See the interview with Ailton Krenak, head of the Union of Indigenous Nations, in Hecht and Cockburn (1985:212).

32. These events parallel the evolution of indigenous movements in other Latin American countries; see, for example, Ehrenreich (1989). COICA, the Coordinating Body for the Indigenous People's Organizations of the Amazon Basin, was also formed in the late 1980s and began meeting with international environmental organizations.

33. For more on the Acre rubber tappers' movement, see Alegretti (1990), Alegretti and Schwartzman (1987), Campbell (1989, 1990), Hecht (1989), Hecht and Cockburn (1989:169–171), Miller (1990), and Schwartzman (1989).

34. Biery-Hamilton (1987) and Castro (1989).

35. Pace (1987).

36. *Jornal do Ouro*, January 1985. They would leave peacefully, but return soon after. Sometimes walking hundreds of kilometers into the forest, they worked at night and practiced their escapes from authorities. Even the rigorous security scheme surrounding the Carajás area failed to stop the invasion of a copper mining site called Salobo in 1984. Conflicts persisted after the civilian government took over in 1985. Data from the DNPM revealed hundreds of conflicts in sixty-four mining areas, involving at least twenty-five cases of violent homicide, during the period from January of 1985 to August of 1986 (MIRAD 1986). Rondônia experienced a resurgence of conflicts in both tin and gold mining areas between 1985 and 1986. Violent conflicts over minerals on Yanomami territory from 1985 on led to more deaths beginning in 1987 (Wright 1987).

37. Castro (1989). Castro and Acevedo Marín (1986/1987) cite various cases of these local political changes and discuss politics in Belém in more detail. Pace (1987) describes another case of a resistance movement that became increasingly politicized in the Amazon town of Itá. The rubber tappers' movement in Acre became strongly identified with the Workers Party, the PT.

38. See *Pará Desenvolvimento*, special issue called "Planejamento e Ocupação Recente," no. 18, 27 January 1986.

39. SUDAM (1986:30).

40. Bentes showed that more than three-quarters of GETAT's titles had been for properties up to one hundred hectares in size and only one for over three thousand hectares. Findings of an internal MIRAD study disputed the figures Bentes presented on the size distribution of GETAT titles. The study, based on data from the GETAT cadaster, indicated that only 13 percent of the titles handed out between 1980 and 1986 were for properties up to one hundred hectares in size. The report charged that during the 1985/1986 period the agency had failed

to carry out its agrarian reform mandate and continued its "concentrationist" tendencies: 44.5 percent of the titles given out had been for properties of over one thousand hectares (MIRAD 1987:29).

41. Whereas under the military government the agency had managed to expropriate 203 properties, the goals of the PNRA would require an average of six expropriations *per day* during the period from 1986 to 1989 (Garcia 1988). Minister Dante de Oliveira, who took over in May of 1986, took a number of steps to make INCRA's functioning more efficient. He also abolished the agency's special office on agrarian conflicts, which had been created in July of 1985 to compile and monitor statistics on conflicts (Almeida 1989).

42. Pinto, *Jornal Pessoal* 1 (4) (March 1988):6 and Almeida (1988).

43. INCRA (1986). Approval of the first state-level plans, including that for Pará, did not come until months later in May of 1986. The revised version underestimated the number of land conflicts reported by INCRA's now-defunct office on agrarian conflicts (Almeida 1988).

44. Almeida (1988).

45. Pinto, *Jornal Pessoal* 2 (40) (May 1989):8 and 2 (47) (September 1989):3. In September of 1990 civilian President Fernando Collor de Melo uncovered a fifteen-year-old secret military program to develop an atom bomb and ordered the Cachimbo facility sealed off (*New York Times*, 9 October 1990).

46. Some of the areas ceded to the military were superimposed on Indian reserves, ecological set-asides, state lands, or federal project zones (*Folha de São Paulo*, 24, 26, and 27 September 1989).

47. Almeida and Oliveira Filho (1985) and Albert (forthcoming).

48. Ricardo (1987:44–46). In preparation, however, the DNPM proceeded to allocate "preferences" for particular areas to mining companies, responding to 537 requests for mining permits that covered 3,771,417 hectares of indigenous lands in Amazonia. A study carried out in 1986 found that the permits would affect 77 of the 302 indigenous areas, or 34 percent of their total 17 million hectare territory, especially in the states of Pará and Rondônia. Nearly all of the Yanomami territory had been requested. The military continued attempts to open up mining in indigenous lands under the civilian government. Five-hundred-sixty requests had been approved by 1987, and 1,685 were pending (Cunha 1989:20–21).

49. Under the New Republic, the institutional reform of FUNAI announced in March of 1986 called for the agency's "decentralization" through the creation of six regional units (CEDI 1987:23). Hundreds of employees were subsequently fired or transferred, causing protests and a strike by FUNAI workers. ABA and UNI protested the intrusion of other ministries in FUNAI's policy making. Further administrative changes under President Fernando Collor de Melo in 1990 transferred FUNAI's land demarcation function to the Ministry of Justice and the agency's other responsibilities (such as provision of health and education services) to the respective Ministries.

50. Ricardo and Oliveira Filho (1987:3), Albert (forthcoming), and Leite (1990).

51. Oliveira Filho (1987, 1990).

52. Albert (forthcoming), Pinto (*Jornal Pessoal* 1 (1) (1987):62–63), Cunha (1989), and Gaiger (1988).

53. Cunha (1989) and Oliveira Filho (1990).

54. Oliveira Filho (1990).

55. Sarney's personal pet project, the North-South Railway, was announced in 1987 over the objections of his own technical advisers. The seventeen hundred kilometers of tracks (from Anápolis in Goiás to Açailândia in Maranhão) would connect the steel exporting ports that served the state of Minas Gerais to the Carajás Itaquí railroad in Sarney's home state. Despite a fraudulent bidding process and the project's astronomical cost (originally estimated at two billion dollars), the first 107 kilometers from Açailândia to Imperatriz were completed in February of 1989 (*Veja*, 22 February 1989).

56. This refers to the rising atmospheric temperatures attributed to the suspected buildup of carbon dioxide and other gases in the earth's atmosphere.

57. Estimate by Brazil's Minister for Science and Technology, José Goldemberg; see Goldemberg and Freitas (1989). According to the same source, the United States contributes 16.9 percent of global carbon emissions, more than any other country.

58. Pandolfo (1990).

59. Ayres (1989) and Imbiriba and Mitschein (1989). The debt-for-nature-swap proposal consisted of negotiated arrangements whereby a portion of a nation's foreign debt could be purchased at a discounted rate on the secondary market. A sum in domestic currency equivalent to the nominal value of the debt purchase (rather than the discounted price) would then be invested in conservation efforts in the country. The swaps were intended not to resolve the foreign debt problem (since they canceled only a minuscule portion of the debt) but to leverage scarce funds to support conservation efforts. In some cases countries set aside or expanded a land area for a reserve. Designated national and international organizations collaborated in the administration of the funds and coordination of the conservation activities, such as training and reforestation.

Some of the first swaps were negotiated in Bolivia, Ecuador, Peru, Costa Rica, and the Philippines. The viability of the swaps depended in part on the value of the country's debt on the secondary market, where private banks tried to sell off their foreign credits at discounted prices. After the secondary market value of Brazil's debt plummeted in 1989, allowing discounts of up to 77 percent, debt swaps began to be considered more seriously (*Jornal do Brasil*, 5 November 1989).

60. Brazil's mounting foreign debt climbed to over one hundred billion dollars in the mid-1980s. The need to generate foreign exchange to service the debt restricted the growth of the national economy, possibly slowing the economic impetus to invest in Amazonia. On the other hand, the debt accentuated the tendency to view the region's resources as a potential source of export earnings. The Amazon's megaprojects also provided a convenient way to channel external funds. During the 1970s state-controlled companies like CVRD attracted international financing that snowballed by the 1980s. New loans were needed to roll over the debt, upping the size of debt service payments and increasing the pressure to cut costs and maximize short-term profits (Altvater 1987). Such economic realities relegated concerns over the environment to secondary priority.

61. Miller (1990:8–39) traces the evolution of concern by U.S.-based conservation groups about global issues such as climate, biodiversity, and deforestation. The U.N. conference on the environment held in Stockholm in 1972 was an important event marking the link between development and global conservation.

The 1980 World Conservation Strategy called for international cooperation on resource issues not bounded by nations and for the incorporation of local populations into decision making about conservation and development strategies. For a detailed discussion of the environmental strategy with the MDBs, see Miller (1990) and Rich (1985).

62. See Mahar (1989:28–40), Wilson (1985), and Milliken (1988).

63. See Aufderheide and Rich (1985), Miller (1990), Rich (1985), and Schwartzman (1986).

64. Also under discussion was the construction of a highway through the state of Acre that would cross the Peruvian border and link Acre to Lima and thus to Asian export markets for Brazilian grains and hardwoods. The idea was popular in Acre but controversial overseas. The Brazilian authorities consulted informally with the Japanese about financing the highway through Acre. However, in early 1989 U.S. President George Bush, presumably in response to the strong U.S. environmental lobby in Congress, took time during his trip to Japan for Hirohito's funeral to urge the Japanese not to finance the road (*Time*, 30 October 1989). Whatever the President's intentions, Bush's intervention in the road question was interpreted in Brazil as a move to defend U.S. soybean producers from competition for Asian export markets.

65. See CEDI's publication series entitled *Povos Indígenas do Brasil* and *Aconteceu*.

66. See Miller (1990) for a detailed analysis of these points.

67. Mendes was well aware of the irony of his international fame. He liked to joke that before the 1987 prizes he was labelled a "communist," afterwards, an "imperialist." His comment reflects the tendency of his political enemies to presume that others were directing the rubber tappers' movement.

68. In 1989 the Better World Society also awarded an environmental medal to anthropologist Mary Alegretti, a principal supporter of the rubber tappers' movement.

69. Extractive reserves have also been established in the states of Amapá, Rondônia, and Maranhão as well as in other tropical countries.

70. They were invited to Miami to attend an international symposium on "Wise Management of Tropical Forests" sponsored by Florida International University. From Miami, the Indians traveled to Washington at the invitation of the National Wildlife Federation and the Environmental Defense Fund. For more details, see Posey (1989).

71. The anthropologist who accompanied them was also charged although he only translated what the chiefs said. The presumption was that the Indians could not have undertaken the denunciation on their own accord. The grim irony of charging indigenous people as foreigners in their own land was reinforced at an October hearing when the judge refused to permit the chiefs to enter because their traditional body paint and headdress (along with shorts and bare feet) did not constitute "proper dress." The Kayapó were adept at using ritual to intimidate their political enemies, including the Belém military police; see Posey (1989) for more details.

72. See, for example, Schuh, Moigne, Cernea, and Goodland (1988). There were also other technical issues involved in Brazil's negotiation of the energy sector loan with the World Bank.

73. Binswanger (1989) and Mahar (1989).

Contesting the Military, 1978–1989

74. This account of the Yanomami controversy is based on CCPY reports, publications of Survival International, two reports by Ação pela Cidadania (*Roraima: O Aviso da Morte*, 1989, and *Yanomami: A Todos os Povos da Terra*, 1990), Albert (forthcoming), and other sources cited in the text.

75. *Folha de São Paulo*, 17 January 1990.

76. Emergency medical teams sent into the area in February of 1990 calculated a mortality rate of 12.6 percent since 1987 and of up to 14.7 percent in villages near the mining sites. The rate had tripled compared to the period from 1984 to 1986 before mining had begun. Of the Indians included in the health census 43 percent had lost at least one member of their immediate family between 1987 and 1989 (Menegola and Albert 1990). A new Yanomami Health program was scheduled to begin in March of 1991.

77. One example was the reaction to a delegation of U.S. senators and legislators who made a hastily planned visit to Brazil in 1989. With little sensitivity to domestic political debates, they publicly urged the government to accept debt-for-nature swaps. The proposal was widely interpreted to mean that Brazil should surrender sovereign control over part or all of the Amazon region.

78. The Brazilian scientific community was also divided. Leftists questioned the links between conservation organizations, multinational corporations, and the U.S. government. They suspected that inexperienced indigenous groups were being manipulated by outsiders. Leftists in the United States also accused the predominantly conservative U.S. conservation organizations of distorting Amazonian grassroots movements and appropriating money purportedly raised on their behalf; see the Hecht and Cockburn article in *The Nation*, 5 May 1989, and the response by Schwartzman and Rich on 18 September 1989.

79. *Carta da Amazônia*, November 1989.

80. *Isto É*, 27 January 1988.

81. Some foreign environmentalists were, however, found to have shares in mining companies in their own countries (*Veja*, 20 September 1989).

82. *Folha de São Paulo*, 29 May 1990, cited in Albert (forthcoming) and in *Rainforest Futures Newsletter*, 1, no. 1 (1990). See also Lima (1990a).

83. At the U.N. conference on the environment held in Stockholm in 1972 Brazil's delegation led by Finance Minister Delfim Neto argued that environmental concerns were irrelevant and that protectionist policies would only perpetuate the development gap between countries of the northern and southern hemispheres.

84. See Foresta (1991). IBDF was housed within the Ministry of Agriculture, and the main thrust of the agency's goals was to exploit, rather than preserve, timber resources in the nation's parks. For example, in 1978 IBDF proposed the concession of long-term "risk contracts" for logging in state and federal parks and forests as a means of generating foreign exchange. The proposal was based on an FAO study by Schmithüsen entitled "Contratos de utilização florestal com referência especial à Amazônia Brasileira." It generated so much public controversy that IBDF abandoned the plan.

By 1984 IBDF policy statements began to respond to the growing criticism of its environmental responsibilities. An edict issued in July required prior studies of soil and logging conditions before permits would be issued for burning of forested areas (*Gazeta Mercantil*, 12 July 1984). Citing LANDSAT data that showed that 12.4 million hectares of Amazonian land had been deforested between 1975 and 1980, the institute's president expressed a new attitude: "We have now reached the conclusion that it is not the smallholders who devastate the forest but the companies responsible for large agricultural and ranching projects."

Paulo Nogueira Neto and Maria Teresa Pádua, heads of SEMA and IBDF's DPN, were awarded the Getty prize for their achievements in establishing protected areas in Brazil.

85. *Jornal do Brasil*, 3 September 1989.

86. See *Amazônia Notícias*, XIV (85 and 86) (March and April 1989) for AEA statements and *O Rio Branco*, 14 May 1989, for a statement sent to the federal ministries by the industry, commerce, and agricultural organizations of the state of Acre.

87. Albert (forthcoming), Gabeira (1989), Gaiger (1988), and Mesquita (1989).

88. Albert (forthcoming); see also Hecht and Cockburn (1989:200–205).

89. PR/SADEN-GTI VI Document, *Programa Nossa Natureza, Anexo D (Memento do relatório dos GEI a NGA do "Programa Nossa Natureza"): Pressupostos econômico-sociais*, 1988, cited in Albert (forthcoming).

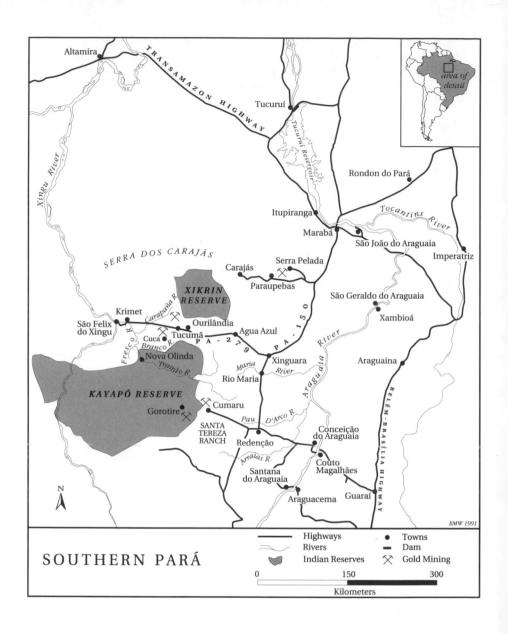

Altamira

TRANSAMAZON HIGHWAY

Tucuruí

Xingu River

Tucuruí Reservoir

Rondon do Pará

Itupiranga

Tocantins River

Marabá

São João do Araguaia

Imperatriz

SERRA DOS CARAJÁS

Carajás

Serra Pelada

Paraupebas

São Geraldo do Araguaia

XIKRIN RESERVE

Carapaña R.

Krimet

Ourilândia

Xambioá

São Felix do Xingu

Fresco R.

Cuca

Tucumã

Agua Azul

PA - 279

PA - 150

Araguaia River

Branco R.

Nova Olinda

Tyairão R.

Xinguara

Araguaina

Maria River

Rio Maria

KAYAPÓ RESERVE

BELÉM - BRASÍLIA HIGHWAY

Gorotire

Cumaru

SANTA TEREZA RANCH

Pau D'Arco R.

Conceição do Araguaia

Redenção

Coùto Magalhães

N

Arraias R.

Santana do Araguaia

Araguacema

Guaraí

EMW 1991

SOUTHERN PARÁ

Highways

Rivers

Indian Reserves

Towns

Dam

Gold Mining

0   150   300
Kilometers

2

❖

Southern Pará

Part two narrows the scope of inquiry to the southern region of the state of Pará. Herein we show how the global and national events recounted in part one intersected with the histories of particular localities in Amazonia to shape the contemporary process of frontier change. Chapter 5 reviews the transportation and related policies that shifted the main axis of southern Pará's economy from waterways and riverboats to dirt roads and diesel trucks. The story of the road to São Felix do Xingu (PA-279) provides a detailed example of the multiple forces that impinged on the planning and execution of development policies. Subsequent chapters follow the road as it pushed westward across the state and document the founding of three major communities along the way. Xinguara, located at the crossroads with the PA-150, sprang up the moment the construction crews set to work on the PA-279. To the west lie the twin towns of Ourilândia and Tucumã. The former was the product of the gold rush in the late 1970s; the latter, built about the same time, was designed by a private colonization company. Chapters 6, 7, and 8 recount the respective histories of the three towns and address the major themes of frontier change in southern Pará: land conflicts (Xinguara), private colonization schemes (Tucumã), and the gold economy (Serra Pelada, Cuca, and Ourilândia). How the events documented in parts one and two played themselves out in the particular community of São Felix do Xingu is the topic of part three.

FIVE

❖

From Rivers to Roads

Current maps of southern Pará show the PA-279 road as a neatly drawn line that travels westward about two hundred kilometers from the town of Xinguara to the village of São Felix do Xingu located at the confluence of the Xingu and Rio Fresco rivers. The state highway department started construction of the road in 1976, a time when migration to eastern Amazonia was particularly heavy. Small farmers, cattle ranchers, and loggers were quickly drawn to the vast areas that were suddenly made accessible by the new road. Migrants established settlements at strategic points along its path, often claiming lands well ahead of the construction crews. Several of the communities founded along the way—Xinguara, Ourilândia, and Tucumã—soon grew into large urban areas. Each of them later played a prominent role in the history of frontier expansion in Amazonia.

The history of the PA-279 itself is an illuminating chronicle of the forces that influenced the geography of land settlement in the state. If today the road appears on the map as a relatively straight line, the cartographer's steady hand conceals the numerous changes of plans that took place before the road became a reality and glosses over the tumultuous political process that decided its final route. Like so many other facets of frontier change, the direction the PA-279 took was the outcome of a dramatic story of power and politics and of the clash of interests between local elites and Indians and between state and federal agencies vying for authority over newly settled areas on the frontier.

The interplay of these complex social and political forces varied from one place to another, depending on the special characteristics of different localities. Of particular importance to contemporary events were the changes in economic and political organization that took place in the three or four decades following the collapse of the rubber trade early in this century. When the extraction of latex was no longer profitable, the town of Marabá, for example, became a center for Brazil nut gathering. Conceição do Araguaia, on the other hand, turned to cattle raising on the natural savannas in the surrounding areas. Far from being a mere backdrop to current events, such differences in land and labor use and the corresponding variations in social and political structure in each setting actively shaped the contemporary evolution of frontier change in the region.

By the time the federal government's ambitious roadbuilding schemes began to penetrate the Araguaia and Tocantins river basins, the economy and population of southern Pará were already growing and becoming more diverse. The highways were only one element in the new policies that had sought since the 1960s to integrate the region into Brazil's national development plans. But the roads stimulated a dramatic spatial reorientation that set in motion a transformation of the socioeconomic and political organization of southern Pará. For one thing, the historical focus of settlements along the region's waterways shifted to the dusty roadside towns of the interior. Even more significant was the power of highway access to turn natural resources, including land, into commodities that could readily be sold in national and international markets. The opening up of roads through southern Pará thus aggravated the contests over land, minerals, and forest resources.

Variations in local histories rarely command the attention they deserve. Most accounts of twentieth-century Amazonia, especially those that concern the years between the two world wars, are prone to general statements about the region as a whole, thereby overlooking the singular aspects that set one place off from another. The stories of Marabá and Conceição do Araguaia, two long established towns in southern Pará, illustrate the interplay of past and present and the way the specific characteristics of each place has influenced the course of frontier change in recent years.

Marabá and Conceição do Araguaia

Southern Pará was a latecomer to the rubber boom. Natural latex had been extracted from the area since the mid-1800s, but it was not until the peak of the rubber trade at the end of the last century that tappers founded villages along the banks of the middle Tocantins and along the Araguaia and Xingu rivers.[1] The *aviamento* system soon extended its reach in every direction and stimulated the first overland supply route that connected river basins separated from one another by hundreds of kilometers. By the early 1900s each of the newly established settlements had carved out its particular role in the complex supply and trade network associated with the collection and transport of natural latex.

The town of Marabá, located on the Tocantins river, was founded by rubber merchants. Many of the warehouses they built along the banks of the wide river still stand today, painted red, blue, and green in the colorful Amazonian style. At the turn of the century the buildings stored heavy balls of smoked rubber as well as an assortment of agricultural products bound for Belém. On the return trip, the boats that traveled the Tocantins to Marabá were laden with dry goods. Most of the items made their way further upstream into the hands of rubber tappers through the *aviamento* credit and supply system that dominated the rubber economy at the time. When the heyday of the rubber trade had passed, the waterfront storehouses were filled with Brazil nuts, the commodity that replaced rubber as southern Pará's main export item.

The Marabá merchants who had grown wealthy from the rubber trade lobbied the state government in the early 1900s for local political autonomy.[2] When their appeals went unheeded, they petitioned the federal Congress to place the town under the jurisdiction of the state of Goiás or to create a new state altogether with Marabá as its capital. The merchants got what they wanted in 1913. Even though the town held only about five hundred people at the time, the state of Pará separated the municipality of Marabá from that of São João do Araguaia and appointed a governing junta to control the newly created county seat. For the next two decades, members of the junta used the municipal power base to consolidate their control over land and the new forms of production that later replaced the extraction of rubber.[3] By 1923 about two thousand people lived in the town of Marabá.[4]

Conceição do Araguaia, the other major town in southern Pará, was established by missionaries who set out to pacify and acculturate Indians who lived in the Araguaia-Tocantins river basin. In 1902, five years after its founding, Conceição held some two thousand inhabitants. In 1904 *caucho* (*Castilla ulei*) trees were discovered nearby, and the town was swept into the rubber trade. By 1911 Conceição's population had grown to around six thousand persons.[5]

Caucho trees, unlike *Hevea brasiliensis*, had to be destroyed to extract the latex they contained. Once an area had been exploited, it was necessary to find new trees further away.[6] The use of pack mules and the substitution of human power by motorized boats were among the changes that facilitated the wider search for *caucho* during the period.[7] In 1908 a supply trail was opened up as far as the Rio Fresco, where trees were said to be so numerous that they occasionally were found in thick stands. The mule trains that traveled back and forth along the overland route made Conceição an important supply depot and transfer point for rubber collected along the Fresco and Xingu rivers.

The mule trail to the Rio Fresco followed a path originally cut by the Kayapó Indians. The first portion of the journey traversed the natural grasslands near the Pau D'Arco river and its tributary, the Arraias. After five days of arduous travel from Conceição do Araguaia, the caravans generally stopped for a few days before following the trail into the dense forest. The resting place was called Solta because it was there that the muleteers turned their animals loose (*soltar*) to graze on the natural pastures before embarking on the last stretch of the trip through the jungle.

Although the mule trail between Conceição do Araguaia and the Rio Fresco fell into disuse after the collapse of the rubber trade, it was the precursor of the roads that were later built in the region (the PA-150 and the PA-279).[8] The trail also serves as a reminder of the long-standing attempts to establish overland transportation routes in the southern region of the state. Today, the place once known as Solta is the site of the cemetery that adjoins Redenção, a town that was founded about sixty years after the end of the rubber trade.[9]

The sudden fall of the price of rubber in 1910 had a devastating effect on both Marabá and Conceição. As in the rest of the state, the depression provoked massive out-migration. But unlike most other places in eastern Amazonia, Marabá was able to retain its importance as a regional center. Local merchants took steps to underwrite the consumption needs of rubber tappers until they could be shifted to the extraction of Brazil nuts. It was this alternative activity that spared Marabá the severe economic downturn that swept most of the Amazon.[10]

The Brazil nut (*Bertholletia excelsa*, called *castanheira* in Portuguese) is a majestic tree found throughout the Amazonian uplands. The richest stands (*castanhais*) are concentrated in the Tocantins river valley near Marabá, extending south and west towards Conceição do Araguaia and São Felix do Xingu. Indians first introduced the oil-rich nuts to the Jesuits at the Cametá mission in 1669.[11] The nuts were used as animal feed when cattle were brought to the Tocantins in the nineteenth century. Later, Brazil nuts were sold to England and eventually to Germany and Russia.

The collection of Brazil nuts rapidly expanded as the tapping of rubber declined. In 1913 Marabá produced about twenty hectoliters (equivalent to about fifty to sixty kilograms) of nuts. The following year production rose to 2,502 hectoliters, and in 1919 it doubled to 5,396. When the full effect of the rubber crisis hit Marabá in 1920, the production of Brazil nuts soared to 17,878 hectoliters and continued to rise, reaching 120,417 hectoliters in 1926. By the end of the decade, Brazil nuts had become the state's primary export commodity and the major source of livelihood for people living in Marabá.[12]

The existing *aviamento* system was easily extended to the gathering of Brazil nuts and with many of the same results.[13] As the rubber traders had done before them, a handful of Marabá families controlled the transport and buying of Brazil nuts and held a tight monopoly over the credit extended to collectors. The Chamon brothers, of Lebanese origin, and the merchant Deodoro de Mendonça and his family dominated the business in the 1920s and 1930s. After World War II, the 1950s witnessed the economic and political ascendance of the Mutrán family, who also made their fortune from the Brazil nut trade. By the end of the decade the Mutráns controlled 45,135 hectares in Marabá and São João do Araguaia.[14]

Unlike the rubber barons before them, Marabá's new economic elite sought legal rights to the vast areas where Brazil nut trees grew. State land legislation passed in 1920 and again in 1954 permitted the legal acquisition of large areas of land through a long-term lease known as *aforamento perpétuo*.[15] In the ensuing decades, the elite's domination of local politics allowed its members to consolidate huge landholdings, a strategy that served mainly to reinforce the labor discipline among the collectors. It was during this period that even the "free" *castanhais* on state and municipal lands in the Marabá area were brought under the control of the Marabá merchants.[16] To expand their control over production, many leaseholders hired foremen to oversee their workers in remote locations. Violence was often used as a means to keep the *castanheiros* tied to their merchant-patrons.[17] The expanded extraction of Brazil nuts in the 1920s and 1930s also led to violent clashes with the Gavião and Kayapó Indians when collectors ventured into Indian lands.

During the Brazil nut collecting season, Marabá attracted migrants from all over Pará and from the nearby states of Maranhão and Goiás. By 1935 the town had grown to some three thousand inhabitants, about half of whom were permanent residents.[18] In the mid-1940s a railroad built from Alcobaça (now Tucuruí) to Jatobal facilitated shipping of Brazil nuts to Belém by avoiding the worst rapids on the Tocantins river.

The 1930s also witnessed the discovery of gold and diamonds near Marabá. Whereas Brazil nuts were collected during the rainy months, mineral prospecting provided a complementary activity for the dry season. During World War II the revival of the rubber trade under the Washington Accords compensated for the slump in the overseas market for luxury goods, such as Brazil nuts. Small-scale mining for gold and diamonds continued, and mining began for quartz, a mineral of strategic importance to the war effort.[19] Some *castanhal* owners began to diversify their activities into agriculture and cattle, and the town of Marabá further consolidated its role as a regional commercial center.[20]

To the south and west, local economies lapsed into an isolation based on subsistence activities punctuated by occasional upturns in the demand for specific products. In Conceição do Araguaia the population fell from 11,000 to 4,715 between 1920 and 1940. At one point in the 1930s the settlement was even denied its municipal status for a brief period.[21] Small-scale mining in the 1930s and 1940s and the rise in the price of rubber during World War II temporarily stimulated the demand for agricultural products and increased the flow of money. But the last load of rubber from the Xingu reportedly came through the traditional stopping place near the Pau D'Arco en route to Conceição in 1946.[22] Agriculture and cattle production continued, interstitial to the Brazil nut extraction in Marabá and primarily for subsistence elsewhere.

The late 1940s and 1950s saw a slow growth in the population of southern Pará. In Conceição the population increased from only 4,715 in 1940 to 6,322 in 1950 and to 11,283 in 1960.[23] Population growth in the state as a whole began to create a market for the beef produced in the region. Since the 1950s cattle produced in Conceição were moved to Araguacema and shipped from there by air to Belém.[24] To the north, Marabá became a center for fattening the cattle on their way from Goiás and Maranhão to Belém. By the end of World War II the economy of southern Pará had diversified to support a growing number of inhabitants.

From Rivers to Roads

A major turning point in the history of eastern Amazonia in the post-World War II period came with the construction of the Belém-Brasília Highway. The road provided the first major ground link between southern Pará and the rest of the country. Together with the other projects launched and funded by the federal government, the highway opened a new chapter in the development of Marabá and Conceição do Araguaia. These changes introduced a new set of actors onto the regional stage. The investments they undertook and the impact they had on local politics and the regional economy in the 1950s and 1960s were a prelude to the massive changes that began to take place from the 1970s onward.

Construction of the Belém-Brasília Highway began in 1956, but the road did not reach southern Pará until 1960. As it slowly pushed northward, waves of migrants moved into Goiás and Mato Grosso. Small producers were pushed aside by large investors who gradually monopolized the roadside lands. In 1961 the *município* of Santana do Araguaia was carved out of the southern portion of Conceição do Araguaia where the properties owned by southerners and multinational firms formed a checkerboard pattern of huge landholdings. The concentration of land ownership meant that the vast majority of the small farmers that had migrated into the area were evicted from the agricultural plots they had claimed. In a pattern that would repeat itself in the 1970s, they ended up living in frontier towns where they offered their labor to nearby ranches or supported themselves by performing odd jobs.[25] Others moved northward into southern Pará, joining the northeasterners who had arrived there years before with the onset of the rubber boom.[26]

Unpaved access roads linked the towns of Conceição do Araguaia and Marabá to the new highway. Before long ground links began to replace rivers as the principal means of transportation. Although many traditional riverine communities were bypassed by these events, the overland flow of commodities imported from southern Brazil only increased the importance of Marabá and Conceição as regional commercial centers.[27] But the road also attracted cattle ranchers and small farmers to southern Pará. It did not take long before the two groups confronted one another in a contest for land that often turned violent. Other forms of confrontation emerged as well. Loggers who had migrated to Amazonia from southern Brazil, for example, squared off against the traditional class of leaseholders who claimed ownership of the timber that the loggers sought to extract from the *castanhais*.

As eastern Amazonia became an attractive investment site, the state of Pará seized the opportunity to sell off its public lands as rapidly as possible, especially from 1959 to 1963.[28] Thus began the practice of selling large tracts of land to wealthy investors while those same areas were being informally claimed by small farmers. It was a policy that the federal government continued in the 1970s, which only intensified the level of violence in the competition for land and resources in the countryside.

One of the original investors in southern Pará was a rancher and auto parts industrialist from São Paulo, João Lanari do Val.[29] Lanari do Val owned a ranch in Goiás and set out to expand the size of his operation. In 1959, before the road to the Belém-Brasília Highway was passable, he flew to Conceição do Araguaia in the company of several associates. From there the party undertook the overland trip to Pau D'Arco to get a firsthand look at the natural grasslands he had heard about. On his return to southern Brazil, he filed no less than sixty-four land requisitions (*requerimentos*), laying claim to some four million hectares of land.[30] Because legal statutes prevented a person from owning more than one lot, Lanari do Val registered the land in the names of relatives, friends, and employees. The properties were then joined together in a holding company of which Lanari do Val was the majority shareholder. In the year after that he began to survey and clear a portion of the land, which the law required before he could receive title. His claim infringed on the area inhabited by the Kayapó, whose reserve at that time had still not been properly surveyed.[31]

Lanari do Val brought in skilled workers and supplies from Goiás, traveling the Belém-Brasília Highway as far as the newly established town of Guaraí. From there to Couto Magalhães his men followed the unfinished path of the road and then traveled by canoe to Conceição do Araguaia before starting off again for Pau D'Arco. Unskilled labor was provided by the Pau D'Arco residents who welcomed the offer of local employment.[32] In addition to surveying and clearing his land, Lanari built a road that followed the old rubber trail to Conceição. The site formerly known as *Solta* came to be called *Escritório*, after the surveying office he established there in 1960. A small landing strip was built alongside. The ranch headquarters itself was built some twenty kilometers away. In 1962 the state issued the definitive title to 250,000 hectares of land that came to be known as the Santa Tereza ranch, the largest Brazilian-owned *latifúndio* in the state, occupying nearly 10 percent of the *município* of Conceição do

Araguaia. In 1976 the enterprise employed fifty workers to attend to ten thousand to fifteen thousand head of cattle.

The pioneering effort to establish the Santa Tereza ranch paid off. Shortly after title to the ranch had been secured, the military government that had taken power in 1964 announced its plans for Amazonian development. Constitutional Amendment No. 18, issued in December of 1965, extended to legal Amazonia the generous fiscal incentives that had been created for the northeastern region of the country. In 1966 SUDAM was created to administer the programs, and Pau D'Arco became an attractive site for the many investors seeking to take advantage of these new programs.[33] There were abundant natural pastures as well as nearby forested areas for agriculture. In 1966 the state highway department announced plans to build state road PA-150 to join Conceição to Pau D'Arco. With the promise of a road link, Lanari do Val and his associates were able to sell much of the land they had just purchased at considerable profit. Furthermore, five areas qualified for SUDAM subsidies. The combined budgets of the five projects amounted to Cr$527 million in direct investments and Cr$354 million in fiscal incentives. The initiative provided jobs for forty-nine permanent workers and some five hundred temporary hired hands.

Between 1966 and 1975 SUDAM approved thirty-three projects in Conceição do Araguaia, the largest number in any Amazonian *município*. Together the projects accounted for about one-sixth of the total area.[34] By early 1975, when some 715,000 hectares were under petition for land title, Conceição do Araguaia had become nationally recognized as a major cattle ranching area in the state.[35] In 1976 President Geisel and other federal and state authorities were present in the town to celebrate the signing of the contract to build a seven-hundred-meter bridge across the Aragauia river. The bridge to Couto Magalhães completed the land link to the Belém-Brasília Highway.

Roadside Towns and the New Face of Local Politics

The ranchers who began to move into the savannas near Conceição required a quantity of labor that was not available locally.

Labor recruiters—called *empreteiros* but better known as *gatos*—were hired to bring in temporary workers from the Northeast.[36] Escritório, with its landing strip and survey office, served as headquarters for the new enterprises. The lot on which it was located was jointly owned by Lanari do Val and a surveyor who worked for him, Luis Vargas Dumont. As was commonly done, the land itself was registered in their wives' names.

In mid-1969, when Vargas was about to leave on a month-long trip, he instructed a colleague to survey thirty 450-square-meter lots along the landing strip for urban residences. On his return Vargas was surprised to find all the lots sold and a substantial proportion of them already occupied.[37] Quick to see the opportunity at hand, Vargas took additional steps to place more lots on the market, and a town soon began to take shape. The landing strip became its first street. The first mass, performed at the end of 1969, christened the new settlement Redenção, or "Redemption." A year later census enumerators counted 767 residents of Redenção and 152 houses of which four were also places of business. By 1980 its population had grown to 12,680.[38]

Vargas bought Lanari do Val's share of the urban lots and laid out plans for the town. He installed water and electricity, but these services were soon unable to keep pace with the rapid growth. This element of initial planning was one of the aspects that set Redenção apart from most other towns that were created as a consequence of the roadbuilding and development programs in the 1960s and 1970s. In other respects the history of Redenção was little different from that of other frontier towns that sprang up in a flurry of round-the-clock activity. One of the first settlers described Redenção's first days this way:

> When Redenção began, ranching companies, such as Santa Tereza, Codespar, Belcon, Santa Ernestina, Arraiapora, Chaparral, were already beginning their first clearings, so there were jobs for the people who came here. I was the first trucker in these parts. I brought in the thatch and wood people used to make their houses. It was quite a sight. In the early morning, after four a.m., you couldn't sleep because of the noise of people beating thatch all over town. Lots of families put the roof on their house at night, by the light of a lantern. During the day they didn't have time because they were working for someone else and most of them were really poor.[39]

As in so many other places in southern Pará, violence came with rapid growth. By the mid-1970s Redenção became known for its crime, prostitution, and gunfights. From 1969 to 1977 there were twenty-six unsolved murders in the town.[40] Local residents joked that the cemetery, now located where mule teams once grazed, was the fastest growing spot in Redenção. Both Conceição do Araguaia and Redenção were especially violent places because of their proximity to the Belém-Brasília Highway, which attracted both small farmers and large ranchers to the region. In July of 1974 a federal minister, Rangel Reis, and the governor-elect of the state of Pará visited the area and decided that federal troops were needed to maintain order.[41]

The thriving new town of Redenção with nearly seven thousand inhabitants in 1976 soon rivaled the older riverside settlement of Conceição do Araguaia as a regional center. Southern investors attracted to Amazonia by the fiscal incentive programs lavishly offered by the federal government began to dominate the local economy. They soon challenged the political power held by the regional elites who were linked to the extractive economy and who had close ties to long-standing factions in the state government in Belém.

The case of Giovanni Queiroz, a young rancher and medical doctor from Minas Gerais, is typical of the kinds of political changes that took place in the mid-1970s. With the support of Redenção's founder, Luis Vargas, Queiroz ran against the incumbent mayor of Conceição in local elections in 1976. In his aggressive campaign, the young doctor criticized both state and local authorities for incompetence. Queiroz repeatedly addressed the disgruntled residents of frontier towns and villages. With an inspired rhetorical flourish, he drove home the idea that it was private initiative that carried the onus of development, no thanks to the government or to the retrograde local politicians whose days were past. He blamed bureaucratic obstacles for the region's rampant land problems and hinted that delays in titling were intended to raise land prices and fill state coffers. His administration, he claimed, represented technical progress that would integrate southern Pará into the modern economic development of Brazil.

Queiroz's charismatic blend of populism and developmentalism was enough to defeat his opponent, a traditional merchant and long-time resident of Conceição. The victory of an "outsider"— a candidate neither linked to the extractive economy nor beholden to the traditional elites—was indicative of the new political winds that began to blow across southern Pará.[42]

In Marabá the forces unleashed by the new roads played themselves out differently. The lands bordering the Tocantins river both upstream and downstream from Marabá had already been occupied by small farmers and cattlemen from the Northeast. Unlike the traditional Amazonian *caboclos*, these migrants established themselves on unoccupied lands away from the rivers.[43] The Belém-Brasília Highway provided a new stimulus to this movement. After 1950 agricultural production increased and the northeasterners were joined by migrants from Goiás, Bahia, and Minas Gerais. In 1964 the state started construction of the PA-150 to link the Belém-Brasília Highway to a point on the Tocantins river just outside of Marabá. The 220-kilometer road took several years to complete, and when it was opened in July of 1969, the area was already occupied by migrants. The road was not fully usable until 1972, and bus service was established the following year.

Of all the roads built in southern Pará during the 1970s, it was the Transamazon Highway that had the most far-reaching effects on the town of Marabá and its surrounding area. The national publicity given to the Transamazon colonization projects located just outside of Marabá and further down the road in Altamira and Itaituba stimulated a wave of in-migration of unprecedented proportions. Officials responsible for settling colonists were soon overwhelmed by far more clients than they could possibly handle. Migrants who were not lucky enough to receive a hundred hectares in the project area could do little else but search for land wherever a road made new areas accessible. The PA-150, which connected Marabá to Conceição do Araguaia and Redenção, became the locus of intense and disorganized settlement and land clearing in first half of the 1970s. In retrospect, it was the Transamazon Highway that marked the turning point when the main axis of southern Pará's transportation system shifted from rivers to roads.

The PA-150 gave rise to several new settlements. The town of

São Felix (not to be confused with São Felix do Xingu), located fifteen kilometers from Marabá on the Tocantins river, had three houses in 1965 before road construction began. By 1970, when it was the site for the ferry connecting the road to Marabá, it had 1,461 inhabitants.[44] Bom Jesus, Abel Figueiredo, and (somewhat later) Morada Nova sprang up farther down the road. São Domingos do Capim, a municipal seat, grew from only ninety-six houses in 1969 to a population of well over ten thousand people by 1976. The most important new settlement was Vila Rondon (now called Rondon do Pará), which began as a construction camp in 1967. By the end of the decade when it became the seat of a new *município*, Rondon had emerged as a bustling commercial center that catered to the needs of wealthy ranchers who claimed vast stretches of land to the northwest of the road.

The state government tried to set aside the roadside for small farmers, but they were quickly bought out by the middle-sized cattlemen, mostly from Bahia and Minas Gerais, or they were forced to move on by land speculators and their hired guns. Aware of the fate that awaited them, many new migrants to the area planted pasture grass when they had cleared their land, knowing they could sell out to ranchers.[45] The area around Vila Rondon, where the largest ranches were located, gained notoriety in 1976 when two *posseiros* were beheaded in one conflict, and three American ranchers were killed in a highly publicized second incident.

In response to violent incidents such as these, migrants moved further west in search of land, but the frontier soon caught up with them. In the interviews we carried out in 1978, it was not uncommon to come across whole families of tired and destitute migrant farmers who in the past few years alone had cleared and planted four or five different plots of land, only to find themselves on the road again, looking for a new place to settle.

The effects of the road were felt profoundly by Brazil nut exporters based in Marabá. Although the road facilitated shipping to Belém, it also broke their control over the collectors, who could more easily escape their debts and who could report grievances to the military commander now stationed in the area. In addition, mining companies, construction firms, ranches, and sawmills hired workers away from Brazil nut collecting, and the productivity of collectors fell as novices to the task had to learn their way around the forest. To make matters worse, the deforestation taking place across the region caused a decline in the volume of Brazil nuts produced per tree.[46]

The arrival of newcomers, including powerful investors from southern Brazil, broke the traditional families' monopoly over land in the *castanhais*, especially after the mid-1970s. As the number of rural properties officially registered increased rapidly beginning in the 1960s, the proportion of land in the Marabá area controlled by the traditional local oligarchy fell from 44 percent in 1972 to 33 percent in 1976 and to only 14 percent in 1981.[47]

As in Conceição do Araguaia, changes in Marabá brought political challenges from outsiders. After Marabá was classified as a National Security area in the wake of the guerrilla movement (see chapter 3), the federal government appointed mayors who owed little allegiance to the traditional local elites.[48] Fading political power was accompanied by an increase in direct challenges to control over the Brazil nut areas. In 1970 the Catholic church appointed as Marabá's Bishop Estevão Cardoso Avelar, whose philosophy was sympathetic to the activist Pastoral Land Commission (CPT) that supported *posseiros* in their struggle against ranchers and other large land claimants. With the support of the church and lay religious members of the CPT, *posseiros* began to invade the Brazil nut lands in the 1970s and 1980s, first individually and later in more organized groups.

The peculiar legal status of the leases—which classified land neither as private nor as public property—became the focal point of legal battles when the Brazil nut merchants of southern Pará began to lose influence to peasants and ranchers. With different land use strategies in mind and different notions regarding the very concept of land ownership the newcomers to the Marabá region posed a radical challenge to this feature of traditional Amazonia. In the late 1970s and well into the following decade the area surrounding the town of Marabá became the site of intense and often violent confrontations.

The fate of the traditional Marabá oligarchy was finally sealed as a consequence of the combined effects of the rapid pace of local change and the shifting political priorities in Brasília. When the military began a process of gradual political liberalization in

1979, regime strategists hoped to control the transition to a civilian administration through the election of a president from the ranks of the proregime party, the PDS (Partido Democrático Social). Aware that the PDS candidate could not win by direct popular vote, the military decreed that the election for president in 1985 would be indirect. In order to ensure a PDS victory, it was necessary to win the congressional and state elections in 1982 since the electoral college would be composed of all federal senators and their deputies together with state delegations.

In Marabá the PDS faced stiff opposition in the 1982 elections from the rival PMDB party. The picture was further complicated by splits within the PDS, one arm of which was firmly in the control of the Brazil nut elite, notably the Mutrán family. From the standpoint of the technocrats and political strategists in Brasília, the traditional oligarchy in Marabá represented an electoral liability that was likely to lose this crucial election to newcomers as had happened in Conceição do Araguaia in 1976. The solution was to direct the campaign to the new entrepreneurial groups in the area, including people who had invested huge sums in the Serra Pelada gold mine (see chapter 8). Thus it happened that Curió, who was then in charge of Serra Pelada, became the candidate for congressional office at the personal request of President Figueiredo. In November of 1982 the strategy worked, and Curió was elected to Congress with a huge vote, mainly from thousands of Serra Pelada *garimpeiros*. Members of the Mutrán family continued to wield power in Pará, but the 1982 election marked the end of the political monopoly exercised by the traditional oligarchy in Marabá. "Garimpeiro votes," as David Cleary aptly noted, "had achieved what over a decade of rural unionization, church activity, and PMDB organization had thus far been unable to manage."[49]

The Timber Boom

The PA-150 opened access to the world's richest stand of mahogany trees—*Swietenia macrophylla*, a tropical upland species.[50] Even before the road between Redenção and Marabá had been built, logs were extracted along the Maria and Araguaia rivers during the 1960s. These operations depended on subcontractors (*empreteiros*) who hired up to a hundred men and organized them into teams. One group felled the trees. Another sawed the huge trunks to manageable size, and the third group cut trails to the riverside. When the rains came and the water level rose, logs were cabled together in enormous rafts (called *jangadas*) that were guided downstream all the way to Belém by men in motor boats.

The construction of the PA-150 transformed the timber industry by providing an overland link to the port in Belém and to domestic markets in central and southern Brazil. The road also opened up southern Pará to medium-sized and large logging firms from the southern states of Paraná and Santa Catarina. Sawmill operators were attracted to Amazonia by the tax credits and exemptions offered by SUDAM and by the strong demand for mahogany on the international market. Production in the state of Pará rose over 4,000 percent during the 1970s. By the end of the decade Pará accounted for 69 percent of Amazonian industrial wood production.[51]

When roads began to penetrate southern Pará in the early 1970s, the sawmills often pioneered the process of land settlement. Near Redenção, the Pau D'Arco sawmill, built in 1972, quickly spawned a new town by that name. In that same year the Maginco company, Brazil's largest mahogany exporter, installed its first sawmill at Xambioá north of Conceição along the Araguaia River. To the company's distress, the mill was situated squarely in guerrilla territory where the military carried out its campaigns against the dissidents. At the first opportunity, Maginco moved its headquarters to a new site along the PA-150, which was then still under construction.

In August of 1973 both the road crews and Maginco arrived at a point some 190 kilometers west and north from Conceição do Araguaia, on the banks of the Rio Maria where a small spontaneous settlement already existed. Maginco acquired rights to 6,000 hectares of land and donated 150 hectares for the site of the new town of Rio Maria. By 1976 Maginco employed eighty to ninety workers in its processing plant and another hundred in logging operations that took place between May and October. The company built a store and housing for some sixty workers and their families. Health care was provided through a contract with the private hospital built in Rio Maria by Giovanni Queiroz, the young doctor who became mayor of Conceição do Araguaia in the elections that year. Rio Maria was home to about six thousand people in 1976 and to some eight thousand people by 1980.

Compared to other groups who migrated into southern Pará, loggers were a special breed. Most of them had learned their skills in Paraná, cutting the so-called Paraná pine trees during an earlier stage of frontier expansion in the 1950s and 1960s. With the opening of the Amazon, many small operators transported their equipment to the north, running their operation as a family business. As soon as a new area was made accessible by a road, sawmills were close behind, buying mahogany trees from ranchers and small farmers who were clearing land.

The presence of sawmills in newly settled areas gave a distinctive cast to frontier towns in the region. Most of the buildings, even sidewalks, were often made out of mahogany, which, at least in the initial stages, was the only wood the mill operators bothered to cut. The sawmills also influenced the pattern of land settlement since the feeder roads that loggers cut into the forest often invited the entry of small farmers. Moreover, the sale of timber played an important role in the economic viability of small farmers and ranchers. For cattle ranchers, the sale of mahogany trees was a source of extra profits. For small farmers it was a source of supplemental income, especially early on when they struggled to get established in a frontier area.

In Pará, the "golden years" of mahogany production were over by 1981. Industrial wood producers in Redenção, Rio Maria, and Xinguara had depleted the most accessible reserves in a few years. Most mahogany trees take one hundred to three hundred years to reach a size ideal for harvesting.[52] The diameter of the trunks carried on the logging trucks along the PA-150 diminished markedly from one year to the next until the operation was no longer viable. Smaller operators generally picked up and moved on down the road to new areas, such as São Felix do Xingu, where the prime trees were in greater supply. Several of the larger mills reacted by exploiting new species and diversifying into the production of veneers. Compared to other frontier enterprises, the larger sawmills offered more stable employment and were one of the few sources of jobs for women.

The cyclical character of the timber trade also affected the geography of land occupation and clearing. The rapid growth followed by the gradual decline in timber extraction had especially significant consequences for smaller roadside villages. Although strategically located towns like Xinguara continued to grow in size as their economy diversified, smaller places—like Agua Azul, which sprang up seventy kilometers west of Xinguara along the PA-279—began to lose population once the surrounding area was deforested and the timber boom had run its course. On our visit to southern Pará in 1987, one informant described Agua Azul as "the most progressive town in the state." "Hardly a day goes by," he added with wry humor, "that somebody doesn't pick up his whole house and move on down the road."

By the mid-1970s southern Pará had become virtually unrecognizable to old-timers in the region. Conceição do Araguaia, once a sleepy riverside village, bustled with automobile and truck traffic and was on its way to becoming a major tourist attraction for vacationers who enjoyed the clear waters of the Araguaia river and the spectacular beaches that lay exposed during the dry season. Marabá, for its part, began to look much more like a city than the small town it had been for so many years. In the countryside, villages sprang up in places where once only a few houses had stood. New settlements located at strategic points along the roadside grew at an explosive rate. The figures in table 5.1 give some idea of the magnitude of the population increase in some

TABLE 5.1

Population Growth and Percent in Urban Areas of Selected Municipalities in Southern Pará

Municipality	1960	1970	1980	Percent Increase 1970–80	Percent Urban 1980
Conceicão de Araguaia	11,283	28,953	111,551	285.3	29.6
Itupiranga	4,298	5,346	15,641	192.6	17.6
Marabá	20,089	24,474	59,915	144.8	69.5
São Felix do Xingu		2,332	4,982	113.6	35.0
São João de Araguaia	297	15,326	35,772	133.4	3.7
Tucuruí		9,921	61,140	516.3	44.6
TOTAL	35,967	86,352	289,001	234.7	37.3

SOURCE: Population Censuses 1960 (Acre, Amazonas,Pará. Série Regional, Vol. 1, Tomo II, 2a parte), 1970 (Série Regional, Vol. 1, Tomo IV), 1980 (Dados Distritais, Vol. 1, Tomo 3, No. 4), Fundação IBGE, Rio de Janeiro.

of the principal southern Pará towns that predated the roads. Between 1960 and 1970 the total number of people nearly tripled. The population had grown by 235 percent by 1980 and continued to expand into the 1980s. Contrary to what might be expected in a frontier area, much of the growing population was concentrated in urban areas.[53]

The Road to the Xingu

Of the many roads built through southern Pará in the 1970s, the PA-279 had a particularly turbulent story. In the 1950s local authorities in São Felix do Xingu pressured the state for a road linkage to southern Pará. River transport was difficult given the rapids on the Xingu that made the river dangerous during the dry season. A few years later an ambitious "Belcan proposal" sought to build a road from Belém to Gorotire, the main Kayapó village. From there it would connect to a road to be built from São Felix. By 1963 São Felix was an independent *município*, and its first prefect, Francisco Sales Bessa, used local funds to construct some thirty kilometers of road in the direction of Gorotire. For more than twenty years, this was to remain the *município*'s only road.

When the state highway department announced plans in 1966 to build the road from Conceição to what soon became Redenção, there was talk of extending this highway to Gorotire. But events elsewhere convinced the highway department of the "inconvenience" of building roads through Indian reserves. The PA-150 linking Marabá to the Belém-Brasília Highway cut through the territories of the Gaviões in 1969. When invaders entered their lands, the Indians attacked and killed a number of people. It was an incident that sent the highway department back to the drawing boards to find a route that would avoid the Gorotire lands inhabited by the Kayapó.

In the meantime, while the PA-150 that linked Marabá and Redenção was still under construction, a new proposal was prepared in 1973 for the PA-279 road that would connect the PA-150 to São Felix do Xingu, avoiding the southern route through Gorotire. According to the plan, the 250-kilometer road would depart the PA-150 at a point 250 kilometers south of Marabá near the Rio Maria. Detailed plans showed the proposed road traveling between the Trairão and Branco rivers, along the northern border of the Gorotire reserve, passing near the settlement of Nova Olinda on the Rio Fresco, and from there to the municipal road to São Felix. But this route was also abandoned when FUNAI announced changes in the boundaries of the Gorotire reserve to compensate for areas to the south that had been invaded by settlers. The new border went as far north as the Rio Branco, and the proposed road would therefore have cut through the reserve after all.

In 1974 and 1975 the prospects for a road to São Felix do Xingu brightened considerably as a result of new funds made available through the POLAMAZONIA project and as a consequence of Projeto Radam, which had shown that the area was endowed with good soils and rich mineral deposits. In August of 1975 the state highway department, after demanding that FUNAI clarify the northern boundaries of the Gorotire reserve, received approval for a new route to start just north of Rio Maria. But the confusion over Indian lands was far from over. This time it was the Xikrin, a group of Kayapó Indians, who presented a problem.[54]

For several years prior to 1975 anthropologist Lux Vidal had worked with the Xikrin and FUNAI to establish the boundaries of that reserve. On the basis of her recommendations, an agreement was reached in October of 1975. Just two months later work began on the road whose projected new route would cut through the reserve's southern portion.[55] FUNAI placed an embargo on the road, and the project was again brought to a halt. In mid-1976 Pará's state highway department sent a representative to Brasília to negotiate with FUNAI. The compromise solution was to shift the route along the Pium river, making the road the southernmost limit of the reserve. Because this trajectory cut off a portion of Xikrin lands to the south, the Indians were to be compensated with additional lands to the north. The northern side of the road, which bordered the reserve, was to be cordoned off by barbed wire. The lands on the south side were to be returned to state jurisdiction.

The latter condition of the agreement turned out to have a profound effect on the subsequent evolution of events in southern Pará. Engineers within Pará's highway department (DER) reasoned that the lands to the south of the road could serve as the site of a state-sponsored colonization program (see chapter 6). A DER engineer convinced FUNAI to consider the plan, pending an on-site investigation. The plan was attractive primarily for political reasons. A few days after his trip to Brasília, the engineer who had negotiated with FUNAI temporarily left his duties in the highway department to become a candidate for prefect of Conceição do Araguaia in 1976. In a place where people were hungry for land, the proposed colonization project along the borders of the PA-279 became a key campaign issue. Eager to promote their candidate, state officials began to distribute lots in an area close to the intersection of the PA-150 and the PA-279. The publicity that the colonization scheme aroused attracted thousands of people from Goiás, Redenção, and Rio Maria. The result was the tumultuous growth of a new town, which came to be known as Xinguara (see chapter 6).

The euphoria generated by the colonization project soon turned sour. First the DER engineer failed in his bid for political office. Then the federal highway department in Brasília published a map in May of 1977 that showed the projected route of another new road (the BR-158) slated to go through São Felix do Xingu and all the way to Altamira. Because of Decree Law 1164, the road project transferred jurisdiction for all of the lands in question from the state to the federal government. Meanwhile, the borders of the Xikrin reserve that had been defined in October of 1975 were still in dispute.

In April of 1976 Vidal was asked to review a request for mineral exploration within the Indian territory. In the process, she unexpectedly discovered a new map that significantly reduced the size of the reserve. The revised boundaries were apparently the work of the regional FUNAI office in Belém. Vidal successfully appealed to the President of FUNAI in Brasília to stick to the original agreement, only to learn in December of that year that the president's decision was overturned by the Minister of the Interior who changed the boundaries of the Xikrin reserve to coincide with the road.[56]

Vidal protested in February of 1977, urging the immediate demarcation of the Xikrin reserve to prevent the invasion of Indian lands. Her petition included the recommendation that the road be shifted to the south to permit the Indians to continue their use of the Rio Seco area. There were three different proposals for identifying the precise boundaries of the Xikrin reserve. One was Vidal's version, based on the Indian's traditional land use patterns. Another was the plan proposed by the regional FUNAI office and the state highway department, which would significantly reduce the size of the reserve. The third version was put forth by FUNAI officials in Brasília, who proposed that the reserve end at the road.

The matter was not resolved until January of 1978 when the reserve was finally demarcated. The result essentially conformed to the compromise proposal of FUNAI in Brasília with an unexplained additional cut of thirteen thousand hectares to the west.[57] The loss of the western strip was apparently included in the final plan so that the area would serve as a buffer zone for the proposed Carajás project based at Serra Norte.

But the struggle to defend the Indians' reserve and to define the precise route of the PA-279 was not yet over. In late 1977 a new FUNAI representative was assigned to the Xikrin. She was prohibited by her superiors in Belém from having any direct communications with anthropologists, medical doctors, or FUNAI in Brasília. About this time, an adulterated map of the reserve—one that conformed more or less to the reduced Belém proposal—began to circulate. Invasions were also taking place on some four hundred hectares of land within the newly demarcated reserve. At the regional level, FUNAI officials insisted that the land invaders were "good faith" investors, and should not be penalized for problems that were not of their own making.[58]

In August of 1979 a FUNAI commission from Brasília arrived in the area to investigate the Xikrin situation. The commission's report noted that the Xikrin were dissatisfied with the demarcation of their reserve and that medium-sized cattle ranchers as well as loggers and *posseiros* had already taken over much of the reserve's southern border. Having accepted the fact that the road itself could not be stopped, the commission's objective was to minimize the damage. In October of that year FUNAI requested that the highway department again revise the route of the PA-279 to a more southerly position, thereby skirting the reserve.

By July of 1978 some 130 kilometers of the road had been completed, and it inched its way ever closer to the fertile soils purchased by the construction firm Andrade Gutierrez, the company that planned to establish a large private colonization project in the area (see chapter 7). The problem posed by the advancing road was especially critical in light of the fact that the Andrade Gutierrez land claim was at that time still stalled in the Senate in Brasília, where it was the object of a prolonged and heated debate. To protect itself from the anticipated onslaught of migrants, the company pressured INCRA in August of 1979 to request that the state highway department suspend work on the road until the land question could be sorted out. In January of 1980 the previous contract for construction of the road to the Xingu was suspended, much to the frustration of the people of São Felix do Xingu who anxiously awaited the road's arrival. In February responsibility for building the remaining stretch was transferred to none other than Andrade Gutierrez, but the company was in no hurry to complete the road all the way to São Felix.

The new route, settled on in March of 1980, took a more southerly path than the previous plan had called for, allowing a small buffer zone between the road and most of the Xikrin reserve. DER asked FUNAI to keep Indians in the northern part of the reserve, away from the construction crews. The plan also better attended to the interests of the new investments going into the region, including the Andrade Gutierrez colonization project, three gold mining areas, and the tin ore operation underway by PROMIX (see chapter 8). Hence, after years of convoluted negotiations between state and federal agencies, the Indian question was resolved, the final route of the road seemed settled, and Andrade Gutierrez—a powerful construction company with its own interest in land development in southern Pará—was in charge of completing the PA-279.

With considerable resources and equipment at its disposal, Andrade Gutierrez completed the road, at least as far as the borders of its property. There the company erected a gate in an attempt to keep migrants from invading land. The barricade, which prevented anyone from entering the area without proper documentation, also served as a means to put pressure on the state government to pay up for the cost of the road work the company had performed. Well inside the property line, Andrade Gutierrez went about building an urban center the company called Tucumã (see chapter 7). The construction within the project included a service road that traveled westward from Tucumã as far as the company's experimental farm along the banks of the Rio Fresco not far from São Felix do Xingu.

Residents of São Felix do Xingu were outraged. After years of waiting for the road to reach them, it became apparent that Andrade Gutierrez had little interest in completing the final stretch to the town, and the makeshift road that did exist as far as the Rio Fresco was not open to public transit. But try as it might, the colonization company was unable to keep the road closed to outsiders for very long. Rumors of gold on Tucumã lands prompted miners to assault the checkpoint, forcing the company to allow free passage (see chapter 7).

Once the gate to the Tucumã project was opened, the service road to the experimental station at Krimet became the de facto link to the Rio Fresco. There small boats carried passengers and cargo downstream to São Felix do Xingu. Realizing that the promised state road was going to stop short of reaching its final destination, the prefecture of São Felix had little choice but to take over the task. In June of 1983 forty or so of the town's residents cleared a four-kilometer path that finally made the link between the Rio Fresco crossing and the municipal road that ran all the way into the town. An enterprising resident, Luís Otávio Montenegro Jorge (a descendant of São Felix's founder in the days of the rubber boom, Colonel Tancredo Jorge) established a ferry service to cross the river. Precarious though it was, the people of São Felix finally got the road that they had awaited for so long. What this would mean for them is the subject of the final part of this book.

NOTES

1. For the sake of consistency, we refer to rubber "tappers" (*seringueiros*) in this chapter although in certain regions where latex was extracted from caucho trees they are properly designated *caucheiros*.

2. Rodrigues (1945:122).

3. Emmi (1985:33–34). Much of the following analysis of political and economic change in Marabá is taken from this excellent study, later published as a book (see Emmi 1988).

4. Velho (1972).

5. Ianni (1978:15–32).

6. Emmi (1985:29–30).

7. Arnaud (1975:14–15).

8. The PA-150 in southern Pará was originally designated the PA-70. In the interest of both clarity and consistency we refer to the PA-150 in our discussion in this chapter and the accompanying map.

9. Silva (1982:11).

10. Velho (1972:47–57).

11. Paternostro (1945:82–85).

12. Velho (1972:47–57).

13. Unlike rubber, Brazil nuts were collected during the rainy season when the mature nuts fell to the ground where they could be collected by the *castanheiros*. The collectors would break open the hard outer shells of the *ouriços* to separate the inner *castanha* nuts (Emmi 1985:66–68). Because the Brazil nut trees grew inland, the nuts had to be transported overland by pack mules, then by small boats or diesel-powered canoes from the small streams to Marabá, and eventually onto small steam-powered boats (*gaiolas*) to Belém (Dias 1958:411). The rapids in the Tocantins river between Marabá and Alcobaça (now called Tucuruí) required that nuts be transported in small boats and temporarily stored in Alcobaça or (after the 1940s) moved on the small railroad between Alcobaça and Jatobal.

14. Emmi (1985:71–87,96).

15. Emmi (1985:73–99). As discussed in chapter 3, these leases were one target of the military's land policy reforms in the 1970s and of the short-lived agrarian reform effort of the 1980s.

16. Emmi (1985:98–99).

17. Emmi (1985:8,67–68) and Weinstein (1983:244–245).

18. Velho (1972:57).

19. Dias (1958:421) and Arnaud (1975:15–17).

20. Dias (1958).

21. Ianni (1978:35–63).

22. Silva (1982:18).

23. Ianni (1978:63).

24. Silva (1982:21).

25. Hébette and Azevedo (1979) and Lisansky (1988).

26. Velho (1972:95).

27. Arnaud (1975:20).

28. Santos (1984:453).

29. Silva (1982).

30. Silva (1982:41–59). The *requerimentos* were for nine hundred *alqueires* of land.

31. *Amazônia*, August/September 1985. For more on the Kayapó Indians, see chapter 9.

32. Silva (1982:53–59). Until this time the grasslands and forested areas of Pau D'Arco had been isolated from contact with the outside world except on the rare

occasion when a traveling salesman ventured by on muleback or a trading vessel appeared on the Pau D'Arco river during the high-water season. Residents only rarely made the five-day, 105-kilometer trip to Conceição to buy the supplies of salt, kerosene, matches, and ammunition needed to last them through the rainy season when the Rio Arraias swelled too wide for crossing. Until a hanging bridge was built in 1945, the crossing meant swimming the pack animals from one side to the other. Cash for required purchases came from selling dried beef, salt pork, or deerskins. Most other needs were supplied by the residents of the remote communities where brown sugar (*rapadura*) and cane liquor (*cachaça*) were used as currency more often than money (Silva 1982:21–27).

33. Silva (1982:62–69).
34. Ianni (1978:93).
35. Pinto (1977:23–24).
36. Silva (1982:72).
37. Silva (1982:79–82). The account of the history of Redenção is based on Silva (1982) and on field interviews.
38. Silva (1982:97).
39. Silva (1982:85).
40. Fernando (1977:10).
41. Silva (1982:90).
42. Despite his local victory, Giovanni was unable to realize his ambitious plans because of the poor relationship with the state government that was the target of much of his criticism. Years later Giovanni went on to become state deputy and the state leader of one of the new parties of Brazil's New Republic.
43. Velho (1972:95). This study is an excellent source of information about the settlement of southern Pará prior to the Transamazon Highway.
44. Velho (1972:138).
45. Velho (1972:137–142).
46. Brazil nut production varies naturally from year to year. Forest clearing contributes to declining production in various ways even though it is prohibited by law to actually cut down Brazil nut trees. Trees that are left standing in a field are often damaged by the smoke and flames during burning. Furthermore, the isolation of the trees from the surrounding forest disrupts the pollinization process on which the tree's reproduction depends. By the 1980s loggers were openly cutting down the remaining *castanheira* trees near Marabá.
47. Emmi (1985:116).
48. Emmi (1985:121–122).
49. Cleary (1990:178).
50. Browder (1984:15).
51. Browder (1986:56).
52. Browder (1984:19).
53. For more information on urbanization in Amazonia, see Becker (1985), Browder and Godfrey (1990), and Godfrey (1990).
54. The Xikrin are part of the group of Gê-speaking Indians referred to as the northern Kayapó whose history is recounted in more detail in chapter 9.
55. Vidal (1981).
56. Vidal (1981:127).
57. Vidal (1981:128).
58. Vidal (1981:129–132).

SIX

The Struggle for Land: Xinguara

"First we'll make an Old West in the Amazon,
then we'll call in the sheriff."
          Antonio Delfim Neto, March 8, 1978,
                    (former Minister of Planning)

The highway department in the state of Pará began construction of the PA-279 to São Felix do Xingu in 1976. The road started about twenty kilometers north of the town of Rio Maria, jutting westward from the PA-150, the heavily traveled link between Conceição do Araguaia and Marabá. Migrants began to settle the area the moment road crews got to work. In a few months time a handful of makeshift houses had sprung up at the intersection. The place was first known as Entroncamento do Xingu ("Xingu Junction"). Later, when the town grew in size, residents took account of the two main rivers in the region—the Xingu and the Araguaia—to come up with a new name: Xinguara.

Xinguara was strategically positioned between the long established towns of Conceição do Araguaia and Marabá. Its location made the town a preferred destination for thousands of migrants who poured into southern Pará in the 1970s. By February of 1977, less than a year after it was founded, Xinguara housed 1,360 residences, 30 retail stores, 25 bars and restaurants, 15 butcher shops, 6 pharmacies, and 5 Protestant churches. Four sawmills exploited the plentiful stands of mahogany trees in the area, and a rice processing machine serviced nearby farmers.[1] By the end of 1977 Xinguara held over four thousand inhabitants. Nearly twice that number lived there by the end of the following year.[2] In November of 1980 the malaria control agency (SUCAM) counted 3,202 houses in Xinguara and a population of 14,398.

The road itself was not the only impetus for migrant settlement at the junction of the two roads. Farmers also were drawn to Xinguara hoping to receive a plot of land in a colonization area promoted by the state government. As it turned out, the project began as part of a campaign strategy in a politician's unsuccessful bid for public office and was never completed. The promise of free land nonetheless stimulated a massive influx of migrants, which in turn sparked violent confrontations between ranchers and would-be colonists. In the end, both state and federal agencies as well as the Catholic church and the rural labor union were drawn into a conflict that grew increasingly complex with each failed attempt to bring the situation under control. The prolonged battle that took place over land bestowed on Xinguara the sad distinction of being one of the most violent places in all of Amazonia.

False Promises and Crisis Colonization

The state-sponsored colonization effort to be carried out in the place that was then still called Xingu Junction was the centerpiece of Ulysses Vieira's electoral campaign against Giovanni Queiroz. At stake in the electoral contest was the position of mayor of the *município* of Conceição do Araguaia. As regional director of the state highway department, Vieira counted on his associates in the government for help in his bid for votes. In a place like southern Pará, the offer of free land was an effective way to get people's attention. In August of 1976 members of the Agricultural Secretariat (SAGRI) and Land Institute (ITERPA) arrived at the crossroads to implement the land distribution program.[3] Vieira inaugurated the settlement in September of 1976. In honor of the governor of the state of Pará, Vieira called it "Agricultural Colony Governor Aloysio Chaves."

The stated purpose of the colonization program in Xinguara was to anticipate, and therefore sidestep, the violence that plagued the rest of southern Pará. The orderly distribution of agricultural plots, Vieira contended, was the only way to avoid the confrontations between ranchers and peasant farmers that had already become widespread in other parts of the state. Yet the outcome of the initiative was quite the opposite. Because the settlement project was part of an electoral campaign, it was highly publicized on radio and television in Pará and in the nearby states of Goiás and Mato Grosso. News of free land quickly set in motion a massive influx of people. Officials were soon overwhelmed by the number of petitions for farm lots. During a period of only two weeks in October more than fifteen hundred families applied for land.[4]

While administrators of the project tried to select colonists from the growing list of applicants, migrant families continued to pour into Xinguara in record numbers.[5] State officials attempted to control the settlement process and to regulate the plunder of timber stands in the area, but they met with little success.[6] *Posseiros* who had already settled near the crossing of the two roads found their properties overrun by newcomers to the area. The already complicated situation grew worse in November when Vieira lost the mayoral election. The priority the state government had once given to the colonization program faded along with Vieira's political ambitions.

Tensions mounted in Xinguara as the size of its population grew. Like Redenção just down the road, Xinguara became widely known for the shoot-outs that regularly occurred on the streets and for the impunity with which gunslingers and crooks carried out their business. After a time, charismatic individuals assumed control of the town. In frontier style, they used a combination of violence and patronage to establish their authority. Among them was the man who called himself the founder of Xinguara, José Ferreira da Silva, better known as "Chapeu de Couro" ("Leather Hat") after the traditional cowboy garb in his native state of Ceará. Silva's reputation as a gunman made him one of the most feared men in southern Pará. Still, in the tradition of rural bosses who so often turn up in the pages of Brazilian history, Chapeu de Couro was not without a civic conscience. It was Silva who organized the initial distribution of urban lots, and it was he who later built the town's first school.

In the early days of the settlement, Chapeu de Couro was a familiar sight in Xinguara. Late in the afternoon he could be found holding court from a hammock slung at one end of the front porch of the ramshackle hotel he owned. He was nearly always in the presence of several brooding henchmen, who were also from the

Northeast. In the 1980s Chapeu de Couro moved to Tucumã where he became a licensed gold buyer and, by all accounts, a reputable citizen. Yet his violent past eventually caught up with him. In 1986 on a trip to Redenção, he was gunned down on the street by an anonymous killer.

As Xinguara suffered its growing pains, the federal government dealt the final blow to the colonization program by assuming jurisdiction over the entire area. The legal device for doing so was Decree 1164 of 1971, which stipulated that one hundred kilometers on either side of a federal road would fall under Brasília's jurisdiction. In 1976 engineers proposed the BR-158 to connect Conceição do Araguaia and São Felix do Xingu. Although the road was never built, the dotted line the cartographers drew across the map of southern Pará was all it took to transfer some twenty million hectares into the hands of the federal government. The site of the colonization project in Xinguara was included in the federal takeover, as state officials belatedly learned the following year when Brasília published a new map of the area.[7]

Federal authorities proved no more effective in dealing with the land problem in Xinguara than did their predecessors in SAGRI and ITERPA. The commander of the army's Jungle Battalion in Marabá grew increasingly disturbed by the chaotic situation in and around the town and pressured INCRA to find a solution. In response to the growing crisis, the INCRA office in Marabá was elevated to the status of "Special Coordinator for the Araguaia-Tocantins" (CEAT). Staff salaries were increased, and the agency was relieved of INCRA's many other responsibilities. The plan was to devote full attention to land conflicts by redefining the objectives of an existing agency and empowering it with sufficient bureaucratic flexibility to contend with the growing emergency.

CEAT sent a team of investigators to Xinguara in June of 1977. The report they filed with the Marabá office warned of the intense disillusionment felt by the people in the town and its surrounding areas. By then many families had been taken in by unscrupulous *grileiros* who sold phony titles to farmers desperate to acquire legal rights to their own plot of land. Others had been pushed off the land they had cleared by cattle ranchers and speculators who commanded greater economic resources and wielded considerable political power among the local police and military personnel. The report pointed to the threat of organized resistance movements of small farmers, migrants, and landless workers.[8]

In September of 1977, CEAT set up a regional office in Xinguara. This decision opened the second chapter in a story that seemed to grow more complicated by the day. Invoking a procedure called *discriminatória branca*—a bureaucratic provision that dispensed with the need to survey land—CEAT quickly set aside 250,000 hectares of land, known as Gleba Rio Maria and Gleba Cabeceiras. By October, well over five hundred families had put their name on the list and waited anxiously for a plot of land. CEAT demarcated four hundred lots that the agency hoped to colonize by November, but the distribution of land was held up by a legal problem. A summary of the contrived legal steps that followed CEAT's initial attempt to get the colonization project underway offers an insight into the knotty bureaucratic challenges that confronted even the most well-meaning official.

The agency first intended to provide settlers with a document called Occupation License (LO) but soon found that under Brazilian law the LO could be awarded only to farmers who had occupied land for at least a year. Under pressure to resolve the legal matter as soon as possible, the CEAT staff then explored the possibility of using an "Occupation Authorization" (AO); yet this too failed. According to the statutes, the AO was permitted only in official INCRA colonization areas, which this project was not. The matter went all the way to the agency president who circumvented the legal obstacle by devising an "Emergency Settlement" procedure as an extension of the existing AO.[9]

Thinking that the legal problems had finally been taken care of, CEAT handed out land to the colonists, many of whom had been waiting in Xinguara for as long as a year. The distribution of emergency settlement papers was accompanied by stern lectures from the CEAT staff, described to us by colonists interviewed in 1978. Settlers were reminded of the importance of not selling their land and of the need to work together for their collective defense against ranchers and others who were vying for the property they received.

CEAT officials who delivered these high-handed admonitions soon regretted having said anything at all. In its haste to find a solution to land conflicts in Xinguara, the agency inadvertently settled fifty-six families on property that on closer inspection turned out to be legally held by fourteen sawmills and eight cattle ranchers.[10] After first urging the farmers to stay put, CEAT now found itself in the awkward position of forcing these same families to move to a new location.

The relocation was easier said than done. By then settlers had borne the cost of a year's wait in town. In addition, the majority of them had already cleared and seeded their newly acquired plots, leaving them few resources with which to start over again. CEAT officials resorted to various tricks to induce colonists to surrender their documents, including deception and threats. If CEAT's first message to the farmers was to stand firm, now the agency did everything it could to break the colonists' solidarity and get them to agree to the resettlement scheme. Some complied. Others did not. "The chief told me I had to stay right here and to work the land," said one colonist with mock humility and a twinkle in his eye. "I've got the documents, so I'm going to do just exactly what he said."

The need to move Xinguara colonists elsewhere gave birth to a new CEAT colony called Mata Geral ("General Forest"). It was located about 121 kilometers south of Xinguara in an area that CEAT had demarcated in 1977 to serve as the receiving place for incoming migrants. Mata Geral was a small "island" of untitled land surrounded by three large properties (including the Santa Tereza ranch, discussed in chapter 5) that had been purchased from the state in the 1960s. CEAT began the process of settling 269 colonists from Xinguara in Mata Geral in June of 1978. Many were "resettled" colonists who had agreed to move from their first plot. Others were drawn from CEAT's waiting list, which now ran to several volumes.

Despite its inauspicious beginnings, the Mata Geral colony's relative isolation contributed to a degree of stability uncommon in this contested region, at least in its initial years. But problems soon emerged. By 1981, just three years after its inauguration, Mata Geral was severely overcrowded. The growing population density was largely due to the influx of relatives and friends who became sharecroppers on the land the original colonists had received. When Mata Geral became saturated, settlers began to invade the vast private landholdings that lay unused on all sides of the colony.

CEAT activities in southern Pará amounted to a process of "crisis colonization." When a particularly volatile situation was identified, the federal government sent in a small and well-trained staff to sort out the problem. The solutions they devised often involved imaginative legal and political maneuvers that sometimes worked, at least in the short run. Yet the stopgap approach to the land problem in Amazonia hardly addressed the larger question of agrarian structure nor did it deal effectively with the huge inflow of migrants to the region. On the contrary, the crisis settlement policy—first carried out by CEAT in the 1970s and later on a much broader scale by an agency called GETAT in the 1980s—often served to aggravate the very problems such measures were intended to solve.

Rural Violence and the GETAT Takeover

The growth of the new towns and the expansion of logging, ranching, and farming activities quickened the pace of forest clearing along the PA-150 and the PA-279. Satellite images showed that the size of deforested areas between Marabá and Rio Maria had risen from 300 square kilometers in 1972 to 1,700 square kilometers in 1977 and to 8,200 square kilometers by 1985 (see Map 5). In thirteen years the proportion of cleared land increased from less than 1 percent to over 17 percent of the total surface area shown in the maps.[11]

LANDSAT images further showed that deforestation occurred well ahead of the expanding road network. Wealthier investors began to clear large patches of land for pasture many kilometers in advance of the road construction crews. Ranchers often built landing strips in order to bring in men and equipment by small aircraft. Similarly, peasant farmers trekked into the forest in search of unoccupied land, following the survey trails engineers had built to mark the projected route. The process of advanced clearing by ranchers and small farmers meant that latecomers to the area found that much of the land had already been claimed,

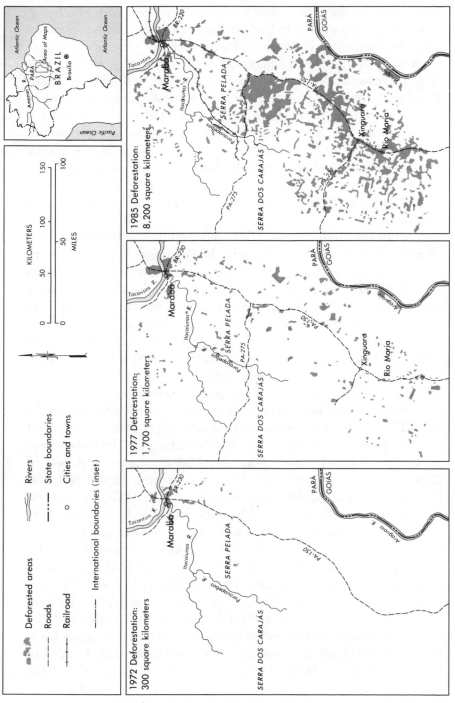

Deforestation in Southern Pará, 1972, 1977, and 1985.

especially the more desirable locations. With no place else to go, newer migrants unable to find land moved into town, where they often fell victim to violence and exploitation.

In 1977 the police in Xinguara tried to extort protection fees from merchants and brothel owners.[12] In one incident, they swept through the town's crowded outdoor market, overturning stacks of produce as they went. In the scuffle that followed, hungry marketgoers fought one another for the rice strewn on the ground.[13] The purpose of the tactic was to leave no doubt among the stall owners and townspeople that the police meant business. In October of that year a coalition of merchants sent a petition to the police commander in Belém denouncing the corruption in Xinguara.

Most of the violence took place in the countryside and involved disputes over land. A particularly shocking incident occurred in 1979 on a ranch called Tupã-Ciretã located twelve kilometers from Xinguara. São Paulo banker Flávio Pinto de Almeida claimed rights to some thirty thousand hectares and tried to expel the four hundred or so families who were already settled there.[14] When the *posseiros* contested Almeida's claim, police and armed guards allegedly entered the area and brutally assaulted its occupants. According to witnesses to the event, they burned houses to the ground and tortured some of the people who lived there.

In response to the Tupã-Ciretã incident, the Catholic church, the CPT, local rural unions, and human rights groups organized a public protest in Xinguara on October 22, 1979. The event drew some six thousand people who marched through the streets of Xinguara chanting "we want land." According to the National Confederation of Agricultural Workers (CONTAG), the protest in Xinguara was the largest public demonstration by rural workers that Brazil had seen since the military takeover in 1964.

Events in Xinguara and elsewhere in the state convinced the military government of the need to better control the process of land settlement on the Amazon frontier. CEAT had succeeded in handing out some 8,500 titles in the Xinguara area; yet the land war in southern Pará grew steadily worse. So volatile had the situation become by the end of the decade that it prompted leading members of the National Security Council to visit the area in October of 1979. On the basis of information gathered on that trip, the federal government established a new agency in February of 1980 called GETAT—the Executive Group for Lands in the Araguaia Tocantins basin. The new organization took over CEAT and INCRA offices, resources, and personnel (see chapter 3, "The Militarization of Land Agencies"). With headquarters in Marabá, GETAT was organized into six "executive units." The unit in Conceição do Araguaia was responsible for southern Pará, including the Xinguara area.

GETAT commanded far more political and economic power and benefited from a greater degree of bureaucratic autonomy than any of the land agencies that had come before it. Topographic services were provided by the army and by private firms contracted for the task. GETAT relied on these services to demarcate large areas of 300,000 to 400,000 hectares that were called *glebas*. The *glebas* were surveyed into individual plots to be handed over to small farmers. To distribute land efficiently, the GETAT high command, with its direct connections to the National Security Council, eliminated much of the red tape that had crippled the effectiveness of other agencies, such as ITERPA, INCRA, and CEAT. In order to prod the local staff to move with dispatch, the headquarters in Brasília set annual title quotas for each of the field units. Progress was monitored every trimester. In the interest of absorbing as many migrant families as possible, GETAT arbitrarily halved the established minimum size of agricultural plots in Amazonia from one hundred to fifty hectares.

GETAT extended its activities far beyond the task of settling migrants. Drawing on its considerable power, GETAT intervened whenever the agency deemed it in the interest of "maintaining order." In Xinguara, GETAT usurped the functions of the Brazilian Institute for Forest Development (IBDF) by seizing lumber trucks whose records were out of order and by suspending IBDF forestry regulations for colonists in settlement areas directly under GETAT control. Through arrangements with the Ministry of Education and the National Agricultural Extension Agency (EMATER), GETAT was also able to channel the meager resources of those agencies into settlement areas it had chosen as priority targets. EMATER employees were housed in GETAT offices, and their activities were restricted to working with farmers settled by the agency. Similarly, the well-publicized "Civic-Social Actions" (ACISO) brought mobile health services to the colonies GETAT had established.

The strategic deployment of these resources was regularly complemented by dramatic public ceremonies. On several occasions GETAT built elevated platforms in the middle of town. The structures were draped with colorful banners proclaiming the wisdom and effectiveness of government action in the region. With much fanfare and after lengthy speeches, GETAT officials and local political supporters would hand out land titles to selected individuals gathered in the expectant crowd. Through these measures, GETAT sought to build grassroots political support in an area where violence and the persistent conflict over land fostered growing opposition to the military regime.

Land Titles and GETAT Colonization

Between December 1980 and April of the following year around one thousand migrants applied to GETAT for land. By June of 1981 the number of applicants had more than doubled. The first GETAT colonies in the Xinguara area were titled in 1980 under the direction of the executive unit in Conceição do Araguaia. Some five hundred titles were issued to colonists in two sections of the Gleba Rio Maria, including most of the people settled there by INCRA two years earlier. In April of 1981 an executive subunit was installed in Xinguara. From March through July several hundred more colonists were selected for settlement in the Glebas Araguaxim, Rio Maria, and Pium and for resettlement from Mata Geral.

Data collected during the selection interviews showed that more than half of the applicants (56 percent) had migrated to the area directly from the previous frontier areas of the Center-West (Goiás, Mato Grosso, Brasília). About a third came from Minas Gerais or from the Northeast (especially Maranhão and Ceará, which accounted for 17 percent of the migrants). Only six percent were from Pará, and the remainder came from other parts of Brazil.

Potential settlers were interviewed using a questionnaire and a point system similar to the form and method that INCRA had developed earlier in the colonization projects along the Transamazon Highway and in Rondônia. Extra points were given to applicants who had larger families and who possessed greater agricultural experience. Yet, for all of its putative objectivity, political and ideological criteria figured prominently in the procedures that GETAT used to distribute land in southern Pará. *Posseiros* from areas that had experienced rural violence were given priority, as were particular individuals whose previous histories suggested that they possessed the ability to organize farmers and landless workers. The offer of clear titles to dispossessed farmers thus became an important weapon in GETAT's attempt to settle land disputes and in its efforts to co-opt leaders of incipient opposition movements.

Other aspects of the application process were intended to control the colonists' behavior. GETAT required applicants to sign a statement that forfeited rights to land in any other GETAT area if the colonist sold or abandoned the lot he was about to receive. Similarly, individuals were penalized if they invaded private property. GETAT followed through with these threats in places like Mata Geral where settlers found encroaching on neighboring cattle ranches were blacklisted and thereby prevented from ever receiving another plot of GETAT land.

Colonists in Mata Geral were driven to invade the surrounding private property by the increasingly difficult circumstances they faced. Overcrowding was only one of the problems that threatened the settlement's long-term viability. A study GETAT commissioned in 1981 found that rice production was adequate, but like most areas of small agriculture in Amazonia Mata Geral suffered from a lack of storage facilities, access roads, and transportation.[15] The colonists were limited to planting a few staple crops (rice, beans, corn, and manioc), which could be harvested for only four or five years before the soil became exhausted. The report concluded that without credit and technical assistance the future of Mata Geral was in doubt.

This diagnosis led to a draft proposal for a rural development project in the colony, but GETAT never followed through with the plan. Instead, the solution chosen was to move farmers from Mata Geral to a new location. GETAT received a total of 261 applications for resettlement. Nearly all (94 percent) of the applicants were already living in the colony, having arrived there sometime during the preceding six months. Compared to those selected for the colonies in Rio Maria, Araguaxim, and Pium, a substantial proportion of the Mata Geral applicants (36 percent) were natives of Pará.

One hundred and fifty applicants were initially approved on the basis of having earned a minimum of five hundred points. The list of winners was read aloud by GETAT's executive officer standing in the back of a pickup truck outside a small church in the colony, surrounded by anxious listeners. Following the announcement, dissatisfaction among those not chosen was so vehement that the GETAT staff spent the next few hours reviewing each claim. Under pressure from the restive crowd gathered nearby, the minimum point level was dropped to four hundred so that 171 colonists were finally accepted.

The case of Mata Geral illustrates key elements of the evolution of colonization policies carried out in southern Pará. GETAT's activities focused mainly on "hot spots" where land conflicts threatened to explode into open warfare. In the interest of expediency, settlement guidelines—such as the minimum plot size and the point system used to select colonists—were arbitrarily changed to attend to the crisis of the moment. Credit and technical assistance and the need for support services essential to long-term agricultural sustainability were matters that received little more than lip service in the crisis colonization agenda GETAT pursued in the 1980s.

GETAT's regional personnel were candid about these strategies in interviews we conducted with them in 1981. They readily admitted that the fifty-hectare lots that were being distributed were not large enough to support viable farms in the long run. GETAT's purpose, unlike INCRA's mandate, was not, after all, to promote colonization. GETAT had been created in order to resolve local land disputes by converting public lands at its disposal to titled, private property. Once this was accomplished, it was understood that GETAT would be abolished.

Titling already occupied land was the principal strategy GETAT employed to bring the situation in southern Pará under control. The legalization of informal claims to land had the important effect of replacing the direct confrontations between farmers and ranchers with impersonal market forces. The effectiveness of this bureaucratic procedure was impressed upon us one afternoon in 1984 when we chanced upon a colonist we had met years earlier. On our first visit to a settlement area called Floresta in 1976, he was struggling to defend his land from encroaching ranchers. With the help of the Catholic church, he was involved in organizing the community for a showdown with the cattlemen. Eight years later, when our paths crossed again in the town of Redenção, we asked him what had finally happened. He told us that he had sold out and moved on to Xinguara. "GETAT finally gave me a title to my land," he explained. "But then my wife got sick, and I had to sell. Because of that piece of paper, I got a pretty good price."

This was the same man who in 1976 had been willing to die rather than lose his land to ranchers who threatened to use force to take the area he had cleared. Once the property was titled, the relationship between the contending parties changed fundamentally. Not only did the document increase the value of the land, it also transformed it into an asset that could be readily converted into cash. The latter was often made necessary by the precarious economic viability of small agriculture in much of Amazonia. In the absence of credit and technical assistance and as a result of many other constraints (e.g., lack of storage facilities, poor soil quality), most farmers operated close to a subsistence level. When a farmer fell victim to an accident or an emergency, or when a family member needed medical attention, he often had no choice but to put his land on the market for sale. In the end the ranchers got what they wanted, even if they did have to pay a little more to expand their pastures. The titling of the *posseiros'* claims and the emergence of a competitive market for land thus contributed to the consolidation of rural holdings in southern Pará.[16]

The concentration of land ownership was further boosted by the policies GETAT used to provide title to contested lands held by cattlemen. When a ranch became the target of an invasion by small farmers, as often happened in Xinguara, GETAT found it impossible to remove the *posseiros* from the area. The solution was to strike a deal with the rancher. In exchange for giving up his claim, GETAT provided the rancher title to a larger area located somewhere else. As with many other stopgap solutions, this one had the unintended consequence of promoting rather than suppressing land invasions, especially in cases when it was in the rancher's interest to have his land overrun. For example, when pastures became degraded and maintenance costs began to rise, a timely land invasion (prompted by the rancher himself) could be parlayed into a more desirable location further down the road.

Data published under the New Republic revealed the degree of land concentration in southern Pará. The figures showed that by 1985 39 percent of the titled estates in Xinguara controlled 85 percent of the municipality's land. Smallholders, who represented 61 percent of total holdings, owned only 15 percent of the land. Just forty-three property owners controlled 163,474 hectares, or about a quarter of the entire *município*.[17]

Contesting Development Ideology: The Catholic Church

The Catholic church figured prominently in the land wars that raged in the Xinguara area in the late 1970s. Tensions between the church and government authorities were hardly new in Amazonia. In the early 1970s the bishops and priests in Marabá and Conceição do Araguaia defended the rights of incoming migrants. They also played an important role in organizing small farmers whose lands were threatened by ranchers and speculators drawn to southern Pará by SUDAM's fiscal incentive programs. The clergy and lay religious leaders instructed *posseiros* in their legal rights and often represented small farmer communities before the various government agencies. At a time when other channels of political expression were closed off by the authoritarian regime, grassroots organizations tied to the church often were the only means for peasants to voice their needs and their opposition to events on the frontier.

Activists in the progressive wing of the Catholic church endorsed the Christian values of equality and solidarity among community members. The outlook fostered by church leaders encouraged the coordinated action of peasant groups in defense of their interests. The church's commitment to social and political change—in Amazonia as in Latin America at large—grew out of the growing incompatibility between the corporatist ethic of traditional church doctrine and the realities of class and class conflict in modern society. In the face of the brutal social conditions in urban and rural Brazil, organic views of humanity's place in the world gave way, both in theological discourse and in the daily practice of laypersons, to a secularism that endorsed the perfectibility of temporal existence. The result was a new form of political expression in Amazonia that was quick to identify and denounce injustice and to push for social change.

The discourse with which peasant farmers legitimized their claim to land drew on the traditional precepts of Catholicism and on a worldview that was deeply rooted in their own origins and personal history. In most cases the *posseiros* themselves, or their parents and grandparents, had come from Goiás, where they had lost their land to speculators before moving on to northern Mato Grosso and southern Pará. Their apparent rootlessness led some to think of migration as a kind of collective search for the "promised land," a place where they would have their own autonomous existence, free of the "captivity" of the past when traditional paternalistic relationships had tied them to local merchants or ranchers. Hence, the *posseiro's* struggle for land was often thought of in mystical terms, laden with biblical overtones.[18]

A concept frequently invoked in the struggle for land was the notion of the "social function" of property expressed in the idea that land belonged to God rather than to the state or to a private person. The peasant vision of the world rested firmly on the assumption that land was to be used to fulfill the divine mandate to produce and multiply. To peasant farmers and to newly arrived migrants seeking land in southern Pará it was reprehensible that an individual could own more land than he could use and thus deprive another person of a source of a livelihood.

The ideas espoused by the Catholic church directly challenged the moral basis of private property and indicted the priorities the military regime endorsed for Amazonia and, indeed, for the country as a whole. The alliance between peasant communities and the progressive branch of the Catholic church led to demands for local improvements that were premised on a fundamental critique of capitalist society. In light of the military regime's intense preoccupation with geopolitical and national security concerns, it is hardly surprising that Catholic priests and peasant leaders were regarded as dangerous subversives.

In 1976 an incident in Perdidos, near Conceição do Araguaia, resulted in the death of two soldiers and in injury to two more. The bishops of Marabá and Conceição do Araguaia were later interrogated about their supposed role in inciting thirty-nine *posseiros* to this violent act. The Perdidos case foreshadowed a pattern of conflict between the church and federal and state authorities that was to emerge more clearly in southern Pará after 1979.

The sequence of events often began with an unsuccessful move by ranchers or land speculators to evict *posseiros* from a desirable area. This was generally followed by an attempt to resolve the conflict through established institutional channels, a course of action that was also ineffectual. When mounting tensions resulted in armed resistance by the *posseiros*, authorities and landowners accused the church of instigating violence and promoting communist ideology.

In 1981 tensions between the Church and GETAT reached a new peak of intensity. One weekend in August, when GETAT President Iris de Oliveira was busy handing out land titles from a platform in Xinguara, we interviewed Father Francisco Gouriou, in town to celebrate a special "Farmer's Day" mass. We knew Padre Chico, as he was called, from 1978 when he had been Xinguara's parish priest. When we spoke to him again, he was assigned to the former guerrilla stronghold São Geraldo, where tensions over land were especially serious. The GETAT executive unit in charge of that area appeared to be on a collision course with the strong peasant organizations there. "My relations with GETAT are not good," said Padre Chico, "although, on a personal level, we get on just fine with those people."

A few days later, on August 8, Padre Chico and another priest, Aristides Camio, celebrated mass in Cajueiro, a place where authorities in the land agency were threatening to evict *posseiros*. The following day a group of settlers ambushed a GETAT topographer who was surveying the area in the presence of his police bodyguards. One person was killed and several others were wounded. Soon thereafter a platoon of federal agents arrested thirteen men from the community. On August 29 Curió visited Cajueiro, demanding that the settlers turn over their hunting rifles. The guns Curió collected were dumped into the river from a helicopter.[19]

Authorities invoked the National Security Law and charged the two priests with leading an armed conflict. The prosecutor's case was based primarily on hearsay and circumstantial evidence. Much was made of the "subversive" literature found in the priests' possession. Ironically, the two French clergymen accused of spreading communist ideas and of inciting violence had come to Brazil in 1977 from Laos, after a communist government had expelled them from southeast Asia.

The trial and sentencing of the two priests and the *posseiros* did much to further tarnish the government's image in southern Pará. The Conceição do Araguaia rural workers union appointed Djalma Farias, a former federal police agent, as lawyer for the defense of the *posseiros*. In its award-winning coverage of the trial, the Belém newspaper *Resistência* reported that the attorney functioned more as accuser of the priests than as defender of the *posseiros*.[20] Conducted under heavy military security, the Belém trial generated national publicity and stimulated the formation of a Movement for Liberation of the Araguaia Prisoners (MLAP). On June 22, 1982, the priests were sentenced to ten to fifteen years in prison for "inciting subversion." The *posseiros* received sentences of eight or nine years each.

If military authorities had hoped that the issue would fade from the headlines once the trial was over, they were mistaken. The decision was first appealed to the Supreme Military Court in Brasília, but was upheld by a majority vote of the fifteen justices in December of 1982. Four dissenting judges voted to absolve Gouriou for insufficient evidence, while two others argued that Camio's case should be transferred to the civilian courts.[21] Later, in December of 1983, the two priests were set free when Brazil's National Security Law was changed in response to the nationwide public demand for the release of political prisoners. Fathers Aristides Camio and Francisco Gouriou spent 837 days in prison.

GETAT and the Rural Workers Union

The threat posed by the Catholic church in Amazonia was one of the main reasons why GETAT was created. The task of titling and colonizing public property was the agency's principal concern, but GETAT did not restrict its activities to the land question. GETAT officials had no qualms about wielding the agency's considerable power in the attempt to undermine opposition political movements and to exert control over any institution that might strengthen the voice of peasant farmers (including the Catholic church). The battle that took place over the presidency of the tiny rural workers union in Conceição do Araguaia in 1980/1981 illustrates the blatant political maneuvers GETAT undertook to contain the burgeoning antigovernment sentiment in southern Pará. In the end such actions only weakened the land agency's credibility and, by extension, that of the military regime it represented.

The union was hardly an opposition stronghold. In addition to the chronic lack of funds, the power of the rural workers union in Conceição do Araguaia, as in the rest of the country, was severely curtailed by federal regulations. The latter included the government's right to directly intervene in union affairs in cases of fraud or mismanagement. When the elected president was accused of corruption in 1974, federal authorities unilaterally gave the position to Bertoldo Siqueira, who remained in power unchallenged until the elections in June of 1980.

Bertoldo was widely perceived as a government lackey, a union man who neither defended workers' rights nor questioned instructions from authorities. GETAT officials told us they relied on Bertoldo to distinguish "good faith" from "bad faith" candidates for colonization areas.[22] In the late 1970s wildcat strikes that occurred with increasing frequency across Brazil signaled the emergence of a union movement opposed to such complicity with government policies. Members of the union in Conceição do Araguaia became increasingly dissatisfied with Bertoldo's control of the organization. The opposition group chose Raimundo Ferreira Lima, or "Gringo," as their candidate in the upcoming elections.

The father of six children, forty-two-year-old Gringo was born in Marabá and served as a community representative in the progressive Catholic church. The fifteen-point platform Lima and his supporters drew together emphasized the need for agrarian reform. His stance on this hotly contested issue soon gained him the support of national opposition groups, including the PT and

PMDB political parties. Gringo's radical views and the national attention he received made him a threat to landowners in the region who had grown accustomed to the presence of a submissive labor union that never challenged the status quo.

On May 29, one month before the election, Lima was shot dead by a gunman on the streets of the nearby town of Araguaina in Goiás. Shortly after his death, four thousand people gathered in Conceição do Araguaia to protest Lima's murder. Despite this setback, a replacement opposition candidate won the election the following June by a margin of 641 to 470 votes. But the last-minute effort was for naught. The results of the election were declared invalid for lack of a quorum. And Lima's assassin—who boasted openly of his deed—was never even arrested.[23]

The date for the new election was delayed as long as possible until it was finally set for May 10, 1981. Once again, violence erupted on the eve of the balloting. On April 3 three peasants were kidnapped by the federal police and accused of inciting an armed conflict. The three *posseiros* were taken to the GETAT headquarters in Marabá where they were beaten and tortured. They were forced to sign a statement that incriminated several prominent critics of government policy: Aristides Camio (the priest in São Geraldo who was arrested a few months later), attorney Paulo Fontelles of the Pastoral Land Commission; and Gringo's widow, Oneide Costa Lima.

The second election for the presidency of the rural worker's union failed again for lack of a quorum. Only sixteen hundred of the eighteen hundred votes that were necessary had been cast. The shortfall was partly due to the last-minute removal of the ballot box from São Geraldo, an opposition stronghold. A third election was held on May 25. The opposition slate won a majority in three of nine polling places: Conceição do Araguaia, Rio Maria, and São Geraldo. But this time the outcome (1,032 to 684) favored the government candidate. Although the remaining ballots required to meet a quorum were either blank or void, the election was declared legal. State deputies Lucival Barbalho and Ademir Andrade immediately denounced irregularities in the electoral process, but their protest was to no avail.

The progovernment victory was the result of "operation union," a coordinated effort that involved the military, the federal police, and GETAT. The radio station run by the Catholic church in Conceição was silenced, and a slur campaign was mounted against its well-known members, including Gringo's widow. Curió himself visited polling places. He arrived by helicopter on election day promising *garimpeiro* cards and land titles to supporters of the government candidate. GETAT contributed personnel to manage the membership books of the union and donated its resources to rural communities in order to win support for the government candidate. Responsible GETAT officials privately admitted that lots in the various colonization projects were given out in return for votes in support of the government's candidate.[24]

Land Reform and Escalating Violence

Federal intervention in southern Pará put two church leaders temporarily in prison and won the battle for the rural union. Yet neither of these actions had the desired effect nor did GETAT's massive effort to distribute land titles. Contrary to the purpose of these strategies, rural violence escalated rather than declined, and opposition political parties gained rather than lost strength in towns across southern Pará. In the elections held in November of 1982, opposition candidates won majorities in the newly created *municípios* of Xinguara, Rio Maria, and Redenção. In Belém, Jáder Barbalho, also a member of the opposition, won the race for governor of the state.

In the countryside *posseiros* devised new and more effective ways to defend themselves. In the early 1970s small farmers had been the victims of one-sided acts of violence by gunmen and police hired by ranchers and land speculators. By the end of the decade, small farmers had learned from their tragic experiences to organize for their collective defense.[25] The new tactics included public protests to attract media attention as well as organized land invasions.

The death toll among agricultural workers in Pará shows the degree to which violence in the state had escalated during the 1980s. The data presented in table 6.1 indicate that the number of violent deaths rose from an average of 2.3 per year between 1964 and 1972 to 9.3 between 1973 and 1979. During the following decade the number of deaths increased still further to an average of around 37 per year.

TABLE 6.1
Number of Workers Killed in Pará State, 1964–1986

1964	4	1973	14	1980	34
1965	3	1974	10	1981	15
1966	0	1975	5	1982	20
1967	3	1976	9	1983	30
1968	1	1977	6	1984	29
1969	4	1978	6	1985	59
1970	1	1979	15	1986	71
1971	2				
1972	3				
TOTAL	21	TOTAL	65	TOTAL	258
(1964–72)		(1973–79)		(1980–86)	
Average/year	2.3		9.3		36.9

SOURCE: *Movimento dos Trabalhadores Rurais Sem Terra* (1987).

In April of 1983 a group of thirteen newly elected federal deputies from three opposition parties (PDT, PT, and PMDB) visited Araguaina, Xambioá, and São Geraldo to investigate the violence against rural workers. The team included federal deputy José Genoino Neto, a former member of the Araguaia guerrilla movement that had once operated in this same area of Pará. Curió prepared for the event by traveling to São Geraldo a week before their arrival. He warned local residents of the impending visit by "a group of communists." In a style that by now had become familiar to most people in the region, Curió threatened anyone who attended the planned public meeting with loss of their land title.[26] On the first day of the deputies' visit, the bus the delegation traveled in was accosted by federal police. Brandishing machine guns, the officers demanded to see the deputies' identification cards.[27]

Documents published by the Catholic church provide estimates of the intensity of the continuing violence in southern Pará in 1983–1984, the last years of the military regime. In 1983 land conflicts led to a reported 403 death threats, 114 imprisonments, and 116 beatings and tortures. Approximately 1,179 families were threatened with expulsion (and 361 expelled), and 272 houses were burned.[28] Land conflicts reported by the CPT in 1984 reportedly affected 13,191 families and resulted in twenty-nine

The Struggle for Land   *187*

deaths and twenty-five injuries. Fifty-seven people were jailed and seven disappeared.[29]

In early 1985, shortly after taking office, President Sarney announced his intention to implement a national agrarian reform. The first state-level plan, submitted in January of 1986 (but not completed until May), singled out Conceição do Araguaia, Xinguara, Redenção, and Marabá as priority areas due to high rates of in-migration and social conflict.[30] The plan also called for a review of private colonization projects, such as the Projeto Tucumã (see chapter 7), to examine the possibility of converting them to small farmer colonization areas.

Violence in southern Pará escalated significantly in anticipation of the reforms (see table 6.1). The large Brazil nut leases near Marabá were the site of such intense violence that people referred to 1985 as "the year of the massacres." The long-simmering land conflicts near Mata Geral, Rio Maria, and Xinguara also heated up, and pressure mounted to expropriate the largest landholdings in the region. In June four areas in southern Pará were expropriated under the agrarian reform. That same month a local branch of the União Democrático Rural (UDR)—the newly formed right-wing organization representing landowners opposed to the agrarian reform—was established in Paragominas (northeast of Marabá). No longer able to count on the support of the military and police, large ranchers in the region began to recruit private militias to defend themselves against land invasions by small farmers as well as federal or state agencies that might attempt to expropriate their property.[31]

The number of gunmen proliferated, reportedly for hire through employment agencies linked to landowners. But times had changed, even for this gruesome aspect of frontier life. In the early days *pistoleiros* had been well-known figures. They were just as often feared for their ruthlessness as they were respected for their occasional acts of charity. Such was the case of Chapeu de Couro, the founder of Xinguara, a man who thought of himself as an urban planner and builder of schools. By the mid-1980s the contract killers were no longer professionals. They were drawn instead from the ranks of unemployed drifters, many of whom did not even own their own weapon. After doing their job, they faded into obscurity in the mining camps, ranches, or frontier towns.[32] Nor was the violence confined to rural areas as it had been in the past. In June of 1987 Federal Deputy Paulo Fontelles (formerly CPT attorney in Conceição do Araguaia) was murdered in the capital city of Belém.[33]

During 1985 and 1986 the powerful federal agencies that had been in control of southern Pará were in limbo. Already discredited by 1984, GETAT came under increasing criticism. It was finally abolished in 1987, the same year that the New Republic revoked Decree Law 1164, thereby relinquishing federal control over Amazonian lands designated as national security areas. Regaining jurisdiction over the violence-torn area of southern Pará was a mixed blessing for the state. The state could not hope to match, much less surpass, the performance of agencies like GETAT that had benefited from federal resources and extraordinary bureaucratic power.

The Outcome of the Struggle for Land in Xinguara

Looking back over the previous decade, the ebb and flow of people in and around the building in Xinguara that housed the succession of land agencies symbolized the various epochs in the grim history of land settlement in southern Pará. At the height of the Mata Geral colonization effort in 1978, hundreds of people milled about what was then the INCRA office, with sacks of belongings strewn across the yard and excitement in the air. Standing in the crowd outside the office doors, people craned their necks to see if their names appeared on the list of colonists regularly posted on the bulletin board. A ripple of impatience would spread through the expectant crowd each time one man's joyful cry was heard.

In 1981 the same office, which now belonged to GETAT, was busier still. Would-be settlers gathered by the hundreds in the front yard. Surveyors came and went at all hours, as did other teams that set out to deliver medical and dental services to colonists. Between 1981 and 1983 GETAT employees complained that they rarely had time to wash their clothes between one trip and the next, sometimes staying on the road for weeks at a time. On special occasions, such as titling ceremonies when colonists were bussed in for the day, the compound was full of people who listened to politicians and GETAT personnel speak from a stage in front of GETAT's door.

By 1984 the tide had turned against GETAT. The compound was surrounded like a fortress by a stout fence that kept people at a distance. Top level personnel were hostile to outsiders, and their subalterns were cautious in providing information. In 1987 the offices were virtually abandoned. The small and demoralized staff that remained had been accused of corruption and would be required to take a competency test if they hoped to keep their jobs as civil servants. Occasionally a newcomer to Xinguara would approach the building to ask when new lands might be available for colonization. The inquiry would elicit a halfhearted and cynical reply. No one in the office had much confidence that the fate of small farmers would improve. Nor did anyone believe that whatever agency came to replace GETAT under the New Republic would be any more effective in controlling the process of land settlement.

By 1987 Xinguara no longer resembled the chaotic frontier town that had begun as Xingu Junction a decade before. The well-financed Carajás project had provided the rationale and the funds to pave the PA-150 highway from Marabá as far south as Xinguara and Rio Maria. Both towns now received electricity from the Tucuruí hydroelectric plant. With a good road and electrical power, Xinguara had become a commercial center of considerable importance to the region.[34] Supermarkets and small businesses lined either side of the main street that now required a stop light to control (if ineffectually) the steady traffic of cars and trucks that came through town. A three-storied building close to the center of town housed the regional headquarters of the Assembly of God church, and a bus station occupied a large structure near the junction of the PA-150 and the PA-279. Ten to fifteen taxis regularly gathered under the shade of a tree across the street, waiting for customers. Xinguara increasingly came to resemble other mid-sized towns one finds in the center-western region of Brazil's interior.

By the mid-1980s most of the remaining public land around Xinguara and along the PA-279 highway had been designated by federal and state bureaucracies for reserves or for crisis colonization programs (see Map 8, chapter 10). A block of land set aside for the Carajás project was partially buffered by the Xikrin Indian reserve and by GETAT's hasty colonization efforts to the north and south of Xinguara. Colonists lucky enough to be settled in these areas faced an uphill struggle to survive without even minimal government support. By the late 1980s many had already been forced to sell out and move on. In the meantime, pressures increased on the lands farther along the PA-279 highway and in the municipality of São Felix do Xingu.

In the countryside around Xinguara the pattern of land ownership that was the outcome of the previous decade of violence could be plainly seen from the window of the bus we boarded in 1989 the last time we traveled the road to São Felix do Xingu. For miles on end fences made of wooden posts and three taut strands of barbed wire enclosed huge tracts of land that had been cleared for pasture. Some of the holdings were so large that they stretched from the roadside clear to the horizon. Although only a few years old, many of the pastures we drove by already showed signs of severe degradation. The small herds of zebu cattle we occasionally saw far exceeded the number of small farmers we encountered on that trip. By then most of the *posseiros* who had pioneered the region years earlier had moved on to try their luck elsewhere.

The bedlam that was Xinguara during its days as a frontier town had given way to a more stable community, to be sure. Yet the underlying problems of land conflicts and rural violence had only worsened in southern Pará. Violent contests over land continued to erupt in each newly settled area. The outcome of these disputes did not always reproduce the victory of ranching interests in Xinguara (for example, see chapters 7 and 9). The outcome of the confrontations depended on the changing economic and political context, the forms of government intervention, and the balance of power between the contending parties in the contest.

Central to the story of the PA-279 was the shift from public to private land colonization. By the mid-1970s Brasília had given up on the kind of public colonization projects that had been the hallmark of Amazonian development policy earlier in the decade (see chapter 3). The INCRA settlement program along the Transamazon Highway had been virtually abandoned along with plans for similar efforts elsewhere in southern Pará. With the exception of extraordinary agencies—such as CEAT and later GETAT, which were designed to implement highly specific crisis settlement projects—the emphasis among federal policy makers shifted in favor of private development schemes. The largest and most ambitious private colonization project in all of southern Pará—Projeto Tucumã—was located along the PA-279, about 150 kilometers from Xinguara.

NOTES

1. Coutinho and Matos (1977), cited in Godfrey (1979:98,100).
2. Godfrey (1982:76).
3. Godfrey (1979:96–101).
4. Godfrey (1979:97).
5. Project coordinators selected 559 settlers. About a third of the colonists came from northeastern states. Another third came from the Center-West (Goiás and Mato Grosso), and the remainder made their way to Amazonia from states across southern Brazil. Only a small proportion (7 percent) were from the state of Pará (Coutinho and Matos 1977, cited in Godfrey 1979:99).
6. Brasil and Patriarcha (1976) and Coutinho (1976, cited in Godfrey 1979:97).
7. Godfrey (1979:100).
8. INCRA (1977, cited in Godfrey 1979:106,109).
9. Godfrey (1979:110,112).
10. Godfrey (1979:110,112).
11. Total surface area shown is 47,270 square kilometers based on images provided by the Companhia Vale do Rio Doce. See also Dicks (1984).
12. *O Liberal*, 13 October 1979.
13. Mendes (1979).
14. Pinto (1979). See also Branford and Glock (1985:170–173).
15. Weigel and Clements (1981:12,21).
16. Landowners' organizations such as the Association of Amazonian Entrepreneurs and the Association of Brazil Nut Exporters nonetheless repeatedly protested against GETAT's actions and policies favoring small farmer settlement.
17. Godfrey (1989:16–17). See also Godfrey (1990).
18. Velho (1972:258–262) and Vieira (1981:218–223).
19. Fon (1981:53).
20. *Resistência*, Ano V, No. 33. See also *A Report of the Trial of Father Aristides Camio and Father François Gouriou, Belém, 21–22 June 1982*, Amnesty International Review, 19 July 1982, cited in Branford and Glock (1985:165).
21. *Resistência*, Ano V, No. 46, 16–30 December 1982.
22. See also Branford and Glock (1985:173).

23. Police inquiry records for the case disappeared from the Araguaina police station, so no judicial proceedings were ever opened (Amnesty International 1988:21).

24. In the first half of 1981 GETAT selected about 315 colonists in Conceição do Araguaia, two-thirds of whom were settled during March and April just prior to the election. Similarly, by the end of June six hundred titles had been handed out in Xinguara and Redenção. The criteria for choosing the election-time settlers differed from those used in the Mata Geral selection, which took place after the vote. The application forms we inspected showed that some preelection documents were nearly blank except for the observation that the candidate was a union member. Later, GETAT authorities admitted that their intention was to sway the election by manipulating the distribution of land titles.

25. Kotscho (1982b) and Vieira (1981:325–326).

26. *Resistência*, Ano VI, No. 55, 16–30 May.

27. Tactics such as these continued to be combined with populist colonization initiatives. In May of 1983, for example, GETAT's new Carajás colonization project (known as CEDERE) was inaugurated in an area along the PA-150 highway between Xinguara and Marabá. The project goal was to create an agricultural settlement of small farmers that would serve as a buffer for the Carajás mining area to the northwest, helping to keep out invaders. As in other GETAT areas, many of the 1,551 colonists settled on fifty-hectare lots were drawn from other areas of conflict. GETAT controlled entry to CEDERE by requiring colonists to show identification cards (and by denying access to researchers). GETAT built over five hundred kilometers of feeder roads and provided other kinds of support to colonists, only to abandon the project later on. In 1985 the administration of all services in the colony was turned over to the *município* of Marabá, already overextended by the demands of explosive population growth.

28. CPT (1984).

29. CPT (1985).

30. INCRA (1986:40).

31. The UDR held fund-raising cattle auctions whose proceeds were used to buy arms (see interview with the UDR President in Goiás, published in *Germinal*, 4 April 1987, cited in Amnesty International 1988:47).

32. Lúcio Flávio Pinto, *Jornal Pessoal*, No. 1.

33. At the time of his murder, Fontelles was defending *posseiros* accused of the December 1986 murder of the son of rancher Tarley de Andrade, UDR treasurer, in Santana do Araguaia. Two weeks before his death, Fontelles was publicly threatened by a known gunman who accosted him during a demonstration in Xinguara against rural violence and in favor of land reform (Amnesty International 1988:18,41,71–76). For details on the still-unresolved Fontelles murder, see the award-winning coverage in Lúcio Flávio Pinto's *Jornal Pessoal*, No. 1.

34. See Godfrey (1990).

SEVEN

❖

Private Colonization: The Rise and Fall of Tucumã

"Guaranteed, with the approval of INCRA
and GETAT, and with incentives linked to the
Greater Carajás Program, Tucumã is the most
secure colonization project in the
country." *(Advertising brochure)*

May of 1978 found us in Belém preparing for an extended trip to São Felix do Xingu to survey the town's population. Several people we interviewed in the city before our trip into the field called our attention to a privately funded and administered colonization project to be located along the PA-279. The project was called Tucumã after a palm tree native to the area. It was to be built about 150 kilometers to the west of Xinguara. The site had once been the intended location of a public settlement program. But with the shift in federal development policies in the mid-1970s the land had been auctioned off to Andrade Gutierrez, one of the largest and most successful construction companies in Brazil.

In contrast to the INCRA and GETAT colonization projects elsewhere in the state, the company's expertise and generous financial backing amounted to nothing less than a "wish list" for an ideal settlement plan. In addition to the company's extensive resources and its administrative competence, the four hundred thousand hectares it set out to develop encompassed the largest expanse of rich soils (a type called *terra roxa* in Portuguese) found anywhere in southern Pará.[1] Moreover, the project was headed by a young management team that was fully cognizant of what the company was getting into. From the beginning, the blueprint for Projeto Tucumã identified the problems associated with previous attempts to colonize the region. Heavy in-migration, and the certainty of land invasions and fraudulent claims to company property were among the issues that project planners anticipated and accounted for.

These advantages notwithstanding, there remained something fundamentally implausible about a project that attempted to build an island of order and tranquility in the midst of the turbulence that was southern Pará at that time. Subsequent events showed that our uncertainties in this regard were well-founded. By 1988, after the Andrade Gutierrez company had invested somewhere between twenty and thirty million dollars in Tucumã, the colonization site was completely overrun by an invasion of *posseiros*, loggers, and landgrabbers. That the project failed despite all that Tucumã had in its favor was a sobering reminder of the power and complexity of the social, economic, and political forces that conditioned the process of land occupation in Amazonia in the 1980s.

Politicians and Landgrabbers

With more than twenty-four thousand people on its payroll and annual profits in the neighborhood of $350 million in the early 1980s, Andrade Gutierrez was one of the largest wholly national corporations in the country. Since its founding in the 1940s in Belo Horizonte, the company had been involved in roadbuilding and a wide array of projects ranging from the Itaipú dam to a nuclear power station and the construction of the subway system in São Paulo. Amazonian contracts included the Belém-Brasília, the Manaus-Porto Velho, and the Northern Perimeter highways as well as the port facilities for the Tombetas bauxite complex and numerous projects in the city of Manaus.[2]

As the company grew, so did its interest in diversifying its activities. Taking account of the high inflation rate in Brazil, investment analysts recognized the potential to make large profits from the rising cost of real estate in the southern part of the country and the availability of relatively cheap land in the north. From 1975 to 1976 the company commissioned studies of the cost-effectiveness of existing private colonization projects in Mato Grosso as well as estimates of the size of the potential demand for Amazonian land by investors in São Paulo and other southern states. The RADAM survey of Amazonia offered a panoramic view of the potential sites for a land development project.[3]

Of the many possible alternatives, Gleba Carapanã, located in southern Pará, was especially attractive.[4] The soils were of high quality and the site was located relatively close to existing highways in the region. Given the likelihood that land invasions would be a problem, Carapanã's strategic location between two Indian reserves was a further advantage of considerable importance to the long-term success of the colony. The land was bordered to the east by the Xikrin reserve and to the south by that of the Kayapó, and it was relatively free of occupants and competing land claims.

Andrade Gutierrez purchased six thousand hectares within the *gleba* from a Belém family, and the company built an attractive guest house. Adjacent to the luxurious facility, agronomists established an experimental farm that became a showcase for visiting officials. The property named Krimet (meaning "big house" in the Kayapó language) provided a local base for the company's colonization plans. It also allowed company employees to build relations with the neighboring Kayapó groups and with the few settlers who were already living there. The latter received compensation for their investments and were moved to alternative sites further down the river. Krimet also served as headquarters for the security force that patrolled the borders of the *gleba* to prevent encroachment by squatters and landgrabbers.

On September 19, 1978, INCRA opened the formal bidding for Gleba Carapanã. Duly registered colonization companies were given sixty days to tender competing proposals. On January 11, 1979, INCRA declared Projeto Tucumã the winner. The decision gave the first official recognition to the plan put forth by the company called Colonizadora Andrade Gutierrez (hereafter referred to as CAG). In early May the National Security Council approved the selection, but this was not the last of the bureaucratic hurdles involved. Before the company could receive title to the property, the project had to be approved by the Senate, a step required of all sales of public lands larger than three thousand hectares.

Senate ratification proved to be far more difficult than anticipated. Four months after CAG had won the INCRA competition, the Tucumã plan was stalled in the Ministry of Agriculture. Under pressure from the company, the agency delivered the proposal to President Figuereido, who passed it on with his endorsement to the Congress for approval. Standard procedures required that the plan be reviewed by three commissions before going to the floor of the Senate. Projeto Tucumã gained quick approval from the Constitution and Justice Commission, but the subsequent steps in the process taxed the best efforts of company lobbyists.

On June 23 the plan was postponed by the Agricultural Commission when key members, noting the rapid progress so far, suspected collusion between CAG and INCRA. Other objections were also raised. A speech by an opposition party member from Pará questioned the selling price of the land (which was 55.5 times the purchase price), and complained about the alleged violence perpetrated by federal police against *posseiros* in the area. A congressman from Amazonia, also a member of the opposition party, contended that CAG was essentially a construction company and therefore had no business posing as a colonization firm. Anyway, the congressman argued, Andrade Gutierrez had already profited from too many government contracts. He proposed the suspension of all land sales in the Amazon until the forest policy then under discussion was established.

INCRA set about clarifying the issues raised during the debate. In August of 1979 the agency's president, Paulo Yokota, made public the documentation of the bidding process. The record showed that only one other proposal had been received, and it had been an inferior one at that. When questions surfaced about the potential consequences for the Xikrin and Kayapó reserves, INCRA disseminated copies of the FUNAI endorsement of the Tucumã project that were dated May 1978. Similarly, when skeptics claimed that CAG's real motives were to make a quick fortune from gold (an allegation prompted by a map published by the National Department of Mineral Research, DNPM), INCRA spokesmen reminded critics that a land title did not extend ownership rights to subsoil resources.

Every month that went by without government approval made

the project more vulnerable to invasions and counterclaims, which began immediately following the INCRA announcement in January of 1979 that CAG had won the bid for the land. In late March *grileiros* under contract from one of the area's largest sawmills invaded the headwaters of the Carapanã river to extract lumber. Others made their way to the proposed colonization site to clear land, knowing full well that they would later be forced to leave. In such cases, the *posseiros'* objective was to extort a handsome settlement from the company in exchange for the "improvements" they had made. Increasingly, Colonizadora Andrade Gutierrez found itself in the awkward position of defending a piece of land it did not yet own.

Competing claims for land in Gleba Carapanã were sometimes quite elaborate. In August of 1979 a group of 120 *posseiros* wrote to a senator in Brasília complaining that they were unjustly expelled by CAG. The petition was accompanied by papers showing the transfer of land rights to them from previous residents. The claim was supported by surveys allegedly carried out in 1975 and by copies of contracts for air transport and wood extraction. The contracts presumably documented their long-time presence in the area, but company lawyers had little trouble pointing out irregularities in the *posseiros'* claim. An INCRA on-site survey, done in April of 1979, found only three occupants in the disputed area; the maps presented to the senator identified airstrips that had not yet been built on the specified date; the contracts for air service and wood products were dated from 1975 in Xinguara, but the town did not even exist until two years later, and the receipts themselves, dated 1975, were printed by a company not founded until 1977. If this particular claim was inept, it nonetheless illustrated the lengths people went to in the contest for land in Gleba Carapanã.

The delay in obtaining Senate approval and the growing threat of land invasion put the colonization company in a dilemma. On the one hand, it was essential to move forward with the project and with the construction of the PA-279, which CAG was contracted to complete (see chapter 5). On the other hand, it was financially unwise to invest too much money into Tucumã before the company received official approval for the project. Furthermore, if the company finished the road before it received title to the *gleba*—thus giving loggers, *posseiros*, and land speculators easier access to the site—there was a serious risk of losing control over the property. The execution of Tucumã in the early years could best be described as a high-stakes gamble in which managers tried to balance the immediate needs of the project against the threat of land invasions and the uncertainties of dealing with politicians and bureaucrats in Brasília.

The Tucumã plan might have been rubberstamped by the Senate had it come before the legislative body years earlier when the military regime was in firm control. But times had changed by the late 1970s. The political *abertura* underway at that time meant a resurgence of debate in the political arena (see chapter 4). Public scrutiny of the Tucumã proposal took place just as political opponents to military rule were gaining a louder voice. As a consequence of these changes in national politics, much of the controversy over Tucumã focused less on the soundness of the colonization plan as such than it did on the fairness of federal policy writ large.

Whatever their particular objections to the Andrade Gutierrez land development scheme, critics sooner or later returned to the same issue. On trial was the perceived tendency of the military regime to favor large capitalist firms over small farmers and to support profit-oriented colonization enterprises instead of state-sponsored programs aimed to distribute agricultural plots to Brazil's poor and landless rural population. Much to the company's chagrin, Tucumã became the lightening rod for a broader dispute about the priorities associated with the growth-oriented development policies that had been promoted by the military regime since the 1960s.

The issue of land distribution and the disputed role of state versus private-sector colonization initiatives were the topics that dominated the debate when the matter finally came before the Senate in 1980. CAG was nonetheless successful in defending the proposal once it had made it through the various bureaucratic channels and reached the Senate floor. By a vote of twenty-five to three the Tucumã project was approved on November 13, 1980. CAG submitted the blueprint for the first phase of the project in

December, and by April of the following year the plan was accepted by GETAT. The land purchase was finally consummated in May of 1982.

The Tucumã Project

Projeto Tucumã was divided into three sections that totalled nearly three thousand proposed lots. The first section, to be colonized within six years, consisted of 1,771 lots that covered 181,358 hectares. The size of the lots and the asking price per hectare depended on the proposed use, the location, and the quality of the soil. Closest to the urban centers, 650 relatively small lots (fifteen to fifty-five hectares) were set aside for the production of vegetables. Areas beyond the urban perimeters were destined for 2,200 larger agricultural plots (55 to 280 hectares). The plan called for cattle ranches (three hundred hectares and over) in places farthest from town. In a concession to INCRA, CAG agreed to set aside 10 percent of the total number of lots to be distributed without charge to colonists selected by the land agency.

The company planned to build one thousand kilometers of roads, three urban centers, and sixty rural communities. Schools, hospitals, administrative buildings, warehouses, and markets were also part of the project design, along with an airport, a bus station, and the provision of water and electricity. Colonists would have access to technical assistance and credit, and the agricultural experiments begun at Krimet would be continued at Tucumã through agreements with the state research and extension agencies, EMBRAPA, EMATER, and CEPLAC.[5]

The town of Tucumã was designed by architects and engineers. It was divided into commercial and residential zones that were separated by straight avenues lined by neat rows of painted houses and buildings.[6] Reflecting the social hierarchy to which CAG's managers were accustomed, the largest and best-served houses, located high on the slope overlooking the town, were inhabited by administrators and engineers and by the professionals who settled in Tucumã at the company's invitation. Managers, foremen, and lower-level office workers occupied smaller and more modest houses located closer to the center of town. Workers inhabited two neighborhoods next to the commercial zone in quarters that lacked electricity and running water.[7]

The transition from planning to implementation was marked by an important shift in the way the project was carried out.[8] The progressive management team that had originally planned Tucumã turned to recruiting colonists in southern Brazil. In Pará, engineers in charge of the road crew took over the on-site construction. The company also hired a security chief who was charged with protecting the Gleba Carapanã from further invasions. By the mid-1980s the technical and security aspects of the project commanded everyone's attention. As a result of the change in personnel and priorities, Tucumã administrators were less adept at dealing with the social and political issues that arose. Ill-advised decisions, especially regarding the treatment of gold miners in the area (discussed below), led to unexpected consequences that posed a serious threat to the success of the project.

The town soon had an airport, hospital, hotel, church, bank, sports club, recreational area, and three schools. A centrally located complex of buildings housed telephone and mail services as well as administrative offices. An agency of the municipality of São Felix do Xingu was established to handle tax collection and urban administration, and a community "Cultural Association" (ACTUC) was created to manage social and educational services. ACTUC published a small monthly newspaper, the *Folha de Tucumã*, which later became a weekly mimeographed newsletter. Eventually, once Tucumã was sufficiently developed, the municipal officers and the ACTUC were expected to assume full administrative responsibility for the community.

In Belo Horizonte, sales personnel embarked on a campaign to attract colonists to Tucumã. Two regional offices were established to oversee twenty-six sales offices operating in São Paulo and in other places in southern Brazil. To compete with the more established and better known colonization projects in Mato Grosso, Andrade Gutierrez developed elaborate promotional materials and used the radio and newspapers to advertise the merits of Tucumã. Interested buyers were offered free transportation by bus caravan to the colonization site where they were housed in specially constructed visitor's quarters.

Sales got off to a slow start.[9] By the end of 1982 (the year CAG finally received title to the land) there were only ten colonist families in Tucumã and many of those were already having a difficult time getting settled. Start-up costs turned out to be much higher than expected, a problem that was compounded by the unusually heavy rains that year.[10] The company offered assistance by providing credit and by loaning the colonists machinery to clear their land. Despite this ominous beginning, CAG continued to invest in the project on the assumption that things would improve in the future. Work crews completed over five hundred kilometers of roads in the first section of the colonization site, and more than four hundred urban lots were sold. In November of 1982 the town of Tucumã itself—which consisted of ninety-three company houses and another eighty-one built by individuals or firms—was inhabited by about seven hundred people.[11]

But matters grew worse the following year, primarily as a consequence of the severe economic crisis that struck Brazil. The macroeconomic plan announced by the federal government in June of 1983 dealt a severe blow to the colonization project. The adjustment policies designed to combat rising inflation meant a sharp rise in interest rates and a cutback in special credit lines such as those colonists used. Especially significant was the impact of the crisis on the land market in southern Brazil. The economic downturn made it difficult for prospective colonists to sell their holdings in order to purchase lots in Projeto Tucumã. The recession also had direct effects on the management of the project. CAG was forced to reduce its workforce by half and cut operating expenses by shifting a greater share of the settlement costs to colonists. Farm families could no longer count on credit or machinery from the company as they had the year before.[12]

Matters improved in late 1984 and early 1985 when Brazil's recession eased somewhat. As the market for real estate picked up in the southern and central regions of the country, so did the prospect of selling land in Pará. The company hired a new sales director who opened thirty-eight new sales offices, expanding the campaign into the states of Espirito Santo, Goiás, Minas Gerais, and Mato Grosso do Sul. Between January and March of 1985—a period of optimism associated with the transition to a democratic political system in Brasília—an average of about three buses a week brought prospective buyers to visit the colonization site.

By May of 1985 CAG had sold 750 lots and had settled 184 farm families at Tucumã.

Closing the Gate

The Tucumã project was officially designated as part of POLA-MAZONIA's Greater Carajás program, which provided special government resources and protection.[13] Having obtained the state contract to build the PA-279 highway (see chapter 5), Andrade Gutierrez then set out to control ground access to the project area. In mid-1981, when the road was completed as far as the project border (160 kilometers from Xinguara), a physical barrier was erected. A guard was posted at the gate, or *guarita*, to screen everyone who wished to pass through. Although the highway was a public road, the firm justified this measure on the grounds that the state government had not yet paid for the construction work.

The *guarita* became the tangible symbol of the project's exclusionary character.[14] The strategy was to preserve the Gleba Carapanã as a planned enclave where investments would be well-protected from the chaos and violence that plagued other frontier towns. The company sought to avoid undesirable elements that might discourage prospective colonists from settling there. The effect was to exclude not only the landless poor who could not afford to purchase lots in the colonization project but virtually anyone who did not have sufficient capital to meet the company's criteria.

Some local entrepreneurs were rejected in favor of southerners invited by the company to run the hospital, hotel, and other businesses. Selected businessmen from Xinguara, Rio Maria, and Redenção were invited to relocate in Tucumã, but many local entrepreneurs could not afford the high cost of urban lots in Tucumã and the licensing fees the company demanded. All-night bars and brothels—the bread-and-butter of the gold economy—were initially prohibited altogether.[15]

The discovery of gold in southern Pará in the late 1970s introduced unexpected pressures on the project and altered the spatial distribution of the population in and around Tucumã's borders. By the time construction had begun on the town of Tucumã, there

Private Colonization

was already an active gold mining area at Cuca, inside the project borders (see chapter 8). Access to Cuca was carefully controlled by CAG, and company officials were determined to prevent further invasions by *garimpeiros*. But the strategy was ill-advised. Not only did it overlook the essential role the gold economy could play in underwriting the colonization effort, it also underestimated the risks of confrontations with the indomitable gold miners.

In July of 1981 the lure of gold on the company's land prompted a group of *garimpeiros* to bypass the gate and set up camp along a creekbed inside of Tucumã called Grota da Taca. Security men soon discovered the settlement. In the violent confrontation that followed, the guards ran the miners from the site, burning their shelters for good measure. Later, the *garimpeiros* claimed that they had been beaten and robbed of their possessions, including large quantities of gold. They gathered in Redenção and Xinguara where the miners spread word of the rich deposits that were there for the taking in the Taca creekbed. As it turned out, this particular site was hardly worth the fuss, but by then a major invasion of Tucumã was in the making.

News of the incident at Tucumã reached us in Xinguara where we joined the rest of the town's population to watch *garimpeiros* amass a long caravan of cars and trucks loaded with hundreds of miners from nearby camps. As they waited in the hot sun for the signal to move out, leaders of the small army of men were only too willing to voice their outrage against the colonization company that was depriving them of their rights. Boasting of the support that they allegedly had from the federal police and the military commander in charge of the nearby Cumaru gold field, the *garimpeiros* reminded us that the colonization company, even if it did hold title to the land, had no rights to subsoil minerals and, therefore, no authority to keep them out.

By mid-morning the caravan started down the PA-279 from Xinguara to Ourilândia. Several hours later the vehicles approached the company gate. The company's security force offered no resistance. The *garimpeiros* immediately took over the disputed creekbed. In the end, Grota da Taca produced very little gold, and it was not long before the miners who had invaded Tucumã moved on to other camps.

The gold rush nonetheless became the mainstay of Tucumã's economy, as it was for so many other towns in southern Pará. From the beginning, farmers comprised only a small proportion of the project area inhabitants. In 1984 less than 10 percent of the town's residents were full-time farmers or farm workers. Most were merchants and service providers (27.7 percent), professionals (8.6 percent), or worked in some other nonagricultural pursuit (40.2 percent).[16] For newly arrived colonists, the gold rush was a mixed blessing. On the negative side, thousands of young men who otherwise might have worked in agriculture were drawn to the gold fields, where earnings were nearly three times as high. The labor shortage that resulted was acute in the dry season when the task of clearing land for agriculture coincided with peak activity in the mining fields. By driving up the cost of labor as well as the price of services and basic commodities generally, the gold rush severely hurt farmers, especially those in the early stages of getting settled in the new environment.

Malaria posed a problem of a different sort. Although the disease was endemic to the region, most incidents of malaria occurred in the *garimpo* where pools of stagnant water provided an ideal breeding ground for the mosquitoes that carried the dreaded fever from one person to another. The disease struck nearly half of the farm families in Tucumã. People who lived closer to the *garimpo* were subject to a higher risk of infection. Prevention and treatment added to the cost of settling in the region as did the debilitating effect of the disease on labor productivity. Malaria accounted for an average yearly loss of ten days of labor per farm family.[17]

On the positive side, the gold economy provided diverse off-farm employment opportunities to earn supplemental income. The latter was particularly helpful during the first year or two when colonists were in need of extra cash to cover the high start-up costs. Later, when their agricultural plots began to produce, farmers were able to sell food crops to the growing population of gold miners in the area. By 1983 there were about fifteen thousand people directly involved in mining activities inside the project area. So great was the demand for rice and other products that suppliers traveled right to the farm gate where they paid a high price for whatever commodities were to be had. The strong market for agricultural products was particularly important to small farmers in 1983 when the company cut its workforce and scaled back its credit assistance and material support to the colonists. The fact that many of the CAG workers who were laid off that year stayed on in the area to try their luck in the *garimpo* was indicative of the promise people saw in the gold economy.

By that time much of Tucumã's economy relied in one way or another on the search for and the sale of gold. In 1983 one out of every five of the town's residents participated directly in mining activities, and 40 percent had lived or worked in mining camps.[18] Servicing the *garimpo* was the major source of income of merchants, lawyers, and doctors, and gold itself became a kind of underground currency. Although it was strictly illegal, those who could afford to do so bought gold as a means to protect their savings from the eroding effects of Brazil's rising rate of inflation.

Ourilândia and Tucumã: A Tale of Rival Towns

The gold rush not only affected the economic viability of small farming among colonists in the project, it also set in motion a series of events that forever changed the urban geography of the region. The influx of gold miners gave rise to a place that became known as Ourilândia, or Goldland, situated on the southern border of the colonization area only ten kilometers from Tucumã. In the fashion of other spontaneous settlements in the region, Ourilândia, with its brothels and all-night bars, had a sprawling, chaotic quality that stood in marked contrast to the neatly surveyed design of Tucumã, the quintessential company town.

The story of Ourilândia began with the short-lived Grota da Taca invasion of 1981. Two men, Candido and Francisco Paiva, tired of the itinerant life of gold miners, invested what resources they had into a small business at the farthest point accessible along the PA-279. Francisco, who had arrived first, established a dry goods store. Candido came later and occupied the other half of the building where he set up a bar-restaurant that sold soft drinks, beer, and fruit juice. The establishment was located just beyond the infamous *guarita* that marked the boundary of the Tucumã project. In reference to the gate, the town that grew up on that site first was known as Gurita, a name that persisted long after the gate itself was removed.[19]

Because the village was strategically located to service Cuca and other *garimpos* in the area, the gold rush stimulated further investment in roadside businesses next to the guard shack. In November of 1981 Gurita held about fifty houses. A few months later, in January of the following year, 150 buildings had been constructed there. When Gurita emerged as a sizable population center along the PA-279, residents under the leadership of people like Candido changed its name to Ourilândia, a town that continued to grow at a rapid pace. By 1984 there were about ten to twelve thousand people living in Ourilândia compared to a population of only about three thousand in Tucumã.

Residents of Ourilândia nursed a special bitterness against Tucumã's security forces, and they continued to hold a general animosity toward the colonization company for years to come. Such attitudes came to have significant negative effects on the development of Tucumã after 1983 when CAG brought in a new administrative team to manage the transition from the construction phase of the project to colonization and community development.

With cutbacks in the massive company presence in Tucumã, it was necessary to prepare the way for local control of the project. The new emphasis required that the colonization site be opened up and that links be strengthened with the towns of São Felix do Xingu to the west and with Ourilândia to the east. New businesses and a larger population were needed to justify Tucumã's eventual dismemberment as a new municipal seat eligible to receive state funds. In August the company sponsored a plebiscite among residents and property holders in Tucumã to elect a municipal agent or subprefect.

Mending relations with Ourilândia, marred by Tucumã's image as a "rich man's town," proved to be more difficult. The detested barrier at the property's boundary was removed, but by this time Ourilândia was a well-established community with a thriving commercial sector.[20] As an incentive to lure Ourilândia residents to Tucumã, the company set aside 480 lots in a new urban zone, called the Vila das Palmeiras, to be distributed by the new subprefect. The meeting to announce the offer, called near the place where the gate once stood, turned out to be a public relations fiasco.

Problems began as soon as the audience realized that the spokesman for Tucumã was none other than the security chief responsible for the heavy-handed expulsion of *garimpeiros* from company property back in 1981. After extolling the advantages of the Projeto Tucumã, he made the mistake of commenting that people should move to Tucumã because, anyway, Ourilândia "was likely to end" (*"a tendencia é de acabar"*). The statement deeply offended those Ourilândia residents who had fought for two years to build their community with no outside support and often in direct conflict with Tucumã. As one listener put it, "When people heard these words, many left the meeting; it was all over. They wouldn't accept a lot in Tucumã if the company gave it away." Instead of lining up to receive a lot in the colonization project, as the company had hoped, Ourilândia residents mounted a rival campaign to make the town its own municipal seat.

The antipathy between them notwithstanding, residents of the twin towns of Ourilândia and Tucumã were intimately bound to one another whether they liked it or not. On the one hand, small farmers in Tucumã depended on the economic activities outside its boundaries, such as gold mining. At the same time, the non-agricultural settlers, both inside the project and in Ourilândia, relied heavily on the services available only in the company town. Butler concluded that it was more accurate to view Ourilândia and Tucumã as "complementary parts of a single whole." His description of the two places in 1984 is persuasive in this regard:

> A fleet of over fifty taxis, four buses, and more than twenty vans provided daily service between Ourilândia, Tucumã, and Cuca. Local businessmen expanded their operations to include shops in both communities. Street vendors from Ourilândia walked the streets of Tucumã. People in Tucumã went to Ourilândia for entertainment or to find services they could not find in Tucumã. For example, if you wanted to employ the services of a goldsmith or have your watch repaired you had to go to Ourilândia. If, on the other hand, you needed to use the bank, the post office, the airport, or the telephone you had to come to Tucumã. (Butler 1985:116)

The Tucumã-Ourilândia complex showed more clearly than most urban places how the contradictions between rich and poor and between planned and spontaneous settlements generated patterns of population distribution that even the best-laid plans had neither intended nor anticipated. Linked to one another through a kind of symbiotic rivalry and interacting to produce a textured and dynamic urban system, the side-by-side towns of Tucumã and Ourilândia stood as a kind of metaphor of contemporary frontier change in Amazonia.[21]

The Demise of Projeto Tucumã

The goals set forth in the original plans for the Tucumã colonization project were far from met by the mid-1980s. Numerous events slowed its development, including the delay in obtaining the government's approval and the disappointing record of land sales due to the downturn in the national economy. At the local level, project managers faced the constant threat of land invasions by *posseiros* and miners and had to contend with the unexpected rise of Ourilândia, which diverted people and capital away from Tucumã. Although the picture brightened somewhat in 1984 when more lots were sold than in the previous three years, new problems arose.

The rains in 1985 were particularly heavy. In January and February alone nearly eight hundred millimeters of rain fell, double the corresponding amount for the previous year.[22] The PA-279 became impassable, and thousands of *garimpeiros* who were no longer able to work their mining sites found themselves stranded in Ourilândia. When food supplies, medicine, and fuel ran short, authorities declared the town a disaster area. The air force flew in provisions from Conceição do Araguaia, and CAG deployed its tractors and trucks in a losing battle to maintain uninterrupted transportation between Tucumã and Ourilândia.

Outgoing President Figueiredo chose this inopportune moment to visit the iron ore project in nearby Carajás. To guarantee the president's safety, all available policemen were transferred to the visit site, leaving Tucumã protected only by the company's security staff, which had been reduced in size during the 1983 cutback in personnel. About 120 settlers in Ourilândia, seeing that Tucumã was more vulnerable than usual, seized the opportunity

stands of mahogany on company property, encouraged the invasion of Gleba II north of the highway. By June of 1985 more than three thousand people had invaded the project, forcing the original colonists to defend themselves against losing their land to incoming *posseiros*.

The events that took place in May and June of 1985 marked the end of Projeto Tucumã, at least as it had initially been conceived. From that point on, CAG's main concern was how to best get out of the colonization project while salvaging as much of its investment as possible. The settling of accounts in Tucumã and the negotiations to decide which agency would take responsibility for the area initiated yet another round of public debate. With a new president in power in Brasília and a markedly different political climate across the country the content of the negotiations that followed the collapse of Projeto Tucumã revealed much about the new economic and political issues that came to affect the process of frontier change in the late 1980s.

Settling Accounts

The transition to a democratically elected president in 1985 profoundly transformed the relationships between the federal and state governments in Brazil. Two changes were of special significance in Amazonia. One was the erosion of federal control over the land settlement process, exemplified by the discredit that had befallen GETAT in the latter years of military rule (see chapters 4 and 6). The other was a shift in the balance of power in favor of progressive political groups in southern Pará that were linked to the Catholic church and to leftist political parties and that made important gains in the state and local elections.

The decentralization of authority and the new political climate intrinsic to the democratization process meant that Projeto Tucumã once again became a target of criticism. For politicians on the left, the colonization project represented what they detested most about the military regime, namely, the favor given to large capital. Moreover, Tucumã—with much of its infrastructure already in place—presented an attractive opportunity. Now that public figures were more accountable to voters than they had been during twenty-five years of military rule, the call to turn

Tucumã over to the landless poor had considerable populist appeal.

Jáder Barbalho, governor of Pará in 1985 and long-time opponent of the Projeto Tucumã from the days when he was still a congressman in 1979, proposed to Nelson de Figueiredo Ribeiro, head of the new Ministry of Agrarian Reform and Development (MIRAD), that Tucumã revert to the public domain and that the remaining lots be distributed jointly by the state government and the federal ministry. Barbalho's letter to the minister described the intense migratory pressure that existed along the PA-279 highway as a result of the movement of thousands of people attracted to the area by construction projects, gold, lumber, and, above all, the desire for land. Appealing to the new political debate in Brasília, the governor argued that the "emergency settlement" of six thousand needy families—a call reminiscent of the crisis colonization policy endorsed by GETAT years earlier (see chapter 6)—was compatible with the goals of agrarian reform. The fact that both Ourilândia and Tucumã were bidding to become independent municipal seats at that time was an additional consideration that surely came into play in the governor's political strategy.

Barbalho visited Tucumã in July 1985 when an independent community development council, the CODETUC, was created to assist the authorities in the transition from private to public governance, which took far longer than most people had hoped. For the next few years, the fate of the colonization project became increasingly entangled in a bureaucratic morass. In Brasília, the MIRAD itself came under heavy fire from landowners who feared expropriation of their land and from conservative politicians who rejected any threat to the sanctity of private property. As a result of the heated controversy at the national level, the agency was headed by five different ministers before it was abolished in 1989. The lack of continuity delayed the solution to the Tucumã dilemma, and CODETUC found itself virtually on its own as it tried to administer the town.[24]

In September of 1985 negotiations began on how much CAG was to be paid for the repossession of Gleba Carapanã. The new president of GETAT notified the company that because there was little prospect that the agency could clear the land of the three thousand invaders, GETAT could no longer approve the proposal for Gleba II . "We recognize that the company built infrastructure

and provided services of significant value in the area of the project." The letter further noted that "We understand that the public authorities, to whose domain the Gleba Carapanã area will
return, also are responsible for making just payment ... which we
wish to describe and quantify."

In CAG's reply, the company estimated the cost of its investments at thirty-one million dollars. GETAT carried out its own
study in October and came to the somewhat lower figure of
twenty-nine million dollars, which was accepted by the company.
In a letter to the Minister of Agrarian Reform and Development,
GETAT concluded that Colonizadora Andrade Gutierrez had fully
complied with its contractual obligations. The letter recommended that the sales contract for Gleba Carapanã be rescinded
by mutual consent of the parties involved and that the company
be reimbursed for its expenditures. But despite this agreement,
the debate continued.

A MIRAD internal commission concluded that the amount the
company asked for was far too high. In the commission's view,
the estimate was inflated due to the unwarranted inclusion of
numerous items, such as the costs associated with administration,
security, publicity, registration of lots, taxes, educational services,
electricity subsidies, and overhead. The commission revised the
amount downward to only ten million dollars—an estimate the
company promptly rejected.[25]

Critics of Projeto Tucumã were incensed that the government
should now be forced to repay the company for the excesses it
committed. Colonizadora Andrade Gutierrez countered that its
investments were far below the estimates of costs for official settlement projects being considered under the new agrarian reform
program. The state-level agrarian reform plan in Pará, for example, called for settlement of a total of 75,200 families between
1986 and 1989, and in 1986 alone for eight thousand families to
receive lots on 378,192 hectares of land to be expropriated. CAG
pointed out that whereas the National Agrarian Reform Plan had
estimated the average cost of settling each family on a plot of
forty-six hectares to be six thousand dollars, the fertile soils of
the remaining 361,200 hectares of the Gleba Carapanã were already equipped to absorb 12,100 families on lots averaging thirty
hectares in size and at a cost (excluding urban investments) of

only $3,160 per family. Curiously enough, the private colonization company found itself endorsing the idea of agrarian reform as a means to recover the investment it had made in southern Pará.

In July of 1986 the new Minister of MIRAD, Dante de Oliveira, sent his secretary-general to visit Tucumã. He recommended that another study be carried out by an independent consulting company selected by public bid and announced in September. In January of 1987 a firm called Sondotécnica was awarded the contract. The six-volume, 850-page report completed in May came up with an estimate of twenty-five million dollars, an amount much closer to the original agreement between CAG and GE-TAT.[26]

The Sondotécnica report was still under consideration when Dante de Oliveira stepped down as minister four days after the report was submitted to MIRAD. In an open letter to President Sarney, Oliveira reviewed the steps that had been taken during his mandate, emphasizing that as yet no resolution to the Tucumã situation had been found. Nor was a decision reached by the next minister, Marcos Freire, before his death in an airplane crash in September of 1987. The paperwork associated with the Tucumã case burned up in the crash.[27] No action was taken by his short-lived successor, none other than Jáder Barbalho.

Throughout the prolonged negotiation period, Tucumã was in limbo. The company maintained water and electrical services at its own expense, but withdrew most of its employees for their own protection. Federal and state authorities likewise left the community to its own devices. Public school teachers who were not paid from February through August of 1985 (despite promises by the governor) threatened to go on strike, until the CODETUC raised money from the community to assume the payroll expenses for the remainder of the year.[28]

Loggers exploited the uncertainty to extract as much valuable mahogany as possible.[29] The round-the-clock traffic of lumber trucks carrying immense loads accounted for much of the severe deterioration of the PA-279. Land pressures continued to lead to violent conflicts. In June of 1986 an estimated five thousand families carried out another mass invasion of Tucumã.[30] When the death toll reached one hundred people, the Pastoral Land Commission and the rural workers unions referred to Tucumã as the latest "powder keg" in the long list of violent places in southern Pará.[31]

In September of 1988 the new Minister Leopoldo Bessone finally authorized payment to CAG of 6.6 billion cruzados (roughly twenty million dollars). The settlement included expropriation of the Colonizadora Andrade Gutierrez and transfer of most of its assets to the municipal government. When local officials elected in 1988 took over the administration of the newly created municipality, they inherited a physical infrastructure that far surpassed anything in the spontaneous frontier towns of southern Pará.

Despite the failure of the colonization project, the future of Tucumã may yet hold the promise of developing into a stable agricultural community. In 1989 most of the original two hundred colonists were still there. State agencies like EMATER and CEPLAC continued to work with settlers, many of whom were planting perennial crops such as rubber, coffee, and black pepper. Cacao plantations were the biggest hope of the colonists since they increased the value of their lots and helped them hold out against the pressures to sell to larger investors. The invasion of *posseiros* created a kind of de facto land reform that at least in its initial stage was more equitable than the massive efforts by GETAT in the Xinguara area.

Indeed, a comparison of the outcome in Xinguara with that in Tucumã reveals a curious irony. In Xinguara, cattle ranchers won control over land in an area ostensibly designated for settlement of landless migrants. In Tucumã, landless invaders turned the tables, carrying out their own land reform program in an area that was conceded to a single large company for sale to relatively wealthy settlers.

NOTES

1. A survey in 1984 by Moran (1987:85–86) of Tucumã colonist lots found their soils to be generally good though not uniform.
2. Butler (1985:32–34). Andrade Gutierrez also had been involved in mineral

research in the Tapajós and in Rondônia. The company's only other agricultural project was on a 240-hectare plot of land in Minas Gerais.

3. Butler (1985:35–38). In 1966 the firm had proposed a private colonization project in the Pindaré Valley of Maranhão to SUDENE, but SUDENE was not interested. Andrade Gutierrez was also part of an unsuccessful proposal by the Association of Amazonian Entrepreneurs to colonize the Cuiabá-Santarém Highway that did not receive INCRA's support.

4. In the mid-1970s SUDAM had considered the same area as a possible site for a colonization project. Part of POLAMAZONIA funds for São Felix do Xingu were allocated to a feasibility study, and a preproposal developed a plan similar to the INCRA model used along the Transamazon Highway. SUDAM then learned that the state land agency (ITERPA) had received a proposal to develop the same area from a group of private investors linked to São Paulo entrepreneur Pedro Ometto and was therefore reluctant to turn over the land to SUDAM. Shortly thereafter, because of the route of a projected federal road (the BR-158) and the provisions of the 1164 statute, Gleba Carapanã passed into the federal domain under INCRA's jurisdiction. INCRA decided to put it up for auction to private colonization companies.

5. Both annual and perennial crops were of interest: cacao, rubber, guarana, coffee, citrus, annatto, papaya, soybeans, rice, corn, beans, passion fruit, black pepper, sugar cane, pineapple, regional fruits, cassava, vegetables, and pasture.

6. Butler (1985:49,68–71).

7. One was known as the Vila dos "Dorme Sujo"—those who "go to bed dirty."

8. Butler (1985:41–44).

9. CAG representatives evaluated candidates in terms of their farm assets and farm management experience, at least initially. Later, when pressure mounted to sell as many lots as possible, the ability to pay became the overriding criterion (Butler 1985:17).

10. Butler (1985:18).

11. *Folha de Tucumã*, Ano 1, vol. 7, November 1982.

12. Butler (1985:54,59). Labor constraints due to the gold economy (see below) meant that manual clearing was not feasible.

13. Carajás was a priority area under the POLAMAZONIA program, and the government sought to control the areas surrounding the core mining zone by control of population movement and settlement in buffer areas (Becker 1990). A similar security strategy was adopted by CAG to protect the Tucumã project. The first major hurdle had already been passed. The company had purchased a practically unoccupied territory protected on two borders by Indian reserves.

14. Becker (n.d.:13) describes how the *guarita* protecting the Carajás mining project area took on similar significance in the eyes of the population. CVRD called it the "gateway" (*portaria*) to the mining company. People living outside called it the "barrier" (*barreira*).

15. Butler (1985:114).

16. Butler (1985:109–110,143).

17. Butler (1985:140–143).

18. Butler (1985:140–143).

19. Ourilândia was still referred to by this name in 1989.

20. Butler (1985:114–115).

21. Similar patterns emerged in other large project sites like Jari (the Monte Dourado/Beiradão complex, see Fisk 1984), Carajás (Serra Norte/Paraopebas), Tucuruí, and Marabá (see Becker 1990).

22. *A Província do Pará*, 9 March 1985.

23. *O Liberal*, 24 April 1985.

24. Jorge (1986).

25. Peter (1986:47).

26. In accordance with MIRAD instructions, the calculations included costs of urban and rural road construction, the demarcation of the *gleba* and individual lots, installation of water and electric energy systems, teachers' salaries, buildings and other community equipment, preparation of the Gleba I and Gleba II proposals, administration, sales agents and transportation of prospective colonists, and agricultural research. It excluded the cost of the land itself and indemnification of its previous occupants, registration of lots, taxes; maintenance of water, electric energy, and other urban services (an obligation not specified in the original contract) and other costs such as promotional materials for which CAG was unable to produce adequate documentation of expenses.

27. Pinto (1988c).

28. The difficulties faced by the community due to the delay in resolving the situation in Tucumã were spelled out in the introduction to the CODETUC annual activities report: "It's not easy to administer Tucumã because, since it's a private colonization project, the government always uses this argument to justify its omission even though the project actually has been totally absorbed by the community. The wealth of Tucumã has become a true warehouse for state and federal authorities, from which they collect all that is their due without, however, returning a single penny to the community."

29. Indeed, logging practices had undermined the success of the Projeto Tucumã in different ways since the beginning when sawmills were among those behind the initial 1979 invasions of the Gleba Carapanã. Six years later, logging companies again contributed to the invasions that finally overran the project area. Once CAG had won rights to the Gleba Carapanã, the company itself began to exploit the mahogany while clandestine logging continued as well. In an effort to control the extraction of wood and to replenish company coffers, contracts were signed in 1983 with three large companies to exploit mahogany on unsold lots. The revenues from this lucrative business brought CAG an estimated twenty-eight thousand dollars per month. Removal of this valuable resource took away an important source of initial capital for colonists that had been promised by the sales agents. It is impossible to calculate the total returns to the project from logging activities, a factor that did not enter into the negotiations over indemnification.

30. *O Liberal*, 1 June 1986.

31. *A Província do Pará*, 24 May 1987.

EIGHT
❖
Amazon Gold

When prospectors found new deposits of gold in southern Pará in 1980, the discovery ushered in a dramatic new chapter in the region's history. Although gold mining was not unknown in the region,[1] three factors accounted for the greater importance of the recent strikes. For one thing, the deposits discovered in the 1980s were much richer than previous finds. For another, the discoveries coincided with an unprecedented rise in the price of gold on the international market. Gold prices had been steadily increasing since the 1970s. But the price peaked at $850 per troy ounce on the London Metal Exchange in 1980, the same year the largest find was made. After that the price fell; yet for the rest of the decade it remained at what in historical terms was an extremely high level. The gold strike in Amazonia also attracted special interest because it occurred just when Brazil's international debt burden sent the national economy into its most severe recession in many decades. The economic crisis promoted the idea that Amazonian gold was the solution to country's economic ills, an illusion that motivated the federal government to pay particular attention to *garimpeiros* in Amazonia.

As always, news of the gold strikes traveled with astonishing speed across rural Brazil. Word of mouth reports, embellished with every telling, reached people from near and far. In a matter of a few days, the informal communications network, nicknamed *rádio peão*, sent people rushing to the site of the newest discovery. By the middle of the decade the population of gold miners in Amazonia reached around half a million. Official statistics and informed estimates from knowledgeable observers suggest that in the late 1980s Brazil produced around eighty-nine tons of gold annually, over 90 percent of which came from manually operated *garimpos*. At the August 1987 price this was worth around 1.1 billion dollars a year. That the volume of Amazonian production surpassed the great nineteenth-century gold rushes in California and the Klondike suggests the magnitude of what took place in northern Brazil in the 1980s.[2]

Of all of the gold mining areas in southern Pará, it was the massive gold strike at Serra Pelada that captured the media's attention, and for good reason. The image of thousands of mud-soaked men working the open pit like a swarm of furious bees made dramatic copy. Pictures of Serra Pelada were soon published in newspapers and shown on television screens in Brazil and across the world. The gold strike became the topic of popular documentaries produced by Jacques Cousteau, the BBC, West German television, and several North American networks. Because of the attention given to it, Serra Pelada came to symbolize the Amazon gold rush although by Amazonian standards it was a thoroughly atypical *garimpo*.

Far more common in the region were the smaller and less concentrated deposits of gold found in the sandy river bottoms and streambeds that fan out across the watershed. Although never on the enormous scale of Serra Pelada, the alluvial gold deposits came to play a major role in the region. Examples in southern Pará included the golds fields of Cumaru near Redenção and Cuca, located inside the Tucumã colonization project. These sites as well as others along the PA-150 (Andorinhos and Paraupebas) form part of a larger gold-bearing zone that lies between the Xingu and Araguaia rivers. It was here that *garimpeiros* discovered innumerable small deposits on ranches and farms across the state. Landowners regularly visited the areas to collect the traditional 10 percent that was their due. In many instances, farmers and ranchers themselves took up the prospector's tools to mine their own land, struggling all the while, usually with little success, to keep others out. So prevalent was gold in the area that residents of towns like Rio Maria sifted and washed the soil they dug up to sink water wells. In the early 1980s about five kilos of gold were sold every day in Redenção, Rio Maria, Xinguara, and Marabá.[3]

At first glance, *garimpeiros* appear to be a distinct social group, living in distant enclaves isolated from the rest of the frontier population. So precarious and transitory does their lifestyle seem that it was tempting to treat them as little more than a subplot in the main story of Amazonian development. For researchers like ourselves—who in the 1970s had come to think of southern Pará primarily in terms of ranchers, small farmers, and land conflicts—mining activities were little more than an exotic curiosity. In fact, as we later discovered, mining was firmly linked to agriculture, as it was also to nearly every other facet of frontier life. Just as small farmers became involved, directly or otherwise, in mining activities, so too did *garimpeiros* find themselves swept into the unresolved contests over land as well as into confrontations with Indians, with mining companies, and, in the case of Serra Pelada, with the federal troops. Hence, the massive influx of people and money that took place in southern Pará in the 1980s not only changed the spatial distribution of the population, it also transformed the size and structure of the regional economy. For people living in the region, both natives and newcomers, the *garimpos* that sprang up all around affected the way they lived and worked and the way families organized themselves and their resources to gain, or to keep, a foothold on the frontier.

What is usually referred to as "*o garimpo*" consists in reality of many different kinds of mining communities. They have undergone rapid and dramatic change as a consequence of military intervention and technological innovation. The recent adoption of high-powered water jets to mine alluvial gold in places like Cumaru and Cuca, for example, thoroughly transformed the character of the traditional *garimpo*. By requiring new skills and larger quantities of capital, technological changes altered the labor process in the fields and gave rise to new financial arrangements. The financial networks associated with gold mining soon penetrated the economies of nearby towns and drew investors from as far away as Rio de Janeiro and São Paulo. The ever more complex system of financing mining activities in the Amazon increased the number of people with a vested interest in the *garimpo*. As a result of the closer integration of the *garimpo* into the regional economy a degree of political power was bestowed on the ragtag army of *garimpeiros* they never had before. How these changes reshaped the character of the conflicts that ensued between miners, mining companies, and the federal government was evident in the tumultuous events that took place in Serra Pelada.

Serra Pelada: The Militarized Garimpo

Legend has it that in December of 1979 a day laborer by the name of Aristeu was hired to sink post holes on the Tres Barras ranch, a modest enterprise located about ninety miles south of Marabá. The point of Aristeu's pickax struck a stone so large he was obliged to get down on his hands and knees to move it to one side. What Aristeu thought was an inconveniently placed rock turned out to be a nugget of solid gold.[4] News of the strike spread with lightning speed. By March of 1980 there were about five thousand people working the site, which became known the world over as Serra Pelada. At its peak in 1983 Serra Pelada produced more than a metric ton of gold a month and held a population of eighty thousand to a hundred thousand miners, merchants, and related tradespeople.

Serra Pelada was a worrying development to the military. The thought of so many people congregated in such a small place conjured troubling memories of the guerrilla movement that had plagued the army in the early 1970s. It also brought to mind the violent land wars that GETAT was unsuccessfully trying to contain in southern Pará. More importantly, Serra Pelada was ominously located on the border with the huge Carajás iron ore mine, the most expensive development project in the entire region. Serra Pelada amounted to nothing less than the richest gold discovery in Amazonian history, and it was apparent to the state agencies that the deposit could be mined more efficiently by CVRD (Companhia do Vale do Rio Doce), the agency that had been awarded mineral rights to the area via the Decreto de Lavra 74.509 issued back in 1974.

On the basis of these technical and national security issues, the military urged President Figueiredo to intervene. On May 1, 1980, federal authorities under the command of the SNI's Major Curió took charge of Serra Pelada. It is said that Curió, in his usual charismatic fashion, stepped off the helicopter that took him to Serra Pelada and opened his address to the assembled *garimpeiros* by firing his Magnum pistol several times in the air. "From now on," Curió declared, "the gun that shoots the loudest is mine." With that unambiguous claim to authority, Curió set out to transform Serra Pelada into a *garimpo* the likes of which had never been seen before.

The effort was orchestrated by a body called simply the Coordenação. It was headed by Curió and staffed by the DNPM, federal police, and SNI agents. Entry into the mining area was controlled, weapons were confiscated, and all women were expelled. The Coordenação built a free clinic, a malaria control post, a telephone office, and established a government store (COBAL) that sold foodstuffs at subsidized prices. In a fashion reminiscent of the way GETAT had carried out its crisis colonization program for small farmers, a total of about fifteen government agencies were mobilized in Serra Pelada to minister to *garimpeiro* needs.

Curió drew on his military background when he instituted a daily regimen intended to bring the obstreperous miners under control. Every day began with a meeting in front of the offices of the Coordenação. The men went to work only after calisthenics, the singing of the national anthem, and listening to a pep talk from Curió. The federal police devised their own means of maintaining order. *Garimpeiros* caught stealing gold had their heads shaved. Before being expelled from the area, the police paraded them in handcuffs before the crowd of jeering *garimpeiros* gathered at the early-morning flag-raising ceremony. The arbitrary system of justice carried out by the federal agents in the region was brought to the nation's attention in a bizarre event that took place in July of 1985 when the chief of police settled a personal quarrel with one of his own detectives by shooting him dead during a live interview on a television broadcast from Marabá.[5]

The majority of the *garimpeiros* had few complaints about the changes that Curió and the Coordenação brought to Serra Pelada. The initial success of military populism was evident in November of 1980 when President Figueiredo visited the gold mine. After he was carried on the shoulders of an appreciative crowd of miners, Figueiredo announced that Serra Pelada would forever remain open to the *garimpeiros*. It was a promise the president would later regret.

The Organization of Work

The social relations of production that evolved in Serra Pelada bore little resemblance to those found in the traditional *garimpo*. In Serra Pelada only a minority of *garimpeiros* worked under the *meia-praça* arrangement.[6] On productive claims, owners preferred to pay day workers or percentage workers who earned from 1 to 5 percent of the take. The concentrated nature of the gold deposit required that the material be carried out of the pit by hand. The task was done by people known as *formigas* ("ants") who comprised the vast majority of workers in Serra Pelada. *Formigas*, who were paid by the load, typically made forty to sixty trips per day, using a latticework of precarious hand-hewn ladders to climb up the steep incline.

The other jobs in Serra Pelada included the *cavador* who dug the pit, and the *paleador* who filled the burlap bags. Both earned about the same amount a *formiga* received on a good day.[7] The *apontador* and the *fiscal* were supervisory positions remunerated on a percentage basis, as were the *batedor*, who tested and purified the gold, and the *alimentador* and *controlador*, who operated the motorized hammers and sluice box, respectively. Over a period of years, the mass of *garimpeiros* gradually dug away at the hill called Babilônia until it became a vast crater. The hill itself reappeared as a huge mound of discarded material called the *amontoeira*. The army of *formigas*—covered with mud and moving in a steady stream up the ladders, each carrying a heavy sack across the shoulders, suspended by a head band—gave Serra Pelada a surreal, biblical appearance that caught the imagination of the national and international media.

Social relations in Serra Pelada evolved rapidly as individual miners and investors sought a toehold in the changing fortunes of Serra Pelada.[8] During the first two years of Serra Pelada, luck favored some more than others, and the process of concentration of ownership of claims ensued.[9] The *bamburrados* (those who struck it rich) bought claims from the *blefados* (those who went broke). Curió attempted to counteract this tendency by instituting a lottery system to distribute new areas to those who had no claims. But in the absence of any provisions for financing the *garimpeiros* who lacked capital, a gradual concentration process was inevitable.[10] Over time, claim owners ran out of money to supply their workers and were forced to sell percentages of their claim to outside investors. While the original owner would retain rights to 1 percent of the claim, the remainder might be divided among ten or twenty investors. Some investors bought up shares in dozens of claims, giving them greater control over production. Unlike the traditional *garimpo*, where economic divisions were less pronounced, Serra Pelada came to be known as the *garimpo* of the "bourgeoisie and the ants." According to data on gold sales released by the MME, more than a quarter of the production was controlled by only 104 persons. Similarly, 990 people—only 2 percent of the total registered *garimpeiro* population of 48,000— garnered 72 percent of the income from gold in Serra Pelada during the boom period.[11]

The Battle for Serra Pelada

The military intervention in Serra Pelada echoed the inconsistency that plagued GETAT's efforts to resolve land disputes in southern Pará, and it had many of the same results. According to the strategy of military populism, the objective was to attend to the needs of the miners as a means of controlling their actions and gaining their political support. The policy was successful, at least in the short run. Indeed, it was the huge *garimpeiro* vote that handed Curió a victory when he ran for Congress in the crucial elections held in November 1982 (see chapter 5). Allies of Curió also took eight out of nine seats on the Marabá council and enjoyed similar successes in the town of Imperatriz. But in the long run there was little doubt that the development policies formulated in Brasília embodied a very different set of priorities. If appealing to the mass of *garimpeiros* was politically expedient for certain purposes at one point in time, it did not take long before the mining companies began to wield their considerable power to shift priorities back to large-scale, capital-intensive projects.

Particularly effective in this regard were the lobbying efforts of the Brazilian Mining Institute (IBRAM), an association representing both public and private sector mining companies. With the 1982 elections out of the way and with Curió and his cronies in office in Brasília and in the local city councils, President Figueiredo acceded to the pressure to turn over Serra Pelada to the CVRD. But what to do with the *garimpeiros*? The plan was to transfer them to the "mining reserves" in Cumaru and the Tapajós by November 15, 1983. As could be expected, the president's proposal was vehemently rejected by the miners even though things were not going at all well at Serra Pelada. By that time the crater was twelve hundred meters in diameter, and some forty to fifty meters deep. Because the floor of the pit was well below the water table, constant seepage made the work site increasingly dangerous. Fractures in the *garimpo* structure caused deadly avalanches that forced the temporary suspension of work in some areas. After one such closing,*garimpeiros* who spent the weekend in Marabá waiting for the mine to reopen were hardly encouraged when they watched the Sunday night television show *Fantástico* that highlighted the unhealthy conditions in the Tapajós, the place where the government proposed to send them. Nineteen more deaths followed soon after the *garimpo's* reopening, bringing the total to forty-five.[12]

DNPM attempted to close off areas that technicians considered unsafe, but they could barely control the *garimpeiros* intent upon extracting as much gold as possible before they might have to leave. DNPM officials went hoarse from blowing the whistles they used to try to stop the entry of *garimpeiros* into the most unstable zones. Many of the *garimpeiros* staunchly believed that someone had actually found the mother lode and that this was the real reason they were being driven off. They accused DNPM of using safety considerations to deliberately sabotage their work and to discourage them from further excavation.

Figueiredo's decision to evict the *garimpeiros* from Serra Pelada placed Curió in the impossible situation of having to close off the mining area to the very people who were his electoral base. Faced with this dilemma, Curió opted to defy the government. Using every means at his disposal, he launched a campaign to keep Serra Pelada in the hands of the *garimpeiros*. With the backing of entrepreneurs and investors from across the country, congressmen and senators were showered with letters and telegrams. In addition, Curió sought support from a wide variety of organizations, including labor unions, professional associations, and the National Garimpeiros' Union based in Rio de Janeiro. A Serra Pelada delegation went to Brasília and told the congressional Committee on Mines and Energy that the *garimpeiros* would resist any attempt to get them to abandon Serra Pelada. In September 1983 Curió presented a bill to the Congress that would extend the stay of the *garimpeiros* in Serra Pelada another five years until 1988. In the months ahead, as the controversy grew more heated, it was Curio's bill before the legislature that was the target of intense lobbying efforts by interest groups both for and against the *garimpeiros* position.

Debate intensified when the Ministry of Mines and Energy (MME) sponsored a national seminar on gold, which was held in Santarém. The purpose of the meeting was to seek ways to increase gold production.[13] Many of the participants, including a *garimpeiro* who seized the microphone, protested that no consideration was being given to the men working in the *garimpos*. Other depositions hardly favored the government's plans for Serra Pelada. The regional director of SUCAM, the malaria control agency, warned of the potentially grave health consequences of relocating the mass of Serra Pelada *garimpeiros* to the remote Tapajós region, where malaria and hepatitis were already a serious problem. In the meantime, two Pará state congressmen favorable to the *garimpeiros*—Gabriel Guerrero of the opposition PMDB party and Haroldo Bezerra, a close associate of Curió's and a former *garimpeiro*—were denied entry to Serra Pelada. Bezerra was allowed on the premises only after he showed the work card he still carried with him from his *garimpeiro* days. He later tore up his identification card to protest the treatment he received and to call public attention to the *garimpeiro* cause.[14]

The newly formed regional branch of the National Garimpeiro's Union sent telegrams requesting support from Brazil's powerful metalworkers union and from state governors, the Congress, the Brazilian Lawyers Organization (OAB), and even the National Council of Bishops (CNBB). The latter was an ironic twist in light of the enmity between the church and Curió that dated back to the major's commanding role in the military campaign against guerrilla forces in southern Pará. If the expulsion order came, the *garimpeiros* planned to stay put and sing the national anthem while sympathetic labor unions elsewhere in the country would strike.[15]

On the first of October a caravan of buses and private cars departed from Serra Pelada carrying more than two thousand *garimpeiros* to Brasília to lobby for Curió's bill. A few hours later, in a surprise move, the government transferred control of both Serra Pelada and Cumaru from the National Security Council to the federal mining agency, DNPM. The decision was made by the Minister of the Interior without even consulting the mining bureaucracies. As a result of the confusion that followed, many of the DNPM technicians became unexpected allies of the *garimpeiro* cause from within the government agency.[16] Meanwhile, *garimpeiros* convinced the congressional leadership to introduce Curió's bill on an emergency basis—a legislative ploy that required a vote within forty-eight hours. In a last-ditch effort, Minister Cals proposed that the closing of Serra Pelada be postponed until the Tapajós and Cumaru *garimpos* were ready to receive the influx of *garimpeiros*. Despite such diversionary tactics, Curió's bill passed both houses of the Congress in a rare demonstration of multipartisan support on October 5, 1983.

DNPM reports of weapons stockpiled in Serra Pelada raised fears of armed resistance, but these warnings were largely ignored. On October 8 IBRAM sent telexes to the president, key ministers, and party leaders urging the president to veto the bill. The Professional Association of Geologists of Amazonia (APGAM) published a statement in favor of the closing although for different reasons. MME technicians argued that it would cost about fifteen million dollars and sixteen months of work to perform the earth-moving operations needed in Serra Pelada.[17] As if to reinforce the point, more accidental deaths occurred in the *garimpo* on October 13.

On October 27 Figueiredo vetoed the bill and recommended a gradual relocation process that would return the men to their home states or send them to "work fronts" in the Northeast (suffering from a severe drought) or to *garimpos* in the Tapajós and Cumaru. This could be accomplished with the natural decline in *garimpo* activity during the rainy season, which was just then beginning. As a precaution, he declared a state of emergency and sent federal police into the area. The *garimpeiros* responded by obtaining a court injunction that insured their presence in the *garimpo* for ninety days while the merits of the case were reviewed. The injunction, ordered by a local judge in Marabá, was upheld by the Federal Appeals Court the day after the veto.

As Curió scrambled to get the two-thirds vote needed to overturn the veto, a congressional study commission looked into ways Serra Pelada might be managed by the *garimpeiros* themselves. In December Figueiredo authorized a committee composed of Curió, Haroldo Bezerra, and a *garimpeiro* representative to organize a cooperative of *garimpeiros* that could maintain control over the *garimpo* under official tutelage. The cooperative was set up in January 1984. The situation became somewhat calmer as a result, but the tranquility did not last long. When the rainy season drew to a close in March, pressures quickly mounted to resolve once and for all the legal status of Serra Pelada. Time was rapidly running out, and the prospect of a violent confrontation became more likely with every day that passed.

After months of political and legal tactics had failed to achieve their objectives, the miners resorted to more direct action in March of 1984. Some twenty-thousand Serra Pelada *garimpeiros* gathered in Imperatriz to pressure for the definitive opening of the *garimpo*. They threatened to block the Belém-Brasília and the Transamazon highways if action was not taken within a week. In May the Congress approved Figueiredo's compromise bill allocating federal resources to expropriate the *garimpo* area, provided that the miners paid CVRD for its investment.[18] Once again, the *garimpeiros* were present in the assembly hall when Congress made its decision. The bill created a *garimpo* reserve and specified that the *garimpeiros* could continue to dig as far down as 190 meters above sea level (the pit was already down to less than 210 meters) or for a maximum of three more years.[19]

Things came to a head on June 6, 1984, when one of Curió's

customary missives was read to the assembled *garimpeiros* in Marabá. Frustrated by his inability to get final action, Curió pleaded
for one more day to negotiate. The message was greeted with
loud jeers from the audience. The first speaker to take the podium
concluded his diatribe against the government's actions with a
further attack on Curió: "Deputy Curió is properly a mediator,
not a leader to give orders or tell us what we should or should
not do," he proclaimed to an approving crowd. In defiance of
Curió's wishes, an overwhelming majority voted to occupy Serra
Pelada.

The next day *garimpeiros* from Imperatriz formed a barricade
across the Belém-Brasília Highway on a bridge over the Cacau
river.[20] A separate group entered Serra Pelada and destroyed the
communications system used by the military police. Another six
hundred armed *garimpeiros* departed from Marabá in trucks and
other vehicles and headed for the CVRD headquarters in Serra
Norte. When they arrived at the first settlement, Paraupebas, they
disarmed the military police. They proceeded to burn several
CVRD buildings before moving on to Curionópolis where they
continued their rampage. The threat that the *garimpeiros* posed
to the Carajás project fulfilled the worst nightmares of the CVRD,
IBRAM, and the security forces that tried unsuccessfully to keep
the unruly *garimpeiros* under control.

Security was tightened at Serra Norte, and no further damage
was done to the installation. Curió, who knew more than most
about the military's response to such demonstrations, traveled
from location to location urging the *garimpeiros* to open up the
highways. The miners agreed to wait until 6 P.M. on Monday, June
11, for a response from the government. In the meantime, some
sixty thousand *garimpeiros* amassed at various locations, one
group of them at Serra Pelada. The largest concentration was at
Recanto das Mangueiras near the Cacau river bridge on the Belém-Brasília Highway. Police managed to open the highway to
traffic, but thousands of *garimpeiros* maintained a hostile vigil just
across the river. Curió warned the president, the Congress, the
various ministries, and anyone else who would listen that he could
not restrain the miners beyond the appointed deadline.

On June 11, 1984, Figueiredo reluctantly signed Curió's bill into
law. The president vetoed objectionable amendments and spec-

ified indemnification of CVRD in the amount of nearly sixty million dollars. He outlined the steps by which the cooperative could take over the *garimpo* and dispatched the earthmoving machines to Serra Pelada to carry out needed repairs. Jubilant celebrations broke out in Marabá, Imperatriz, Serra Pelada, and the other places where *garimpeiros* had congregated.

The *garimpo* was reopened in September of 1984. Yet the dramatic political victory the miner's had won failed to produce the economic returns they had hoped for. As it turned out, CVRD was largely correct when it concluded that it was both dangerous and inefficient for *garimpeiros* to work at such depths. After the mine was reopened under *garimpeiro* control, Serra Pelada was plagued by a series of accidents, and production plummeted from 13.9 tons in 1983 to 3.5 tons in 1986.[21] Three years later, in 1989, only a few thousand *garimpeiros* remained in the place where nearly a hundred thousand miners had once worked.

The political mobilization that kept Serra Pelada in the hands of the *garimpeiros* marked a new era in the history of mining in Brazil. As David Cleary noted, it was the first time that *garimpeiros* "were able to confront the formal mining sector and the state on its own terms—within the political and judicial apparatus which had previously been used to define the parameters of law and debate on the mineral question in Brazil."[22] Still, the impressive lobbying effort headed by Curió was only one aspect of the change that took place. Equally important was the solidarity forged among the *garimpeiros* themselves. The latter was fostered by the working conditions in Serra Pelada and by the extraordinarily high population density in the mining camp. The *garimpeiros'* consciousness of their strength in numbers and the perception of their capacity for collective action were undoubtedly bolstered by the platoonlike formations and the regimented calisthenics that Curió initially used to keep the *garimpeiros* under control. That such efforts later contributed to the very conditions the military wished to avoid in Serra Pelada was an irony similar to the one faced by GETAT officials, whose actions to contain the land wars in southern Pará only strengthened the peasants' resolve (see chapter 6).

The role *garimpeiros* played in Brazil's economy in the midst of its international debt crisis was not lost on the men whom Curió commanded to sing the national anthem each morning before work. "We are the ones who are paying off the debt," was a statement we repeatedly heard during interviews carried out among *garimpeiros* in the 1980s. Invariably the comment was made with a combination of pride in their country, dismay at the treatment they received in Serra Pelada, and undiluted anger at the mining companies, the military, and the officials that staffed the various government agencies. Whether the gold miners were truly saviors of the nation as they claimed was less significant than the attitude itself. The essential point is that in addition to giving them experience in the art of political lobbying the contest for Serra Pelada prompted miners to define themselves as a group, to act in concert to defend their interests, and to invoke a nationalist theme to legitimize their claim to mineral resources. In so doing, *garimpeiros* became a powerful and independent political force in Amazonia.

Cumaru

Cumaru was the name given to a rich gold-producing area near Redenção on the borders of the Gorotire reserve of the Kayapó Indians. It was discovered in 1979, just before the great find at Serra Pelada. Unlike Serra Pelada with its highly concentrated deposits of gold, the Cumaru gold district consisted of dozens of *garimpos* spread over the countryside.[23] In other respects, the phenomenon was the same. Word of the gold strike spread and thousands of *garimpeiros* began to converge on the spot. Pilots dropped supplies for the miners from small planes, merchants set up shop, and the *garimpo* of Cumaru was launched.

João Lanari do Val, pioneer in the region and owner of the Santa Tereza ranch (see chapter 5), had taken the precaution of securing a license to exploit mineral resources on his own land through a contract with the Paranapanema mining company. Lanari initially sought help from the state military police to expel the intruders, but they were unsuccessful in doing so. Unable to control access to his land, Lanari was allowed to carry out his own experimental mining and to monopolize the lucrative commercial centers that sprang up to service the *garimpeiros*. The merchants and suppliers who operated clandestine landing strips were evicted and their property was confiscated.

In February of 1980 the federal police set up a base in Redenção in order to control events in Cumaru, but these modest efforts soon proved inadequate. The rising price of gold and the discovery of Serra Pelada triggered a massive influx of miners into the region. Later that year about ten thousand *garimpeiros* invaded the Cumaru area. In a few months *garimpos* spread further into Lanari do Val's property and into public lands and two creekbeds inside the Gorotire Indian reserve (see chapter 9). According to official statistics, Cumaru produced 1.7 metric tons of gold in 1981. Two years later the production reached 6.4 metric tons.[24]

Conflicts emerged between landowners and *garimpeiros* and between *garimpeiros* and the Kayapó. The Indians either expelled the miners or conceded them temporary permission to work within the reserve, provided that the *garimpeiros* paid them a percentage of the gold they produced. In an area wracked by intense land conflicts, it was inevitable that a sudden increase in the *garimpeiro* population would affect the political struggles underway in this part of southern Pará (see chapter 6). Community organizers affiliated with the Catholic church as well as unionists and opposition politicians stood to gain from the social tensions that mounted in the region. As the 1982 elections grew nearer, these political trends and the possibility of a bloody clash between the *garimpeiros* and the Kayapó caused the military great concern.

In March 1981 federal authorities reacted by taking charge of Cumaru. Following the example of Serra Pelada, albeit on a smaller scale, roadblocks were set up, and basic services were provided. The area was restricted to those with *garimpeiro* identification cards, and the Caixa Federal, a subsidiary of the official Banco do Brasil, became the exclusive buyer of gold in the *garimpo*. But the geography of Cumaru stood in the way of the attempt to repeat the Serra Pelada experience in Cumaru. Compared to the highly concentrated deposits in Serra Pelada, the widely dispersed alluvial gold fields in Cumaru meant that *garimpeiros* were spread out over a much larger area, which made it exceedingly difficult to bring the *garimpo* under the same degree of centralized control.

The similarities between the two *garimpos* lay in the reasons that prompted the federal government to intervene. In both cases the motivation was predicated on a concern for national security and on a desire to exert political influence in the area. Instead of forming part of a consistent policy agenda, military interventions in the *garimpos* in Amazonia were mainly ad hoc initiatives adopted in response to unexpected political and security crises. In the case of Cumaru, the new relationship that emerged between the state and the mining sector in the 1980s was further complicated by the technological changes that revolutionized the production process in the gold fields. To illustrate the ways technological innovation restructured the traditional *garimpo* and to show how these changes led to new forms of social conflict, we turn to the history of Cuca, one of the smaller gold fields that was part of the Cumaru gold district.

Miners and Machines in Cuca

At the height of the gold rush in southern Pará, prospectors discovered alluvial gold deposits midway between Xinguara and the Xingu river.[25] Among the pioneers in this area was Petrônio Dias Alves, who began searching for gold from Xinguara and Agua Azul in 1978. Another was Ari Navas, a native of Barra do Corda, Goiás, who had worked as a prospector in the *garimpos* of the Tapajós from 1962 to 1974. After a run of bad luck, he moved to Imperatriz where his brother drove a truck for a living. In 1977 he returned to *garimpagem* in the newly opened Rio Branco *garimpo*. When FUNAI expelled the miners from Rio Branco, Ari began to explore other areas. In July of 1979 he set off into the jungle to search the area around the Cabano airstrip built by PROMIX (Produtora de Minérios Xingu, S.A.), a local company that was holding rights to this area in reserve for mechanized mining. The airstrip was located on property that belonged to the Projeto Tucumã colonization company. In February of the following year, in a place about twenty kilometers from PROMIX, Ari found gold in the Jibóia, Ferro, and Júlio creekbeds. The Andrade Gutierrez construction company later built an airstrip nearby and allowed Ari to set up a *cantina* where he controlled commerce in a benign version of the "closed" *garimpos* of the Tapajós. The area Ari discovered became known as the Cuca *garimpo*.

Drawing on his past experience in the Tapajós, Ari was among the first *garimpeiros* in this area to use hydraulic machines called *chupadeiras*. He purchased the equipment in Imperatriz and flew it to Cuca. Because *chupadeiras* were virtually unknown in southern Pará at the time, he brought *garimpeiros* from the Tapajós region to operate them.[26] Ari Navas' innovation started a process of rapid technological change that profoundly altered the organization of gold mining in southern Pará.

In the traditional manual system, workers first cleared the designated claim or "work front" and then dug down to the level of the ore-bearing material or *cascalho*.[27] They reinforced the walls of the pit with tree trunks and palm leaves and built canals to divert stream water. The *cascalho* was then removed with shovels and dumped outside the pit. Next, the work team mounted a sluice box next to the extracted material in order to wash it. This was accomplished by adding water—manually or with the aid of a 3.5 horsepower pump—to the *cascalho* that was poured over the cloth-lined rungs of the box, to catch the valuable ore as it descended. A sieve at the top of the sluice box removed the largest pieces, which were discarded by hand. Skill was required to ensure that the water flowed strongly enough to remove the unwanted material yet slowly enough for gold to cling to the rungs of the sluice box.

At the end of a day's washing (a *puxada*) came the *despescagem*, the removal of material collected in the sluice box. One worker held a *bateia* (a shallow, cone-shaped zinc pan) at the bottom of the box while another carefully removed the rungs one at a time while squeezing out the cloth lining. Water running through the box was controlled by another *garimpeiro*. The gold was heavy and therefore collected in the *bateia* instead of floating away. The man holding the *bateia* controlled the level of water to prevent spillage. If oil or grease had contaminated the water, soap was added to diminish the surface tension between the grease and the fine particles of gold, causing the latter to sink. Periodically material from the *bateia* was dumped into a bucket to be purified later. When the cloth and rungs were all removed, the last of the ore was caught in a small vessel called a *cuia*. Finally, the contents of the bucket and of the *cuia* were purified (*apurado*) by a skilled *garimpeiro* who manipulated the *bateia* with a smooth circular motion to gradually concentrate the gold at the bottom of the zinc pan.

The *chupadeira* system consisted of motorized hydraulic units that more efficiently accomplished the tasks of extraction and washing. There were three components to the system.[28] First, a small, motorized water pump connected to a large hose was used to produce a powerful jet of water used to cut through the river bank. Once the pit had reached the ore-bearing gravel, a second pump sucked the *cascalho* out of the bottom of the pit and piped it into the processing component. This third element of the *chupadeira* system was a metal drum attached to the head of a sluice box, where the *cascalho* was received and processed.

The hydraulic system was based on different skills and a new division of labor among the *garimpeiros* who worked alluvial deposits of gold. One man, the *jateiro* or *pistoleiro*, used the jet of water as a digging tool. A second man, the *maroqueiro*, fed a mixture of water, dirt, and gravel into the suction tube connected to the second water pump. During the digging phase, this discarded material was piped several yards away where it spewed out forming a lake of discarded mud known as *melexete*. Once the pit had reached the level of the ore, the suction tube was hooked up to the sluice box managed by two workers mounted on precarious platforms of sticks. Dirt and gravel poured into the metal drum, which served to slow down the flow of water. Mercury was usually added to the water in the drum. The mercury would cling to the gold, making it heavier and therefore separating it more easily from sand and gravel. One worker, called the *raleiro*, supervised the entry of material into the drum, removing the large rocks caught in the drum's built-in sieve. Another, the *embarcador*, guided a slower stream of water over the rungs of the "long-ton" box (a longer version of the traditional sluice box). As in the traditional system, the gold collected in the cloth that covered the rungs of the sluice box and in the reservoir below the box.

At the end of the day, the *despescagem* and *apuração* took place. Mercury added to the *bateia* in the final *apuração* phase agglutinated the gold. Depending on the characteristics of the particular deposit, this mixture might be washed with vinegar (said to remove the copper impurities) or salt (to make the gold shinier). The gold was wrapped tightly in a cloth and squeezed to remove and recover most of the mercury. The *garimpeiro* then used a butane torch to burn off the remaining mercury, leaving a shiny lump of gold in the bottom of the pan. Generally, few precautions were taken to avoid skin contact with the mercury or to guard against inhaling the toxic fumes released in the final stage of the process.

The *chupadeira* used water power to increase the productivity of the *garimpo*. Greater productivity permitted the expansion of *garimpagem* into less rich areas. The new technology also actually increased the number of people employed in the mining fields. The system required four to six steady workers, sometimes aided by day laborers to yield far more gold per worker than manual techniques. The *chupadeira* modified the traditional system of *garimpeiro* work relations in several ways. Increased capital requirements widened the gap between the owners of the machines and the workers. This reinforced the growing importance of the "*garimpeiro*-entrepreneur" who had sufficient resources to purchase equipment.[29] Specialization among workers led to internal differentiation in skills and earnings. There was also increased use of day workers on a wage basis although nothing approaching the extremes of Serra Pelada. Employment in the *garimpo* became more stable and less variable from one season to the next. These technical and financial changes altered the relationships between workers in the gold fields.

In the traditional system, suppliers paid for the workers' food and provided the minimal equipment necessary (picks, shovels, *bateias*, sluice box, small pumps). The relatively small amount of capital involved meant that the divisions between supplier and worker were minimal.[30] In the Tapajós, for example, there was some degree of mobility between *garimpeiro* and owner, a process that strengthened the sense of identity and solidarity among them.[31] In the traditional *garimpo*, the owner of the claim received 50 percent of the gold produced. If a pump was used, its owner received 10 percent. The remainder was divided equally among the *garimpeiros*.

This began to change in the 1970s largely due to technological change and the increasing costs of gold extraction. Because many *garimpos* were accessible only by airplane, transport costs added significantly to the capital needed by investors. Pilots increasingly came to play a critical role, which allowed them to capture a larger share of the profits and to expand their control over production and commerce. As in other *garimpos*, pilots were often part owners in mining claims in Cuca.[32] With the introduction of the *chupadeira* system, claim owners not only supplied the workers' food but also purchased the expensive equipment. In 1982 and 1983 two sets of motorized pumps and the pipes and tubing that the system required cost between five thousand and eight thousand dollars. In addition, claim owners had to pay for about ten to twenty liters of fuel per day, approximately six liters of lubricating oil, and expenses for repairs and maintenance. Total costs amounted to over one thousand dollars a month.[33]

The distribution of profits also differed in the hydraulic system. Equipment owners took 60 percent, and sometimes more, of the gold produced. *Garimpeiros* working in teams with the *chupadeiras* still divided the remaining product. But the specialization associated with the new technology meant that shares were no longer evenly divided among the team members. Rather, set portions were established according to the job. The more demanding positions, such as *jateiro* or *maroqueiro*, were rewarded with larger shares of the product (7 to 8 percent depending on the size of the work team). A worker who simply removed stones and other debris from the pit might earn 5 to 6 percent, while a cook was generally paid 4 percent of the take. These changes altered the character of the relationships between the men working the claim. Whereas the *meia-praça* was a partner, the *garimpeiro* who worked for a percentage was considered an employee.[34] Day workers were also occasionally hired for some construction and earthmoving tasks, but wage work was not predominant in Cuca as it was in Serra Pelada. In the latter, the peculiar characteristics of the deposit led to a reliance on the ubiquitous *formigas* to carry the excavated material manually away from the work areas.

The high cost of the hydraulic system led to a degree of capital accumulation in Cuca that was greater than that in the traditional *garimpo* but not nearly as extreme as in Serra Pelada. In 1983 most owners used one or two *chupadeiras* although one individual owned eighteen claims worked by 110 men.[35] By May of 1984, when production in Cuca began to decline from its peak the year before, about two hundred claims were being worked. Three-quarters of the sites were concentrated in two principal creekbeds. *Chupadeiras* were used on about 80 percent of the claims. Nearly two thousand *garimpeiros* were employed in Cuca, and the number of machines totalled about three hundred.[36]

The use of *chupadeiras* soon spread throughout the *garimpos* in southeastern Pará, at least in those deposits that permitted their use; *chupadeiras* were banned in Serra Pelada. DNPM technicians in charge of the Cumaru area promoted the new technology.[37] Until the end of 1981 the work in Cumaru had essentially been manual. By then about half of the principal areas had already been exhausted. A large volume of alluvial material of lower quality remained that could only be worked using the semimechanized hydraulic method. Moreover, the *chupadeiras*, which required abundant water, could be used during the rainy season when the large volume of water in the creeks exceeded the capacity of the smaller pumps used in the traditional system. These considerations led DNPM to promote the replacement of conventional manual methods with the more productive technology beginning in 1982.

DNPM initially limited the machines to areas that had already been worked manually, but this restriction was later dropped. By June of 1982 there were forty-five *chupadeiras* operating in Cumaru, employing twenty-two hundred people. They had produced forty-three kilos of gold in that year.[38] The number of machines rose to 327 by December of 1982.[39] By the end of the next year 1,616 hydraulic units operated in Cumaru, providing jobs for some sixteen thousand *garimpeiros*. Beginning in March of 1981, when federal intervention in Cumaru took place, official production in Cumaru rose from 1,707 kilos (March to December of 1981) to 1,912 kilos in 1982. A year later the production amounted to 6,383 kilos of gold.[40]

Mining companies bitterly disputed the way the DNPM chose to deal with the technological changes underway in the *garimpo*. As far as the mining companies were concerned, the use of the more productive *chupadeiras* meant that the *garimpeiros* were in reality engaged in mechanized rather than manual operations.

The distinction was important because of the legal statutes that governed the mining sector. According to Brazilian law, mechanized mining was subject to a host of requirements that did not apply to traditional, manually operated extraction. By allowing the *garimpeiros* to use machinery, the companies claimed that the DNPM was permitting the *garimpeiros* to avoid the regulations that properly applied to them. The effect, the companies argued, was to discourage investments from the formal mining sector.

The DNPM, on the other hand, based its policy on different grounds. As early as 1977, with the creation of Projeto Garimpo, many of the DNPM's technicians sided with the *garimpeiros* who resisted attempts by mining companies to take over production. By 1984 DNPM technicians defended their pro-*garimpeiro* stance as a means to combat the potential "social tensions" that arose among a poorly educated population that was vulnerable to "demagogic ideas" and unscrupulous vote-hunters.[41] From the perspective of DNPM, the increasing use of *chupadeiras* was a welcome development inasmuch as it increased the employment capacity of the gold fields.

The rise in productivity associated with the new technology thus did much more than change the division of labor and the social relations of production within the *garimpo*. Technological innovations blurred the distinction between formal-mechanized and traditional-manual production, thereby raising legal ambiguities that have yet to be clarified. Moreover, the equipment and the capital required by the new methods transformed the relationship between mining and other sectors of the regional economy and brought about different forms of conflict in the gold fields of southern Pará.

Mining Conflict in Cuca

Before the PA-279 highway reached the Tucumã colonization project, the Cuca *garimpo* was accessible only via the Cabano airstrip that PROMIX had built. The company had been licensed since 1977 to extract cassiterite from two thousand hectares of the upper Rio Branco basin.[42] After staking claim to production rights in the tin fields, PROMIX extended its research rights to a larger area of 6,143 hectares through licenses issued in 1978 and 1980. The strategy of claiming more land than the company could reasonably expect to work was common practice in Amazonia. It granted the license holder the legal basis for taking control of mineral deposits *garimpeiros* might discover.

When Ari Navas and other prospectors discovered gold in nearby Cuca, PROMIX found it profitable to sell its mineral rights to another company, Mineração Ouro Norte, in 1983. Like PROMIX, Ouro Norte was a small company with little mining experience.[43] In addition to securing the mining rights from PROMIX, Ouro Norte also purchased land in the Tucumã colonization area. The problem facing the company was how to deal with the thousands of *garimpeiros* who by then were well established in Cuca.

In January of 1984 Ouro Norte hired fifteen men as security guards and began the risky business of moving heavy equipment into the Cuca area. The *garimpeiros* claimed that the guards threatened a massacre if the miners failed to move on. Other allegations blamed the Ouro Norte men of injuring a child when they fired their guns in an attempt to intimidate the *garimpeiros*. A few days later, a helicopter arrived from Cumaru carrying DNPM technicians and company representatives under the protection of federal police. The guards denied any wrongdoing, while the Ouro Norte staff reiterated the company's legal right to the area.[44] The precise details of what took place at this point in the story remain unclear, but there was little doubt that tempers ran high in Cuca the moment that Ouro Norte threatened to evict the miners from the area.

The actions the *garimpeiros* in Cuca took to defend themselves resembled what had happened in Serra Pelada although on a much smaller scale. In March a delegation of the National Garimpeiro's Union arrived in Cuca. Union representatives enlisted new members and secured agreements with many of the claim owners to hire only unionized workers. The union sent telegrams to the minister of Mines and Energy and to the minister of Social Welfare in Brasília protesting the DNPM's decision to extend the company's mineral rights for another two years. The messages noted that it was the *garimpeiros* who had discovered the Cuca deposits and that in any case the license that Ouro Norte had purchased from PROMIX applied to tin, not to gold. By May 1984, when the union had recruited about two hundred members in Cuca, the *garimpeiros* enlisted the support of federal deputy Haroldo Bezerra. In a speech to the state legislature, Bezerra denounced the speculative activities of outside mining companies (Ouro Norte's office was in Brasília) that had blanketed the southern Pará region with research licenses for huge areas that they had no intention of actually exploring.[45]

As in Serra Pelada, the mining dispute in Cuca mobilized people in nearby towns. Merchants and farmers in Tucumã and Ourilândia opposed the expulsion of the *garimpeiros* because the miners were of direct economic benefit to the community.[46] Whereas the *garimpo* employed several thousand workers, the mining company hired only about forty people. Even if Cuca were completely turned over to Ouro Norte, the operation would provide jobs for only about two hundred workers. Moreover, the semimechanized *garimpo*—unlike the enclave character of corporate mining activities—generated a brisk commerce in machines, diesel fuel, and other supplies and services that benefited a wide range of people outside of the mining camp itself.

Wary of a dangerous confrontation with the *garimpeiros*, the Ouro Norte staff decided to take charge of Cuca by increments. The miners countered every move. The company first built a small dam that diverted the water from one of the areas where *garimpeiros* were working. The *garimpeiros* responded by pressuring DNPM to force the company to build a spillway that would provide the necessary water for the miners to continue their excavations.[47] In April of 1984 Ouro Norte then tried to remove some of the miners' equipment and replace it with its own. This second action was more than the *garimpeiros* were willing to tolerate. The incident provoked a violent response that resulted in the shooting death of three of the company's security guards. The federal police moved in to confiscate weapons from the *garimpeiros*, but no one was arrested. The exact circumstances of the killings were never clarified. Ouro Norte immediately halted its operations in Cuca. The company withdrew altogether at the end of 1984.[48] The incident reportedly was Brazil's first case of violent death resulting from a conflict between *garimpeiros* and a mining company.

Farmers, Miners, and the Southern Pará Frontier

By the mid-1980s mining had become an integral part of the economic and political life of southern Pará. At the height of the gold rush, the influx of small farmers into the region was already well underway and may even have begun to slacken somewhat. The lure of the gold fields stimulated an additional wave of migrants who found employment in urban centers and in *garimpos* that sprang up in remote areas of the countryside. The discovery of gold and other valued minerals increased the size of the frontier population and radically changed its spatial distribution.

The rapid growth of Serra Pelada and Cumaru prompted novel forms of federal intervention in Amazonia. The initiatives undertaken by the security forces and federal mining agencies were in many respects uniquely tailored to the *garimpos*. But there were also striking parallels between the land and mining policies that the military regime carried out in the region. In both cases federal action was predicated to one degree or another on a concern for national security and on an attempt to elicit grassroots political support from the local population. From this perspective, both GETAT's crisis colonization policy as well as the DNPM's decision to allow *garimpeiros* to work the gold fields were outcomes of the military populism the regime pursued in the late 1970s and early 1980s in its unsuccessful attempt to offset its declining political legitimacy.

In Pará, the banking system, the financial markets, and the patterns of investments were reshaped by the gold rush. Serra Pelada—which was less than half a square kilometer in size—was closely tied to the economies of the nearby cities of Marabá, Imperatriz, and Araguaina. These municipalities benefited from the increased taxes they received from mining. The head of the Chamber of Commerce in Imperatriz estimated that half of the town's four thousand registered businesses owned a share in the *garimpo*. Many more benefited from the business the gold economy generated.[49] Serra Pelada and the other *garimpos* affected farmers, truck and taxi drivers, merchants, bankers, politicians, and others who competed for their share of the extraordinary flow of wealth in the region. The benefits from the gold economy spread throughout the regional economy although, over time, the resources became concentrated in the hands of a relatively small group of investors.

The *garimpos* stimulated the demand for goods and services and provided a market for the foodstuffs that small farmers produced. Gold mining thus became closely intertwined with the process of land settlement in the region, often in the wake of tense confrontations between various interest groups. Administrators of the Tucumã colonization project, for example, initially tried to keep *garimpeiros* out of the project area (see chapter 7). The miners who gathered just outside the security gate contributed to the founding of the town that later came to be known as Ourilândia ("Goldland").[50] When *garimpeiros* gained access to land inside of Tucumã in the early 1980s, the population of Ourilândia continued to grow as a consequence of the influx of small farmers in search of land. In the meantime, the colonization company ceded urban lots to the mining community in Cuca. The new settlement became a permanent part of the Tucumã project and a source of income to small farmers who sold rice and beans to the *garimpeiros*.

The gold fields also provided jobs to people who otherwise would have been unemployed. *Garimpeiros* were drawn from the general population of small farmers, rural workers, and small-scale merchants. "Professional" *garimpeiros*—those who spent a lifetime moving from one *garimpo* to another—were a minority. In one of the few studies of its kind, a survey of Poxoréo in Mato Grosso found that only 15 percent cited mining as their sole occupation. The majority combined mining with work in agriculture.[51] In southern Pará, the gold rush attracted migrants from the surrounding area. Many had been employed as wage laborers on ranches or in urban areas. Small-scale merchants and farmers with their own plots of land often worked in the *garimpos* on a seasonal basis.

Many migrants had come to southern Pará in the hope of acquiring their own piece of land only to find that most of the territory was claimed by large landowners. The *garimpo* presented a means of earning the money it took to hold on a little longer. Other *garimpeiros* migrated from the Northeast to escape the prolonged drought that beset the region. In government-controlled Cumaru, the majority of *garimpeiros* were migrants from the neighboring state of Maranhão. When the rainy season interrupted work in the *garimpo*, many returned to Maranhão, only to come back to Pará after the rains subsided.[52] As a result, the *garimpeiro* population fluctuated from an average of twenty thousand in the peak summer months of 1982 to only three thousand during the height of the rainy season in January and February. The constant movement in and out of mining areas contributed to the fluidity of the region's already complicated migration patterns.

The *garimpo* was an attractive alternative to those unable to find land or a job.[53] The gold fields also offered the bright, if unlikely, prospect of striking it rich. While a few fortunes were made, especially in Serra Pelada, the Cumaru deposits yielded modest returns typical of the southeastern Pará gold zone. *Garimpeiros* in Cumaru earned an average of three times the regional minimum salary.[54] Even the unskilled *formigas* in Serra Pelada earned far more than the wages available elsewhere.[55] For those working as *meia-praças*, the gold fields offered the kind of work that eliminated most living expenses. Furthermore, in contrast to working clearing land for ranchers—with the dreaded *jagunço* (security guard or hired gun) as overseer—mining offered a greater degree of independence.

The *garimpo* was a mixed blessing for the southern Pará region. The gold economy contributed to local development, but it also undermined other activities. If mining provided men a much-needed source of income to help finance their family's economic future, their absence left women and children to fend for themselves. The lure of the gold fields often undermined the already precarious stability of family relations and stimulated prostitution. Similarly, mining provided an avenue for upward mobility and served as a refuge for the landless and unemployed, but it did little to resolve the underlying problem of unequal access to land.

The malaria epidemic that came in the wake of the gold rush presented another threat to the well-being and productivity of the region's population. The increasing use of hydraulic methods contributed to the deterioration of health conditions for *garimpeiros* and people living in nearby communities because the abandoned pits filled with stagnant water that served as a breeding place for malarial mosquitoes. In 1982 there were nearly seventeen thousand cases of malaria in Marabá and Conceição do Araguaia. In the Cumaru district alone, twenty thousand cases were reported by 1986.[56]

A 1984 survey of 388 miners in four *garimpos* within the Tucumã colonization project found that 66 percent suffered at least one occurrence of malaria; 62 percent reported more than one episode.[57] The longer the time spent in the *garimpo*, the higher the probability of contracting the disease. Income was also positively correlated with reported cases, suggesting that *garimpeiros* working in more profitable areas ran a higher health risk. The average case of malaria cost the miner 5.9 working days. To retain his share of production a stricken worker had to pay a substitute to take his place. The going wage was approximately ten thousand cruzeiros per day—considerably higher than the median expected income share of Cr$4,667 per day. With medical expenses added to the estimate, the cost of an average bout with the disease came to 12 percent of the miner's average salary for the eight-month dry season, or to a total amount of $50,758 for the whole mining community. In 1988 and 1989 a special program by the public health agency, SUCAM, contributed to a decline in malaria in the Tucumã and São Felix mining areas, but the disease was far from eradicated.

The *garimpeiro* population and the wide network of people with vested interests in the gold fields introduced new issues and new actors into the arena of local, state, and national politics. In the countryside, the contest between *garimpeiros* and mining companies and confrontations between miners and Indians brought to life new forms of social antagonism. The conflicts were made all the more complex by the technological changes that increased the productivity of the production process and that revolutionized the social relations within the *garimpo*. Increased productivity blurred the distinction between formal and traditional mining activities, thereby raising a number of intractable issues that played themselves out in the legal system and administrative bureaucracies at all levels of government.

Despite direct federal intervention—in some ways, because of it—the conflicts over land and mineral resources in southern Pará were far from resolved by 1985 when the military turned over political power to a civilian president. Subsequent democratic regimes faced a legacy of intense violence, increasing political mobilization, and a general mistrust of government mediation among the farmers and miners in southern Pará. How these issues played themselves out in the specific context of São Felix do Xingu is the topic of the third and final part of this book.

NOTES

1. Gold mining in southern Pará began in the 1960s inside the Gorotire Indian reserve when pelters stalking the prized spotted jaguar found traces of gold on the right bank of the Rio Fresco, a tributary of the Rio Branco (Lestra and Nardi 1982:168). After they were expelled from Indian areas in the late 1970s, *garimpeiros* explored nearby prospects, including the Cabano airstrip, which functioned like the "closed" *garimpos* in the Tapajós. Operating from these small airstrips and from the ranches and frontier towns, prospectors began to penetrate every corner of southern Pará in the late 1970s.

2. These figures are from the first chapter of David Cleary's (1990) book, *Anatomy of the Amazon Gold Rush*.

3. DNPM (1982a:33).

4. The exact circumstances of the discovery are not known. According to one version, gold was first discovered by a *garimpeiro* panning a streambed on the Três Barras ranch. Another claims that the ranch owner, Genésio, contracted a geologist to examine his land after hearing of gold strikes in nearby areas (see Cleary 1990; Kotscho 1984). Whatever the precise details, there remains little doubt that this was one of the largest deposits of gold ever discovered in Brazil and that the gold rush that followed was the greatest extractive enterprise in Amazonia since the rubber boom.

5. See the account in *Veja*, 7 August 1985.

6. DNPM (1982c). Even traditional forms of generosity were co-opted. In Serra Pelada, Curió used the traditional *reque* as a populist tactic, granting license to some thirty-five hundred miners to reclean the *cascalho* that had been worked during 1980. The recleaning process improved the efficiency of mining in Serra Pelada, reducing the gold found in rejected gravel to only .4 to .7 grams per ton (Guimarães et al. 1982).

7. *O Liberal*, 1 December 1983.

8. A *garimpeiro* interviewed in 1986 by Gay Biery-Hamilton described five different claims he had worked there in different ways. First, he and five companions dug a pit down ten meters before hitting sand. The federal police prohibited them from further digging for safety reasons, so they had to start again elsewhere. Working with ten other men in a new area, he found a modest amount of gold at a depth of nine meters, but then got sick and had to leave the *garimpo* for treatment. In his absence, his partners sold the claim and left. His third attempt, working with one other man as a partner over a two-month period

similarly produced no gold. Next he hired on with a patron for a five percent share and was forced to see the work through to protect his meager share of another weak claim. Finally, he invested his own capital to buy twelve percent of a claim that he hoped would be more profitable. Such stories were typical of the fluid nature of mining relations in the uncertain Pará setting.

9. *Informe Amazônico* 1 (3) 16–30 October 1980:4–5.

10. Kotscho (1984:18–19).

11. *A Província do Pará*, 21 September 1983.

12. *O Liberal*, 24 August 1983.

13. *O Liberal*, 17 September 1983.

14. *O Liberal*, 14 September 1983.

15. Kotscho (1984:72).

16. Although the Serra Pelada *garimpeiros* accused DNPM officials of sabotaging their work, DNPM reports in 1982 and 1983 questioned the wisdom of closing the *garimpo*. In 1982 they predicted that closing Serra Pelada would cause "social tensions" and provoke invasions by *garimpeiros* all over the Carajás area (DNPM 1982c). The following year the team's annual report recommended that a reconstruction effort would provide more long-term support for the *garimpo* (DNPM 1983b).

17. *Correio Brasiliense*, 16 October 1983.

18. DNPM technicians also questioned the methods used to calculate the indemnification for CVRD, a fixed amount based on the 9.6 kilos of gold the company expected to extract from the area (*Folha de São Paulo*, 13 June 1984). In their view this estimate was too high.

19. The members of congress made some of their own changes that were not to the president's liking, however. They established a ceiling on the amount of indemnification and conditioned payment on proof that sufficient gold could be found in CVRD's area. Figueiredo opposed this amendment because of the limitations it placed on the receipt of full reimbursement for CVRD.

20. *Diário do Pará*, 8 June 1984.

21. Cleary (1990:184).

22. Cleary (1990:181).

23. *Diário do Carajás*, 30 May 1981.

24. Cleary (1990:Table 1.2).

25. Typically, there are different accounts of the discovery and opening up of any *garimpo*. This discussion draws on interviews by the authors and an interview with Ari Navas in 1984, taped by John Butler.

26. Hydraulic mining techniques, which had also been important in the California gold rush, dated from the nineteenth century when they replaced simple panning on the surface (Eaken 1985:13).

27. DNPM (1982b:16–17).

28. Vale and Pereira (1983:234).

29. Salomão (1984:65) and Cleary (1990).

30. Cleary (1990).

31. Salomão (1981:41–42).

32. Butler (1985:73).

33. DNPM (1982a).

34. Lazarin and Rabelo (1984:115).

35. Ferreira (1984:20).

36. Calculated from field notes of Afonso Borges Ferreira (1984).

37. DNPM (1982a:10–12).

38. DNPM (1982a:14).

39. DNPM (1982b:32).

40. DNPM (1982a, 1982b, 1983a).

41. Carvalho (1981) and Willig (1979:38); see also DNPM (1982b:34).

42. PROMIX was the only mining company operating in the area that had origins in the region itself. It was founded by two merchants who invested the capital they had accumulated through the export business in a new diversified enterprise that continued to operate out of their storefront in the Porto do Sal zone of Belém. In an interview conducted there in 1980, one of the owners described the company's history. Their firm began as a tile company in 1966 and in doing research on ceramics was led to become involved in mining in the Xingu area. In 1970 the company took the name PROMIX and became exclusively a mining company. The firm was like many Amazonian ventures in having little previous experience in mining.

43. Mineração Ouro Norte was not registered as a mining enterprise until October of 1983.

44. From field notes of Afonso Borges Ferreira (1984).

45. From field notes of Afonso Borges Ferreira (1984).

46. Butler (1985:104).

47. Butler (1985:104).

48. Butler (1985:104). In August of 1986 Tucumã witnessed another violent confrontation when a local merchant attempted to claim the land occupied by the Manelão and Gavião *garimpos* near Cuca. José Ferreira da Silva was known as "Zé dos Motores" because of his successful business in the town of Tucumã selling machines for the mining operations. Using a falsified map, he convinced a local judge to issue a court order expelling five thousand *garimpeiros* and sixty families of *posseiros* from the area he claimed (MIRAD 1986:31–32). A detachment of 150 military police from São Felix do Xingu, Conceição do Araguaia, and Xinguara apprehended the miners' tools and occupied the area to impede further work. The incident ended tragically a few days later when Zé dos Motores was shot down and killed on the street of Tucumã after an argument with the police.

49. *O Liberal*, 11 June 1984.

50. The place, first known as Gurita—named after the infamous gate that kept miners and others out of the project—and later called Ourilândia, is today, known as Ourilândia do Norte.

51. Baxter (1975:193,211).

52. DNPM (1982b).

53. Baxter (1975:232,354).

54. DNPM (1982b:5).

55. *Informe Amazônico* 5, 16–31 November 1980.

56. Palmquist (1986:38).

57. Vosti (n. d.). These figures underestimated the impact of malaria since they did not include indirect and long-term costs, and the sample probably omitted seriously ill miners who were hospitalized or undergoing treatment elsewhere.

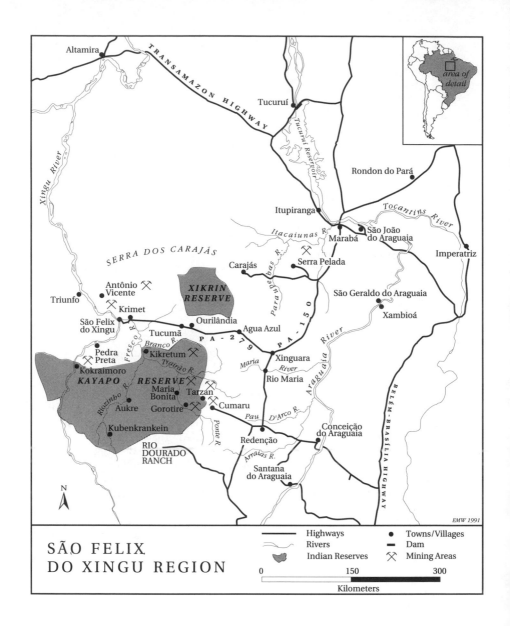

SÃO FELIX
DO XINGU REGION

Highways	Towns/Villages
Rivers	Dam
Indian Reserves	Mining Areas

0   150   300

Kilometers

3

❖

São Felix do Xingu

Part Three shows how the events documented in parts one and two of this book played themselves out in São Felix do Xingu, located at the end of the PA-279. Because of the early and significant presence of indigenous and nonindigenous peoples in the region, São Felix differed from other frontier towns in southern Pará, such as Xinguara, Tucumã, and Ourilândia. Chapter 9 recounts the remarkable history of the Kayapó, how they drew on their warrior tradition to expand their land claims and how they rose to international visibility as political actors in defense of Indian rights and the environment. The expansion of national political and economic institutions into São Felix—punctuated by the disputes over land, timber, and gold described in chapter 10—effectively closed off resources to migrants who made their way to São Felix in search of a better life. Chapter 11 draws on survey data to analyze the background characteristics of the migrant population and to measure the consequences of frontier change on the life chances of people in São Felix do Xingu.

NINE

❖

The Kayapó and the Battle for the Xingu

Contests over the land and the natural resources of the middle Xingu river basin began well before roads and airstrips penetrated the area in the 1970s and 1980s. The first major battles were fought over one hundred years ago between settlers and a remarkable group of Indians called the Kayapó—a warrior tribe whose people survived long after many other groups had perished. Beginning in the 1970s the Kayapó waged a successful campaign to secure the borders of their territory, and in so doing they underwent a rapid process of cultural transformation. Once a barely organized collection of village groups with little tradition of tribal unity, they emerged as articulate and internationally known leaders of a powerful indigenous movement in Amazonia. Through sophisticated political negotiations and the skilled use of the media, the Kayapó were successful in securing—even expanding—the borders of their territory. They played a leading role in the past history of contested frontiers in São Felix do Xingu, and there is every reason to suspect that the Kayapó will continue to do so in the future.

The Northern Kayapó

The first inhabitants of the middle Araguaia, Tocantins, and Xingu river basins that make up southern Pará were primarily tribes belonging to the Gê-speaking plains Indians of Brazil's central plateau.[1] Chavante and Cherente groups occupied the Araguaia-Tocantins headwaters. The Krahó, Apinagé, Gaviões, and Canela settled near the confluence of the two rivers while two groups of Kayapó occupied areas to the south and north of the point where the rivers met. Descendants of the northern Kayapó now inhabit the two reserves in the area influenced by the PA-279 highway.[2]

During the gold rush in Mato Grosso and Goiás in the early eighteenth century, the southern Kayapó clashed with miners in camps along the Araguaia-Tocantins river system. Beginning in the 1770s cattlemen traveled the Tocantins river in search of the natural grasslands believed to stretch from that river to the Xingu.[3] The warrior tribes that inhabited the area were a formidable obstacle to the settlers' westward expansion. Efforts to entice the Kayapó, Chavante, and other tribes to live in "model villages" along the Tocantins constituted the "most important official attempt to settle Indians anywhere in Brazil during the Directorate period."[4] But the experiment failed. By the end of the Directorate period, fighting continued between Indians and settlers, mainly along the road opened between Goiás and Cuiabá. Forts were established at Alcobaça (now Tucuruí) in 1780 and at São João das Duas Barras, a site at the junction of the Araguaia and Tocantins rivers, in 1797. A fort called Santa Maria, located along the main rapids on the Araguaia, was destroyed three times by the Indians, in 1813, 1852, and 1861.

By the 1830s the Krahó, Apinagé, and Timbira had been subdued and their lands invaded, never to be regained.[5] More belligerent tribes, like the Chavante and Kayapó, continued to resist, moving westward to relative safety beyond the Araguaia river. In 1850 there were reportedly three groups of northern Kayapó.[6] The largest was the Gradaús tribe, which consisted of some three thousand members, living along the Araguaia river. The first to split off from the Gradaús settlement were the Xikrin, whose five hundred members settled at the headwaters of the Itacaiunas River.[7]

The threats posed by the cattle frontier and by missionaries were greatest for the Gradaús group, also known as the Ira-am-ranirea. Beginning in the midnineteenth century, church and state authorities encouraged missionaries to assist in "pacifying" the Indians. Friar Gil Vilanova, a thirty-seven-year-old Dominican from Marseilles, attempted to contact the southern Kayapó as early as 1888. A few years later, in 1891 and 1896, he was more successful in winning the trust of the northern Kayapó. In 1897 he performed the first mass at Conceição do Araguaia—the mission he founded on a bluff overlooking the Araguaia river. Five hundred Kayapó from the Gradaús group moved to a site one kilometer away. The new mission also attracted a thousand white settlers, many of them refugees from the civil wars that had erupted in Maranhão and Goiás after the proclamation of the Republic in 1889.[8]

A second French priest, Guillaume Vigneau, arrived in 1898 to assist with the mission work. In the early 1900s the mission relied on the financial support that Friar Gil mustered on his annual trips to Belém, where he carried Kayapó artifacts to sell in the city. A few years later, malaria claimed the lives of both priests. Vigneau died in 1903 and Vilanova in 1905. The settlement of Conceição do Araguaia they had founded persisted (see chapter 5), but the Indians were not so fortunate. By 1921 only one Gradaús village remained. The tribe's population dwindled to about thirty individuals in 1940. The last surviving Gradaús Kayapó died in 1960.[9]

The Xingu

The Xingu River—one of the major tributaries of the Amazon—lies some three hundred kilometers to the west of the Araguaia-Tocantins basin. Early in the seventeenth century, Jesuits had established *aldeamentos* along the river's lower reaches. Rapids impeded river travel any farther upstream. By the time the first explorers penetrated into the middle and upper Xingu searching for rubber in the late nineteenth century, all the other major tributaries of the Amazon had long since been explored and mapped.[10]

Authorities were under growing pressure to pacify the Indians who stood in the way of access to the grasslands that settlers found along the Pau D'Arco and Arraias rivers at the site of present-day Redenção. In 1896 an expedition set out from the fledgling settlement of Itacayuna (near present-day Marabá; see chapter 5) in search of grasslands. Their report that vast savannas had been discovered—in fact, they end long before reaching the Xingu—led to the first proposal for a road link to the river, an idea that did not become reality for nearly a century. The expedition nonetheless discovered rich stands of *caucho* trees (*Castillea ulei*).

The middle reaches of the Xingu river were inhabited by the Gorotire Kayapó, who settled along the Fresco river and its tributary, the Ponte.[11] At the turn of the century most of them reportedly lived in one large village in the southern part of what is today the Kayapó reserve.[12] Feuds between the different groups of the northern Kayapó—who referred to themselves as the Me-bêngôkre, or "people from the water's source"—contributed to their dispersal in the early twentieth century.[13] In 1905 the original village (Pyka-Toti) broke up and part of the group—the Mek-rãgnoti—moved westward to the Iriri River, where they were later joined by other Kayapó.

The Rubber Boom

With the discovery of rubber along the Xingu, the various groups of Kayapó found their new homelands invaded by rubber tappers. The first ground route to the Xingu from Conceição do Araguaia was opened in 1908, and hostilities against the Gorotire began later the same year.[14] Tappers led by Antônio Firmino attacked twice and succeeded on the second attempt in destroying a Kayapó village. Indian hunters from the Araguaia reportedly threw their bloodied victims into a nearby river that came to be known as Rio Vermelho, or "Red River."[15] It was from the rubber tappers that the warrior Kayapó acquired their first guns. The Kayapó began annual attacks on the inhabitants along the Xingu, Araguaia, and Fresco rivers, frequently kidnapping women and children.

At the turn of the twentieth century, the river basin was under the control of the powerful Altamira rubber merchant and supplier José Porfírio de Miranda, who controlled the strategic confluence of the Xingu and Amazon rivers.[16] José Porfírio, a colonel in the now-extinct National Guard, was born in Piauí but had lived much of his life in Bahia. One of the Bahians he recruited to help control his expanding empire was Tancredo Martins Jorge—also a former National Guard colonel—who arrived in Pará in 1900 to set up a rubber trading post on the island of Ilhota near present-day São Felix. After a flood in 1914 wiped out the entrepôt, the settlement was moved to its present location at the confluence of the Xingu and Fresco rivers. The place was named after the image of Saint Felix that Colonel Tancredo brought to his new *barra-cão*.[17]

With José Porfírio's backing, Tancredo became one of the most powerful rubber barons in the region. For over a decade he exercised monopoly control over as many as two thousand rubber gatherers, or *machadinhos*, named after the small ax the tappers used.[18] In the brutal style of the day, Tancredo used his *capangas* to enforce his rule and to meet his every wish. On one occasion, Tancredo's men kidnapped the wife of a tapper named Sepaúba, forcibly delivering the beautiful woman to their boss. Several years later Tancredo paid for his deed when Sepaúba ambushed Tancredo and put a bullet through his former patron. Luis Santana—São Felix's self-taught historian—described the Sepaúba affair to us in great detail in an interview with him in 1984. The incident, Santana explained, illustrates the power the rubber barons wielded in the region. It was a time, he said, when the "law in the Xingu rested on Article 44." He was referring to the forty-four caliber gun, the preferred weapon of the day.

But by the end of the rubber boom, Tancredo's hold over the region was already beginning to slip. The overland cattle trail to Conceição do Araguaia provided an alternate supply line to São Felix that permitted the entry of migrants and of meat and other merchandise that bypassed the colonel's hold over transportation and commerce. In early 1915 health problems caused Tancredo to travel to Bahia, where he was hospitalized for a time. In his absence—which was longer than expected—a rumor started that Tancredo had broken relations with Porfírio and had disappeared for good. Competition between rivals seeking to take over Tancredo's operation led to a period of intense violence that ended only when he returned.

In 1918 Tancredo in fact had a falling out with José Porfírio. During a heated discussion in Altamira, Porfírio, backed by a legion of bookkeepers, demanded that Tancredo immediately settle accounts. When Tancredo claimed that he owed nothing, Porfírio took steps to appropriate all of Tancredo's possessions. Tancredo returned to the Xingu to collect the thirty-five tons of rubber still owed him by collectors. When Porfírio heard that Tancredo had arrived in Altamira with a boatload of rubber to sell, he sent twenty of his men to seize all the merchandise. Tancredo returned to the Xingu, where he died penniless in 1920. In the 1980s his heirs were still fighting in court to gain title to the lands that the colonel had once claimed.

Warfare and Pacification

With the decline of the rubber trade, productive activities diversified in São Felix, as they did in other parts of Pará. Supplied by *aviadores* in Altamira, gatherers collected Brazil nuts in the "free" *castanhais* along the Rio Fresco during the rainy season from January through May. One Major Basílio Lima is said to have been the first to begin trade in Brazil nuts in 1927.[19] By 1940 the nonindigenous population along the Xingu had fallen to a few hundred people engaged in the collection of latex and Brazil nuts.[20] By then most of the rubber barons had died, and the few who remained had little power. A dozen or so *regatões* disputed the meager profits to be made from supplying the *caboclos* living up and down the riversides.

During the 1930s and 1940s contacts between the Kayapó and the *castanheiros* intensified. The increased interaction with outsiders and the deadly consequences of the spread of European diseases that came with it further contributed to the tendency for villages to divide.[21] In 1936 one group of Kayapó left the main village of Kubenkrankein and formed a separate village that took the ancestral name of Gorotire. Armed conflicts between Kubenkrankein villagers and settlers led in 1940 to the formation of a yet another village, called Kokraimoro.[22] The three villages— Kubenkrankein, Gorotire, and Kokraimoro—still survived in the 1980s, but by then their location and composition had changed.

The Kayapó themselves sometimes initiated the contacts with white settlers that eventually led to their "pacification."[23] Warfare, disease, and village divisions had so undermined the subsistence of Gorotire that 844 Indians approached the small community of Nova Olinda at the confluence of the Fresco and Riozinho tributaries in 1937.[24] Although the Indians had long been using European clothes and weapons, glass beads, axes, and cooking pots, this was their first direct contact with alcohol and prostitution.[25] By 1941 a church publication in Conceição reported that the previous decade had seen the death of about fifty settlers and the kidnapping of an equal number of white children.[26]

It was during this period that missionaries and government authorities established a firmer presence in the Kayapó area. Between 1931 and 1935 the bishop of Conceição do Araguaia, Friar Sebastião Thomas, traveled three times to the Rio Fresco to make contact with the Kayapó. Beginning in 1934 priests from the newly established Prelazia in Altamira also began regular journeys along the Xingu, Riozinho, and Iriri rivers to perform baptisms and marriages in the riverside communities.[27] The first permanent contact with the Kayapó was made in 1937 by Father Eurico Krautler. Brazil's Indian Protection Service (SPI) established the Gorotire Indian Post in 1938, the same year that Englishman Horace Banner of the World Evangelical Mission established a well-equipped settlement near Nova Olinda. Banner remained in the Xingu for nearly forty years in an attempt to "civilize" the Kayapó and convert them to his religion.

The 1940s saw an increased demand for natural latex and renewed hostilities against the Kayapó villages. With the participation of the United States government, many of the old *seringais* along the Xingu were revived—this time with direct subsidies from the Banco de Crédito da Borracha (BCB), which took the place of the patrons who had once stood at the top of the *aviamento* hierarchy (see chapter 2). The population of the Xingu grew once again as "rubber soldiers" recruited under the Washington Accords moved into the region. For a brief period the region's rubber trade provided a new source of power for the merchants who controlled the rubber-producing areas.

The revival of rubber extraction during World War II brought new threats to the Xingu Kayapó. Many of those in the Kubenkrankein village were induced to extract rubber and Brazil nuts for local traders. The activity so interfered with their subsistence agriculture that the SPI had to distribute food to the villagers.[28] Conflicts with settlers and rubber tappers intensified in the 1940s, but the outcomes were no longer as one-sided as they had once been. By now the Indians were more experienced and better armed than they had been during the first rubber boom period. Indeed, many of their attacks against whites had the specific purpose of obtaining firearms.[29] In response, the rubber traders appealed to authorities to supply them with rifles to defend themselves. It was a time when interethnic conflicts became more widespread and more openly hostile in this region than they were anywhere else in the country.

Starting in 1945 the rubber traders mounted an attack on the Indian protection agency.[30] Reports surfaced in the press accusing the SPI of furnishing guns to the Kayapó. The Indians were described as a semiwesternized group who spoke Portuguese and were accustomed to handling firearms. In the eyes of those involved in the rubber trade, the Indians amounted to little more than "semicivilized bandits." SPI personnel countered that the Indians only responded in kind to the violence visited upon them by the rubber tappers. The SPI further charged that the rubber traders were simply using the Indians as a scapegoat for their own low productivity and inability to repay bank loans.

After the wartime rubber effort ended, interethnic conflicts dragged on. In the early 1950s several state and federal commissions were formed to study the Kayapó problem.[31] President Getúlio Vargas himself met with the Xingu rubber traders, and land concessions were discussed in the national Congress. In 1953 the new SPVEA program for Amazon development was created (see chapter 2), and funds were allocated to support the pacification effort proposed by anthropologist Darcy Ribeiro of the SPI. Airstrips were built in the area as well as radio and telegraph facilities. When the SPI was brought into the Ministry of Agriculture in the mid-1950s, new administrators were recruited among politicians and military officers with little experience or sympathy for Indian affairs. Dedicated anthropologists like Ribeiro left the agency because it became increasingly hostile to indigenous interests. By the 1960s the SPI had become a public disgrace and was replaced by the National Indian Foundation, FUNAI (see chapter 3).

During the 1940s and 1950s more than half of the contacted Indians died. Mounting evidence showed that rather than those who had become "pacified" it was the more hostile Kayapó groups that survived in greater numbers and in better health. In 1960 there were probably only 600 to 650 Kayapó left.[32] It was not until 1966 that all of the various groups were pacified, although this hardly put a stop to the threat to Indian lands or to the violence that continued between Indians and settlers in the upper Xingu. Despite these continuing difficulties, the Kayapó population began to recover slowly, reaching a number of approximately fifteen hundred by 1970 and remaining stable for the next two decades.[33]

The Contest over Indian Lands

In 1945 the governor of Pará signed a decree that set aside twenty-eight thousand hectares of land for a forest reserve and for the Gorotire Indian reserve, but the decree was never implemented.[34] Further attempts to demarcate the Gorotire territory did not resume until the end of the 1960s. A rough description of the borders of the reserve was prepared in the mid-1970s after FUNAI officials and three Kayapó chiefs overflew the area.[35] But the actual demarcation of Gorotire lands was postponed to the "second phase" of FUNAI's program development.[36]

By this time the Kayapó—particularly those in Gorotire—had attended white schools and were accustomed to interacting with anthropologists and missionaries. They had also learned to communicate by radio and had traveled to Belém and Brasília to participate in Indian assemblies. Internal divisions between more and less acculturated Kayapó stimulated additional village fissioning in the 1970s and 1980s. The divisions in turn contributed to the expansion of Kayapó land claims.[37] At Gorotire, disagreements in 1976 between two chiefs, Kanhonk and Pombo, prompted the latter to leave the village with 150 followers. Pombo, an acculturated Indian who had partly been raised in Altamira, held the honorary title of coronel, granted to him on "Indian Day" by his military allies in that city.[38] At the Nova Olinda site on the Rio Branco, Pombo founded a new village called Krikretum. Other Kayapó chiefs extended their claims in other directions. A fifth Kayapó village, called Aukre, was established in 1981 under the leadership of Chief Paiakan. Both Pombo and Paiakan would play important roles in the battle for the demarcation of the Gorotire reserve.

A 1978 decree defined an area of 2,738,085 hectares for the Gorotire reserve. The boundaries more or less conformed to the area identified years earlier by the commission headed by Darcy Ribeiro.[39] Although the demarcation process began that year, it was halted in 1979 because of irregularities in the surveying process and later because the firm that had contracted with FUNAI for the job went bankrupt. Leaders from the Krikretum and Gorotire villages demanded that the borders of the reserve be extended to include their traditional burial ground and the site of their ancestral village, Pyka-Toti, located about fifty-five kilometers southeast of Gorotire.[40]

By the mid-1970s the Kayapó had become one of the better organized Indian groups in Brazil. Using shortwave radios, they established a communication system among villages to notify each other of incursions into their land. Warriors began to patrol the disputed southeastern border of the reserve regularly, keeping a close watch on the cattle ranchers who were beginning to move into the area. In 1980 the Kayapó prodded FUNAI to stop the new clearings taking place inside the reserve. When the land invasions continued, a group of Gorotire Kayapó took matters into their own hands. Painted for battle and armed with clubs, bows, and arrows, two young chiefs led an attack on a group of workers clearing land for the Espadilha ranch. They killed twenty people, including several women and children.

The event called national attention to the conflicts underway in the Kayapó territory.[41] The attack and the publicity it generated stirred up anti-Indian sentiment in São Felix do Xingu, where the memory of prepacification battles was still fresh in many people's minds.[42] Local ranchers armed their employees and threatened to kill Indians on sight. Meanwhile, there was dissension among the Gorotire villagers themselves. Some of the women and older chiefs censured the young warriors for indiscriminately killing women and children. Shocked by the sudden violence of the Indians, FUNAI blamed an anthropologist for instigating the attack.

For all of the publicity it brought the Kayapó, the incident did little to advance their effort to get their lands demarcated. In the meantime, the territory the Kayapó claimed was increasingly invaded by ranchers, miners, and loggers, prompting the Indians to adopt new forms of resistance. In 1981 sixteen Kayapó chiefs came together for an unprecedented ten-day meeting to discuss a unified strategy to defend themselves.[43] Some of participants in that historic gathering reportedly had not seen one another for nearly forty years. The urgent need to protect their territory brought the Kayapó together on several more occasions.

In June 1984 the chiefs met in Gorotire with the head of FUNAI to demand immediate action.[44] But the problem was farther than ever from solution. As the threat to Indian lands grew in scope and intensity, the federal bureaucracy seemed to become increasingly bogged down by red tape, overlapping authorities, and Byzantine procedural requirements. New measures passed by the military government in November of 1983 meant that FUNAI was no longer solely responsible for setting the boundaries of Indian reserves. The revised procedures required studies by the ministries of Land Affairs and Interior and approval by an interministerial working group before the demarcation could be approved by the president (see chapter 4). Faced with the disturbing prospect of long delays, the Indians issued subtle threats about taking matters into their own hands if these obstacles that stood in the way of the survey were not overcome soon. Although there were sharp differences among the Kayapó chiefs regarding other issues—namely, the presence of loggers and miners on Indian lands—all agreed on the urgent need to secure the demarcation of their reserve.

Meanwhile, contracts with logging companies became a source of intervillage tension.[45] In 1982 FUNAI approved contracts with several sawmills to exploit timber on Kayapó lands—ostensibly a forest reserve under IDBF jurisdiction.[46] One sawmill had a contract with FUNAI to extract mahogany from the Gorotire lands near Krikretum in return for building a hundred-kilometer road to the village and providing the Indians with lumber. The logging company was also building a road to the Kokraimoro village, where Indians sought permission from FUNAI to strike their own deals with the loggers. But members of the Aukre village remained hostile to the idea. In June of 1987 Aukre warriors attacked and killed three men found carrying out illegal logging on their lands.[47] In a similar dispute the following year, several Kokraimoro men walked into São Felix where they shot and seriously wounded a man in the lobby of one of the town's hotels.[48]

The Pyka-Toti area, bordered by the Trairão stream, had not been included in the 1978 decree that created the Gorotire reserve. Because of its importance as a ceremonial center and because its resources had long been exploited by the Kayapó, the study commissioned by FUNAI in 1981 recommended that Pyka-Toti be added to the reserve.[49] Problems arose when the state land agency, ITERPA, issued some two dozen titles to enterprises located there, several of which received fiscal incentives from SUDAM. A working group was formed to propose a solution, but by then it was too late. In February of 1985, before the commission completed its investigation, ITERPA went ahead with its plan to sell the land in a public auction. The land sale was the first phase of a larger state initiative, called Projeto Integrado Trairão.[50] In response to FUNAI's vehement objections, ITERPA officials produced a letter, signed the year before by governor Jáder Barbalho, an outspoken member of the opposition party. In the letter, Barbalho insisted that the state of Pará was the rightful owner of the land in question. The sale primarily benefited those landholders who already occupied some three hundred thousand hectares of the disputed territory. The Trairão affair illustrates once again how competing bureaucratic authorities and political divisions between the state and federal governments affected the process of demarcating Indian lands in Amazonia.

Indian Gold

The Kayapó's prolonged struggle to get FUNAI to survey the boundaries of their territory was made all the more difficult by the dispute over the mineral wealth their lands contained. In the late 1970s two sections of Kayapó territory were invaded by gold miners. Small "closed" *garimpos* sprang up in the northeast corner of the reserve near the Rio Branco. Other deposits were discovered near Chief Pombo's Krikretum village. A much larger invasion was linked to the military-controlled *garimpo* inside the reserve's eastern border, close to the main Kayapó village of Gorotire (see chapter 8).

The Indians themselves were bitterly divided over how best to deal with the presence of gold miners on their land. Some, like Pombo, favored doing business with them. Others wanted nothing to do with the *garimpeiros*. One way or another, the experience gained in dealing with the contests that ensued further developed the arsenal of strategies the Indians used to contend not only with gold miners but also with Brazilian society in general. Ironically, it was negotiations over mineral rights that ultimately provided the basis for resolving the land question.

Rio Branco

Even before the gold rush began in Serra Pelada, a *garimpeiro* nicknamed "Bateia" (after the shallow dish miners use to pan for gold) had discovered a deposit in the Rio Branco area inside the northeastern corner of Kayapó territory. By 1978 there were approximately six hundred *garimpeiros* working along two airstrips, called Bateia and Filomeno—the latter named for a supplier from São Felix do Xingu who was later elected mayor of the town. For three years, these "closed" *garimpos* functioned quietly at their remote location about a week's trek from the village of Krikretum.

In 1980 Chief Pombo led thirty-five Krikretum warriors to Rio Branco where they ambushed three hundred *garimpeiros* working the Bateia airstrip.[51] The Indians seized the miners' gold, radios, weapons, equipment, even their clothes. The Indians expelled the *garimpeiros* from the mining site, clad only in their shorts. Bateia was taken back to the village but later released. With the support of the federal police, FUNAI completed the expulsion of the miners from the Rio Branco area. But it was not long before the *garimpeiros* returned.

In December of 1980 a company called Stannum appeared with a research permit to reopen the Rio Branco *garimpo*. The attempt to mine Indian lands proved controversial, prompting a special interministerial directive, issued in January of 1981, that limited such activities to state mining companies. Based on this directive, FUNAI refused permission to Stannum. In March FUNAI relied on help from the Brazilian air force to remove twenty-five hundred *garimpeiros* who had entered the area.

By this time the Krikretum chief had begun to have second thoughts about his initial opposition to the *garimpo*. With the southern Pará gold rush now in full swing, Pombo turned to his contacts in Altamira, São Felix do Xingu, Tucumã, and other nearby towns to devise a way to turn a profit. Ignoring the advice of FUNAI officials, he negotiated a series of deals with various suppliers to operate the Bateia and Filomeno airstrips, now called Rio Branco and Nova Olinda. In April of 1982 he signed a formal agreement that gave Stannum exclusive rights to work the area for a three-year period, using up to four hundred men. The company agreed to pay Pombo 5 percent of the production from mechanized mining and 10 percent of the gold extracted through *garimpagem*. Pombo in turn was responsible for the security of the area.

The agreement was struck without the approval of upper level FUNAI officials. The head of the local post whose signature appeared on the papers was removed from his job soon afterwards. FUNAI later made several attempts to put a stop to Pombo's mining operation, which was opposed by other influential Kayapó chiefs.

Disputes soon arose over the amount of the payments due the Indians, which were sometimes made in kind. Planes loaded down with goods—including loaves of white bread, meat, soft drinks, and clothing purchased from merchants in Tucumã—landed daily in Krikretum. The Indians rapidly grew accustomed to the consumer goods their new income provided. In mid-1982 Pombo expelled a number of *garimpeiros*, accusing them of smuggling gold in bars of soap. After the arrangement with the company broke down, the two thousand *garimpeiros* who stayed on to work the streambeds were obliged to pay a 10 percent fee to the Indians. One mining technician commented with considerable irony that in Rio Branco it was the Indians who exploited the whites.

Cumaru

The discovery of the Cumaru gold fields in 1980 prompted a second invasion of Kayapó land about twenty kilometers from the village of Gorotire.[52] By 1983 there were about four thousand miners working the Tarzan and Maria Bonita sites. Unlike the Indians in the gold fields in Rio Branco, the Gorotire Indians had little say about decisions regarding the Cumaru *garimpo*, which was controlled by the Brazilian military (see chapter 8). The Kayapó received only the amount legally due the owner of gold-bearing land—one percent of the mining tax. The Cumaru *garimpo*, which was far less lucrative than the mining in Rio Branco, was also the cause of a number of problems. One was the pollution of the Arraias, Ponte, and Fresco rivers, where the Kayapó fished and from which they drew their water. Another was the spread of malaria that posed a serious health threat to the Kayapó.[53]

The objections by Gorotire chiefs, such as Kanhonk, to the presence of *garimpeiros* on the Indians' lands was one of the principal complaints that led the Kayapó to step up their pressure on FUNAI to survey their territory. When several Kayapó chiefs met with the agency's president, Jurandir Fonseca, in June of 1984, they demanded that some of the mining sites be closed. They agreed to allow Tarzan and Maria Bonita to stay open on the condition that royalties from the two *garimpos* be raised to 10 percent of production over and above the 1 percent of the mining tax they already received.[54] Fonseca was sympathetic to their demands, but his attitude did little good to his career. Three months later he was fired from his post, reportedly because he refused to sign new legislation allowing mining on indigenous land.

In early 1985 the contract that had required the federal bank to pay the Gorotire Indians 1 percent of the mining tax expired. When the bank stopped payment on the proceeds from the Maria Bonita *garimpo*, Chiefs Kanhonk and Totoi (of Gorotire) and Paiakan (of Aukre) took control of the mining field. They suspended work in the *garimpo* and stopped all air traffic on the airstrip. Several thousand miners were held captive for a few days. The Indians demanded the overdue fees and an increase in their percentage of future production. When the late payments were finally turned over to them without monetary correction, the Indians announced that the *garimpo* would not reopen at all. They further demanded a ransom payment before they would release the 789 hydraulic mining units and the 47 mechanical crushers that had been seized.

The air force assisted in removing approximately five thousand miners to Belém, Conceição do Araguaia, Marabá, and Imperatriz. Most of them ended up in nearby Redenção, where they soon became an unruly mob. Military police tried to keep order but with little success. Four *garimpeiros* were injured in shootings, and a car was burned. Ten were arrested for sacking a supermarket. Others attempted to invade a store but were stopped by the owner who fired his revolver into the air. About fifty *garimpeiros* threatened the local radio station, where authorities broadcast messages pleading for calm. Small groups of *garimpeiros* tried to return to Maria Bonita in the next few days, but they were intercepted by the Indians, who turned them over to the federal police. On April 29 over thirteen thousand *garimpeiros* blocked the Belém-Brasília Highway for twenty-four hours, demanding that Maria Bonita be reopened.

The new FUNAI President, Nelson Marabuto, flew to Maria Bonita where he announced that mining in Gorotire would be discontinued—a position consistent with his goal to end mining in indigenous land. A few days later he too was removed from the FUNAI presidency. But the Indians stood their ground. By this time the Kayapó recognized that the mining crisis was their best hope for resolving their land claims, which by then had dragged on for decades. In effect, it was the army of *garimpeiros* who fought the final battle for them. Chief Paiakan went to Brasília to negotiate a solution to the impasse, insisting that they would reopen the *garimpo* only after the land question was settled.

The strategy worked. On May 3, 1985, the interministerial working group—now representing a civilian rather than a military regime—agreed to the demarcation of the Gorotire and of six other indigenous areas.[55] At the last minute, Paiakan, the chief who represented the Kayapó at the meetings in Brasília, refused to sign until the word "delimitation" was changed to "demarcation." The agreement finally was signed on May 4 by Paiakan, the Minister of the Interior and the Minister of Agrarian Reform and Development. Accordingly, FUNAI defined a 3,262,960-hectare reserve, increasing the size of the territory by more than 500,000 hectares above the original 1978 decree. In return, the Kayapó agreed to reopen the Maria Bonita *garimpo*. They were to receive payment of 5 percent of the profits from the mining area. The state of Pará reluctantly accepted the agreement, but ranchers threatened to charge indemnification for their investments in the disputed area.[56]

In keeping with the agreement, mining resumed in Cumaru. The Indians, for their part, closely monitored subsequent events. They made it a regular practice to interdict boats traveling on the Xingu and Fresco rivers when they passed through Kayapó territory. They also kept a vigilant watch for *garimpeiros*, whose presence could be detected by mud in the streams the Indians fished. The Indians expelled intruders after seizing their gold, equipment, and belongings. In some cases, the Indians shaved the miners' heads and pierced their ears before sending them on their way.[57]

The Kayapó Victory

The Kayapó warrior tradition, honed in battle with *seringueiros* and *castanheiros* earlier in this century, gained them more time and territory than most other tribes in Brazil. It also brought them notoriety, which itself was turned to their advantage. Even after winning their land rights, the Kayapó continued to make use of their tradition of ritualized warfare. On several occasions, hundreds of Indians—decorated in war paint and wielding clubs— put on spectacular demonstrations in Belém and in Brasília in successful attempts to call media attention to indigenous rights.

To the average person living in the rural areas of southern Pará, such displays only reinforced the long-held image of the Kayapó as violent and uncivilized. One resident of São Felix do Xingu explained to us that the Kayapó were merely savages, lacking even the most simple agricultural skills.

In fact, Kayapó agriculture provided one of the best-documented examples of indigenous resource management in Amazonia. A long-term research project, organized by anthropologist Darrell Posey, showed that Kayapó resource use strategies were adapted well to the fragile and variable Amazonian ecology.[58] When their territories were still unlimited, the Indians dispersed into small hunting groups during the dry season, returning to their villages once the rains began. To adapt to a fixed land base, the Kayapó developed an array of techniques to maximize the use of the different microenvironments. Near the Gorotire village, for example, the Kayapó exploited eight major ecological zones and two types of transitional zones. Separate agricultural plots were devoted to food crops, to medicinal herbs, to plants with religious applications, and to the preservation of wild varieties in a kind of germ plasm bank. The Kayapó also created and nurtured "forest islands" of woody vegetation in their scrub savanna habitat. Moreover, their soil management practices appeared to be far more productive than those of colonists or ranchers in the region.

These findings gave impetus to international interest in the Kayapó. In 1987 nearly one hundred Kayapó went to Belém to attend the opening of a scientific exhibit at the prestigious Emílio Goeldi Museum entitled, "Alternatives to Destruction: Science of the Mebêngôkre."[59] Other participants included the state governor, the head of Brazil's National Research Council, and scholars from around the world. The Kayapó were subsequently invited to attend an international symposium on "Wise Management of Tropical Forests" sponsored by Florida International University in Miami in January of 1988. At a time when U.S. environmental groups were consolidating their links to grassroots Amazonian movements (see chapter 4), these contacts provided the Kayapó with the credibility and opportunity to serve as spokesmen for the region's indigenous peoples.

After the Miami meeting, environmentalists invited Kayapó representatives to visit Washington, D.C. To the chagrin of the

Brazilian government, the Indians met with officials at the World Bank, the U.S. Departments of State and Treasury, and with members of the U.S. Congress. They expressed concern about proposals to use World Bank funds to build a series of dams along the Xingu river (see chapter 4). For most Washington bureaucrats and politicians, this was the first direct contact with the people who would be affected by the policies that were being considered in the various offices. For the Kayapó, this was their international public relations debut.

Their visibility on the international stage was only heightened on their return home when the Brazilian government brought charges of foreign sedition against the Kayapó chiefs who had traveled abroad and against the anthropologist who had served as their translator. With the assistance of environmentalists, the Kayapó used this incident to expand their support network to European capitals. Each step in the judicial process presented an opportunity for mass demonstrations that were reported around the world. The government eventually dropped the charges.

One of the defendants—Chief Paulo Paiakan of the Aukre village—emerged as a spokesperson for the group. In 1989 he was presented with an environmental award by the Better World Society. Known for his defense of traditional customs, Paiakan was criticized for his western ways and his lucrative economic dealings. Skeptics insisted on seeing Paiakan and others like him as pawns in the hands of self-serving anthropologists or as the naive agents of foreign environmental groups and transnational corporations bent on thwarting Brazilian economic development. But as Paiakan himself explained, the Kayapó "used to defend themselves with war clubs and spears. Today," he said, "we defend ourselves with words, our heads, and the press."[60]

In February of 1989 the Kayapó hosted a six-day meeting of six hundred indigenous leaders. The "First Encounter of Native Peoples" was held in the town of Altamira in Pará. The Xingu dam proposals were a key focus of the gathering, to which ELE-TRONORTE officials had also been invited. The media high point came when a Kayapó woman delivered an impassioned tirade while holding a machete to the throat of an ELETRONORTE representative. Less picturesque but more lasting achievements of the meeting were contained in a document entitled "Strategies for the Preservation of the Amazon and its Peoples." The Kayapó went on to use similar tactics to protest the treatment of other native groups, such as the Yanomami, and to bring political pressure to bear on the 1988 constituent assembly's deliberations over Indian rights.

When the Kayapó finally secured the rights to their land, the victory assured them access to income from the logging and mining carried out within the reserve. For years the Indians used every means to keep out such activities, but they were continually defeated. Over time, they learned to adopt a more pragmatic approach and to negotiate agreements that were mutually advantageous to interested entrepreneurs. For better or for worse, the wealth they earned set them apart from other groups. In 1985 the Kayapó purchased their own aircraft and hired a pilot to carry them between villages. They used the plane to make regular shopping trips to nearby towns like Redenção and to patrol the reserve's borders. They also bought video cameras to document their interviews with officials in Brasília and to record their own ceremonies and dances.[61]

In a curious synthesis of the old and the new, the Indians were thus able to draw upon modern resources to revive ancient traditions that threatened to lapse from the memory of the younger generation. On the other hand, their new-found wealth introduced western customs and life styles into Kayapó culture. Where the continuing process of cultural redefinition will lead them is an open question. If they display in the future the cultural resilience they have persistently shown in the past, there is little doubt that in the years ahead the Kayapó will remain powerful players in the ongoing contests over the land and resources of the Xingu river basin.

NOTES

1. Hemming (1987:62).
2. The term "Kayapó," which is of Tupi origin and means "monkey-like," was first used to refer to the southern Kayapó groups in the seventeenth century. In reality, these groups are only distant relatives of the northern Kayapó that

are the focus of this chapter, having separated many centuries ago according to Arnaud (1989:433). See also Nimuendajú (1952) and Dreyfus (1972).

3. Velho (1972:30).

4. Hemming (1987:75).

5. Hemming (1987:195).

6. Arnaud (1989:436).

7. Hemming (1987:416) and Nimuendajú (1952); on the Xikrin, see also Vidal (1979).

8. Hemming (1987:400–402).

9. Arnaud (1989:437), Nimuendajú (1952:428), and Verswijver (1978:10).

10. Hemming (1987:403).

11. Arnaud (1989:437).

12. Posey (1979a), who visited the site of the original village in 1978, calculated that it might have supported three to four thousand inhabitants, making it one of the largest in the Amazon basin.

13. Arnaud (1989:438), Hemming (1987:399–404), and Verswijver (1978).

14. Nimuendajú (1952:428).

15. Couto (1980).

16. Kelly (1975).

17. The image was believed to provide protection against Indian attacks (Santana n.d.). Unless otherwise noted, the next five paragraphs are based on this source and on interviews with Luís Ferreira Santana.

18. Nimuendajú (1952:436), who had travelled along the Xingu upriver from Altamira in 1914, commented that at that time there were thousands of inhabitants ruled by *barracão* owners, some of whom had hundreds of henchmen who enforced their rule with violence.

19. Nunes (1982).

20. Nimuendajú (1952:436).

21. Posey (1987:148). For example, the population of Gorotire, already weakened by disease, fell drastically from 356 to only 85 in the first six months after contact (Posey et al. 1987). Posey (1987) argues that the spread of disease led to more accusations of sorcery that contributed to fissioning and that increased intragroup hostility after the breakup of the ancestral village lent a more warlike appearance to the Kayapó than had been true prior to the epidemics and fissioning of the 1930s. Bamberger (1979) points to differences of opinion between men's groups and their leaders about policies and relations with outsiders as another factor that probably contributed to village splits.

22. Verswijver (1978).

23. Nimuendajú (1952:429–452).

24. Arnaud (1989:339–441).

25. Posey (1987:142).

26. Ianni (1978:70). The hostility of Xingu society toward the Kayapó was also described in Nimuendajú's account of his 1940 Xingu voyage upriver from Altamira (Nimuendajú 1952:433–452).

27. Paróquia (1988:12–21).

28. Arnaud (1989:442).

29. Arnaud (1989:443–444).

30. Arnaud (1989:445–446).

31. Arnaud (1989:446–459).

32. Verswijver (1978:16). The first ethnographic studies of the Kayapó were carried out in 1954 and 1955 by Alfred Métraux and Simone Dreyfus (see Dreyfus 1972).

33. Posey (1979a). Arnaud (1989:477) reports that there were a total of 1,598 Kayapó in five villages in 1986.

34. CEDI (1987:221).

35. *Informe Amazônico*, Ano 1, No. 1, 15–30 September 1980 and Pinto (1977:87–88).

36. Arnaud (1989:469).

37. Arnaud (1989:469). See Bamberger (1979) for a discussion of Kayapó fissioning as a mechanism for dealing with differences over relations with outsiders.

38. Arnaud (1989:473).

39. Arnaud (1989:470).

40. Arnaud (1989:470) and Posey (1979b).

41. This discussion draws on the following sources: *Informe Amazônico*, Ano 1, No. 1, 15–30 September 1980; *Estado de São Paulo*, 4 September 1980; *O Liberal*, 5 September and 9 September 1980; *Jornal do Brasil*, 7 September 1980; *Veja*, 10 September 1980. Sources disagreed on exactly how many people (seventeen to twenty-two) were killed.

42. A statement by one old-timer illustrates the bitter feelings: "The Indian is the most distasteful creature there is. I won't even look at them. The government should kill them all. They killed my father, broke him into little pieces with their clubs. They are intrepid and kill treacherously."

43. *O Liberal*, 10 June 1981.

44. CEDI (1985:160–161).

45. Darrell A. Posey, personal communication, 1988.

46. Arnaud (1989:474–475).

47. *O Liberal*, 9 September 1986.

48. Based on field interviews and on *O Liberal*, 21 June 1987.

49. Pinto (1985d).

50. Pinto (1985a, 1985b) and CEDI (1987:221).

51. The following discussion of the Rio Branco *garimpos* is based on field interviews and on the following sources: *Jornal de Brasília*, 27 July 1980 and 7 October 1982; *O Tribuna*, 22 March 1981; *Jornal do Brasil*, 17 July 1982 and 29 May 1983; *Estado de São Paulo*, 10 October 1982, 12 June 1983, 8 October 1983, and 6 December 1983; *Folha de Tucumã*, October 1982; *A Província do Pará*, 14 June 1983; *O Liberal*, 15 June 1983; Lea (1984); and Ricardo (1985).

52. The following discussion of the *garimpos* near Gorotire is based on field interviews and on the following sources: *O Estado do Pará*, 19 November 1980; *A Província do Pará*, 27 July 1983; *Jornal do Ouro*, May 1985 and 27 August 1985; CEDI (1985:160–164); and CEDI (1987:200,215–228).

53. The Maria Bonita *garimpo* was notoriously unhealthy. According to the state Health Secretary, in 1986 it accounted for half of all cases of malaria in the state (*A Província do Pará*, 29 March 1986).

54. Since April of 1981, the Gorotire gold fields had yielded an estimated 1.8 tons of gold.

55. CEDI (1987:215–228).

56. Pinto (1985c). New conflicts arose in August when Indians patrolling the southeastern border questioned the demarcation process and ranchers brought in the military police who attempted to disarm the Indians (*O Liberal*, 7–9 August 1985).

57. Kent H. Redford field notes, 1985.

58. Anderson and Posey (1989), Hecht and Posey (1989, 1990), and Posey (1982, 1983, 1987, 1990).

59. Posey et al. (1987).

60. Posey (1989); this article also carries a rich description of the Kayapó demonstration in Belém when Chief Kube-i was summoned to give testimony on the foreign sedition charge. See also the videos by anthropologist Terence Turner in the *Disappearing Worlds* series, entitled *The Kayapó* and *The Kayapó: Out of the Forest*.

61. The tribe's first video camera was acquired from a gold miner (Smith 1989).

TEN

❖

The Closing Frontier in São Felix do Xingu

By the time the PA-279 reached São Felix do Xingu, the major contests over land and minerals had already been fought. Unlike the newer roadside towns—such as Redenção, Xinguara, Ourilândia, and Tucumã—the area surrounding São Felix had long been settled by Indians, rubber tappers, fishermen, and Brazil nut collectors. Moreover, regional studies carried out by the Brazilian government in the 1970s showed that the municipality was potentially rich in minerals and contained some of the best soils in southern Pará. Land speculators and mining companies moved quickly to lay claim to these resources well before the road link was completed. As a result of that and of the beginning of the heavy migration to São Felix nearly a decade after the influx of population into other places in southern Pará, redistributive experiments attempted elsewhere—for example, the state colonization project in Xinguara—were never tried in São Felix do Xingu.

For migrant families who traveled the PA-279 in the hopes of finding a plot to cultivate, this meant that São Felix was, literally and otherwise, the end of the road. After being evicted as many as three or four times from lands they had claimed, many arrived in São Felix only to find that their prospects of becoming a landholder had hardly improved. Contests for land, gold, and timber did take place as the road moved westward across the state but not with the scope and intensity that had occurred elsewhere in the state. The story of São Felix do Xingu, more than that of most other places in the region, exemplified the "closing" of the Amazon frontier in southern Pará.

The Decline of Traditional Extractivism

After a brief resurgence during World War II, the rubber trade declined in importance in São Felix as it did in the rest of Amazonia. But the fall in prices was only one of the factors that eroded the labor and credit arrangements that had grown up in association with the collection and sale of natural latex. High rates of monetary inflation in the 1950s undermined the *aviamento* system, as did the change in financial markets brought about by government credit policies. The objectives spelled out in Operation Amazônia in the 1960s replaced the supports provided to traditional extractive activities with a preference given to modern industry and agriculture. The Rubber Credit Bank was abolished and the Banco da Amazonia (BASA) took its place.[1] What little credit for rubber extraction had flowed to São Felix all but dried up although some river traders still purchased rubber. By the 1970s rubber collection in São Felix had fallen to less than thirty tons per year from its peak of about four hundred tons per year in the 1950s.

Some rubber tappers were drawn into other extractive activities also based on the *aviamento* system. Hunting of wild animal skins, such as the giant river otter and the prized spotted jaguar, began in the postwar period and flourished throughout the 1960s in response to world market demand for rare pelts. The trade in wild animal skins provided a profitable alternative to rubber or Brazil nut extraction until it was outlawed in 1971.[2] The figures in table 10.1 show that at the peak in 1969 and 1970, about nine tons of wild animal pelts per year were officially registered in the municipality of São Felix do Xingu alone. Their value was nearly twice that of the over eighty tons of Brazil nuts and rubber. Jaguar and *maracajá* (a small wild cat) pelts commanded the highest price. In 1969 six-tenths of a ton of *maracajá* skins was valued at Cr$139,800 while 2.4 tons of deerskin were worth only Cr$3,600.[3] After the prohibition, the export of officially registered pelts dropped significantly.

TABLE 10.1
Extractive Production in São Felix do Xingu, 1968–1973

Commodity	1968	1969	1970	1971	1972	1973
A. Volume[1]						
rubber	15	6	—	29	27	32
Brazil nuts	181.5	78.2	87.1	209.0	°	°
animal pelts	6.2	9.1	8.5	6.5	°	°
deer	2.5	2.4	2.1	1.4	°	°
maracajá	0.4	0.6	0.2	0.1	°	°
jaguar	°	°°	0.1	°°	°	°
armadillo	0.1	°°	0.1	°°	°	°
otter	0.1	°°	°°	°°	°	°
boa	—	—	°°	°°	°	°
waterboa	°°	0.1	0.1	°°	°	°
white-lipped peccary	2.0	3.0	3.0	3.0	°	°
collared peccary	1.0	3.0	3.0	2.0	°	°
cayman	0.1	—	—	—	°	°
B. Value[2]						
rubber/Brazil nuts	145	90	91	123	773.8	163.2
animal pelts	112.9	172.3	157.4	74	60.5	51.9
minerals	39.8	72.6	108.4	185.9	318.9	639.3

SOURCE: *Sondotécnica*, 1974, vol. 2, 296–417.
NOTES: [1]in tons
[2]in Cr$1,000 (Sept. 1974)
°missing
°°less than 0.1

Extraction of Brazil nuts continued to grow at a modest level into the 1980s, gradually overtaking rubber in importance (see table 10.2). But new activities stimulated by the development policies of the 1970s began to replace traditional forms of livelihood. Rubber production significantly dropped again beginning in 1978, probably due in part to the impact of the tin *garimpo* that drew workers away from rubber tapping during the dry season. When mahogany extraction began in São Felix do Xingu in the early 1980s, it soon eclipsed other products in the regional economy.

TABLE 10.2
Extractive Production in São Felix do Xingu, 1975–1981

Commodity	1975	1976	1977	1978	1979	1980	1981
A. Volume[1]							
rubber	24	20	22	7	10	9	12
Brazil nuts	76.5	82	98.4	67	83	62	78
fuel wood & charcoal	182.2	202.5	324	404	463	523	502
wood	—	—	—	—	—	—	5,400
B. Relative Value							
rubber	61.8%	58.7%	48.5%	19.2%	22.8%	28.1%	5.1%
Brazil nuts	33.7	38.0	48.1	77.0	73.1	69.6	13.1
fuel wood & charcoal	4.5	3.2	3.4	3.8	4.1	2.3	0.3
wood	—	—	—	—	—	—	81.5
TOTAL (%)	100%	100%	100%	100%	100%	100%	100%
(Total value in $Cr)	227,838	323,430	654,780	839,000	1,137,000	2,868,000	29,820,000

SOURCE: IBGE, Superintendência de Estatísticas Primárias: Produçao extrativa vegetal, 1979, vols. 3, 4, and 5; 1981, vols. 6 and 7; 1982, vol. 8; 1984, vol. 9.
NOTE: [1]For wood in m³; for other commodities in tons.

In 1981, the first year timber extraction appeared in official statistics for the municipality, the value of logging was more than four times that of rubber and Brazil nuts combined.

São Felix residents typically combined extractive activities with subsistence hunting and fishing. Despite the area's endowment with relatively good soils, agricultural production was minimal and restricted to subsistence crops of rice, beans, manioc, and corn as well as some fruits (bananas and citrus) grown on small plots. Unlike the flood plain available to *caboclo* communities along the Amazon river and its proximities, the middle Xingu lacks rich *várzea* for agricultural cropping. As a result, the area never supported the diverse subsistence economy found in some Amazonian towns.[4] The richer *terra firme* soils in the municipality of São Felix were not cultivated until the 1970s when the road provided access to the areas. Table 10.3 shows that agricultural pro-

TABLE 10.3

Agricultural Production in São Felix do Xingu, 1968–1973

Commodity	1968	1969	1970	1971	1972	1973
A. Volume[1]						
rice	12	9	27	7	29	10
beans	5	4	11	4	7	4
corn	4	6	24	10	13	5
cassava	3	3	4	15	11	92
B. Area[2]						
rice	17	13	37	6	24	8
beans	9	6	20	4	8	4
corn	10	20	60	16	32	16
cassava	5	6	8	7	6	38
C. Value[3]						
rice, beans, corn, cassava	40	38	112	84	158	248

SOURCE: *Sondotécnica*, 1974, vol. 2, 6–31 (tables I through XV).
NOTES: [1]in tons
[2]area cultivated in hectares
[3]in Cr$1,000 (Sept. 1974)

duction was of little significance in the municipality compared to the extractive products. The INCRA cadaster for 1972 counted only 172 properties in São Felix. The number of cattle registered grew from 118 to 152 head between 1970 and 1973.[5]

Politics and Urbanization

The decline of traditional extractive activities triggered an incipient process of urbanization in São Felix do Xingu. Rural-to-urban migration was further stimulated by political changes that made it attractive to abandon the countryside and move into town. When twenty-two new municipalities were created in Pará in 1961, the *município* of São Felix was officially separated from Altamira.[6] Although the boundaries of the municipal seat were never precisely established, the new municipality became the third largest in Brazil, occupying 116,577 square kilometers. When São Felix was still part of the huge municipality of Altamira in 1960, it had a population of only 1,558, of which only 604 lived in towns. The 1970 census counted a population of 2,332 of which 1,441 lived in town. Whereas the "urban" population had more than doubled since 1960, the rural population had actually dropped slightly from 954 to only 891. Between 1980 and 1983 nine traditional riverside settlements inhabited by fifty people disappeared altogether.[7]

When the traditional *aviamento* system began to decline and the last of the trading posts began to shut down, civil service became a new source of patronage. Contests for public office were fraught with corruption as local office holders were in a position to reward the loyalty of family and friends with municipal jobs and access to land and equipment. The first prefect, Antonio Marques Ribeiro, was inaugurated in 1962. All but one of the elections for prefect until 1982 were uncontested. Town council members, who had large families and little if any education, invariably supported the decisions of the prefect on whom they depended for their livelihood. As in many other communities in the region, denunciations of misuses of the paltry municipal budget and other assets were a constant throughout the municipality's short history.

Public revenues permitted some infrastructural development during the early 1960s. An airstrip was built, two generators were purchased, and the municipal government constructed about seventeen kilometers of road. The dirt trail headed in the direction of Gorotire, and for many years it was the municipality's only road. In 1971 there were twenty public lights in town, and thirty homes were connected to the town's generators.[8] In the early

1970s the *município* gained a parish priest and buildings to house the prefecture, police station, and market. The number of local stores grew slightly from only two in 1962 to eight in 1965 and then to thirteen in 1972.[9] Nearly three-quarters of the population was illiterate, and school facilities were far from adequate.[10] In 1972 the state governor visited São Felix do Xingu to inaugurate the town's new water system. At the time of the public ceremony, the faucet the governor opened was the only one that flowed in the entire town. It was not until 1975 that the town's water system began to function.

Mining Research

Several mining companies began to carry out research near São Felix in the 1960s. Deposits of gold, silver, lead, zinc, diamonds, copper, manganese, nickel, wolframite (for tungsten), and cassiterite (from which tin is made) were known to exist in the municipality. By 1975 hundreds of requests for mineral research permits for São Felix had been filed with the National Mineral Research Department (DNPM). Several national and multinational firms set up temporary operations in the town and hired local residents familiar with the surrounding jungle.

The state research company, Companhia de Pesquisa em Recursos Minerais (CPRM), carried out research for lead and copper in a sixteen thousand-hectare area beginning in 1969 but failed to find economically viable deposits of the minerals.[11] From 1973 to 1978 Mineração Serras do Sul, a subsidiary of a Canadian mining firm, looked unsuccessfully for promising deposits of copper, zinc, or lead in areas covering over sixty thousand hectares.[12] The company received FUNAI authorizations in 1975 and 1976 to explore a site near the Cateté river within the territory claimed by the Xikrin Kayapó. Mineração Serras do Sul employed about fifty people. The staff included a geologist, three mining technicians, one nurse, a mechanic and driver, three boat pilots, six cooks and helpers, six overseers, and twenty-nine locally hired laborers. The number of jobs created was small (relative to the size of the research areas involved), and the impact on the local economy was minimal because most of the supplies were shipped from Altamira to São Felix.

The search for cassiterite, carried out by the Belém-based mining company PROMIX, was more successful. In 1972 PROMIX secured rights to fifteen areas of one thousand hectares each along the Rio Branco, some ninety kilometers from São Felix, where they discovered concentrated secondary deposits of tin ore.[13] The company opened a *garimpo* operation along an airstrip at an isolated site that was ten days travel by boat from São Felix.[14] The area worked by PROMIX was later the site of violent conflicts when gold was discovered there (see chapter 8). As with Serras do Sul, PROMIX found it more economical to purchase supplies elsewhere even though São Felix was much closer. Unlike the multiplier effects of traditional *garimpagem*, the enclave character of the mining companies contributed little to the development of small towns like São Felix do Xingu.

Development Planning

The first planning documents for São Felix appeared in 1970. A preliminary integrated development report on São Felix do Xingu proposed research on the area's resource potential and recommended that the area be linked to the municipalities of Marabá and Conceição do Araguaia. By this time the military government had improved the landing strip in the town as part of a series of strategic support points throughout the Amazon basin. RADAM satellite images published in the mid-1970s revealed fertile soils that caught the eye of planners and investors. Approximately ten percent of the municipality's soils were classified as fertile *terra roxa*. Fully half of the 1.5 million hectares were suitable for cultivation of perennial or annual crops, and an additional 200,000 hectares could be used for pastures or reforestation.[15] By 1973 more than two thousand land requests had been filed with state agencies.

The POLAMAZONIA program, published in the mid-1970s, contained the first real plans for São Felix. Though the municipality was not initially part of any of the ten designated development poles, the limits of the Polo Carajás were later extended to include it. The POLAMAZONIA program sought to break the isolation and backwardness of the *município* by linking it to road networks and to take advantage of the area's resource potential. Nearly twenty million dollars were allocated to projects in São Felix, including land demarcation, an urban development plan, a colonization feasibility study, and the construction of the PA-279 to link São Felix to the rest of Brazil. Funds released between 1975 and 1977 permitted the construction of the new airport, the completion of the city's water system, and the expansion of schools.

São Felix was also included in an integrated development plan for the Xingu and Tapajós valleys, which was prepared in 1974 but never published.[16] The study noted the existence of deposits of iron, coal, and manganese in sufficient proximity to one another to potentially support a steel industry. Large-scale mining, cattle ranching, and forestry were priority activities that would contribute to Brazil's balance of payments. With a prescience uncommon for the day, the report further noted that such enterprises would not lead to a higher standard of living for the local population. To achieve this objective, the report recommended an emphasis on small farmer colonization and reduced food costs through specific measures, such as accelerated land titling, the creation of credit and price supports, and the construction of warehouses and feeder roads. None of these recommendations were implemented. As a result, most of the post-1970 changes took place in the same unruly fashion that had characterized the growth of other towns, such as Redenção, Xinguara, and Ourilândia.

Migration and Urban Expansion

Anticipation of the PA-279 highway set in motion irreversible changes in São Felix. Road construction began in 1976 and continued in fits and starts over the next seven years (see chapter 5). In the mid-1970s *posseiros* began to migrate into the municipality of São Felix, hoping to clear and stake their claim before the completion of the road. Some traveled on foot from the Araguaia area or came by boat from Altamira—the two means of entry dating from the time of the rubber trade. Other migrants paid high prices to get there by private plane from Rio Maria, Redenção, and Xinguara, several hundred kilometers away. Nearly three-quarters of the São Felix migrant households we surveyed in 1981 had traveled primarily by boat or plane from their previous place of residence. All of the people we spoke to had used these two modes of transport for the last leg of their journey.[17] The opening of the road in August of 1983, albeit precariously, meant that by 1984 nearly half of the migrants in São Felix had come by bus, car, or truck.

In 1978, when the new road was still less than one-third complete, the town boasted a new neighborhood of approximately fifty migrant households. The workers constructing the airport helped transport materials for the new residents of the neighborhood called Novo Horizonte, situated around the bend from

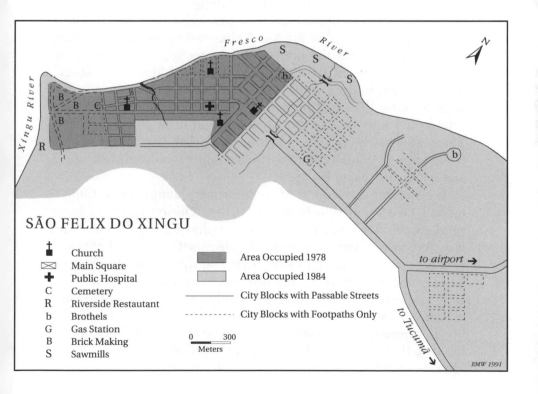

SÃO FELIX DO XINGU

✝   Church
⊠   Main Square
✚   Public Hospital
C   Cemetery
R   Riverside Restautant
b   Brothels
G   Gas Station
B   Brick Making
S   Sawmills

      Area Occupied 1978
      Area Occupied 1984
——— City Blocks with Passable Streets
-------- City Blocks with Footpaths Only

0   300
Meters

EMW 1991

The Closing Frontier

the old town center. As the town grew, it expanded away from the river, and eastward along the road to the airport.

Municipal authorities distributed urban lots at nominal cost to newcomers wishing to build houses. The process was complicated by the fact that the municipality still did not have an officially demarcated urban patrimony. Depending on the map, the town was superimposed on the indigenous reserve or on the forest reserve. Decree Law 1164, passed in 1971, had transferred jurisdiction over the land occupied by the town to the federal domain. A special provision passed in 1977 authorized the federal government to donate portions of such federalized land to municipalities. But the efforts by the São Felix prefecture to resolve the issue were continually frustrated. The problem was partly political, stemming from the prefect's alliance with Alacid Nunes, the state governor whose feud with former ally Jarbas Passarinho caused the latter to block the flow of federal funds (see chapter 3). PO-LAMAZONIA funds for completion of the PA-279 highway and for the expansion of water and electricity systems in São Felix were channeled to other localities. Similarly, the proposed SU-DAM urbanization plan for São Felix was never implemented, despite the fact that the prefect shifted factions within the pro-government party in an attempt to accomplish this goal. Hence, the municipal budget of São Felix was one of the smallest in the state because the exact boundaries of the town had never been established and because the *município* had little political power. The municipality had only slightly more than five hundred registered voters in 1976 although their number would triple by 1982 and quadruple again by 1988.

The prefect carried out his own urban planning even though he had no authority to issue land titles. The provision of basic services could not keep pace with the physical expansion of the city. As a result, the proportion of houses with electric lights and running water declined between 1978 and 1981, respectively from 47.5 percent to 21 percent and from 36.7 percent to 29.4 percent. In 1984 electricity was available for only 28.4 percent of the population and water for only 26.9 percent. The newer neighborhoods where most migrants settled were those most likely to be without these services. A growing proportion of the town's residences supplied their drinking water from their own or a neighbor's well (34.6 percent in 1978, 48.3 percent in 1981, and 64.5 percent in 1984). The use of well water increased the potential for public health risks in a town almost wholly lacking in sanitation facilities.[18] In 1984 less than ten percent of the homes had inside bathrooms, and about one-quarter had none at all. The water problem was complicated by the pollution of the Rio Fresco by upriver mining, which forced the town to shift to the Xingu for its supply in 1983. Water was pumped directly from the river into people's homes.

Social Change, the Church, and Politics

The urban-based patronage system typical of townships like São Felix do Xingu in the 1960s began to erode with the influx of new migrants into the area in the 1970s and 1980s. The change was partly reflected in responses to a question included in the surveys that asked people about the sources of assistance in time of need. In 1981 nearly half of the sample (41.1 percent) referred to "local leaders." Three years later only 21.4 percent of the respondents so indicated. Similarly, the percentage of people who said that "merchants" were a source of assistance fell from 13.8 percent in 1981 to 7.1 percent in 1984. As the ties to local leaders and merchants declined, the reliance on "acquaintances and friends" grew in importance. In 1981 only 2.3 percent indicated they received help from friends. By 1984 the comparable figure rose to 25 percent of the people interviewed.

Few sources of government assistance were available to the residents of the town. Only twelve of the households surveyed in 1984 had ever received anything from the national health and retirement system, INPS. Only five reported receiving medical help from FUNRURAL, the rural assistance fund. In the late 1970s local branches of nongovernmental organizations began to appear in São Felix. A chapter of the rural workers union was founded in 1978 and gained autonomy from Altamira the following year. By 1981 it had 360 members, 194 of whom were up-to-date in their monthly dues. The membership grew to 737 by 1984 when 29.6 percent of the households surveyed reported that at least one member of the household was a member of the union. Although the union provided some medical assistance and tried to assist agricultural producers with transport and marketing, it was unable to accomplish much with its meager resources.

The local Catholic church played an important role in organizing the community of São Felix beginning in the 1970s. From 1972 to 1978 the church brought in goods from Altamira and sold them in São Felix at no profit. When local merchants complained, the church formalized the arrangement by founding a consumers' cooperative in January of 1979. Rice, beans, flour, sugar, margarine, soap, powdered milk, and cooking oil were purchased in Altamira and sold in São Felix at cost plus freight and taxes. The cooperative was founded with forty-eight members and operated under church supervision. The sick, elderly, and unemployed were granted "special" membership status that exempted them from the fee and allowed purchases on credit. By July of 1980 there were 412 members of the Christian Brotherly Assistance Cooperative. A year later membership had dropped to 238, of whom 158 were not paid up. The decline in the number of active members was partly due to the fact that the presence of the cooperative forced local merchants to lower their prices. When it was no longer an advantage to belong to the cooperative, the people who continued their membership tended to be those unable to pay for the food they received. By 1984 the cooperative was disbanded when the road connection improved the town's provisioning system.

The six Christian Base Communities (CEBs) that provided much of the volunteer labor to the cooperative nonetheless survived. The CEBs turned their attention to problems related to health and to land, which they had identified as priority issues in São Felix. In the early 1980s members of the CEBs and church officials became targets of the same pressures that affected progressive organizations elsewhere in southern Pará that were accused of fostering tensions over land. After the arrest of the two priests in São Geraldo (see chapter 6), church organizations in São Felix helped organize the opposition party victory in the local 1982 elections, as they had done in many other municipalities in the region.[19] The increase in land conflicts in São Felix that took place in later years inevitably drew the church more deeply into the fray. After a group of *posseiros* was expelled from the contested Gleba Maguari in 1987, two priests who came to their defense received death threats from ranchers seeking to claim the land. An open letter to authorities signed by four bishops denounced violent police actions in São Geraldo and São Felix do Xingu.

Until the changes of the late 1970s, a one-party political system had functioned in São Felix do Xingu as it had in nearly every other municipality in Pará. A local chapter of the opposition party MDB was created in 1966, but its candidate for prefect, Luís Ferreira Santana, was defeated in the 1967 election. Three years later, Santana rejoined the government party, ARENA, to run successfully as vice-prefect in 1969. In 1978, with the influx of new migrants unrelated to the traditional political system, proposals to revitalize the MDB again circulated in the town. As occurred in Conceição do Araguaia (see chapter 5), it was doctor-ranchers from southern Brazil who provided the first leadership for the incipient political opposition. In 1981 one of the state physicians unsuccessfully attempted to create a chapter of the new opposition party, PTB. Eventually he became one of the two candidates for the PMDB in the 1982 elections.

The influx of newcomers changed the character of local politics in São Felix do Xingu, but the old-timers in town did not immediately lose their power and following. The man elected mayor in 1982 on the PMDB ticket was not an outsider but a populist *aviador* and long-time São Felix resident who had financed his campaign with the profits he had made in the Rio Branco gold mining area. Similarly, in the local elections of 1988 a leading candidate for prefect was Luís Otávio Montenegro Jorge, an able young man with years of experience in city government in São Felix and Tucumã. Montenegro was heir to rubber baron Colonel Tancredo Jorge, the founder of the town of São Felix.

Anticipating the Road

The construction of the PA-279 was at a standstill from 1978 to 1979. Several factors accounted for the delay. FUNAI and the highway department were in the process of negotiating the boundaries of the Xikrin reserve. In the meantime, the funds the state had budgeted for the project were running low. In addition, the Andrade Gutierrez construction company was in no hurry to complete the road before the firm had received approval from the Senate in Brasília to purchase Gleba Carapanã, the Tucumã colonization site (see chapters 5 and 7). From 1980 to 1981 the road was open to the public only as far as the company's property. A year later, the colonization company had built a service road along the Rio Fresco as far as Krimet, but the firm had little interest in going much farther.

Local authorities in São Felix were outraged. They sent a report to Jarbas Passarinho to complain that the company was deliberately holding up the road. The document urged the government to release funds to complete the construction. The president of the local union circulated a similar petition. With the road stalled, both resources and population were being drained from São Felix in favor of the new towns, such as Ourilândia and Tucumã. SUCAM figures showed that the population of São Felix grew between 1980 and 1983 from 2,597 to 5,239, but its proportion of the total population along the road fell from 17.2 percent in 1980 to 14 percent in 1983.[20] The population of the other settlements along the road to São Felix more than doubled during this period from 15,112 to 37,539.

Migrants who had already traveled to São Felix do Xingu held high hopes for the changes that the road would bring about. "We think only of the road," one migrant said. He went on to add that "If it weren't for the road project, we wouldn't stay. We suffer here, but with the road coming we're well-situated." Old-timers were more ambivalent about the changes that were already beginning to take place. They complained about the noticeable increase in crime and prostitution and the presence of so many strangers.[21] One long-time resident predicted that "With the road, everything will change. There will be 20 percent improvement and 80 percent problems, principally with regard to land. This is progress. Progress arrives the same way in every place; it homogenizes everything."

Uncertainty about what the road would bring, especially with regard to land rights, was repeatedly expressed by those inter-

SÃO FELIX DO XINGU

viewed in the 1981 survey. One migrant who had lost his land in
Conceição do Araguaia in 1975 had moved to São Felix do Xingu
in 1977 to stake another claim. Still waiting in 1981, he predicted
that "The road will bring improvements: things will get cheaper,
transport easier. But in terms of land it will get worse for us. The
poor either sell out cheaply or they leave for fear of the sharks
[large landholders]. Who knows," he went on to speculate,
"maybe now the government will take pity on the poor." Subsequent events in São Felix do Xingu would show that his tentative
faith in "the government" was unfounded.

Fishing and Logging Conflicts

Fishing was a mainstay of the traditional subsistence system of
the people of São Felix. Fish, often combined with manioc flour,
played an important part in the diet of both Indians and *caboclos*.
By the 1980s changes were beginning to affect fishing. The most
important was the upstream pollution of the Rio Fresco due to
mining, especially after the introduction of hydraulic techniques.
The soil runoff and other pollutants that escaped during the washing and purifying processes—sewage, diesel fuel, detergent, and
mercury—caused the Rio Maria, Paraupebas, and Itacaiunas rivers
near Xinguara and Marabá to run red and muddy.[22] At one point,
the Rio Fresco, the center of Gorotire village life, was so polluted
by mining camps that FUNAI had to pipe water for the Indians
to use from another stream more than a mile away. The river's
fish population was reduced, and the murky water made it difficult
for the Kayapó to use the traditional bow and arrow method of
fishing. In São Felix, the water system was shifted to the Xingu
river. North of the town, where the two rivers joined, the clear
waters of the Xingu on the western shore ran alongside the muddy
waters of the Fresco on the eastern bank. The sharp division
between the two rivers, which only mingled after many miles,
served as a living, moving symbol of the confrontation between
traditional and contemporary Amazonian life.

The influx of population and the growth of markets in other
towns along the road also placed new pressures on the fish population. Sport fishermen appeared for the first time in 1983 when

tourists came into town. They fished up and down the river, taking hundreds of kilos of fish they loaded into styrofoam containers. In 1984 there were about five merchants who purchased fish regularly in São Felix for sale in Ourilândia and Tucumã. Ice trucks belonging to one entrepreneur carried about five hundred kilos of fish out every week.

Much of the local fish was still caught for home consumption or sold in the streets of São Felix during the early morning hours. One newcomer complained about the persistence of the traditional market: "The fishermen around here are a sorry lot. They'd rather turn their catch over to a kid who walks around town than to sell it to me. The guy thinks it's a better deal because he can sell a fish in town for two thousand cruzeiros per fish. What he doesn't realize is that I'll pay one thousand cruzeiros per kilo, but I'll buy on a regular basis. When he sells fish on the street, he never knows whether he'll sell all of them or not. I can guarantee purchase, but a lot of them around here haven't got much interest in it."

Local fishermen were concerned with the influx of outsiders fishing in the rivers of São Felix, where fish were becoming noticeably scarcer. Long-time resident Belmiro Santana organized a fishing cooperative in 1984 that would license fishermen, organize sales in the Sunday fish market, and provide assistance with credit and medical care. He had collected more than the required three hundred signatures to register a cooperative. "I've been a fisherman here for forty years, along with all my friends," Santana exclaimed. "Everything I own was earned fishing these rivers. But now we have the outsiders who come in here and just think they can do anything they want. We will not sit by and let this happen."

The logging boom also came to São Felix with the road. In 1978 there was only one dilapidated sawmill in town and another extracting mahogany from a nearby *castanhal* called Triunfo. Most sawmills at the time were concentrated in and around Redenção, Rio Maria, and Xinguara. By 1980 and 1981 the mills had moved westward from Xinguara as far as Agua Azul along the PA-279. Once the prime timber was cut in the surrounding area, they moved further down the road. When the Andrade Gutierrez company permitted access to the colonization site, three logging companies operated in the Tucumã project area for a time. The first large sawmill was established in São Felix just after the road was opened. By 1984 five sawmills that occupied the banks of the Fresco River in São Felix had moved there from Agua Azul, Redenção, or Rio Maria.

Conflicts over access to mahogany were not restricted to the Indian areas described in chapter 9. While there was abundant standing timber near São Felix, gaining legal access was problematic because of the confusion over land rights. The sawmills tried to divide up areas between them, but they were unsuccessful because lots were neither demarcated nor legalized. Logs were often purchased from *empreiteiros* hired to clear an area. The sawmills with Belém offices tried to obtain licenses from IDBF for landowners who held some proof of ownership. Just about the only legal documents that could be used as proofs of ownership were those issued by ITERPA for lots in the colony created just before the 1982 elections (see below). Since these lots were not demarcated, a sawmill might buy the rights to the lot from the owner while another sawmill purchased rights to log the same area from a *posseiro* settled there. As a result, loggers sometimes found themselves in armed confrontations.

Ranchers and small farmers who were clearing the land would indicate where mahogany could be found. A *mateiro* or *explorador* would then locate the trees for a fee. The logging company would build the roads needed to extract the logs, often paying a lower price for the timber in exchange for opening up side roads. The loggers with their roadbuilding equipment improved transport conditions for some of the small farmers in São Felix. This primitive method of extracting mahogany trunks from the forest contrasted with that of the bigger sawmills. Each produced about six hundred cubic meters of mahogany a month, worth about four hundred thousand dollars. Their operations were financed by letters of credit and purchase orders from importers in the United States and Great Britain, which were kept in a company safe, along with the dubious land documents and IBDF licenses. The sawmills seemed out of place in the town of São Felix, and the town's mayor in 1984 was openly hostile to the loggers. One sawmill owner described the reception he got when he first visited the mayor's office: "When I mentioned I was a logger, the first thing he did was cross himself and mutter a prayer. It was as though he were talking to the devil himself."

The resources available to the industrial wood producers were far greater than those of the municipal government. As in other places, the loggers ended up maintaining roads and bridges themselves although it was also their heavy trucks that took the greatest toll on the precarious infrastructure. The local bank was incapable of handling the payroll needs of one of the larger sawmills. Checks took about two weeks to be issued because there was rarely enough money on hand to cash them. So the company simply flew the cash in from Belém on payday and kept it in its own safe.

Skilled employees of the sawmills were brought in from southern Brazil. The wooden houses (often constructed of mahogany) built by the company stood out from the rest of the town. The company store carried soft drinks, canned goods, milk, vegetables, rice, and beans—all trucked in from outside. The companies had a separate electrical power system to run their plant and illuminate the nearby workers' homes. Fuel to run the plant was stored on the premises. Operating as an enclave community and economy, the sawmills purchased almost nothing on the local market. The same was true of the mining companies that claimed rights to vast areas surrounding São Felix do Xingu.

Garimpeiros and Mining Companies

Mining became increasingly important in São Felix in the 1970s as other extractive activities declined. Word spread in the mid-1970s about the cassiterite deposits at the site called Antônio Vicente north of São Felix on the Xingu river, first detected by geologists working for DOCEGEO in 1972. A *garimpo* landing strip called Jabá was opened up there in 1976. By this time Brazil's largest tin-producing company, Estanífera (owned by the Bolivian Patiño), held a research license for the area. The company advanced the money for building the airstrip to a pilot who owned two small single-engine planes. In the initial months, the role played by Estanífera was limited to this financing and to buying the ore from the airstrip owner, who operated a "closed" *garimpo* through his monopoly over transportation and commerce. In July of 1976 there were about two hundred *garimpeiros* in the area. The ore they extracted was mixed with impurities that added to its weight and decreased its value. Within a year about three thousand *garimpeiros* invaded the area, and several new airstrips were constructed. Some of the new areas contained higher quality ore for which research licenses were held by DOCEGEO and by BEST (another large tin producer in Brazil). The short airstrips were insufficient to allow planes to take off with full loads of ore. Instead, they took half-loads about fifty kilometers to São Felix, then took off from the town's excellent new airstrip bound for Redenção or Santarém and flew from there to southern Brazil or Manaus.

The *garimpo* prospered because competition from the smaller buyers—often little more than "phantom" companies—bid up the price that miners received for tin. By 1978 there were about eight thousand to ten thousand *garimpeiros* working along five active airstrips. At their peak between 1978 and 1979, the tin mining sites supported thirty-six brothels and about four hundred prostitutes. The movement of workers into the *garimpo* caused the population of the town of São Felix to drop, reversing the earlier urbanizing trend.[23] Mining techniques were manual, using only pumps to move water, and there were only a few specialized jobs in the tin *garimpo*: the *cabeça de caixa*, who controlled the flow of ore through the wash box, and the *telador*, who separated the cassiterite from impurities.

New directives issued by the DNPM in 1978 sought to protect legitimate mining companies from competition from "phantom" buyers. The agency did so by granting the companies exclusive buying rights in the *garimpos* where they held research licenses. In April a special decree signed by the Ministries of Finance and Mining and Energy turned over the rights to purchase cassiterite in the São Felix *garimpos* to two licenseholders: DOCEGEO and Mamoré, a subsidiary of Paranapanema, one of Brazil's largest producers. DOCEGEO held rights to three areas that produced about two hundred tons of cassiterite a month, while Mamoré controlled one area that contained the richest ore. The other buyers were given thirty days notice to move on.

Since the miners themselves were permitted to remain, the directive effectively amounted to an eviction of buyers who had large investments sunk into the *garimpo*. The new regulations amounted to an attempt to turn over a traditional *garimpo* to mining companies. Problems arose because in the traditional system it was the buyers who advanced credit to miners and who were closely involved in nearly every aspect of the supply system. The mining companies, on the other hand, were unprepared to assume responsibility for such tasks. As a result, the mining conflicts that took place in the São Felix area were quite different from what took place in gold fields of Serra Pelada and Cumaru.

São Raimundo

The largest single *garimpo* at the time of the takeover was Pista Nova, also known as São Raimundo, where approximately four thousand *garimpeiros* worked eight or nine different streambeds accessed by the same airstrip. A small company, called Espeng, had made the initial investment to open the area. Founded by a prospector, Espeng cultivated an image of solidarity with the *garimpeiros*. In typical *garimpagem* fashion, buyers controlled the transport of both ore and supplies to and from the *garimpo*, cooperating with merchants operating on the airstrip. Generally, for each kilo of ore merchants sold to the company, they were entitled to bring in one kilo of supplies on the planes that would otherwise be flying empty into the area. This agreement saved on freight for merchants and kept the cost of provisions down. More importantly, the arrangement was maintained even during periods of low production, such as the rainy season. On these occasions, buyers provided merchants with advances to cover the freight cost of provisions. For the *garimpeiros*, the system provided the certainty that they would not go hungry, whether production at that moment was high or low. The *garimpeiros* also profited from the price competition among buyers.

The Mamoré mining company held rights to the São Raimundo site. Once the new regulation was passed, Mamoré expected its competitors to immediately leave the area. The Mamoré staff failed to appreciate the full extent of the disruption this would cause. Merchants suddenly found themselves without credit. The handful of larger suppliers who had made it a practice to sell ore directly in southern Brazil could no longer do so. Their response was simply to stop providing any supplies. The *garimpeiros*—their lifeline suddenly cut—descended en masse on the Mamoré headquarters to demand a solution. Faced with a potential riot, Mamoré made some concessions. The main buyers were given an additional ninety days to continue to buy ore (and sell it to Mamoré) and to collect on their outstanding debts. Merchants selling ore to Mamoré at the official price were granted a small commission on each kilo.

This solution soon created its own problems. Mamoré now purchased ore at a fixed price from anyone in the *garimpeiro* social system. Miners therefore had the option of selling either to their supplier or directly to Mamoré. The latter option provided a means of avoiding repayment of debts to the supplier. The merchants again threatened to stop supplying the *garimpo*. At this point Mamoré agreed to buy ore only from the merchants and at the official minimum price. At the same time, the company began stockpiling supplies in a warehouse nearby in the event of a similar emergency. Although it had no interest in becoming merchant-suppliers, Mamoré needed a back-up system in order to bargain with the merchants. Its ultimate objective was not to support the *garimpo* system but rather to see it slowly decline, leaving the company in a position to begin mechanized production.

The transition from *garimpagem* to mechanized mining was completed by 1982. Three different methods were used to extract the tin-bearing ore from the streambeds: dredges, washing plants, and hydraulic units. All consisted of more sophisticated versions of the semimechanized methods common in the *garimpo*. The company produced five or six tons of tin each day from the fifty to sixty tons of material dredged up. The selling price of the tin was variable, primarily due to the actions taken by the tin producers' cartel, of which Brazil was not a member.

Stratified company housing was provided for three levels of employees at São Raimundo, including about 20 professionals, 50 mid-level technicians, and 420 manual laborers. Unmarried workers received free meals. Those with families were permitted to

TABLE 10.4
Mining Licenses in Southern Pará as of May, 1986

Municipality	Research Requests		Research Licenses Already Granted		Production Concessions	
	No.	Hectares	No.	Hectares	No.	Hectares
Conceição do Araguaia	60	433,632	104	771,128	3	30,000
Marabá	153	1,231,580	278	2,088,898	4	54,650
Marabá/São Felix do Xingu	7	10,000	16	148,807	—	—
Marabá/Xinguara	19	177,569	10	46,000	—	—
Redenção	13	118,072	8	29,830	—	—
Redenção/São Felix do Xingu	—	—	9	87,334	—	—
Rio Maria	1	9,000	—	—	1	1,000
São Felix do Xingu	257	2,150,640	613	4,509,254	14	84,648
Xinguara	—	—	3	3,000	—	—
Total Southern Pará	510	4,130,493	1,041	7,684,251	23	170,298
% of total Pará	22.9%	20.4%	26.1%	27.2%	11.2%	20.6%
Total Pará	2,226	20,236,365	3,994	28,297,221	205	825,935

SOURCE: *IDESP* 1986: 1–4, 8, 9, 11.

purchase their food at the company store at São Paulo prices plus a 10 percent markup. Goods were brought in by boat from Altamira. There was also free health care and schooling up to the fourth grade. Approximately two hundred to three hundred temporary workers, mostly from Altamira and São Felix, were hired through *empreteiros* to cut the lumber necessary to fuel the plant's generator. Their wives and daughters sometimes worked as domestic servants for other employees. Like the sawmill complexes in São Felix, mechanized mining was an enclave operation that had little to do with the local economy or population.[24]

The mineral resources in São Felix had attracted even more interest than its land since the 1970s when there were already hundreds of requests for research permits there. As of May 1986 there were more mining concessions in São Felix than anywhere else in the state of Pará (see table 10.4). About one-quarter of the requests in the state were in southern Pará, and over half of these were in São Felix. Requests for research concessions covered an area of 45,092 square kilometers in São Felix, and licenses had already been granted for research in 4.5 million hectares of the municipality's land and for production in 84,648 hectares.[25] Eleven of the fourteen production licenses were for tin. Access to minerals was officially reserved for mining companies, but the firms had to do continual battle with the *garimpeiros* and merchants who claimed the same deposits.

DOCEGEO

Similar events occurred a little later at the airstrips DOCEGEO took over. Having learned from Mamoré's experience, the DOCEGEO took the precaution of permitting a longer grace period to the companies previously in the area. Out of respect for tradition and aware of the useful function these customs performed in the *garimpo*, the company also continued to pay a landing fee to the airstrip owners although there was no legal basis for the payment. But DOCEGEO faced special problems because it was part of the state-controlled Vale do Rio Doce (CVRD). *Garimpeiros* feared that the army would show up and that the site would be closed, as had happened in Rondônia years earlier (see chapter 3). The buyers raised the price paid for cassiterite, hoping to bring in enough ore to pay off their outstanding debts in the short time left to them. The result was an artificially high price that worked to the benefit of the *garimpeiros*—at least for a time.

When the DOCEGEO representatives arrived on the scene, the *garimpeiros* viewed them with undisguised suspicion. Now that prices were determined at the official rate based on the latest posting on the London Metal Exchange, the price of tin fell. As a result of the drop in prices and the prevailing atmosphere of uncertainty, merchants were reluctant to supply the *garimpeiros*, and production began to drop off. DOCEGEO tried to underwrite the merchants, but the transition was tense.

The supply problem was particularly acute on the airstrip called Jabá, originally opened by Estanífera in 1976 and later known as "Bomsuccesso." When DOCEGEO took over, the airstrip owner made every effort to make the site attractive to other miners and investors. He suspended the payment of "royalties" for landing rights. The move prompted *garimpeiros* to pour into the area even though the deposits were of low quality. As a result of the influx of miners, the work crews had many men but few pumps, which contributed to the demand for food and kept productivity low. Faced with a potential crisis, DOCEGEO granted credit to one of the merchants so that he could supply the *garimpeiros*.

But new problems arose with the procedures DOCEGEO adopted for evaluating ore quality. The company did not use the "acid test" but rather established a minimum weight of four hundred grams, below which it would not purchase the ore at any price. The supplier thus ended up with a stock of unsalable ore. Because he was still unable to pay off his debt, provisioning came to a standstill. DOCEGEO rushed to install an electromagnetic separator to purify the ore (for a fee). The *garimpeiros* now had to produce a greater volume of ore than before when the other companies had bought lower quality ore at a lower price.

Despite the efforts by buyers, merchants, suppliers, and *garimpeiros* to disrupt the transition, the tin-ore sites eventually came under the control of the two licensed companies. The companies' lack of interest in supporting the *garimpo* system and the exploitation of the most readily accessible ore led to the virtual abandonment of the *garimpos* by the end of 1978. In January of 1980 DOCEGEO suspended its operations there, partly because the gold rush had created new priorities for the CVRD elsewhere in the state.

The Garimpeiro Victory at Pedra Preta

In September of 1980 several thousand miners opened up a new area called Pedra Preta, where they extracted a black stone called wolframite from which tungsten is made. The *garimpo* was accessible from São Felix by river and small aircraft. The secondary surface deposits could be worked easily, even by children. Living conditions were precarious with only one small spring to supply drinking water to the whole population. Malaria was rampant. A somewhat ineffectual military presence was established to control the entry of weapons and drink and to enforce the prohibition against gambling. Even so, nightly bingo games were common for prizes such as clothing, radios, chickens, watches, and even weapons.

A mining company called Canopus held research rights for tantalite and cassiterite in the area. In March of 1981 the police expelled the *garimpeiros* from Pedra Preta, causing an uproar akin to that in the tin mining areas. The merchants refused to leave, including the landowner, who claimed rights to the area and who had invested heavily in the *garimpo*. The *garimpeiros* gathered in São Felix to appeal to authorities. The mayor held a town meeting in which he argued in favor of reopening the *garimpo* on the grounds that Pedra Preta was important to the town because it stimulated commerce and provided jobs. In Belém, lawyers hired to represent the *garimpo* suppliers managed to overturn the decision, and the *garimpeiros* returned. The Pedra Preta incident was hardly as dramatic as other confrontations that took place later in southern Pará. Nonetheless, it was one of the first victories of *garimpeiros* over mining companies.

The Struggle for Land in São Felix do Xingu

Despite the importance of mining in São Felix do Xingu, most of the migrants who traveled the PA-279 came in search of land to farm. By the time they got there, most of the land in the municipality of São Felix had already been claimed. The victory of the Kayapó in securing their territory was especially resented by the newcomers. People struggling for a small plot of land had little sympathy for the Indians. As far as most peasant farmers were concerned, the Kayapó were "savages" who claimed an unreasonably large territory.

The municipality's first agricultural colony was initiated by the prefecture in the early 1970s along the few kilometers of road that headed out of São Felix in the direction of Gorotire. Because the area, like the town itself, fell into the confused, undemarcated zone that appeared on some maps as a forest or as an indigenous reserve, no titles could be issued. Instead, the prefecture issued INCRA receipts in return for taxes paid on the lots, but such documents had no legal standing as definitive proof of ownership. In 1984 GETAT established a temporary office in São Felix and carried out a survey of the colony, which it dubbed Gleba Gorotire. In May GETAT called a meeting of the colonists to demand that they justify their land claims. By July some 413 occupants complied, but the agency left São Felix before issuing any titles. In 1987 the status of the colony was still in limbo.

ITERPA controlled most of the land along the Xingu river (see Map 8, p. 305). In 1979 the agency auctioned off about half a million hectares in the Gleba São Felix, just across the Xingu river from the town, in lots of up to three thousand hectares. The Maginco logging firm purchased a block of thirteen lots. The Veríssimo group, associated with the São Paulo-based company Moinho Paulista, purchased an even larger block. But by 1984 there was only one functioning ranch, the Barra do Triunfo, the owner of which was a businessman from São Paulo with properties in other states. He brought in equipment and cattle by boat and built an airstrip and sawmill on his property. Most of the other property owners did little more than sell the mahogany trees on their land to the new sawmills that had set up operations in São Felix do Xingu.

A state colonization program in São Felix was announced by ITERPA immediately prior to the 1982 local elections. The state agency divided up a small piece of land that had been set aside for a forest reserve in the Gleba São Felix. The colonization program was a means of purchasing political support. Titles were handed out for lots that were undemarcated. In some cases their location was not even indicated on the document. Some of the "colonists" who received titles lived not in São Felix but in Belém. However, the titles to land in the colony soon circulated on the land market. They also served as the basis for loggers to secure IBDF licenses for mahogany extraction.

In 1985 ITERPA opened up approximately 1.5 million hectares in the Projeto Integrado Trairão in an area claimed by the Kayapó Indians (see chapter 9). The agency was able to transfer some of the claims from the Gleba São Felix to this new area, thus freeing up land close to the town for distribution to small farmers. The Gleba São Felix was renamed the Colonia Linhares de Paiva. For the first time a government agency began to hand out actual titles to a few of the migrants seeking land in São Felix. In 1988, 196 titles were distributed by ITERPA. In June of 1989 ITERPA's president, Walcir Monteiro, made his third visit to São Felix in order to inaugurate a new ITERPA office there. The town council celebrated the occasion by granting honorary citizenship to Monteiro and to state governor Hélio Gueiros.

Despite all the fanfare, the state titling effort fell woefully short of an effective program supporting small farm agriculture. In the absence of roads, technical assistance, and credit, even those who had been awarded titles had difficulty subsisting. This reality caused embarrassment at the ITERPA inauguration ceremony when a dozen titles were to be delivered to colonists by the agency's president, but only one of the lucky farmers was still around to receive the document.

São Felix was not a priority area for GETAT colonization efforts, which were concentrated in areas of tension (see chapter 6). Instead, the agency limited its activities in São Felix to *arrecadação*, or registration of public lands.[26] This task consists of identifying areas for which no claims exist and which are therefore available for colonization or public auction. The process also sets aside land for which there are existing claims that must be examined. Even though registration does not confer legal rights to those who claim these lands, it is the first step toward conversion to private property. The bureaucratic process temporarily removes the territories in question from the potential stock of public land.

Land in the municipality of São Felix do Xingu accounted for a third of the total land area registered by GETAT between 1980 to 1983 and for over three-quarters of the land registered during the first half of 1983.[27] Of all the *municípios* under GETAT's jurisdiction, São Felix do Xingu showed the highest proportion of landholdings of twenty thousand hectares or higher. Most of these properties were located in the southeastern portion of the municipality beyond the Kayapó reserve and closer to Redenção than to the municipal seat. Some consisted of old *aforamentos* for rubber or Brazil nuts. For the latter, GETAT was considering bending the rule called "index 3" that limited land claims to a maximum of three times the amount already in use to permit larger areas to be titled.

In 1984 an area of 359,000 hectares across the Rio Fresco from the town of São Felix (Gleba Maguari) became the site of land conflicts. Three persons claimed ownership of the huge area based on state titles that had been issued without the benefit of a survey of occupants. They were extracting mahogany from the land and planned to install a palm hearts factory. Yet the area was already occupied by several hundred *posseiros*. GETAT officials doubted the validity of the title, and the agency's 1984 work plan for São Felix included the demarcation of thirty thousand hectares of the Gleba on which to settle two hundred colonist families. Another two hundred families were to be settled on thirty thousand hectares to be demarcated in the Gleba Xingu, an area of over three hundred thousand hectares down the Xingu river from São Felix beyond the Gleba Maguari. GETAT's plans for the *município* included registration of the Glebas called Araguaxim and Luciana and located to the east of the Kayapó reserve near Xinguara and Ourilândia. But the land agency never settled farmers in any of these areas before its technicians were withdrawn from São Felix.

GETAT's presence had some unexpected repercussions. Uncertainty about what the agency would do temporarily slowed illegal activities related to land clearing and logging in São Felix, causing a slump in the town's growing economy. People from the outside who were considering land purchases waited to see what would happen. Those who had bought land or were merely occupying it were reluctant to begin clearing or to hire workers who might subsequently claim *posse* rights. This in turn put the brakes on logging activity, which depended on land clearing for ready access to lumber.[28]

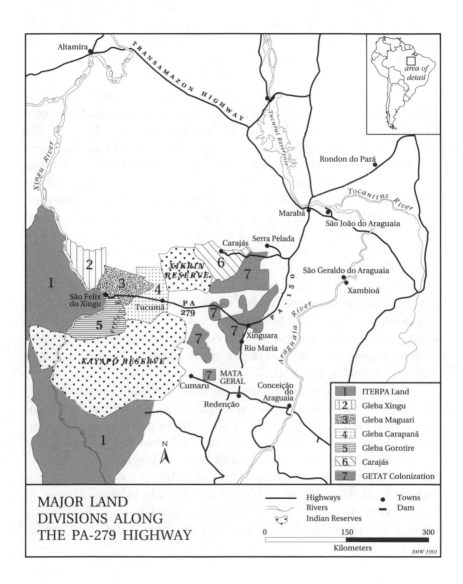

MAJOR LAND
DIVISIONS ALONG
THE PA-279 HIGHWAY

1	ITERPA Land
2	Gleba Xingu
3	Gleba Maguari
4	Gleba Carapanã
5	Gleba Gorotire
6	Carajás
7	GETAT Colonization

Highways — Towns •
Rivers ～ Dam —
Indian Reserves

0   150   300
Kilometers

EMW 1991

The Closing Frontier

By the mid-1980s state and federal land agencies had already allocated much of the land along the PA-279 highway and near São Felix do Xingu. Map 8 illustrates the outcome of bureaucratic procedures that closed off the frontier to migrants moving along the highway. Near Xinguara and Ourilândia, GETAT had distributed thousands of lots in its hasty colonization efforts to the south of the Carajás project area (see chapter 6). Two Indian reserves had been set aside following protracted negotiation with the Xikrin and Gorotire Kayapó (see chapters 5 and 9). The private colonization company Andrade Gutierrez had laid claim to the rich lands of the Gleba Carapanã for its Tucumã Project (see chapter 7). State land controlled by ITERPA along the Xingu river had been auctioned off to ranchers, distributed in preelection colonization efforts, or ceded to the Kayapó reserve. Most of the remaining land accessible to the migrants in São Felix do Xingu was either occupied or already in dispute. Under these conditions of uncertainty, people in São Felix spoke fearfully of conflicts over land. Those who had previous experiences of expulsion pondered how they would respond to new threats. One was resigned to lose: "I planted a field, and when it was ready, they took it away from me. I'm a fundamentalist, and, you know, fundamentalists obey like sheep. We do what God wills and can't complain. I'm going to make some charcoal to raise money and then leave." Another had nearly reached his limit: "We see this happen a lot: someone works a plot of land, clears it, and plants a crop. Then along comes someone else who says he's the owner. I don't want to create problems, but there are some kinds of humiliation that we can't tolerate anymore."

Despite apparent abundance, the land available for small farmers near the town of São Felix was quite limited. While vast areas remained unoccupied, much of the municipality's land was already claimed when the migrants arrived. São Felix was a place where the usual frontier cycle had been "closed" off by the actions of government agencies and the attempts by mining companies, land developers, and large ranchers to take possession of huge tracts of land.[29] One migrant summed it up: "People say there's lots of public land here. You get here—and it all has an owner."

NOTES

1. Mahar (1978:10–12).
2. Trade in pelts was outlawed in 1967, but the IBDF permitted dealers to continue trading skins until 1971, ostensibly to clear their inventories (McGrath 1986; Smith 1980:1).
3. Sondotécnica (1974, vol. 2:399–400).
4. See Wagley (1964).
5. Sondotécnica (1974, vol. 2:85,100).
6. This was the second attempt to create a *município* in São Felix. The municipality of São Felix de Gradaús, created in June of 1955, was abolished in December of that same year due to political disputes in the state (Paróquia 1988:46).
7. Based on SUCAM data reported in Monte-Mór (1984:19). This trend towards declining riverside settlements in favor of the municipal seat is reported for other *caboclo* communities as well; see chapter 2.
8. Sondotécnica (1974, vol. 2:633).
9. Sondotécnica (1974, vol. 2:489).
10. Sondotécnica (1974, vol. 3B:438,445,469). In 1973 there were only six classrooms. Each held an average of seventy-four students per class under the instruction of thirteen teachers, only one of whom had training beyond the primary level. Half of the school-age population did not attend school at all.
11. CPRM (1969).
12. Castro Filho and Heim (1978) and Mattos and Heim (1978). However, in 1989 the company was preparing to begin extraction and processing of nickel and iron.
13. PROMIX (1973).
14. Also in 1972 DOCEGEO, the research subsidiary of the powerful state-controlled Companhia Vale do Rio Doce (CVRD), began research for lead in five research areas of ten thousand hectares each. The company did not find lead and paid little attention to the rich tin ore detected at a site called Antônio Vicente, forty kilometers from São Felix. In 1976 the area was invaded by *garimpeiros* (see below).
15. SUDAM (1976).
16. Sondotécnica (1974).
17. For details on the household surveys carried out in São Felix do Xingu in 1978, 1981, and 1984, see chapter 11.
18. Monte-Mór (1984:27).
19. The Xingu church was not directly involved in the southern Pará struggles until an ugly incident involving Altamira bishop Erwin Krautler, who had been in the Amazon region since 1965. In June of 1983 the bishop joined a group of sugar cane growers who blockaded a bridge along the Transamazon Highway between Altamira and Itaituba. The nonviolent protest was arranged to demand payment from the local processing cooperative for their 1982 harvest, guarantee of payment for the 1983 harvest, and the removal of the cooperative from control of the processing facility. When the federal government threatened to intervene, Governor Jáder Barbalho sent in his military police with tear gas and rifles. In

the ensuing violence, the bishop and other religious were beaten and arrested along with the protesters.

20. Monte-Mór (1984:14).

21. The town's mayor had proposed to relocate São Felix residents who were used to the *caboclo* way of life and unlikely to adapt to frontier change. His plan was to create a new riverside community where they might still maintain their isolation and former lifestyle. But he was unable to motivate the former rubber tappers and Brazil nut collectors to move. For the moment, they still benefited from their ties to the established social and patronage systems in the growing community. They recognized that the frontier had brought with it possibilities of improving their standard of living in ways the *caboclo* life did not offer.

22. Lea (1984:683).

23. This trend continued even after the mining boom had ended. According to SUCAM data, between 1980 and 1983 the movement of some 370 persons to new mining communities more than compensated for the loss of population in traditional extractive settlements. As a result, the riverside population grew during this period even more than the town and its agricultural colony (Monte-Mór 1984:19). However, after the road had reached São Felix in 1983, the urban and road-based populations expanded far more rapidly.

24. By the mid-1980s some mining companies were also seeking rights to land in the areas where they carried out their mining operations in São Felix. Espeng, one of the small buyers in the tin mining areas, had purchased a *seringal* consisting of nineteen lots, or about fifty-seven thousand hectares. The company also had ranches in Goiás. Mamoré had cleared about seventy hectares of land to plant pasture and agricultural crops and was seeking title to the claim. The company had approached GETAT about building a road to São Felix in exchange for title to the land on one side of the road. The agency was not interested in the proposal. These land claims sometimes caused the mining companies to be drawn into disputes over land. In 1985 a group of *posseiros* in São Felix accused a mining company called COMIPA of threats, destruction of property, and invasion of their lots (MIRAD 1986:35–36).

25. IDESP (1986:1–4,8–11).

26. The analysis in this and the following paragraph is based on Almeida (1985).

27. Almeida (1985).

28. There was considerable uncertainty among the town's population surveyed as to precisely what the agency was up to in São Felix. In 1984 of the fifty-two people who responded to the question: "What is GETAT doing in São Felix?," 26 percent responded with either "nothing" or "don't know." Nearly half (47.9 percent) of the respondents indicated they thought GETAT was dividing up and distributing lots for colonization, while another 26 percent thought the agency was dealing with some aspect of land conflicts.

29. Silva (1979) and Schmink (1985).

❖

ELEVEN

The End of the Road: São Felix do Xingu, 1978–1984

Images of our trip to the town of São Felix in 1987 tell how the tenor of daily life had changed compared to what we had seen there a decade earlier. The original part of town had become a commercial center after many families sold their lots to business establishments and moved from the center of São Felix to new residential neighborhoods. In the places closest to the center, houses once made of clay walls and thatched roofs were now constructed of cement blocks and asbestos sheeting, giving an established appearance to the area despite its recent origin. Further from town, newcomers to São Felix had cleared acres of land for housing. The builders had set fire to piles of dried underbrush, leaving gray mounds of ash that smoldered for days. Row after row of bare corner posts and roofing trusses, lined up at regular intervals along would-be roads, gave the appearance of a matchstick village waiting to be completed.

Along the road leading into town, clouds of crimson dust hung in the dry air, churned up by the incessant traffic of logging trucks, tanker cars filled with gasoline, and the comings and goings of battered vehicles of every description. Gasoline stations, auto repair shops, and tire mending shops dotted the roadside. Each garage was surrounded by shredded tires and the gutted remains of discarded Volkswagen cars, Ford pickups, and overturned Mercedes flatbed trucks. Overhead, a low-flying plane buzzed the town to catch the ear of one of the town's twenty-eight taxi drivers, who would rush off to the airstrip for a fare. At the river's edge, dozens of small boats were lashed to a makeshift dock that serviced the sawmills and other enterprises.

To the east of town, the waters of the Rio Fresco now ran pale yellow, stained by the effluents of the upstream mining for gold. The *garimpos*, once operated by hand, now relied on powerful water jets to cut deep trenches into the river banks and surrounding hillsides. The quantity of water used to dig and wash the ore exceeded anything needed for the manual technologies that had still been used as late as four or five years before. Stripped of valuable minerals and laced with deadly mercury, the tailings poured into streams that emptied into the Fresco, causing untold damage to the river's fish and plant life and forcing the town of São Felix to shift its water supply to the Xingu.

The downtown port on the Rio Fresco, where six to eight riverboats had formerly docked every month bringing supplies from Altamira, was relatively quiet. By 1987 the vessels that once came to São Felix had shifted their regular routes to the Iriri and other rivers where the roads had not yet reached the riverside towns. Where the Fresco widens before converging with the Xingu, flotillas of huge logs awaited their turn at the sawmill. From the distance of a mile or so, the high-pitched scream of the enormous circle blade could be heard as it sliced thick, rose-colored slabs from the trunks of mahogany trees several hundreds of years old. The lumber would be trucked down the road through Xinguara and Marabá and on to the port city of Belém where it would be sold on the international market.

A company called Vegetex, a subsidiary of the German pharmaceutical company Merck, occupied a large compound complete with helicopter landing pad in the new part of town. The company's helicopters continually overflew the town, stirring up dust as they brought in sacks of *jaborandi* leaves (*Pilocarpus jaborandi*)—used in the treatment of glaucoma—collected by approximately three hundred men in the forest around São Felix.

In the morning hours, before the bustle of the day began, women gathered by the gates of the rice husking mill. Quietly and with shaken dignity, they would ask for a handout of the broken rice kernels that sifted from the cracks of the ancient machine and gathered in dusty piles on the wooden floor. Throughout the day, a motley stream of people, mostly men, flowed in and out of town: a farmer with a sack of rice to sell; a *garimpeiro*, hauling a heavy water pump on his bruised shoulder, in search of a replacement part; a carload of engineers from the nearby mining camp looking for a hearty lunch and more than a few cold beers.

In the center of town and in the more affluent sections of the new neighborhoods, the early evening was a time when families moved dining room chairs just outside the front door to escape the afternoon heat that lingered inside the house. Cradling aluminum pots of water in one hand, women used the other hand to sprinkle the dirt road to keep the dust down. In earlier times the family would have faced the street, greeting passersby and chatting among themselves. Nowadays the chairs mostly faced inward, people's eyes riveted on a television set prominently displayed against a wall in the living room, under a crucifix and perhaps a framed wedding picture. The flickering neon light the screen cast against their faces grew steadily brighter as the sun set behind the rolling hills across the Xingu.

In the twilight hours in late August, when small farmers and ranchers in the surrounding area set fire to the trees felled on newly cleared land, children in town made a game of catching the inch-long cinders that drifted silently from the sky like flurries of black snow. Late into the night on the outskirts of town, rock music, mostly sung in English, blared from battered stereos propped in the doorways of the string of bars that catered to sawmill hands, miners, cattle ranchers, and to a new clientele of transients who made their living from the road one way or another.

Newly built supermarkets, warehouses, hardware stores, and restaurants as well as the presence on main street of a branch of a national bank were physical manifestations of changes in the rhythm of work and leisure in the town of São Felix. In 1978 people went about their main chores in the morning hours, beginning at daybreak. The noon meal of rice, fish, and manioc flour was taken at home. The heat of the day, from one to about three o'clock, found most residents napping behind closed doors. By mid-afternoon, the pace would pick up somewhat but rarely to what it had been earlier in the day. If a general pattern existed in the way people allocated their time, the customary schedule nonetheless expanded and contracted in response to the weather and the seasons. An exceptionally hot day or one when the rains came at an odd hour would find people staying home longer or venturing out earlier as the case required. Except for Sundays, when the priest conducted mass in the blue and white Catholic church that stood on the hill above the main square, the days of the week could hardly be distinguished from one another.

By 1987 time had taken on a measured quality it did not exhibit before. The change was plainly evidenced by the shrill whistle that blew at the sawmill, marking the start and the end of the day shift, and by the line of customers that gathered by the bank, waiting for the doors to open at the appointed hour. Beyond the mill yard and the bank, the change was equally apparent. Both the morning and afternoon hours saw a bustle of people and traffic that paid little mind to heat or rain. Midday took on the appearance of a distinct lunch hour, a time when the restaurants and sandwich stalls did most of their business.

The weekends acquired new meaning as well. Saturdays and Sundays became a time of leisure and entertainment, to be enjoyed in special places that assumed that function. During the dry season, when the river was low, people from town and the surrounding areas gathered at the new bar and snack shop on the banks of the Xingu to swim in the clear, swiftly moving water. By nine or ten o'clock in the morning on a typical weekend in 1987 you could easily count twenty to thirty cars or trucks, parked in a semicircle around the thatch-roofed establishment that sold beer and plates of fried piranha fish.

Later in the afternoon, after the families had departed, the men and women who stayed on would continue to drink well into the evening. On a particularly rowdy weekend, it was not uncommon to hear a gunshot late at night, echoing from a riverside bar or, more likely, from one of the establishments along the road in the new part of town. On Monday morning, when everyone went back to work, the air would be filled with stories of a trucker or rancher who had tangled with someone in a bar, leaving a body sprawled on the floor and no witnesses to the killing.

New means of communication also transformed people's reckoning of time and space. In 1978 direct communication with the outside was possible only by radio. Popular stations set aside time slots during which they would broadcast letters from their listeners. For hours on end messages addressed to people in towns across Amazonia brought news of a wedding, a birth, a death in the family, a plea for money. The public telephone post was closed down for repairs most of the time. On occasions when the equipment functioned, the dingy building became the site of the town's own soap opera. Residents lined up to await their telephone connection to loved ones or business partners. Just outside the building, an audience of eavesdroppers gathered to pass the time listening to people shouting their intimate dealings into the black plastic receiver.

By 1987 television had come to those São Felix homes and businesses that had electricity. In the evening, less fortunate residents were permitted to stand in the street outside some bars to watch the programs through a doorway or window. A newsstand now stood next to the newly constructed municipal market. Popular magazines were pinned to cotton strings draped across the front and sides of the wooden structure. Rows of glossy images hung like brightly colored shirts on a clothes line: a soccer player kicking a goal in Rio, an Israeli plane flying low over a town in the Middle East, a soap-opera star on Brazilian prime-time television, the naked torso of a pregnant woman framed by bold letters announcing a new contraceptive. Below the magazines lay stacks of newspapers headlining last week's events in Rio, São Paulo, and Brasília. The advent of television, magazines, and newspapers—indeed, the coming of the road itself—meant that São Felix do Xingu was now connected to Brazil and to the rest of the world.

By 1984 the majority of the people who lived in São Felix were recent arrivals. Most newcomers had lived in other frontier towns in southern Pará—such as Redenção, Rio Maria, and Xinguara—only to move further down the road once those places had become more settled and once they had lost hope of finding land of their own. The transformations that took place in São Felix as a result of the influx of migrants raised a number of questions about the process of frontier expansion: Where were the migrants from and how did they make a living in São Felix? What factors motivated them to undertake the journey to this remote town? How well did newcomers fare in terms of such indicators as income, property, health, housing, and nutrition? How did the sociodemographic profile of São Felix's population change after the PA-279 reached the town? Did some social groups benefit more than others from the changes that took place?

To answer these questions, we turn to the data gathered in the surveys we carried out in São Felix do Xingu in 1978, 1981, and 1984. The questionnaires recorded information on a wide range of social, economic, and demographic variables. Together they provide crude, yet revealing, measures of living standards among the town's population.[1] A comparative analysis of these indicators in 1978 and 1984 allows us to estimate the magnitude and direction of the changes in well-being that took place in São Felix do Xingu.[2] The survey results presented here show how the structural transformations in the socioeconomic and political organization analyzed in earlier chapters affected the quality of life among people in one frontier town in Amazonia.

Migrants to the Town of São Felix do Xingu

The interviews we carried out with residents of São Felix do Xingu at three points in time showed how people's personal histories were intertwined with the profound changes that had taken place in the southern Pará region. The results of the 1978 survey indicated that the migration to São Felix had begun well before the PA-279 actually reached the town. Nearly a quarter of the 1,396 residents were newcomers and had arrived there after 1975. The influx of migrants caused the population of São Felix to increase from 2,032 inhabitants in 1981 to 3,840 in 1984.

Prefecture records showed an accelerated demand for urban lots. The office received 80 petitions in 1978, 112 in 1979, and 162 in the first seven months of 1980. By 1981 the new neighborhoods that had been marked off were completely occupied. A new block was opened up in 1982 and a second one in 1984 as the town's population continued to expand along the existing road away from the old center (see Map 7, chapter 10). The commerce and business sector also grew in size and complexity from 34 establishments in 1978 to 67 in 1981 and 108 in 1984.

Most of the people in São Felix had their origins in northeastern Brazil, as shown by the information on the parent's birthplace in table 11.1. The household heads and their spouses interviewed in 1984 were about equally likely to have been raised—and to have lived for the longest portion of their lives—in Amazonia, the Northeast, or the Center-West.[3] Nearly half of the respondents (43 percent) were born in the Northeast. By the time they got married, 50.5 percent of those interviewed were already living in the Amazon region. Similarly, household heads who had grown children in 1984 reported that more than half of their adult offspring (58.9 percent) also lived in São Felix. Another quarter resided elsewhere in Pará.

TABLE 11.1
Region of Origin and Migratory History, Heads of Household and Spouses in São Felix do Xingu, 1984

	Amazonia[1]	Northeast[2]	C/West[3]	C/South[4]	TOTAL (N)
Birthplace of parents	18.4	50.4	17.7	13.5	100.0 (385)
Place of birth[5]	23.1	43.0	19.8	14.1	100.0 (121)
Place where raised	31.6	33.5	25.5	9.4	100.0 (212)
Lived longest	36.4	29.4	26.2	7.9	99.9 (214)
Place married	50.5	20.1	26.2	3.3	100.1 (214)
Current residence of parents	44.9	26.1	24.8	4.2	100.0 (379)
Birthplace[6]	43.6	26.6	23.7	6.2	100.1 (629)

NOTES: [1]Includes the states of Pará, Rondônia, Acre, and Amazonas and the territories of Amapá and Roraima.
[2]Includes the states of Maranhão, Piaui, Ceará, Rio Grande do Norte, Paraiba, and Alagoas.
[3]Includes the states of Mato Grosso and Goiás.
[4]Includes the states of Minas Gerais, Espírito Santo, Rio de Janeiro, Guanabara, São Paulo, Paraná, Rio Grande do Sul, and Santa Catarina.
[5]Heads of household only.
[6]For entire sample.

Data on place of birth show a change in the regional composition of the São Felix population between the time of the two surveys (table 11.2). In 1978, 68.8 percent of all people living in São Felix were born in Amazonia. The Northeast and the Center-West contributed 12.8 and 14.6 percent, respectively, to the town's population. Six years later, the proportion of people born in Amazonia fell to 43.6 percent while the proportion from the Northeast and Center-West rose to 26.6 and 23.7 percent (lower panel of table 11.2). In both years, the proportion of people from the Center-South remained small: 3.8 percent in 1978 and 6.2 percent in 1984.

TABLE 11.2
Birthplace and Region of Previous Residences, 1978 and 1984
(in percent)

Year of Survey	Region[1]	Birthplace[2]	Previous Residence[3]			
			1	2	3	4
1978	Amazonia	68.8	83.9	64.7	58.8	50.1
	Northeast	12.8	3.2	14.7	17.7	24.9
	C/West	14.6	14.5	17.6	11.8	25.0
	C/South	3.8	—	2.9	11.8	—
	TOTAL	100.0	100.0	99.9	100.1	100.0
	(N)	500	62	34	17	12
1984	Amazonia	43.6	69.4	37.5	20.5	13.3
	Northeast	26.6	11.6	20.5	24.4	33.3
	C/West	23.7	18.4	39.4	53.8	46.7
	C/South	6.2	6.7	2.7	1.3	6.7
	TOTAL	100.1	100.1	100.0	100.0	100.0
	(N)	629	147	112	78	45

NOTES: [1]Same as table 11.1.
[2]Total population.
[3]Heads of household. 1 refers to region of residence immediately prior to moving to São Felix do Xingu. 2 refers to place of residence before 1, and so on.

Information on the regional location of four previous places of residence further shows the growing importance of the Northeast and Center-West as sending areas. In 1978 the vast majority of migrants (83.9 percent) had lived somewhere in Amazonia immediately before coming to São Felix do Xingu. The same held true for earlier moves. Data on the second, third, and fourth places of residence indicate that more than half of the migrants had also lived in Amazonia earlier. But the information on the previous place of residence in the 1984 survey, given in the lower panel of table 11.2, shows a different pattern. Whereas 69.4 percent of the migrants came to São Felix from someplace in Amazonia, the proportion of people having lived in Amazonia during earlier stages in their migratory histories was only 13.3 percent (fourth region of residence). On the other hand, the proportion of people who declared the Northeast or Center-West as their earlier region of residence steadily increased with more recent moves in the migrants' histories. On the basis of the information given in the upper and lower panels of table 11.2, we conclude that migration to São Felix do Xingu shifted from a predominantly intraregional movement to a pattern of migration in stages, mainly from the Northeast and Center-West. The change in the composition of the population altered the cultural and socioeconomic profile of the town, as we will note in later sections of this chapter.

In both years, the place of residence just before moving to São Felix was somewhere in the Amazon region. A more detailed analysis of the place of previous residence (table not shown) found a change in the composition of the migrant stream to São Felix and an increase in the pace of geographic mobility. In 1978 almost two out of three households had lived in Altamira or some place in Amazonia other than southern Pará immediately before moving to São Felix. Moreover, nearly 60 percent had arrived in their previous place of residence in Amazonia well before 1970. Analyses of the interviews carried out in 1984 revealed a different migration pattern. Newcomers were twice as likely to have moved to São Felix from nearby southern Pará towns, such as Conceição do Araguaia, Marabá, Xinguara, and Rio Maria, than from Altamira. Most of them had arrived in their previous residence after 1975. Hence, in contrast to the earlier period—when migrants to São Felix were gradually drawn from riverside *caboclo* communities in the region—new arrivals in São Felix were now mainly drawn from the highly mobile populations in the frontier towns of southern Pará.

The journey to São Felix was often fraught with difficulties. One family with six children had steadily made its way in the direction of São Felix after the husband first found work in a sawmill in Xinguara in 1979. In late 1983 they moved further down the road to Ourilândia where they bought a house. There the wife opened a corner store while the husband tried his luck in the gold fields. When he lost all his money in the *garimpo*, they sold the house to pay off the debts owed the local grocery. In May they borrowed money to make the trip to São Felix in the back of a truck together with six other families and additional passengers. Because of the precarious condition of the road, the one-day trip took a week longer than expected. The passengers survived by eating from a sack of rice someone happened to have taken along. At the time of the interview, the man had yet to receive his first earnings from the sawmill in São Felix, where he was lucky enough to find a job. Since their arrival, the only food the family had consumed was the game and fish given to them by the woodsman (*mateiro*) who worked for the sawmill.

Most migrants to São Felix reported that they had left their previous residences for reasons related to land or work. A significant proportion specifically mentioned the desire for land as the main reason for their move. The search for land was the main reason given for having chosen São Felix as their destination. However, the reported motive for leaving the prior residence changed somewhat between 1978 and 1984 (see table 11.3). The desire for work, especially in the *garimpo*, was more frequently mentioned in 1984, and that for land was cited less often. The choice of São Felix as a destination was more often related to the search for work or land in 1984 than it had been in 1978—a change that probably reflected the increasing difficulty in making a living elsewhere on the frontier. Compared to 1978, more of those interviewed in 1984 chose São Felix because they had already visited the town or because they had a job there.

Two-thirds of the 1984 population thought that São Felix was a better place to live than their previous residence. Three-quarters of the population interviewed in 1984 said they intended to stay in São Felix—up from 60.8 percent in the 1981 survey. Paradoxically, the reasons they gave for staying on indicated a less positive assessment of their situation in São Felix. In 1981, for example, over half of the people interviewed intended to stay because they felt they had a good situation in São Felix or because they expected conditions in the town to improve. In 1984, however, less than one-third of the respondents made such optimistic statements. To the contrary, people were far more likely to mention a lack of alternatives as the main reason for staying on. The change in attitude suggests that hopes and expectations for the road had still run high in 1981 but that people were beginning to face up to a less promising future three years later. We can draw the same conclusion from responses to another question in the

TABLE 11.3
Reasons for Migrating, 1978 and 1984[1]

	Reason for Leaving Previous Residence		Reason for Choosing São Felix	
	1978	1984	1978	1984
Work or land	55.6	51.9	35.0	46.9
Desire for land	33.3	23.9	25.0	28.6
Desire for employment	9.3	11.9	—	5.1
Desire for autonomous employment	7.4	3.0	5.0	4.4
Garimpo	3.7	8.3	5.0	8.1
Decline of rubber	—	2.4	—	0.7
Decline of logging	—	0.6	—	—
Drought	1.9	1.8	—	—
General betterment	14.8	13.7	15.0	10.3
Health, education	7.4	1.2	8.3	0.7
Contacts	13.0	25.0	25.1	41.9
Family	11.1	13.7	21.7	16.9
Mayor	1.9	0.6	5.0	—
Acquaintances	—	1.2	6.7	—
Job	—	8.9	—	12.5
Previous visit to São Felix	—	0.6	—	8.8
Other	9.3	8.3	8.3	3.7
TOTAL	100.1	100.1	100.1	99.8
(N)	(54)	(168)	(60)	(136)

NOTE: [1]Includes multiple responses.

1984 survey. When household heads were asked if they intended to invite their relatives to come and live in São Felix do Xingu, 55.5 percent said that they would not.

Agricultural Production and Employment

The people who lived in São Felix do Xingu had a predominantly rural background. Two-thirds were born in the countryside, and fewer than half were raised in urban settings. Yet their migratory histories showed that over their lifetime the migrants had been increasingly exposed to an urban environment. More than half of the migrants had lived in a town immediately before moving to São Felix do Xingu. Most had previously worked in agriculture, and another 15 to 20 percent had prior experience in extractive activities. The occupational background of the population surveyed in 1984 was not significantly different from that found in 1978.

Many people came to São Felix in search of land for agricultural production. In 1984 slightly more than half of the population of the town of São Felix had their own land. A few (less than 10 percent) owned more than one piece of property. Nearly all of these land claims were located somewhere in the *município* of São Felix. More than 60 percent were within ten kilometers of the owner's residence. The vast majority of the land claimed in the *município* of São Felix was located either along the Xingu or Fresco rivers or in the municipality's agricultural colony a few kilometers from town.

These landholdings were small by Amazonian standards. The average size of a plot was 55.8 hectares. About half were twenty hectares in size, well below the official minimum for the Amazon region of one hundred hectares. Most of the land had been acquired either by purchase (42.4 percent) or by *posse* (22.7 percent). A few plots of land had been given out by the state land agency, ITERPA, (7.6 percent) or by the municipality (3 percent). The rest had been obtained through inheritance or exchange. Only 11.3 percent of the acquisitions had taken place before 1975. More than half of the landholdings reported in 1984 had been obtained between 1982 and 1984.

As in the rest of Amazonia, people who claimed land in the São Felix area had a hard time documenting their ownership of the plot (see table 11.4). In 1981, 38.5 percent of "landowners" had no supporting documents whatsoever. Three years later the proportion of landholders without documents rose to 59.7 percent. In both years the percentage with clear title was quite small—less than 10 percent. In the absence of legal titles, people held on to any piece of official-looking paper they had in their possession, hoping it would suffice. Receipts of purchase from the previous claimant—who, likewise, had had no title—were carefully stored away for this purpose. Other claims to ownership were based on the INCRA tax receipts. But even these papers were increasingly difficult to come by. As a result of the increase in the tax rate that took place between the two years, the percentage of landholders with INCRA tax receipts fell from 53.8 percent in 1981 to 14.5 percent in 1984.

TABLE 11.4
Type of Land Documentation[1], 1981 and 1984

Type of Document	1981	1984
None	38.5	59.7
Definitive title	1.9	4.8
Provisional title	1.9	4.8
ITERPA title	—	3.2
INCRA tax receipt	53.8	14.5
Receipt for purchase	—	12.9
Other	3.8	—
TOTAL	99.9	99.9
(N)	(104)	(62)
$\chi^2 < .001$		

NOTE: [1]In percent; includes multiple responses.

Fewer than a third of these landowners had anything planted on their land in 1984. Most of those who had crops in the field held land in the agricultural colony or along the Fresco river. They reported planting altogether an average of seven to ten hectares of subsistence crops: rice and corn (an average of about four and a half hectares each, often intercropped), as well as beans and manioc (about one and a half hectares each). The larger farmers reported devoting as much as twenty hectares to rice and corn and up to four or five hectares to beans or manioc. A few had planted pasture, ranging from seven to fifty hectares. Another 30 percent were clearing their land for the first time and intended to plant about three hectares each of rice, manioc, and beans. Production may have been somewhat depressed during the 1984 survey because of the effects of GETAT's presence in the town described in chapter 10.

Farmers reported selling six different agricultural products from 1983 to 1984, including manioc, manioc flour, rice, beans, corn, and bananas. They also sold chickens, eggs, pigs, game, fish, lumber, charcoal, and Brazil nuts. The proportion of urban households that reported raising domestic animals declined between 1978 and 1984, especially those raising chickens (52.5 percent in 1978 compared to 35.2 percent in 1984). Only 10 percent had pigs (down from 15 percent in 1978) and only 8 percent raised ducks (similar to the 1978 proportion).

Producers frequently sold directly to consumers or, in about one-third of the transactions, to local merchants. Rice was by far the most commonly sold item, mentioned fifteen times out of a total of fifty-seven reported transactions. One of the town's two rice processing mills reported purchasing twelve hundred sacks of rice in 1984, up from one thousand in 1983. The marketing of these products was severely hampered by transportation problems and by the lack of a local farmers' market. Farmers often had to sell for a low price or turn over half their rice to the processors in return for the threshing service. By 1987 conditions for farmers had improved somewhat with the establishment of a Sunday market and the expansion of logging roads that facilitated transportation.

In some cases urban residents did not care for their agricultural plots themselves. About one-fourth of the thirty-five subsistence plots in 1984 were under the care of someone besides the owner: a sharecropper, family member, or other acquaintance. A small number of landowners interviewed reported hiring day workers (eleven) or task workers under the *empreitada* system (thirteen). Extrapolating from the sample to the whole town's population would suggest that approximately 240 persons were hired as rural workers by urban dwellers in São Felix during the 1983/1984 season.[4]

Social Class and Economic Change

Few residents of São Felix had much education to prepare them for anything besides rural employment. Only 17.5 percent of the household heads had completed primary school. About one-quarter (27.9 percent) of the population and 38.8 percent of the household heads were illiterate. At the same time, 57.1 percent (43.7 percent of the household heads) reported that they were partially literate or had attended but not completed primary schooling. Although there were no significant differences in education between men and women, we did find differences in educational attainment by region of origin. Compared to those from the Center-West—half of whom had some schooling—new migrants to São Felix who had lived for most of their lives in the Northeast had never attended school.

Education was highly correlated with urban employment (primarily in commerce and services), which absorbed 82.4 percent of those with completed primary school or higher. This was a substantially higher proportion compared to workers with some literacy, 44.2 percent of whom held urban jobs. Of the illiterate population, 26.5 percent worked in commerce and services. Only two of the seventeen household heads in the highest educational group (with completed primary schooling or more) worked in agriculture or extraction. One respondent in that category combined urban and rural jobs. The majority of the population with less than primary education were ill-equipped to compete in the urban labor market.

By the 1970s the rubber trade in São Felix do Xingu had declined substantially, just as it had across the rest of Amazonia. The *aviamento* system that had flourished during the rubber boom a century earlier was in decline although vestiges of the earlier system remained. When we carried out the first survey in 1978, the patron-client relationship continued to be the basis for much of the collection and marketing of different forest products, mainly Brazil nuts. In fact, 15.9 percent of the migrant population reported having worked as *aviados* when they first arrived in São Felix. Six years later the second survey in 1984 found that *aviamento* had been replaced by wage work.

The fourfold social class distribution of heads of household shown in table 11.5 reflects the changes that took place in the structure of the town's economy. Between 1978 and 1984 the proportion of owner/employers (those who hired others) rose by 17.3 percentage points. Similarly, the proportion classified as employees (those who worked for a monetary wage) increased from

TABLE 11.5
Class Distribution of Household Heads, 1978 and 1984
(percent)

Class	1978	1984	(1984)–(1978)
Owner/Employer	2.9	20.2	17.3
Employee	27.9	37.6	9.7
Self-Employed	57.7	42.2	−15.5
Aviado	11.5	0.0	−11.5
TOTAL	100.0	100.0	
(N)	(104)	(110)	
$\chi^2 < .001$			

27.9 to 37.6 percent. On the other hand, the proportion of self-employed, which included small farmers, tenants, and sharecroppers, fell by about 15 percentage points. The category of *aviado* disappeared altogether.[5]

The greater importance of the wage sector—consisting of owner/employers and employees—in 1984 was partly due to the influx of migrants and the jobs that newcomers took when they got to São Felix. To explore the effects of migration on employment patterns, we can compare jobs held by the heads of households interviewed in 1984 and classified according to three categories of migratory status. Natives and those who had arrived before the changes associated with the road in 1975 were the smallest group. The second group included migrants who arrived in the years just before the road was constructed, i.e., between 1975 and 1982. The third group, which comprised nearly half of the population, consisted of those people who had come to São Felix after the road had reached the town. The comparison showed that most natives were self-employed rather than being engaged in the wage labor market. Migrants, on the other hand, were predominantly in the wage sector regardless of when they had arrived in São Felix.

The greater prevalence of wage labor and the reduced importance of traditional nonwage employment can also be attributed to the modest, but statistically significant, change in the industry profile of the town's economy shown in table 11.6. Between 1978

TABLE 11.6

Distribution of Household Heads by Industry, 1978 and 1984

Industry	1978	1984	(1984)–(1978)
Agriculture	29.7	33.9	4.2
Extraction	17.8	16.1	−0.9
Manufacturing	4.2	1.8	−2.4
Construction	4.2	1.8	−2.4
Transportation	4.2	1.8	−2.4
Commerce	10.2	16.1	5.9
Public Services	10.2	14.3	4.1
Personal Services	5.9	12.5	6.6
Other	13.6	1.8	−11.8
TOTAL	100.0	100.0	
(N)	(118)	(112)	
$\chi^2 = .01$			

SÃO FELIX DO XINGU

and 1984 the proportion of household heads engaged in commerce and public service rose somewhat. Agriculture and extraction nonetheless remained the principal sectors in both years.

The continued importance of agriculture and extraction has implications for interpreting changes in class structure (shown in table 11.5). The increase of wage work took place as a consequence not so much of the rise of new (wage-based) industries but primarily as a result of transformations within agriculture and extraction. The change in the internal class composition of the two principal industry categories is reflected in a shift in the proportion of workers who received a monetary wage in exchange for their labor. Between 1978 and 1984 the proportion of employees in the agricultural sector rose by 8 percentage points. In the extractive sector, the proportion rose by 20.6 percentage points. The rise in the proportion of employees in extractive activities was accompanied by the disappearance of *aviados*. In 1978 *aviados* accounted for 52.4 percent of the total extractive labor force. By 1984 there were no workers in this type of relationship. Hence, we can trace the disappearance of *aviamento* to the rise of wage-based logging jobs, which took the place of traditional forest collection activities in the extractive sector of the local economy.

Gender and Work

In 1984 the economically active population of the town of São Felix was roughly twelve hundred people. One out of every four workers was a woman. The distribution of the total work force by industry and occupation at the time of the survey differed little from that of the household heads, but there were significant differences between male and female workers. About half of the male working population was in either agriculture or extraction, compared to only 18.9 percent of the female labor force (table 11.7). Most of the women in our sample worked in personal services (43.1 percent) or in the public sector (17.2 percent). Only in commerce was the proportion of women workers similar to that of men—about one in seven workers.

In terms of social class, nearly half of the working women (49.2 percent) were employed by others. Women were also less likely

TABLE 11.7
Distribution of Workers by Industry and Gender, 1984

Industry	Total Population	Men	Women
Agriculture	35.5	42.6	10.3
Extraction	15.3	17.2	8.6
Industry	2.7	1.5	6.9
Construction	4.6	5.9	—
Commerce	13.0	12.7	13.8
Public Services	9.9	7.8	17.2
Personal Services	16.4	8.8	43.1
Other	2.7	3.4	—
TOTAL	99.8	99.9	99.9
(N)	(262)	(204)	(58)

than men to be owner/employers or to be self-employed. Compared to men, women were more concentrated in a small number of specific occupations and class categories. Nearly half (43.1 percent) worked either on their own or for others as domestic servants, laundresses, and seamstresses. Another 17.2 percent were employed by the government, mostly as schoolteachers.

Between 1978 and 1984 there was a noticeable increase in the number of prostitutes in São Felix. The change was largely due to the *garimpo*, which had attracted many young women to the area. After the tin mining areas shut down, some prostitutes moved to the town. In 1981 there were three brothels in São Felix, mainly catering to the *garimpeiros* on weekends. Other prostitutes lived on their own, sharing nearby houses. Six prostitutes interviewed in one São Felix neighborhood during the 1984 survey had similar biographies. All were from the Northeast and had borne children while they were still very young. Their children were being raised by relatives or acquaintances. Despite their low standard of living, the prostitutes we interviewed valued their ability to make an independent income. Several spoke of the rewards of seeing the world as "adventurers."

Income, Housing, and Property

Monetary income is a poor measure of the standard of living of people in small communities like São Felix do Xingu. Accurate information on income is difficult to collect even in urban, industrialized settings. The concept is even more elusive in rural settings where in-kind income is prevalent and where earnings from agricultural and extractive activities are highly seasonal. Moreover, the high inflation that characterized Brazil's economy over the past decade made it difficult to compare levels of monetary income over time. In light of these problems, we collected information on the sources of income and on other measures of well-being, including property ownership.

Homeownership was the most important form of property ownership in São Felix. Three-quarters of the town's inhabitants owned their own home—a proportion that remained unchanged between 1978 and 1984. Most had either purchased the lot from someone else (48.9 percent) or acquired it through a petition to the prefecture (31.9 percent). The remainder had received their lot through inheritance, exchange, as a gift, or they had simply taken possession of the property. The house itself was sometimes purchased already built (30.1 percent). More often, the house was built by the family alone (40.9 percent) or with the help of family, friends, or hired labor (14 percent). Only 10.8 percent of the households surveyed paid for the construction of their house. Of those surveyed, 4.3 percent had received the house from the prefecture or from some other source.

Migrants in the town of São Felix had owned little property before moving there. In 1984, for example, only eight (6.4 percent) had owned a car or truck. Less than one-third reported owning their own home, and only half that proportion owned a rural lot. In São Felix, on the other hand, they were far more likely to be property owners. More than three-quarters owned their home, and about half had an urban and a rural lot. One third of the sample owned a second house, and 16.7 percent ran a business. Easy access to urban real estate at minimal cost in São Felix was a significant advantage over other places. Urban lots provided a place to live and, in some cases, a place to set up a small enterprise. They were also a source of cash through rent or resale, albeit without the benefit of legal titles.

In addition to the earnings of working household members, one in five families received additional income from some other source, a proportion that remained the same in 1978 and in 1984.

The sources of the extra income reported in the two surveys changed somewhat, however. Retirement pensions were the most important source of revenue in both years, but in 1978 the second most likely source was income from rent. In 1984 profits from commerce and contributions from persons outside the household had taken on greater importance.

However, there was more likely to be a shortage rather than a surplus of available income from all sources. Most households (60 percent) had resorted to purchases on credit during the previous year, usually to buy food, clothing, domestic goods, or to pay for medical treatments. Many had also called on help from relatives, neighbors, or others to get them through difficult times. For many people, finding sufficient monetary income to cover their needs was a constant struggle. "We work a month to eat for one day," said one woman we interviewed in 1981. "I work, my man works, and even so sometimes we go through the day without eating."

Housing Quality

Houses in São Felix were constructed in the typical rustic Amazonian style with dirt floors, mud walls, and thatch roofs. Between 1978 and 1984 the quality of walls and roofing materials improved somewhat, as is shown in table 11.8. The sawmills that began to arrive in the town in 1983 provided wooden planks that began to

TABLE 11.8
Indicators of Housing Quality, 1978 and 1984

		1978	1984	(1984)–(1978)
A.	Wall	8.5	57.3	48.8°
	Roof	29.6	50.4	20.8°
	Floor	29.1	30.4	1.0
	Stove	30.5	58.4	27.9°
	Electricity	47.8	28.0	−19.8°
	Water	36.4	46.4	10.0
B.	Index of Housing Quality			
	Mean	1.02	2.06	1.04°
	Standard Deviation	.89	1.65	

NOTE: Statistical significance .05 or less indicated by °.

replace the traditional wattle-and-daub constructions. Tile roofs began to replace thatch in a significant number of houses. There was also an improvement in the quality of cooking stoves. The overall index of housing quality—a composite of the other indicators—rose from 1.02 to 2.06. The increase in the standard deviation (from .89 to 1.65) further shows that the quality of housing became more varied in 1984 than it had been six years before, reflecting an increase in social differentiation in São Felix do Xingu.

If the overall housing quality index rose, the proportion of houses with electricity nonetheless dropped by 19.8 percentage points from 47.8 percent in 1978 to 28.0 in 1984. The decline in the relative number of houses with electricity was the result of the pace of the construction boom that outstripped the town's ability to expand public facilities. Despite the improvements between the two years, by 1984 more than half of the houses still had thatched roofs, dirt floors, and no running water. Only one house in three had electricity.

Diet

In 1978 little food was produced locally in São Felix. Canned goods and a number of staples sold in town were brought upstream from Altamira by boat. People supplemented their diets with fish taken from the rivers and with wild game that could still be hunted in the surrounding areas. By 1984 local production had increased. Moreover, the arrival of the PA-279 and the feeder roads built by the logging companies improved the transport of food supplies. Yet, the traditional river-based supply system had been replaced by overland routes, and prices of basic food items remained high in São Felix. With the road still in precarious condition, especially during the rainy season, the loss of the river trade led to shortages in São Felix.

Putting food on the table was a problem for many families. As one woman told us in 1984: "We went hungry in the winter [rainy season]. I'm not ashamed to tell you because it was true hunger. We didn't have anything to eat. God knows what will happen this coming winter." Recent migrants were at a special disadvantage because of the cost of moving and other misfortunes that often wiped out whatever they had managed to accumulate.

We were particularly interested in understanding dietary changes as a measure of the dramatic shifts underway in São Felix. A complete assessment of nutritional adequacy required complex methods that were beyond the scope of what we were able to apply in the field. The survey questionnaire nonetheless provided information on various indicators of food consumption. One measure was based on foods consumed on the day prior to the interview. The results in table 11.9 show that the main food items—those consumed by at least 50 percent of households in 1978 or

TABLE 11.9
Food Consumption, 1978 and 1984[1]

Food Group	Food Item	1978	1984	(1984)–(1978)[2]
Grains, Legumes	Manioc	85.6	60.0	−25.6°
	Rice	96.4	95.2	−1.2
	Beans	65.5	69.6	4.1
	Pasta	11.8	14.4	2.6
	Bread	73.5	45.6	−27.9°
Meat, Eggs	Beef	36.0	36.8	0.8
	Fish	35.7	28.8	−6.9°
	Chicken	7.2	3.2	−4.0
	Eggs	12.6	12.8	0.2
	Pork	9.0	8.0	−1.0
	Tapir	18.6	1.6	−17.0°
	Venison	3.6	2.4	−1.2
	Turtle	4.5	0.0	−4.5°
	Other Game	6.3	3.2	−3.1
	Canned Meat	2.7	0.8	−1.9
Dairy Products	Milk	33.0	25.6	−7.4
	Butter	9.0	5.6	−3.4
	Cheese	1.8	2.4	0.6
Fruit, Vegetables	Greens	3.6	5.6	2.0
	Onions	4.5	6.4	1.9
	Tomatoes	11.6	8.0	−3.6
	Potatoes	6.4	6.4	0.0
	Yams	4.6	4.0	−0.6
	Squash	3.6	3.2	−0.4
	Bananas	42.3	11.2	−31.1°
	Oranges	13.5	1.6	−11.9°
	Other Fruits	6.4	6.4	0.0
Beverages and Sweets	Coffee	89.3	84.8	−4.5
	Tea	6.4	8.0	1.6
	Beer	3.7	0.0	−3.7
	Sweets	11.9	1.6	−10.3°

NOTES: [1]Percent of households consuming food item the day before the interview.
[2]Statistical significance .05 or less indicated by °.

TABLE 11.10
Measures of Dietary Complexity, 1978 and 1984[1]

Food Groups	1978	1984	(1984)–(1978)[2]
Meat, Fish, Eggs	79.7	76.0	−3.7
Dairy Products	37.3	30.4	−6.9
Fruits, Vegetables	48.3	30.4	−17.9°
Grains, Bread, Legumes	95.8	99.2	3.4
Beverages, Sweets	90.7	90.4	−0.3
General Index	7.1	5.8	−1.3°

NOTES: [1]Percent of households that consumed one or more food items on the day before the interview.
[2]Statistical significance .05 or lower indicated by °.

1984—were coffee, manioc, rice, beans, and bread. Only about one-third of the households consumed beef, fish, and milk. Except for bananas, the rest of the food items were rarely eaten.

Did food consumption change between 1978 and 1984? The data presented in the third column of table 11.9 indicate that twenty-one of the thirty-one food items—or 68 percent of the total number of items—showed a decline. The drop between the two years was statistically significant with respect to the percentage of households that consumed manioc, bread, tapir, turtles, bananas, oranges, and sweets on the day prior to the interview. Another measure, derived from the number of times a given food was eaten during the previous week (not shown), confirms the decline in these items and also provides additional information on dietary change. The weekly measure indicated a statistically significant drop in the consumption of fish from an average of 2.8 days in 1978 to 1.9 days in 1984. The consumption of beef, on the other hand, rose from an average of 1.7 to 3.0 days a week from 1978 to 1984.

Although more kinds of foods were readily available in São Felix in 1984 and though some households had a very diversified diet, the range of foods consumed by most families was quite limited. The degree of dietary complexity can be measured in several different ways. One method is to assign a value of "1" to every household that consumed at least one item within each of the five food groups shown in table 11.10. With the exception of the category of grains, bread, and legumes, all groups showed a decline between 1978 and 1984. The change was statistically significant in the case of the category of fruits and vegetables.

The End of the Road 1978–1984

Another method of measuring dietary complexity is to sum up the number of food items consumed from the total list of foods shown in table 11.9. This general index is presented at the bottom of table 11.10. The index showed a significant decline from an average of 7.1 items in 1978 to an average of 5.8 items in 1984.

Limitations in food consumption were undoubtedly related to the scarcity of income with which to purchase food. Lack of income posed a greater problem in 1984 than it did in 1978 because of the increasing commercialization of the food supply. The figures given in table 11.11 show a significant rise in the proportion of households that purchased the key items that compose the São Felix diet, such as manioc, bananas, oranges, fish, pork, and eggs. With the exception of eggs and pork, these were the same items that people were eating less frequently in 1984 than they had six years earlier. This relationship suggests that changes in consumption were partly associated with the decline in home-based production and the increased commercialization of food.

TABLE 11.11
Percent of Households Purchasing Selected Food Items, 1978 and 1984

Food Items	1978	1984	(1984)–(1978)
Manioc	77.8	88.6	10.8°
Rice	75.0	74.8	−0.2
Beans	18.1	17.0	−1.1
Bread	97.1	90.8	−6.3
Bananas	55.8	80.0	24.2°
Oranges	33.9	82.4	48.5°
Fish	23.3	67.5	44.2°
Beef	95.9	100.0	4.1
Pork	37.5	87.0	49.5°
Chicken	26.7	51.9	25.2
Eggs	37.9	67.2	29.3°
Game	35.3	55.6	20.3

NOTE: Statistical significance .05 or less indicated by °.

Analyses of the 1984 data showed that diets varied according to the migrants' place of origin. The consumption of bananas, fish, and manioc flour—basic Amazonian foods—was significantly higher among natives of the region than among people who had come to São Felix from other places in Brazil. Migrants from the Center-South states were less likely than any others to eat manioc flour. Consumption of beans and vegetables was highest among migrants from the Center-South, followed by people from the Center-West and the Northeast. Native Amazonians were the least likely to eat beans and vegetables.

Although we have no measures of the quantity of food consumed, the pattern of change described above suggests that diets in the town of São Felix probably deteriorated over the six-year period. All of the statistically significant changes involved declines rather than increases in food consumption. Reduced consumption was associated with an increase in the tendency to purchase food rather than produce it at home. Changes in the index of dietary complexity between 1978 and 1984 further indicated a narrower range of foods people consumed. The analysis of particular food items also suggested a shift away from the traditional Amazonian diet. Manioc flour, fish, and wild game along with bananas and citrus fruits have long been the staples of *caboclo* cuisine. The decline in these items and the increase in the consumption of beef are indications that the São Felix diet was rapidly becoming less regional in character.[6]

Health and Child Mortality

Health services improved in São Felix after 1978 when the town's only two health practitioners had been a lay midwife and a nurse-pharmacist. Until 1980 a state hospital sat empty for lack of equipment and personnel, serving as a dormitory for the airport construction crew and for visiting researchers like us. In 1978 a dozen local residents were trained as midwives in a course offered by the Andrade Gutierrez company in São Felix. Two southern doctors interested in acquiring land in São Felix arrived in August of 1980 and set up business in the state hospital. A third doctor had arrived earlier that same year and built his own private clinic.

In 1981 the lack of reliable electricity and water at the state hospital limited the services provided by the two doctors and their five attendants to treating malaria and delivering occasional babies. In any case, the population of São Felix tended to have more confidence in the nurse who had been in the community for some time and went to the hospital only as a last resort. The main health problems were related to malnutrition (especially among recent migrants) and, beginning in 1980, the outbreak of malaria primarily due to the expansion of mining. Testing and treatment of malaria were also carried out by an employee of the state agency SUCAM with the help of community volunteers. But a shortage of lab technicians at the SUCAM office in Altamira meant that diagnosis was sometimes delayed for up to two months. By 1984 the two doctors had opened their own private hospital after one of them had been defeated in his 1982 bid for the prefecture.

Survey information from 1984 indicated that doctors had become the most popular health practitioners and were sought by the local population in 42 percent of the reported cases of treatment during the past year.[7] Another 23 percent consulted a nurse, 16 percent went to SUCAM (exclusively for malaria treatment), and 12 percent consulted a pharmacist. Most (55 percent) of the eighteen women who had given birth during the previous year had done so at home, 26.2 percent had gone to a private hospital, and 18.7 percent had gone to the public hospital. The attendant at birth was most often a midwife (40 percent) or a doctor (37 percent) while 15 percent received help from a nurse and 7.6 percent from relatives or friends. Most women's last experience of childbirth (whether or not within the past year) had been without problems; 82 percent reported a normal birth, 10.3 percent had had a Caesarean birth, and in six cases (5.6 percent) the child had died at birth.

Despite improvements in medical services, health problems were still common in 1984. Nearly half (48 percent) of the households surveyed reported that someone living there had suffered an illness during the past year, and in 42.4 percent of the households at least one member was ill at the time of the interview. About one in six (16.8 percent) had members who suffered from some permanent disability, including blindness, deafness, retardation, or paralysis. The most important health problem was malaria, which accounted for half of the 137 cases of illness suffered during the past year. Malaria also accounted for the vast majority of workdays lost due to illness, an average of seventy-seven days for the twenty-three cases reported (or a total of 1,776 workdays lost to a population of 3,840 individuals). Three cases of influenza and two injuries accounted for another seven months of lost working time. Altogether, three out of four health problems during the previous year and half of the current problems were infectious and parasitic diseases, especially malaria, measles, and worms. Worms and dysentery were the most important current diseases, probably related to dietary deficiencies.

One startling finding of our survey was the increase in the death rate of children under two years of age. The child mortality rate provides an especially robust measure of a population's quality of life because it is sensitive to the public health services, the availability of clean water, and an array of individual character-istics, such as income, which affect health through nutrition, hous-ing, child care, and education; the latter is associated with the speed and efficiency with which people respond to illness and injury.[8] The level of child mortality is determined by the com-bined effect of all these factors. Hence, the death rate provides a summary measure of living standards. The mortality rate, as one study graphically put it, "is the bottom line of the social balance sheet."[9]

In 1970 the probability that a child in São Felix would die before reaching the age of two was 133 per thousand—somewhat higher than the average rate for rural Brazil in that year. Between 1970 and 1980 the rate increased by 9 percent to 145 per thousand.[10] From 1980 to 1984, the year of our last survey, the figure rose by another 17.9 percent, reaching 171 per thousand. In just four-teen years from 1970 to 1984 the probability of infant mortality increased by 28.6 percent. The upward trend in the child mor-tality rate and the data on dietary change point to the same con-clusion: the quality of life in São Felix declined from 1978 to 1984.

Social Differentiation and Quality of Life

Revealing as the changes in the various social indicators may be for the population of São Felix as a whole, aggregate measures offer little insight into the character or the degree of differentia-tion among different subgroups of the town's population. This raises a pertinent question: Did the transformations in socioec-onomic structure privilege some groups more than others? The answer is important inasmuch as analyses of quality of life indi-cators disaggregated by social criteria provide a means to identify the distributional outcomes of the processes associated with frontier expansion.

Initially we expected to find that the small group of owner/employers would have the highest standard of living. We further reasoned that the self-employed—by virtue of their access to the means of production—would be ranked next in terms of quality of life, followed by employees. The results of numerous analyses confirmed that owners did indeed have larger, better homes and more diverse diets and that they were less likely to be ill. Yet, contrary to what we anticipated, the findings showed a consistent tendency for employees to rank very close to owner/employers on nearly every measure of living standards. *Aviados* (in 1978) and the self-employed (in both years) were consistently found at the bottom of the socioeconomic scale.

These findings suggest that early in São Felix's transition from a subsistence economy to a capitalist system of production owner/employers did not live very differently than their hired employees. When capital accumulation still was not very pronounced, the distinction between owners and workers was less important in terms of living conditions than was the distinction between people employed in the cash economy—either as owners or wage workers—compared to nonwage workers. Hence, differences in well-being were determined largely by whether households had access to monetary income to purchase food and other goods and services—although this did not imply that wage earners always thought of themselves as better off. Indeed, the benefits of the transition to wage work came at the expense of the workers' highly valued autonomy. As one migrant explained, "Farming is difficult—but working as an employee is like being a slave."

The transformation of the town's class structure can therefore be expressed by combining employers (those who pay wages) and employees (who receive wages) into a single category we label the "wage sector." By extension, the "nonwage sector" consists of people who are self-employed or *aviados* or unpaid family workers. A comparison of the results of the two surveys presented in table 11.12 shows that the proportion working in the wage sector increased from 30.8 percent in 1978 to 57.8 percent in 1984. The nonwage sector declined in importance over the six-year period from 69.2 to 42.2 percent.

TABLE 11.12
Distribution of Heads of Household, by Economic Sector, 1978 and 1984[1]

Sector	1978	1984	(1984)–(1978)
Wage	30.8	57.8	27.0
Nonwage	69.2	43.2	−26.0
TOTAL	100.0	100.0	
(N)	104	110	

NOTES: [1]Derived from table 11.5.

The greater proportion of the labor force employed in the wage sector together with the increasing importance of monetary income suggest that the determinants of quality of life in São Felix do Xingu may have changed between 1978 and 1984. To explore this topic, we selected two indicators of living standards for further analysis—the measure of housing quality and the index of dietary complexity. The first step was to identify the individual characteristics (age and education of the household head) and the structural-level factors (employment in the wage or nonwage sectors of the economy) that explained variability in the two indicators. For this purpose, we used a technique called multiple classification analysis (MCA).[11] The results of the method are easily interpretable because they can be thought of as an extension of the crossclassification tables already presented. In the case of MCA, the results are expressed as deviations from the overall mean value of the quality of life indicator. The advantage of the technique is that the deviations are statistically "adjusted" for the effects of other variables in the analysis. Hence, we can determine the impact of, say, education while holding constant the effects of the economic sector. The second step was to compare the MCA results for 1978 to those for 1984. The comparison illustrates how the transformations in the town's economic organization altered the determinants of social differentiation once São Felix do Xingu was firmly swept into the process of frontier change.

Table 11.13 presents the results of the multiple classification analysis of housing quality and dietary complexity in 1978 and 1984. Columns 2 and 6 of panel A confirm that the average value of the housing index rose from 1.03 in 1978 to 2.05 in 1984 (as noted earlier in table 11.8).[12] Similarly, columns 2 and 6 of panel

TABLE 11.13

Effect of Age, Education, and Economic Sector on Housing Quality and Dietary Complexity, 1978 and 1984
(Multiple Classification Analysis)

Depen. Variables (1)	Grand Mean (2)	Indep. Variables (3)	1978			Grand Mean (6)	1984	
			Adjusted Deviation (4)	Sig (5)			Adjusted Deviation (7)	Sig (8)
A. Housing Quality	1.03	Age		n.s.		2.05		n.s.
		Under 30	−.19				−.21	
		31–45 yrs.	−.14				.04	
		over 45 yrs.	.23				.14	
		Education		n.s.				°
		Illiterate	−.32				−.76	
		Literate	.07				.11	
		Primary	.16				1.24	
		Economic Sector		n.s.				n.s.
		Wage	−.10				.40	
		Nonwage	.04				−.48	
B. Dietary Complexity	7.14	Age		n.s.		5.77		n.s.
		Under 30	.05				−.20	
		31–45 yrs.	−.84				.22	
		over 45 yrs.	.87				−.16	
		Education		n.s.				°
		Illiterate	−1.15				−.71	
		Literate	.19				.33	
		Primary	.75				.61	
		Economic Sector		n.s.				°
		Wage	.87				.48	
		Nonwage	−.38				−.59	

NOTE: Statistical significance .05 or less indicated by ° ; non-significant relationships indicated by n.s.

SÃO FELIX DO XINGU

B show that the index of dietary complexity fell from an average of 7.14 in 1978 to 5.77 in 1984 (noted in table 11.10). These aggregate level changes raise two questions central to the analysis of social differentiation: What factors accounted for variability in the two measures? Did the strength of these factors change over time?

To address these questions, we turn to the adjusted deviations from the overall mean of the indexes in 1978, which are given in column 4. In 1978 none of the independent variables had shown a statistically significant relationship to the measure of housing quality (column 5). In other words, what kind of house people lived in was little influenced by the household head's age, education, or sector of employment. In 1984, on the other hand, the relationship between housing and education was statistically significant. Other things being equal, families headed by someone with higher education tended to live in better houses. Specifically, the value of the index among illiterate household heads was 1.29— derived by subtracting from the overall mean the adjusted deviation associated with being illiterate (2.05 -.76=1.29). The index rose to 2.16 for those who knew how to read (2.05 + .11=2.16). It reached 3.29 for heads of household with at least primary education (2.05 + 1.24=3.29). Hence, between 1978 and 1984 housing quality rose for everyone, but people with more education experienced a substantially greater improvement than less educated subgroups of the population.

The results given in panel B present the same pattern with respect to people's diet. In 1978 none of the variables were statistically significant. In 1984, on the other hand, both education and the economic sector showed a statistically significant relationship to the measure of dietary complexity. Households enjoyed a more complex diet if the household head was more educated or was employed in the wage sector of the town's economy. Hence, between 1978 and 1984 dietary complexity declined for the population as a whole, but the magnitude of the deterioration was greater among people with less education and among those working in the nonwage sector.

Since both education and economic sector were statistically significant determinants of dietary complexity in 1984, a further question concerns the relative importance of each factor. The issue can be addressed by estimating a β statistic that measures the relative impact of different independent variables.[13] In this case, the β values were virtually identical: .31 for education and .30 for economic sector. We conclude that individual and structural characteristics had about the same effect on people's diet in 1984.

The findings with respect to housing quality and dietary complexity suggest several conclusions. In 1978 the houses people lived in and the food they consumed showed little variation when we compared different subgroups of the population. In the years after 1978 the quality of housing improved, but diets deteriorated. These changes did not affect everyone equally, however. People who had higher levels of education and who participated in the wage economy fared better than those who had less schooling and who were employed in the nonwage sector. More generally, we conclude that São Felix—once a town in which everyone lived under more or less the same conditions—was rapidly becoming a more differentiated place in terms of living standards.

São Felix do Xingu: The End of the Road

The socioeconomic and demographic changes brought on by the construction of the PA-279 transformed São Felix do Xingu from a sleepy riverside village into one more bustling frontier town in southern Pará. The influx of migrants, mainly coming from the Northeast and Center-West, increased the size of São Felix and changed the social composition of its population. The center of town quickly evolved into a commercial district, and new residential neighborhoods sprang up in the surrounding areas. The quality of housing improved primarily as a result of the new sawmills in town that produced building materials. Nonetheless, public services were unable to keep pace with the housing boom, causing a decline in the proportion of houses with electricity.

Agriculture and extraction remained important industries, but wage work became the predominant form of labor recruitment and remuneration within these activities. The increased proportion of the labor force receiving wages and the evidence that a greater percentage of household necessities were purchased rather than produced at home or bartered pointed to the growing importance of money in the local economy. The rapid transformation to a more monetized system was associated with greater social inequality. Increasingly, quality of life in São Felix came to depend on factors such as education and employment in the wage sector.

The changes in life and work that took place in São Felix do Xingu between 1978 and 1984 brought a measurable deterioration in key indicators of living standards. Although we were unable to precisely determine the quantity of food people consumed, all of the statistically significant changes in the measures at our disposal suggested a decline rather than an increase in food consumption. Changes in the index of dietary complexity further indicated a narrowing in the range of foods that people ate. But the most revealing change was the increase in the child mortality rate, which rose by nearly 18 percent between 1980 and 1984. Taken together, the various measures point to a decline in the quality of life in São Felix do Xingu—at least in the first years after the road had reached the town. Whether this trend will continue or be reversed in the medium and the long term is a question that can only be answered by future studies.[14]

For the migrants who had traveled the PA-279, São Felix do Xingu was—literally and metaphorically—the end of the road. For many families this was the third or fourth place where they had tried to find a piece of land to support themselves. As one migrant put it, "We're tired of wandering so much in this world. . . . There is public land for us to work here. In Xinguara (his previous residence) we couldn't do that." Sadly enough, São Felix turned out to be the most recent setback in a series of bitter disappointments.

The development plans for the municipality of São Felix do Xingu left little room for smallholders. As in so many other places in southern Pará, it was the wealthy who laid claim to most of the land the migrants sought. Nor did the traditional extractive economy remain sufficiently viable to absorb the rural poor who previously had access to resources for their subsistence needs while depending on traders for credit and other commodities. With most of the land taken, the cash-oriented economy of São Felix left few alternatives. For the majority of men, making a living amounted to a choice between temporary wage work or clearing public land as a *posseiro*, without the benefit of titles or documents of any kind to protect their claim. For women, the options—when they existed at all—were limited to self-employment (including prostitution) and low-paying service jobs. From these earnings, families pieced together an uncertain livelihood, made all the more difficult by the growing realization that, after a long and grueling journey, São Felix, too, was a false hope.

It is no wonder then that the cruel realities of the frontier prompted migrants, Indians, miners, and *caboclos* to engage in the increasingly organized forms of resistance described in the preceding chapters of this book. As victims of violence and all manner of disappointments, their desperate struggle to survive in the face of ever more limited options was a potent force that redefined the strategies people pursued to contend with the rapidly changing economic and political conditions in Amazonia.

NOTES

1. Random household surveys of the town of São Felix do Xingu were carried out in 1978, 1981, and 1984. In 1978 the 120 households surveyed represented 50 percent of the total population of the town. The survey instrument was refined and expanded in 1981 when it was applied to 181 households (also 50 percent of the population). The 1984 survey, which used an almost identical questionnaire, was carried out with 125 households that represented one of every six in the town. The surveys collected information on basic measures of standard of living for each household, demographic information on every person living in the household, and detailed information on up to three economic activities for each person. Detailed migratory and occupational histories were collected from a senior male and senior female member of each household.

The analysis in this chapter focuses primarily on a comparison of findings from the 1978 and 1984 surveys. Data from 1981 are presented only when they reveal a striking change in the intervening period or when they help analyze information not collected in 1978 but added to the revised questionnaire in 1981.

2. Only six years passed between the first and the last survey of the population of São Felix do Xingu. From the perspective of a larger and more established place, this time span would be considered quite short. On the other hand, the marked changes evident from the comparative analysis of the 1978 and 1984 surveys reflect the speed with which things change in a frontier setting. The fact that we do not have more recent data is not meant to imply that we assume that changes underway in São Felix do Xingu had run their full course by 1984. To the contrary, the findings we present in this chapter refer only to the initial stage of the change process that, undoubtedly, continued for many years later.

3. Heads of household were identified by the respondents at the time of the

interview. Migratory and occupational histories were collected from them and their spouses or from other senior male and female members of the household.

4. Estimates of agricultural production in this section are based on a sample survey of people living in the town of São Felix do Xingu. Hence the findings do not allow us to generalize to agricultural production in the *município* as a whole, which covers so immense an area that it was impossible to canvas. Unfortunately, official data on municipal-level agricultural and livestock production for São Felix are of dubious validity. For example, census bureau statistics on cattle production show an increase from 120 head to 22,534 between 1979 and 1980! Agricultural production data also show (less dramatic) increases beginning in 1980 when the last census was carried out.

5. Wesche (1985) also reports an increase in year-round wage employment after an all-weather road reached the *caboclo* town of Itacoatiara in Amazonas.

6. The study by Ayres, Lima, Martins, and Leme (forthcoming) of a Mato Grosso town before and after a road connection also found a decrease in consumption of wild game and an increase in beef consumption. They attributed the change primarily to sociocultural rather than to ecological changes directly affecting the game population or hunting practices.

7. Comparable data on health conditions were not collected in 1978.

8. For a discussion, see Birdsall (1980) and chapter 4 in Wood and Carvalho (1988).

9. Young, Edmonson, and Andes (1983:66).

10. From our survey data. The indirect methods of mortality estimation can also be used to calculate the probability of death to exact ages 3 and 5 (based on the child survival ratio among women 25–29 and 30–34 years of age, respectively). These estimates are not used here because the $3q0$ and $5q0$ values refer to a past time period of anywhere from 6 to 8 years. The retrospective nature of the measure biases the estimate in a migratory population to the extent that child deaths may have occurred before migrants came to São Felix. Although the bias cannot be eliminated altogether, it can be minimized by using only the $2q0$ value, as we have done here, which refers to a retrospective time period of only 2 to 3 years.

11. The use of ordinary least squares regression produces the same conclusions as multiple classification analysis. In fact, the deviations from the grand mean generated by multiple classification analysis can be converted into unstandardized regression coefficients. Although regression techniques are more commonly used in the social sciences, we used multiple classification analysis here because compared to regression techniques the results are more readily interpreted and therefore more accessible to a wider audience.

12. The slight discrepancy in the mean value of the housing index in 1978 in table 11.8 (value of 1.02) and table 11.13 (value of 1.03) is due to the presence of missing cases in the MCA analysis.

13. The β statistic in MCA analysis is analogous to a standardized beta coefficient in ordinary least squares regression.

14. In light of the diversity of local conditions described in earlier chapters, it would be risky to generalize the findings of this study of one town to the fate of residents in all other frontier towns in Amazonia. The value of our quantitative data is greatest when the findings are considered within the historical and structural changes that occurred in this particular place.

The End of the Road 1978–1984   *343*

TWELVE

❖

Contested Frontiers in Amazonia: Conclusion

When we began this study fifteen years ago, what little attention was given to Amazonia was cast in markedly different terms compared to the polemic surrounding the topic today. In the early 1970s the drive to populate the region and exploit its natural resources was of concern to a relatively small number of specialists and observers. The astonishing changes that have taken place since then have transformed Amazonia's role in the country's economy, in the Brazilian national consciousness, and in the global debate regarding the environmental consequences of conventional development models.

Our analysis of these changes was predicated on the idea that what we observed and documented in the field—for example, deforestation, land use and settlement patterns, the rise and decline of different economic activities, and the assault on Indian rights—were net outcomes of a contest for resources between social groups capable of mobilizing varying forms of power. Our perspective recognized that the initiatives taken in a given conflict as well as the power hierarchies that prevailed at a particular point in time were heavily contingent upon the changing alignment of economic and political factors. Many of these operated in places far afield from Amazonia. In our work, we paid close attention to time and chronology and to the relationships between the multiple levels of social organization from local to international arenas.

Throughout this volume we have shown how the actions taken by one government agency or social group led to outcomes that were unanticipated by the people involved. The surprises that history presented to the people of Amazonia were often the result of the convergence of socioeconomic and political influences that propelled the course of events in different and unexpected directions. Underlying the idiosyncratic and contingent properties of history were the patterned transformations of social organization that took place. Our concluding remarks thus refer as much to unique events as they do to the analyses of structural properties that yielded systematic and more or less predictable outcomes. Similarly, our closing observations are inspired as much by the changes that occurred in the region as they are by the continuities that persisted both in Amazonia and in the rest of Brazil.

When the federal government embarked on its Amazonian venture in the early 1970s, Brazil's national economy was expanding rapidly and the military was firmly in control. The combination of rapid economic growth and strict political repression—the hallmark of the "Brazilian model of development"—gave the regime a free hand in economic planning and social engineering. Public funds were plentiful, and private sector entrepreneurs were easily induced to invest surplus capital in the region. Within the national modernization agenda, the commitment to occupy Amazonia's "empty spaces" and to promote modern agro-industrial development was evident in the Carajás iron ore project, the Tucuruí hydroelectric dam, the infrastructural investments financed by POLAMAZONIA, and the Transamazon settlement program.

In the countryside, fleets of yellow construction machines pushed roads into places that until then had rarely seen a surveyor's rod. On either side of the new highways, gangs of men wielded axes and chain saws, converting the forest to agricultural plots and pasture. In the short span of a decade or so the main axis of the region's transportation and communication system shifted from river boats and waterways to diesel trucks and dirt roads. The transition was soon followed by changes in land and labor use and in the structure of local political power. The value of land had once been measured solely by the natural products that could be extracted from the forest cover, and personal relationships and debt obligations had been the main ties that bound people together. Now fence posts marked off private claims to property, and money became the currency of labor remuneration and exchange. In towns and hamlets across the region, these transformations brought new political actors to prominence, usually at the expense of the traditional elite's long-standing control.

Like other facets of the modernization agenda, the Transamazon colonization areas in Marabá, Altamira, and Itaituba bore the imprint of the military's commitment to centralized planning. It was a perspective that was as flagrantly insensitive to the local environment as it was to the needs of the people in the region. Draftsmen in the Brasília planning offices envisioned a grid-square system of land distribution that bore little relationship to the hydraulic and topographic reality of the undulated, and highly varied Amazonian terrain. The cost of such plans was borne by the legion of small farmers and their families who came to Amazonia in search of land. They were the ones to suffer the severe, sometimes fatal, consequences of the ill-conceived project.

More generally the settlement policy, like other federal megaprojects of the 1970s, only replicated the long-standing tradition of subordinating Amazonia to the needs of the national economy and to the will of technocrats in Brasília. Decree Law 1164—which transferred to the federal government the jurisdiction over all land one-hundred kilometers on either side of federal roads, whether actually built or only planned—resulted in the most far-reaching usurpation of state authority in the country's modern history. An intense and prolonged jurisdictional battle between state and federal agencies began. Time and again, actions taken at one level ran directly counter to the intent of actions taken at another. Overlapping authorities and conflicting intergovernmental mandates added bureaucratic confusion to an already complicated process of settlement and change.

At the vortex of the many contradictory agendas were both natives and newcomers to the region. Their attempts to secure their position on the frontier were repeatedly jeopardized by policies and events over which they had little control. It was the poor, as always, who suffered most. But the problem extended to other groups as well. Even people who came to Amazonia with resources to invest often found themselves in an impossible situation. They were unable to secure clear title to the land they claimed or to establish the minimum conditions of predictability required of any entrepreneurial venture.

The developmentalism endorsed by the civilian technocrats in charge of planning between 1964 and 1985 gave preference to large, capital-intensive rather than small, labor-oriented projects. Carajás and Tucuruí were only the more salient examples of large-scale investments whose value to the nation, in the developmentalist view, was self-evident and beyond reproach. This perspective evoked a quasi-religious belief in the virtues of advanced technology as a means to promote the general welfare and as a way to resolve the externalities associated with economic growth, such as environmental degradation and the social costs of displacing local peoples. In the technocratic vision that prevailed, poor farmers—as well as rubber tappers, miners, forest extractors, and native peoples—were either ignored, or, more ominously, were treated as obstacles in the way of progress and civilization. Indians suffered, in addition, the visceral disdain of those who saw their distinctive ethnicity as a threat to the very concept of a united and homogeneous citizenry and hence to the security of the nation.

During the 1970s activists on the political left paid scant attention to *caboclos* and Indians. Such groups were small and politically inconspicuous. For theoretical reasons they were viewed as marginal to the "primary" struggle between capital and labor in urban industry. Questions raised about Amazonian development were mostly couched in terms of the "growth versus equity" debate that dominated policy and academic discussions. In the context of rural Brazil—and, by extension, in Amazonia—the dispute turned on one element or another of the "agrarian question": the concentration of land ownership, agrarian reform, the economic viability of small farming, and the capacity of credit policies and integrated rural development projects to reduce rural out-migration, thus sparing cities the ravages of further population growth.

Conclusion   *347*

By the 1990s the character of the Brazilian Amazon, like the content of the national and international debate concerning its past and future, had taken on a different form. The region had witnessed the rise and defeat of a counterinsurgency movement and had experienced the effects of a strong military presence. Other tumultuous events included the massive in-migration of small farmers who appropriated land along the new roads that were built, a shift in development priorities from public to private colonization schemes with the accompanying abandonment of welfare criteria in the plans to populate the region, and a decline in the legitimacy of the authoritarian military regime, followed in 1985 by the transition to a democratic system. In southern Pará, the scope and intensity of the violent contests for land, gold, and timber spread to ever more distant places in the countryside.

In frontier towns like São Felix do Xingu, agriculture and extraction remained important industries, but wage work became the predominant form of labor recruitment and remuneration. The transformation to a more monetized system was associated with greater social inequality. The changes in life and work that took place in São Felix do Xingu between 1978 and 1984 brought a measurable deterioration in key indicators of living standards. Estimates derived from the surveys we carried out showed a decline in food consumption, a narrowing in the range of foods that people ate, and an increase in the child mortality rate. For many families, São Felix was the third or fourth place where they had tried unsuccessfully to find a piece of land to support themselves. The desperate struggle to survive in the face of ever more limited options was a potent force that prompted people to redefine their strategies for coping with the rapidly changing economic and political conditions in Amazonia.

Beginning in the late 1970s and throughout the following decade, peasants, miners, and Indians increasingly mobilized their efforts to defend themselves. They marshaled their respective sources of economic, political, and ideological power and drew on alliances with other interests both inside and outside of the country. Each group devised its own means to combat the expropriation, displacement, and violence wrought by the massive development projects. This resistance led to a change in their self-conception and to new ideas about how their place in society could be justified. This is the "constitutive" aspect of historical change—the processes through which groups of social actors formulate a common agenda based on shared self-identity in the course of defending or furthering their particular interests. This common agenda makes them potent forces to be reckoned with on the frontier.

Over time the various groups defined and redefined their particular claims to legitimacy. Small farmers from the Northeast, drawing on and inspired by the alliances forged with the Catholic church, constructed a public stance that explicitly contradicted the accumulative ethic of capitalism. They rejected the trend toward land concentration that granted more property to an individual than he could productively use. Ranchers appealed to values of modernity and to the principles of economic rationality to justify their claim to vast stretches of land. A well-oiled lobby machine disseminated ranchers' views within the planning bureaucracy and to the public at large. *Garimpeiros* came to see themselves as saviors of the country, paying off Brazil's foreign debt with the gold they dug from the ground. Similarly, the military promoted its image as defender of the nation against foreign threats and the dangers of internal subversion. With the finesse of a modern public relations firm, Indians and rubber tappers cannily manipulated the national and international press to establish alliances with domestic and international human rights activists and conservationists.

Whatever their respective goals and interests, the process of social change set in motion on the frontier at times led to the very situations that particular actors wanted to avoid. Examples abound. The government planned to open Amazonia as a means to counter the concentration of land ownership in rural areas and as a way to attenuate urban squalor. Actual policies led to an even more skewed distribution of land in the northern countryside and only reproduced the urban ecology of metropolitan Brazil on the frontier. Similarly, the military resorted to a crisis colonization policy to dampen the intensity of rural violence. In response, small farmers began to organize themselves and engage in the very kinds of collective resistance that the generals feared most. Likewise, attempts by the military in the 1970s to centralize control over state and local politics in the Amazon merely added strength to the opposition parties. This led to the regime's undoing in the local elections in 1982. More dramatic still was the military's failed effort to control the unruly *garimpeiros* at Serra Pelada. They sent their favorite henchman, Curió, to establish order. After a bitter struggle, the miners were increasingly defiant and better organized. Ultimately they turned the tables on the army, using military tactics to interdict the Belém-Brasília Highway and to successfully force the hand of the president of the Republic.

The large private investment projects so favored by the government suffered their share of defeat in southern Pará. Andrade Gutierrez was a company with greater economic and political resources at its disposal than any private Amazonian enterprise except Daniel Ludwig's Jari project in Amapá. The company set out to capture the best soils in the *município* of São Felix and to carry out the orderly sale and colonization of Tucumã. Despite the best-laid plans, Tucumã was the site of one of the largest spontaneous land invasions in all of Amazonia in the late 1980s. While politicians debated the matter in the state and federal legislatures and the construction company waged a battle for compensation in the halls of the bureaucracy, people took matters into their own hands. The outcome was a kind of de facto agrarian reform in which the richest agricultural lands, once set aside for relatively wealthy investors from southern Brazil, ended up in the hands of poor migrant farmers.

Contrary to the modernization plan and much to the consternation of the soldiers and technocrats, the people of Amazonia neither passively acquiesced nor unquestioningly embraced the onslaught of change. Novel features of the social structure emerged from the multiple and overlapping contests borne of the specific, sometimes bizarre, combination of old and new types of production, modern and traditional forms of labor use, and the grafting of national cultural traits onto the more tenacious features of Amazonian life.

The collective mobilization of local peoples was an important condition underlying the subsequent changes. However, resistance movements were not the only forces at work. Significant new directions were the product of their interplay with the political and economic context that prevailed at a particular historical moment. As an analytical framework, we thus considered the contests for resources, power, and bureaucratic control that pervaded the system from Brasília to the hinterland. We interpreted these contests with reference to the matrix of shaping influences operating within regional, national, and international arenas. Contextual factors proved essential to the interpretation of events because they structured the profile of opportunities and constraints, incentives and disincentives, that the various actors confronted at a given point in time and because they influenced the relative degrees of power that contenders were able to mobilize to defend or advance their respective interests.

Few macroeconomic contingencies figured more prominently in the changing matrix of influences than did the demise of the Brazilian economic miracle in the 1970s followed by the deep recession in the 1980s. The downturn in growth and productivity associated with the military regime's ever more fragile claim to legitimacy was accompanied by a process of political liberalization that finally resulted in a civilian, direct-election system of governance in 1985. However dramatic the changes in Amazonia may have been during the last decade, the rates of in-migration, deforestation, and land settlement that took place probably would have been much greater had the economy been in a period of rapid growth.

The central themes of the academic and political discourse changed dramatically in content and direction in response to the new context. The "growth versus equity" controversy that had infused development economics in the 1970s waned in importance as it became increasingly evident that neither component of the argument obtained. If social justice was to be achieved at all, hopes were pinned not on economic growth but on the process of democratization and on finding ways to influence the political restructuring that was underway. When President Geisel and his successor, João Figueiredo, embarked on a program of controlled political liberalization, the long stifled opposition became a public force. In the 1982 elections opposition candidates won across most of the region. For the first time, Indian representatives were elected to Congress. The environmental and human rights consequences of Amazonian development policy became the target of headline stories in Brazil and across the world.

With the transition to the New Republic in 1985 a new era of development planning for Amazonia appeared to be imminent. In contrast to the previous decades, progressive legislation regarding land reform and a host of other initiatives were publicly supported by a wide spectrum of increasingly vocal interest groups at the national, regional, and local levels. Cattle ranching, once the mainstay of the modernization program, was condemned in favor of extractive activities that would leave the forest intact. Subsidies to ranching were cut back, and plans to divide vast areas of forest into small farming plots were criticized by most knowledgeable observers. Indigenous cultures were promoted as the repositories of practical knowledge, and the resource management systems of Indians and peasants were treated as credible alternatives in the search for new policy directions.

By the late 1980s political alliances had extended beyond Brazil's national borders. Links were made with environmental organizations and Indian rights groups elsewhere, and they provided a new and potent source of information and resources. Before long, ecological and conservation themes were appropriated in one form or another by nearly all of the actors involved. In what amounted to the widespread "greening of the development discourse," even ranchers who continued to deforest and military strategists who persisted in the attempt to open Indian lands to mineral and timber exploitation did so by invoking environmental concerns. Similarly, sawmill owners proclaimed that selective logging was a sustainable method of forest extraction while rubber tappers and Indians proposed new forms of multiple land use based on their traditional practices. In the terms of the new debate, forest extractors ironically emerged as heroes—the same people who had been regarded as anathema to the development agenda only a few short years ago. Even more extraordinary was the fact that, at least in some cases, grassroots mobilization led to significant changes in policy.

These trends did not go unchallenged. In the first years of the civilian regime, a forceful and well-organized opposition campaign by ranchers and investors managed to stymie most reform-minded proposals. Chico Mendes' murderer was convicted in the state of Acre, but violence against the leaders of grassroots resistance movements in Amazonia continued. More troubling still was the fact that although now one step removed from the decision-making power they once enjoyed, the military maintained control over the main thrust of Amazonian development. The Calha Norte project, for example, remained explicitly hostile to the rights of native peoples. A survey of events during the latter half of the 1980s indicated that despite everything that had taken place over the last two decades—the change in regime from military to civilian rule; the mobilization of peasants, Indians, rubber tappers, and miners; and the fundamental change in the content of the development discourse—the main thrust of Amazonian policy continued to invoke the precepts of developmentalism. Moreover, government policies remained heavily colored by the national security doctrine, and the preference given to capital-intensive projects went unchanged. In the countryside, grassroots resistance movements occasionally were successful, but overall they were far from tipping the balance of power in their favor.

Disturbing continuities notwithstanding, much had indeed changed. The most important transformations may be those that took place at the bottom rather than at the top of the social and political hierarchy. Significant concessions in Amazonian policy—such as the proposal for extractive reserves and the limits on multilateral funding of dams and roads—were the result of the political pressure mobilized by local and regional interest groups. Under more open political conditions, subordinate groups now had a greater number of alternative channels through which to pursue their political objectives: via unions, federations, nongovernmental organizations, and political parties. They could also draw on their own cultural repertoires and historical traditions of everyday life and collective resistance to strengthen their political agenda. Similarly, new forms of political organization as well as alliances within and outside Brazil could provide the means for traditional Amazonian inhabitants to gain a stronger role in decision making. The point is not to wax romantic about the grassroots movements. These remained small and perched at the edge of power. Still, the process of resistance had educated people in the art of exploiting political openings that allowed for new initiatives.

What does the history of southern Pará suggest about the future of the Amazon region? The massive Carajás project and the other activities underway will undoubtedly continue to attract people. Migrants in search of land will have an increasingly difficult time in southern Pará, as land in long-settled areas is monopolized and access to more remote areas like São Felix do Xingu is closed off. Land ownership will most likely become more concentrated as speculators, ranchers, and investors parley their assets into larger holdings. In remote areas, ragged legions of *garimpeiros* will still prospect for new deposits of cassiterite, gold, and other valued minerals, bringing them into confrontations with Indians and mining companies. Although the *garimpeiros* will staunchly resist with every available resource, many of the richer streambeds will most likely be taken over by mining companies that use mechanized technology and employ salaried workers housed in private compounds. These changes signal the decline, but probably not the disappearance, of traditional arrangements, such as the *aviamento*, and the growing dominance of the wage-based and cash-oriented economy.

There is little reason to believe that deforestation will abate, at least not as long as the incentives for it remain. Still, in the São Felix area, the unimpeded destruction of the forest that characterizes much of the rest of the lower Amazon is likely to be contained, at least to some degree, by the presence of the Kayapó, who have developed a remarkably effective strategy to defend their lands and to partake of the profits made from the natural resources they contain. With increasing sophistication and economic power, the Indians will have an impact on the São Felix region and on the whole Xingu basin. There is no guarantee, of course, that in the long run Indians will be any better stewards of the environment than others. Wistful hope in the intrinsic attributes of Indian cultural dispositions is unwise, if for no other reason than that these traditions have been and still are in a process of rapid change. Much will depend on whether the defense of the environment remains in the interest of the Kayapó, however they choose to define it, and on their collective capacity in the face of internal differences to defend themselves against those who would put their land and resources to different uses.

More specific predictions about Amazonia's future are unwarranted. After all, the competition for resources continues, as does the evolution of the contextual factors, both national and international, that shape the outcome of the ongoing confrontations. But it is this very uncertainty that provides room for cautious optimism. The challenge is to identify and exploit those limited but potentially significant degrees of freedom that permit new directions. In this regard the message contained in the previous chapters has profound implications for anyone interested in altering the course of future events in Amazonia, be they politicians or planners, ecologists or conservationists, grassroots activists or members of the myriad lobby groups that have taken up one cause or another. To have the desired effect, proposals for change must be formulated in light of the constellation of socioeconomic, political, and ideological factors whose interplay and frequent collision account for the events we have chronicled in this book.

REFERENCES

A Capa, No. 2, May 1976

A Provincia do Pará, 14 June and 27 July 1983

Albert, Bruce. (forthcoming) "Indian lands, environmental policy, and military geopolitics in the development of the Brazilian Amazon: The case of the Yanomami." *Studies in Comparative International Development.*

Albuquerque, Apolo S., Aldenor P. Pontes, Pedro Albuquerque Neto, J. A. F. Uchôa, and R. Larsen. 1984. "Estudo da viabilidade de implantação de cooperativas de garimpeiros no estado do Ceará." *Anais do XXXIII Congresso Brasileiro de Geologia*:5088–5096.

Alegretti, Mary Helena. 1990. "Extractive reserves: An alternative for reconciling development and environmental conservation in Amazonia." In Anthony Anderson, ed., *Alternatives to Deforestation*, 252–264 New York: Columbia University Press.

Alegretti, Mary Helena, and Stephan Schwartzman. 1987. "Extractive reserves: A sustainable development alternative for Amazonia." Research Report to the World Wildlife Fund.

Almeida, Alfredo Wagner B. de. 1985. *O GETAT e a arrecadação de áreas rurais como terra devoluta.* Belém: IDESP.

Almeida, Alfredo Wagner B. de, and João Pacheco de Oliveira Filho. 1985. "Demarcações: uma avaliação do GT-Interministerial." *Povos Indígenas no Brasil/1984* Aconteceu Especial (15)48–52.

Almeida, Alfredo Wagner B. de, Márcia Anita Sprandel, Andréa Dias Victor, and Célia Maria Corrêa. 1986. "Os garimpos na Amazônia como zona crítica de conflito e tensão social." *Pará Desenvolvimento*, 19(Jan./June):3–10.

Altvater, Elmar. 1987. "Consequencias regionais da crise do endividamento global no exemplo do Pará." In Gerhard Kohlhepp and Achim Schrader eds., *Homen e Natureza na Amazônia*, 169–187 Tübingen, Germany: Universität Tübingen.

Alves, Francisco E. 1984. "Um novo modelo de garimpo." *Brasil Mineral* 6 (May): 9–11.

Amazônia, August/September 1985.

Amnesty International. 1988. *Brazil: Authorized Violence in Rural Areas.* London: Amnesty International Publishers.

Anderson, Anthony B., and Darrell A. Posey. 1989. "Management of a tropical scrub savana by the Gorotire Kayapó Indians of Brazil." In Darrell A. Posey and William Balée, eds., *Resource Management in Amazonia: Indigenous and Folk Strategies*. New York: New York Botanical Garden.

Anderson, Perry. 1980. *Arguments within English Marxism*. London: Verso.

Anderson, Robin. 1985. "The caboclo as revolutionary: The Cabanagem revolt 1835–1836." *Studies in Third World Societies* 32:51–88.

Arnaud, Expedito. 1975. "Os Índios Gaviões de Oeste, Pacificação e Integração." *Publicações Avulsas*, 28. Belém: Museu Paraense Emílo Goeldi.

——1989. *O Índio e a Expansão Nacional*, Belém: CEJUP.

Aufderheide, Pat, and Bruce M. Rich. 1985. "Debacle in the Amazon." *Defenders of Wildlife* (March/April):20–32.

——1988. "Environmental reforms and the multilateral banks." *World Policy Journal* 4(Spring):301–321.

Ayres, José Márcio. 1989. "Debt-for-equity swaps and the conservation of tropical rain forests." *TREE* 4 (11) (November):331–332.

Ayres, J. Márció, Deborah de Magalhaes Lima, Eduardo de Souza Martins, and Jose Luis K. Barreiros. (forthcoming). "On the track of the road: Changes in subsistence hunting in a Brazilian Amazonian village." In John G. Robinson and Kent Redford, eds., *Neotropical Wildlife Use and Conservation*, Chicago: University of Chicago Press.

Baer, Werner. 1965. *Industrialization and Economic Development in Brazil*. Homewood, Ill.: Irwin.

Balée, William. (forthcoming). "People of the fallow: A historical ecology of foraging in lowland South America." In Kent Redford and Christine Padoch, eds., *Conservation of Neotropical Forests: Working with Traditional Resource Use*. New York: Columbia University Press.

Balée, William, and David G. Campbell. 1990. "Evidence for the successional status of liane forest (Xingu River Basin, Amazonian Brazil)." *Biotropica* 22(1):36–47.

Bamberger, Joan. 1979. "Exit and voice in Central Brazil: The politics of flight in Kayapó society." In David Maybury-Lewis, ed., *Dialectical Societies*, 130–146 Cambridge: Harvard University Press.

Bandeira, Luís Antonio. 1985. "As conseqüências do garimpo em Carajás." *Brasil Mineral* 20 (July):109–112.

Barbalho, Jáder. 1986. "Problemas e perspectivas do setor mineral no Pará." *Pará Desenvolvimento* 19:33–35.

Baxter, M. W. P. 1975. *Garimpeiros of Poxoréo: Small-Scale diamond miners and their environment in Brazil*. Ph.D. diss. University of California, Berkeley.

Becker, Bertha K. 1982. *Geopolítica da Amazônia: A Nova Fronteira de Recursos*. Rio de Janeiro: Zahar.

——1985. "Fronteira e urbanização repensadas." *Revista Brasileira de Geografia* 47 (3/4):357–371.

——1990. *Amazônia*. São Paulo: Atica.

——n. d. "Gestão do território e territorialidade na Amazônia." Unpublished paper.

Benchimol, Samuel. 1989. *Amazônia: Quadros Econômicos da Produção*. Manaus: Instituto Superior de Estudos da Amazônia.

Benton, Ted. 1984. *The Rise and Fall of Structural Marxism: Althusser and his Influence*. New York: St. Martin's Press.

Biery-Hamilton, Gay M. 1987. *Coping with Change: The Impact of the Tucuruí Dam on an Amazonian Community*. Master's Thesis, University of Florida, Gainesville.

Binswanger, Hans P. 1989. *Brazilian Policies that Encourage Deforestation in the Amazon*. Environment Dept. Working Paper No. 16. Washington, D.C.: The World Bank.

Birdsall, Nancy. 1980. *Population and Poverty in the Developing World*. Working Paper No. 404. Washington, D.C.: World Bank.

Bittar, Nassri, Cloris de A. Oliveira, Roberto G. Freire, and Eduardo Gebrim. 1985. *Levantamento preliminar sobre a poluição ambiental em áreas garimpeiras na bacia do Rio Crixás-Açu*. Goânia: Secretaria de Minas, Energia e Telecomunicações and Secretaria de Saúde, Goiás.

Bourdieu, Pierre. 1978. *Outline of a Theory of Practice*. Cambridge: Cambridge University Press.

Branford, Sue, and Oriel Glock. 1985. *The Last Frontier: Fighting over Land in the Amazon*. London: Zed Books.

Brasil, Napolitão, and José C. M. Patriarchia. 1976. "Relatório." Unpublished report, September 23. Belém: Instituto de Terras do Pará.

Brass, William A., Ansley I. Coale, Paul Demeny, Don F. Heisel, Frank Lorimer, Anatole Romanintz, and Etienne Van de Walle. 1968. *The Demography of Tropical Africa*. Princeton: Princeton University Press.

Brito, Apolonildo. 1987. "O lado oculto de Serra Pelada." *Enfoque Amazônico* 4:12–14.

Browder, John O. 1984. "The Brazilian mahogany timbershed." Unpublished report.

———1986. "Logging the Rainforest: A Political Economy of Timber Extraction and Unequal Exchange in the Brazilian Amazon." Ph.D. diss. University of Pennsylvania.

———1987. "Brazil's export promotion policy (1980–1984): Impacts on the Amazon's industrial wood sector." *The Journal of Developing Areas* 21 (April):285–304.

Browder, John O., and Brian J. Godfrey. 1990. "Frontier urbanization in the Brazilian Amazon: A theoretical framework for urban transition." Working Paper 90-1. Blacksburg, Va.: Virginia Polytechnic Institute, Center for Urban and Regional Studies.

Bunker, Stephen G. 1982. "Os programas de crédito e a desintegração não-intencional das economias extractivas de exportação no Médio Amazonas do Pará." *Pesquisa e Planejamento Econômico* 12(1):231–260.

———1985. *Underdeveloping the Amazon*. Champaign-Urbana: University of Illinois Press.

Burns, E. Bradford. 1965. "Manaus, 1910: Portrait of a boom town." *Journal of Inter-American Studies* 7(3)(July):400–421.

———1970. *A History of Brazil*. New York: Columbia University Press.

Bush, Mark B., Dolores R. Piperno, and Paul A. Colinvaux. 1989. "A 6,000-year history of Amazonian maize cultivation." *Nature* 340:303–305.

Butler, John R. 1985. "Land, Gold, and Farmers: Agricultural Colonization and Frontier Expansion in the Brazilian Amazon." Ph.D. diss. University of Florida, Gainesville.

Campbell, Constance. 1989. "Community mobilization and education for con-

References 359

servation: A case study of the rubber trappers in Acre, Brazil." *Latinamericanist* 24(2)(May):2–7.

——1990. "The Role of Popular Education in the Mobilization of a Rural Community: A Case Study of the Rubber Tappers in Acre, Brazil." Master's Thesis, University of Florida, Gainesville.

Carnoy, Martin. 1984. *The State and Political Theory.* Princeton: Princeton University Press.

Carvalho, Yvan. 1981. "Uma política para o desenvolvimento do setor aurífero do pais." Paper presented at the Bahian Nucleus of the Brazillian Geographical Society, Salvador.

Castro, Edna M. R. 1989. "Resistência dos atingidos pela barragem de Tucuruí e construção de identidade." In Edna M. R. Castro and Jean Hébette, eds., *Na Trilha dos Grandes Projetos: Modernização e Conflito na Amazônia,* 41–70 Belém: Cadernos NAEA, No. 10.

Castro, Edna M. R., and Jean Hébette, eds. 1989. *Na Trilha dos Grandes Projetos: Modernização e Conflito na Amazônia.* Belém: Cadernos NAEA, No. 10.

Castro, Edna M. R., and Rosa E. Acevedo Marin. 1986/1987. "Estado e poder local: Dinâmica das transformações na Amazônia brasileira." *Pará Desenvolvimento* 20/21:9–14.

Castro Filho, Luís Werneck de, and Steven Lawrence Heim. 1978. "Projeto Puma-Onça, Pará: Relatório final de pesquisa, VI." Unpublished research report. Goiânia: Minerasul, Mineração Serras do Sul.

CEDI (Centro Ecumênico de Documentação e Informação). 1985. *Povos Indígenas no Brasil/1984.* Aconteceu Especial 15.

——1987a. "A política indigenista da 'Nova República.' " *Povos Indígenas no Brasil/1985/1986*:23. Aconteceu Especial 17.

——1987b. *Povos Indígenas no Brasil 1985/1986.* Aconteceu Especial 17.

Chase, Jacquelyn. 1984. "Evolução demográfica no município de São Felix do Xingu, 1970–1980." Unpublished research report. Belo Horizonte: CEDEPLAR.

Cleary, David. 1989. "Mercury contamination in the Brazilian Amazon: A report." Unpublished.

——1990. *Anatomy of the Amazon Gold Rush.* London: Macmillan.

Coelho Neto, Rogério. 1981. "Uma ampla operação de guerra." *Jornal do Brasil,* 16 March.

Costa, Raymundo. 1981. "Na solidão de Belém." *Veja, 8 July.*

Coutinho, Raimundo Eloy. 1976. "Relatório." Unpublished report. Belém: Secretaria de Estado da Agricultura, September 1.

Coutinho, Raimundo Eloy, and Maria Carmela G. Matos. 1976. "Relatório." Unpublished report. Belém: Secretaria de Estado da Agricultura, October 10.

Couto, Lucinerges. 1980. "Odisseia do Pucá Crãne." *O Estado do Pará,* 14 September.

CPI (Comissão Parliamentar de Inquérito). 1980. *Relatório da Comissão Parliamentar de Inquérito destinada a investigar distorções ocorridas na execução dos planos de desenvolvimento da Amazônia.* Brasília: Diário do Congresso Nacional, Seção I, Ano XXXV Suplemento ao No. 156, 5 December.

CPRM (Companhia de Pesquisa em Recursos Minerais). 1969. "Projeto São Felix do Xingu: Relatório final." Vol. 1 Unpublished research report.

CPT (Commissão Pastoral da Terra). 1984. *Nas Terras do Araguaia*. Conceição do Araguaia: CPT.

———1985. *Conflitos de Terra no Brasil*. Belo Horizonte: SEGREC.

Cunha, Manuela C. da. 1989. "Native realpolitik." *NACLA Report on the Americas* 23(1)(May):19–27.

Dall'Agnol, Roberto. 1982. "Tecnologias de exploração mineral na Amazônia." Paper presented at the 34th annual meeting of the Sociedade Brasileira para o Progresso da Ciência, Campinas, July.

Dean, Warren. 1987. *Brazil and the Struggle for Rubber*. Cambridge: Cambridge University Press.

De Janvry, Alain. 1981. *The Agrarian Question and Reformism in Latin America*. Baltimore: The Johns Hopkins University Press.

Denevan, William. 1976. "The Aboriginal Population of Amazonia." In William Denevan, ed., *The Native Population of the Americas in 1492*, 205–234. Madison: University of Wisconsin Press.

Dias, Catharina Vergolina. 1958. "Marabá: Centro comercial da castanha." *Revista Brasileira de Geografia* 20(4)(Oct./Dec.):384–427.

Dicks, Steven E. 1984. "Monitoring deforestation in the Brazilian Amazon using Landsat MSS data." *Florida Journal of Anthropology* 9(2):37–63.

DNPM (Departamento Nacional de Produção Mineral, Ministério das Minas e Energia, Brazil). 1979. *Inventário sócio-econômico da Provincia Aurifera do Médio Tapajós*. Belém: DNPM.

———1980. "Garimpagem no Brasil." Unpublished working group report.

———1982a. Projeto Estudo dos Garimpos Brasileiros, Área Cumaru, Relatório Semestral.

———1982b. Projeto Estudo dos Garimpos Brasileiros, Área Cumaru, Relatório Anual Texto.

———1982c. Projeto Estudo dos Garimpos Brasileiros, Área Serra Pelada, Relatório Anual Texto.

———1983a. Projeto Estudo dos Garimpos Brasileiros, Área Cumaru, Relatório Anual Texto.

———1983b. Projeto Estudo dos Garimpos Brasileiros, Área Serra Pelada, Relatório Anual Texto.

Doria, Palmério, Sérgio Buarque, Vincent Carelli, and Jaime Sautchuk. 1978. *A guerilha do Araguaia*. São Paulo: Alfa-Omega.

Dreyfus, Simone. 1972. *Los Kayapó del Norte*. Ediciones Especiales No. 64. Mexico: Instituto Indigenista Interamericano.

Ehrenreich, Jeffrey, ed. 1989. "Indigenous Peoples and Nation-States." *The Latin American Anthropology Review* 1:2.

Emmi, Marília Ferreira. 1985. "Estrutura Fundiária e Poder Local: O Caso de Marabá." Master's Thesis, Núcleo de Altos Estudos Amazônicos (NAEA), Federal University of Pará, Belém.

———1988. *A Oligarquia do Tocantins e o Domínio dos Castanhais*. Belém: NAEA/ UFPa.

Estado de São Paulo, 10 October 1982; 12 June, 8 October, and 6 December 1983; 1 December 1984.

Evans, Peter. 1979. *Dependent Development: The Alliance of Multinational, State and Local Capital in Brazil*. Princeton: Princeton University Press.

References

Falesi, Ítalo. 1976. *Ecosistema de Pastagem Cultivada na Amazonia Brasileira.* Belém: *EMBRAPA Boletim Técnico* 1.

Fearnside, Philip M. 1980. "Jari and Development in the Brazilian Amazon." *Interciência 5(3)* (May/June):145–156.

——1982a. "Deforestation in the Brazilian Amazon: How Fast Is It Occurring?" *Interciência* 7(2):82–88.

——1982b. "The New Jari: Risks and Prospects of a Major Amazonian Development." *Interciência* 7(6) (Separata, Nov./Dec.):329–339.

——1985a. "Jari Revisited: Changes and the Outlook for Sustainability in Amazonia's Largest Silvicultural Estate." *Interciência* 10(3) (May/June):121–129.

——1985b. "Brazil's Amazon Forest and the Global Carbon Problem." *Interciência* 10(4) (July/Aug.):179–186.

——1986a. "Agricultural Plans for Brazil's Grande Carajás Program: Lost Opportunity for Sustainable Agricultural Development?" *World Development* 14(3):385–409.

——1986b. *Human Carrying Capacity of the Brazilian Rainforest.* NY: Columbia University Press.

Fernandes, Francisco Rego Chaus, Ana M. B. da Cunha, Saulo R. Pereira Filho, and Maria J. R. Marques. 1987. "Recursos minerais de Amazônia." In Francisco Rego Chaves Fernandes et al., *A Questão Mineral da Amazônia: Seis Ensaios Críticos,* 7–29 Brasília: MCT/CNPq.

Ferreira, Afonso Borges. 1984. "Evolução recente do garimpo de ouro no Brasil." Unpublished research report. Belo Horizonte: CEDEPLAR.

Ferreira Reis, Arthur César. 1973. *A Amazônia e a Cobiça Internacional.* Rio de Janeiro: Companhia Editora Americana.

Fisk, Brian. 1984. "The Jari Project: Labor Instability in the Brazilian Amazon." Master's Thesis, University of Florida, Gainesville.

Folha de Tucumã, October 1982.

Fon, Antônio Carlos. 1981. "A guerra do Araguaia." *Isto É,* 16 December:49–53.

Foresta, Ron. 1991. *The Limit of Providence: Nature and Development in the Brazilian Amazonia.* Gainesville: University of Florida Press.

Foweraker, Joe. 1981. *The Struggle for Land: A Political Economy of the Pioneer Frontier in Brazil, 1930 to the Present.* London: Cambridge University Press.

Freitas, Maria de Lourdes. 1986. "Metodologia de avaliação ambiental aplicada para um caso de enfoque preventivo Projeto Ferro Carajás." *Espaço, Ambiente e Planejamento* 1(1) (Jan.):4–26.

Furtado, Celso. 1963. *The Economic Growth of Brazil: A Survey from Colonial to Modern Times.* Berkeley: University of California Press.

Gabeira, Fernando. 1989. "Militares são únicos interlocutores da questão ambiental, diz antropólogo." *Folha de São Paulo,* 28 March 1989.

Garcia, Ronaldo Continho. 1988. "PNRA: As intenções e as possibilidades." *Reforma Agrária* Ano 17(3) (Dec. 1987–March 1988):58–71.

Garrido Filho, Irene. 1984. "Garimpos de cassiterita em Goiás: Pesquisa geográfica." *Anais do XXXIII Congresso Brasileiro de Geografia*:5064–5070.

Gibbon, Ann. 1990. "New view of early Amazonia." *Science* 248:1488–1490.

Giddens, Anthony. 1979. *Central Problems in Social Theory: Action, Structure, and Contradiction in Social Analysis.* Cambridge: Cambridge University Press.

——1984. *The Constitution of Society: Outline of the Theory of Structuration.* Berkeley: University of California Press.

———1987. *Social Theory and Modern Sociology.* Stanford: Stanford University Press.

Godfrey, Brian John. 1979. "Road to the Xingu: Frontier Settlement in Southern Pará, Brazil." Master's Thesis, University of California, Berkeley.

———1982. "Xingu Junction: Rural migration and land conflict in the Brazilian Amazon." In Kristyna P. Demaree, ed., *Continuity and Change in Latin America,* 71–88 Proceedings of the Pacific Coast Council on Latin American Studies, vol. 9.

———1989. "Frontier settlement and the emerging urban hierarchy of eastern Amazônia." Paper presented at the Annual Meeting of the Association of American Geographers, Baltimore.

——— 1990. "Boom towns of the Amazon." *The Geophysical Review,* 80(2)(April):103–117.

Goldenberg, José, and M. L. Davies de Freitas. 1989. "Energy strategies for Latin America." Unpublished paper.

Gómez, Augusto J. 1988. "Llanos orientales: Colonización y conflictos interétnicos 1870–1970." *Universitas Humanística* 17(29):45–89.

Gouldner, Alvin. 1980. *The Two Marxisms.* New York: Seabury.

Guimarães, Gerobal. 1982. "Garimpo do Tapajós: Relatório de viagem." Projeto Estudo dos Garimpos Brasileiros. Brasília: DNPM.

Guimarães, Gerobal, Julio F. Brandão, and Luis R. Guimarães. 1982. "Garimpos brasileiros: Da história aos fatos atuais." In Projeto Estudo dos Garimpos Brasileiros, Informativo No. 1. *Palestras & Trabalhos.* Brasília: DNPM.

Harris, Marvin. 1979. *Cultural Materialism: The Struggle for a Science of Culture.* New York: Random House.

Harvey, David. 1989a. *The Condition of Postmodernity: An Enquiry into the Origins of Cultural Change.* Cambridge, MA: Blackwell.

———1989b. *The Urban Experience.* New York: Oxford University Press.

Hébette, Jean. 1986. "A resistência dos posseiros no Grande Carajás." *Cadernos da CEAS* 102:62–75.

———1988. "A colonização na Amazônia Brasileira: Um modelo para uso interno." *Reforma Agrária* Ano 17(3) (Dec. 1987–March 1988):20–27.

Hébette, Jean, and Rosa Acevedo. 1979. *Colonização Para Quem?* Série Pesquisa, Ano 1, No. 1. Belém: Universidade Federal do Pará, Núcleo de Altos Estudos Amazônicos, Amazônia/NAEA.

Hecht, Susanna B. 1985. "Environment, development and politics: capital accumulation and the livestock sector in eastern Amazonia." *World Development* 13(6):663–684.

———1989. "Murders at the margins of the world." *NACLA Report on the Americas* 23(1)(May):36–38.

Hecht, Susanna B., and Alexander Cockburn. 1989. *The Fate of the Forest: Developers, Destroyers, and Defenders of the Amazon.* New York: Verso.

Hecht, Susanna B., Richard B. Norgaard, and Giorgio Possio. 1988. "The economics of cattle ranching in eastern Amazonia." *Interciência* 13:(5)(Sept./Oct.):233–240.

Hecht, Susanna B., and Darrell A. Posey. 1989. "Preliminary results on soil management techniques of the Kayapó Indians." In Darrell A. Posey and William Balée, eds., *Resource Management in Amazonia: Indigenous and Folk Strategies,* 174–188. New York: New York Botanical Garden.

References	*363*

————1990. "Indigenous soil management in the Latin American tropics: Some implications for the Amazon Basin." In Darrell A. Posey and William L. Overal, eds., *Ethnobiology: Implications and Applications.* Belém: Museu Paraense Emílio Goeldi.

Hemming, John. 1978. *Red Gold. The Conquest of the Brazilian Indians, 1500–1760.* Cambridge: Harvard University Press.

————1987. *Amazon Frontier: The Defeat of the Brazilian Indians.* Cambridge: Harvard University Press.

Hiraoka, Mário. 1985. "Cash cropping, wage labor, and urbanward migrations: Changing floodplain subsistence in the Peruvian Amazon." *Studies in Third World Societies* 32:199–242.

Hobsbawm, Eric J. 1975. "Revolution." Paper presented at Fourteenth International Congress of Historical Sciences, San Francisco, August.

Horak, Christine A. 1984. "The Formation of Public Policy on the Amazonian Frontier: The Rise of the Association of Amazonian Entrepreneurs." Master's thesis, University of Florida, Gainesville.

Hoyos, Juan L. Bardáliz. 1986/7. "Capital social, projetos de desenvolvimento e transformações: Contribuições para uma reflexão." *Pará Desenvolvimento,* 20/21:19–25.

Hurrell, Andrew. 1991. "The politics of Amazonian deforestation." *Journal of Latin American Studies* 23:197–215.

Ianni, Otávio. 1978. *A Luta pela Terra.* Petrópolis: Vozes.

IBGE (Instituto Brasileiro de Geografia e Estatística). 1960. *Censo Demográfico de 1960, Acre-Amazonas-Pará.* VII Recenseamento Geral do Brasil, Série Regional, Vol. I, Tomo II. 2a. Parte. Rio de Janeiro: IBGE.

————1970. *Censo Demográfico, Pará.* VIII Recenseamento Geral 1970, Série Regional, Vol. I, Tomo IV. Rio de Janeiro: IBGE.

————1979. *Produção Extrativa Vegetal,* Vols. 3, 4, and 5. Rio de Janeiro: IBGE, Superintendência de Estatísticas Primárias.

————1981. *Produção Extrativa Vegetal,* Vols. 6 and 7. Rio de Janeiro: IBGE, Superintendência de Estatisticas Primárias.

————1982. *Produção Extrativa Vegetal,* Vol. 8. Rio de Janeiro: IBGE, Superintendência de Estatísticas Primárias.

————1982/3. *Censo Demográfico: Dados Distritais.* IX Recenseamento Geral do Brasil–1980, Vol. 1, Tomo 3, no. 4. Rio de Janeiro: IBGE.

————1984. *Produção Extrativa Vegetal,* Vol. 9. Rio de Janeiro: IBGE, Superintendência de Estatísticas Primárias.

IBRAM (Instituto Brasileiro de Mineração). 1983. "Garimpo x empresa de mineração." *Minérios Extração e Processamento* 6(78) (August):23–25.

IDESP (Instituto de Desenvolvimento Econômico e Social do Pará). 1986. "Setor Mineral. Autorizações de Pesquisa e Concessões de Lavra no Pará." Belém: IDESP.

————1987a. *Estatísticas Demográficas do Estado do Pará.* Belém: IDESP.

————1987b. *Pará Agrária,* No. 1, January–December. Belém: IDESP.

Imbiriba, Maria de Nazaré, and Thomas A. Mitshein. 1989. "Amazônia: Um novo mito leva à omissão política." *Brasil 21 Perspectivas Internacionais* 5 (Jan./March):1–3.

INCRA (Instituto Nacional de Reforma Agrária). 1977. "Relatório de pesquisa:

levantamento sócio-econômico realizado junto aos chefes de família do entroncamento do Xingu e Agua Fria." Marabá: Mimeo.

——1986. *Plano Regional de Reforma Agrária*. Belém: INCRA, Superintendência Regional do Norte.

Informe Amazônico, Ano 1, No. 1, 15–30 September 1980.

Inquérito Civil Programa Grande Carajás. 1989. Informativo No. 1. Rio de Janeiro: Instituto Apoio Jurídico Popular, January.

Jorge, Luís O. Montenegro. 1986. "Relatório de atividades/86." Conselho de Desenvolvimento Comunitário de Tucumã, December.

Jornal de Brasília, 27 July 1980 and 7 October 1982.

Jornal do Brasil, 4 and 7 September 1980; 17 July 1982; 29 May 1983; and 29 November 1984.

Jornal do Ouro, May 1985; 27 August 1985.

Katzman, Marvin T. 1976. "Paradoxes of Amazonian development in a 'resource-starved' world." *Journal of Developing Areas* 10:445–460.

Keller, Francesca Isabel Vieira. 1975. "O homem da frente de expansão: Permanência, mudança e conflito." *Revista da História* 102:665–709.

Kelly, Arlene M. 1975. "The Xingu and José Porfirio." Master's Thesis, University of Florida, Gainesville.

Kohlhepp, Gerhard. 1987. "Problema do planejamento regional e do desenvolvimento regional na área do Programa Grande Carajás no leste da Amazônia." In Gerhard Kohlhepp and Achim Schrader, eds., *Homen e Natureza na Amazônia*, 313–346. Tübingen, Germany: Universität Tübingen.

Kotscho, Ricardo. 1982a. "Posseiros resistem quanto podem." *Folha de São Paulo*, 15 August.

——1982b. "Situação muda com os mutirões de roça." *Folha de São Paulo*, 15 August.

——1984. *Serra Pelada: Uma Ferida Aberta na Selva*. São Paulo: Brasiliense.

Kucinski, Bernardo. 1979. "A Amazônia e a Geopolítica do Brasil." *Encontros com a Civilização Brasileira* 11:12–20.

Lathrap, Donald W. 1970. *The Upper Amazon*. London: Thames and Hudson.

Lazarin, Marco A., and Francisco C. Rabelo. 1984. "Garimpeiros no nordeste de Goiás." In Gerôncio A. Rocha, ed., *Em Busca do Ouro: Garimpo e Garimpeiros no Brasil*, 107–120. Rio: Marco Zero.

Lea, Vanessa. 1984. "Brazil's Kayapo Indians: Beset by a golden curse." *National Geographic* May:675–694.

Leite, Jurandyr C. F. 1990. "Terras indígenas no Brasil: O governo Sarney." *Resenha & Debate* 1 (June).

Lestra, Alain, and José Nardi. 1982. *O Ouro da Amazônia Oriental: O Mito e a Realidade*. Belém: Grafisa.

Lima, Antônia Carlos de Souza. 1990a. "A face ESG do Brasil Novo de Collor." *Resenha & Debate* 2 (September):8–12.

——1990b. "Indigenismo e geopolitica: Projetos militares para os índios no Brasil." *Antropologia e Indigenismo* 1 (November):60–86.

Lisansky, Judith M. 1988. *Santa Terezinha: Life in a Brazilian Frontier Town*. Boulder: Westview.

Loureiro, Violeta R. 1985. *Os Parceiros do Mar: Natureza e Conflito Social na Pesca da Amazônia*. Belém: CNPq/Museu Goeldi.

Mahar, Dennis J. 1979. *Frontier Development Policy in Brazil: A Study of Amazonia.* New York: Praeger.

——1989. *Government Policies and Deforestation in Brazil's Amazon Region.* Washington, D.C.: The World Bank.

Mainwaring, Scott. 1986. *The Catholic Church and Politics in Brazil, 1916–1985.* Stanford: Stanford University Press.

Mallas, J., and N. Benedicto. 1986. "Mercury and goldmining in the Brazilian Amazon." *Ambio* 15(4):248–249.

Margolis, Maxine L. 1973. *The Moving Frontier.* Gainesville: University of Florida Press.

——1979. "Seduced and abandoned: Agricultural frontiers in Brazil and the United States." In Maxine L. Margolis and William E. Carter, eds., *Brazil: Anthropological Perspectives, Essays in Honor of Charles Wagley,* 160–179. New York: Columbia University Press.

Martinello, Pedro. 1988. *A "Batalha da Borracha" na Segunda Guerra Mundial e Suas Conseqüências para o Vale Amazônico.* Cadernos UFAC, Série "C", Estudos e Pesquisas, No. 1. Rio Branco: Universidade Federal do Acre.

Martins, Ana Luiza. 1984. "Breve história dos garimpos de ouro do Brasil." In Gerôncio Rocha, ed., *Em Busca do Ouro: Garimpos e Garimpeiros no Brasil,* 177–215. Rio de Janeiro: Marco Zero.

Martins, José de Souza. 1975. *Capitalismo e Tradicionalismo: Estudos sobre as Contradições da Sociedade Agrária no Brasil.* São Paulo: Pioneira.

——1980. *Expropriação e Violência: A Questão Política no Campo.* São Paulo: Hucitec.

——1984. "The state and the militarization of the agrarian question in Brazil." In Marianne Schmink and Charles H. Wood, eds., *Frontier Expansion in Amazonia,* 463–490. Gainesville: University of Florida Press.

——1987. "O poder de decidir no desenvolvimento da Amazônia: Conflitos de intereses entre planejadores e suas vítimas." In Gerhard Kohlhepp and Achim Schrader, eds., *Homen e Natureza na Amazônia,* 407–414. Tübingen, Germany: Universität Tübingen.

Martins, Ruy Célio, and José Maria N. Pastana. 1983. "Garimpos de ouro da região do Rio Tapajós." In Walter H. Schmaltz and Gerobal Guimarães, eds., *Garimpos do Brasil,* 91–115. Brasília: DNPM Avulso No. 5.

Maybury-Lewis, David. 1975. "The Kayapó." In David Maybury-Lewis, ed., *Dialectical Societies,* 129. Cambridge: Harvard University Press.

McGrath, David G. 1986. "The animal products trade in the Brazilian Amazon." Unpublished summary of a final report to the World Wildlife Fund-US, November 10.

Meggers, Betty J. 1954. "Environmental limitations on the development of culture." *American Anthropologist* 56:801–824.

——1971. *Amazônia: Man and Nature in a Counterfeit Paradise.* Chicago: Aldine.

Meira Mattos, Carlos de. 1980. *Uma Geopolítica Pan-Amazônica.* Rio de Janeiro: José Olympio.

Mendes, Armando Dias. 1985. "Major projects and human life in Amazonia." In John Hemming, ed., *Change in the Amazon Basin, Vol. 1: Man's Impact on Forests and Rivers,* 44–57. Manchester: University of Manchester Press.

Mendes, Carlos. 1979. " 'Chapeu de Couro' diz que a Igreja só cria confusão." *O Estado do Pará,* 28/29 October:11.

Merrick, Thomas W., and Douglas H. Graham. 1979. *Population and Economic Development in Brazil: 1800 to the Present*. Baltimore: Johns Hopkins University Press.

Merrill, Charles W., Charles W. Henderson, and Oscar E. Kiessling. 1937. *Small-Scale Placer Mining as a Source of Gold, Employment, and Livelihood in 1935*. Philadelphia: U.S. Works Progress Administration National Research Project and Bureau of Mines, Department of the Interior.

Mesquita, Rodrigo Lara. 1989. "Ministro explica plano para ecologia." *O Estado de São Paulo*, 6 April 1989.

Miller, Darrel. 1985. "Highways and gold: Change in a caboclo community." *Studies in Third World Societies* 32:167–198.

Miller, Marialisa. 1990. "International Coalition Building: A Case Study of U. S.-Based Conservation Organizations in the Amazon." Master's Thesis, University of Florida, Gainesville.

Milliken, Brent. 1988. "The Dialectics of Devastation: Tropical Deforestation, Land Degradation, and Society in Rondonia, Brazil." Master's Thesis, University of California, Berkeley.

Mills, C. Wright. 1970. *The Sociological Imagination*. New York: Oxford University Press.

MIRAD (Ministério de Reforma Agrária e Desenvolvimento). 1986. *Garimpo e Tensão Social: Conflitos de Terra, Vol. V*. Brasília: MIRAD, Coordenadoria de Conflitos Agrários.

MIRAD (Ministério de Reforma Agrária e Desenvolvimento) and Conselho Nacional de Direitos da Mulher. 1987. *Violência Contra Mulheres e Menores em Conflitos de Terras*. Brasília: MIRAD, Coordenadoria de Conflitos Agrários/ Conselho Nacional de Direitos da Mulher.

Monbeig, Pierre. 1952. *Pionneurs et planteurs de São Paulo*. Paris: Armand Colin.

Monosowski, Elizabeth. 1990. "Lessons from the Tucuruí experience." *Water Power & Dam Construction* (February):29–34.

Monte-Mór, Roberto Luís. 1980. "Espaço e Planejamento Urbano: Considerações sobre o Caso de Rondônia." Master's Thesis, Federal University of Rio de Janeiro.

———1984. "São Felix do Xingu: O avanço da fronteira amazônica e um novo espaço em formação." Unpublished research report. Belo Horizonte: CEDEPLAR.

Monteiro, Benedicto. 1980. *Direito Agrário e Processo Fundiário*. Rio: PLG Comunicação.

Moran, Emilio F. 1979. "Criteria for choosing successful homesteaders in Brazil." *Research in Economic Anthropology* 2:339–359.

———1981. *Developing the Amazon*. Bloomington: University of Indiana Press.

———1984. "Colonization in the Transamazon and Rondônia." In Marianne Schmink and Charles Wood, eds., *Frontier Expansion in Amazonia*, 285–303. Gainesville: University of Florida Press.

———1987. "Monitoring fertility degradation of agricultural lands in the lowland tropics." In Peter D. Little and Michael M. Horowitz, eds., *Lands at Risk in the Third World: Local-Level Perspectives*, 69–91. Boulder: Westview.

———1989. "Models of native and folk adaptation in the Amazon." *Advances in Economic Botany* 7:22–29.

Moreira Neto, Carlos de Araújo. 1959. "Relatório sobre a situação atual dos índios Kayapó." *Revista do Museu Paulista* 7 (1/2):49–64.

——1988. *Índios da Amazônia: De Maioria a Minoria (1750–1850).* Petrópolis: Vozes.

Moura, Clóvis (apresentação). 1979. *Diário da Guerrilha do Araguaia.* São Paulo: Alfa Omega.

Movimento dos Trabalhadores Rurais Sem Terra. 1987. *Assassinatos no Campo: Crime e Impunidade, 1964–1986.* 2d edition. São Paulo: Global.

New York Times, 9 October 1990.

Nimuendajú, Curt. 1952. "Os Górotire." *Revista do Museu Paulista,* Nova Série 6:427–453.

Nunes, Wilson da Silva. 1982. "No meu diálogo biográfico do Xingu." Unpublished manuscript. São Felix do Xingu.

O Estado do Pará, 19 November 1980.

O Liberal, 13 October 1979; 7 August, 5, and 9 September 1980; 10 June 1981; 15 June 1983; 7–9 August 1985; 9 September 1986; 23 May 1987; and 21 June 1987.

O Tribuna, 22 March 1981.

O'Donnell, Guillermo. 1973. *Modernization and Bureaucratic Authoritarianism: Studies in South American Politics.* Berkeley: University of California Press.

Offe, Claus. 1985. *Disorganized Capitalism.* Cambridge, Mass.: The MIT Press.

Oliveira, Adélia Engrácia de. 1983. "Ocupação humana." In Eneas Salati, Wolfgang J. Junk, Herbert O. R. Shubart, and Adélia E. de Oliveira, *Amazônia: Desenvolvimento, Integração e Ecologia,* 144–327. São Paulo: Brasiliense/ CNPq.

——1988. "Amazônia: Modificações sociais e culturais decorrentes do processo de ocupação humana (séc. XVIII ao XX)." *Boletim do Museu Paraense Emílio Goeldi, Série Antropologia* 4(1):65–115.

Oliveira, Luiz Antonio Pinto de. 1985. *O Sertanejo, o Brabo e o Posseiro. (Os Cem Anos de Mudança da População Acreana).* Rio Branco: Fundação Cultural do Acre.

Oliveira Filho, João Pacheco de. 1979. "O caboclo e o brabo: Notas sobre duas modalidades de força-de-trabalho na expansão da fronteira amazônica no século XIX." *Encontros com a Civilização Brasileira* 11:101–140.

——1987. "Terras indígenas: Uma avaliação preliminar de seu reconhecimento oficial e de outras destinações sobrepostas." In *Terras Indígenas no Brasil,* 7–32. São Paulo: CEDI.

——1990. "Segurança das fronteiras e o novo indigenismo: Formas e linhagem do Projeto Calha Norte." *Antropologia & Indigenismo* 1 (November):15–33.

Ortner, Sherry. 1984. "Theory in Anthropology since the Sixties." *Comparative Studies in Society and History* 26(1):126–166.

Pace, Richard. 1987. "Economic and Political Change in the Amazonian Community of Itá, Brazil." Ph.D. diss. University of Florida, Gainesville.

Palmquist, Sérgio. 1986. "Serra Pelada: A outra face do Eldorado." *Pará Desenvolvimento* 18:36–39.

Pandolfo, Clara. 1990. *Considerações sobre a Questão Ecológica da Amazônia Brasileira.* Belém: SUDAM.

Parker, Eugene Philip. 1981. *Cultural Ecology and Change: A Caboclo Varzea*

Community in the Brazilian Amazon. Ph.D. diss., University of Colorado, Boulder.

——1985a. "The Amazon caboclo: an introduction and overview." In Eugene P. Parker, ed., *The Amazon Caboclo: Historical and Contemporary Perspectives, Studies in Third World Societies* Publication No. 32, xvii–li.

——1985b. "Caboclization: The transformation of the Amerindian in Amazonia 1615–1800." *Studies in Third World Societies* 32:1–50.

Parker, Eugene, Darrell Posey, John Frecchione, and Luis Francelino da Silva. 1983. "Resource exploitation in Amazonia: Ethnoecological examples from four populations." *Annals of the Carnegie Museum* 52(8):163–203.

Paternostro, Júlio. 1945. *Viagem ao Tocantins.* São Paulo: Editora Nacional.

Pereira, Neuclayr Martins. 1983. "É à empresa que se deve confiar o aproveitamento econômico das substâncias minerais: O exemplo da cassiterita." *Mineração Metalurgica* 444:14–19.

Perin, Orivaldo. 1986. "Brasil é uma potência sem controle sobre seus minérios." *Jornal do Brasil,* 13 July:20.

Peter, Cynthia. 1986. "Os frutos secos de Tucumã." *Senhor,* 28 October:46–48.

Pinto, Lúcio Flávio. 1975. "O trabalho escravo nas fazendas: vai acabar?" *O Bandeira,* Ano 1, No. 5, 12–18 February:7.

——1977. *Amazônia (O Anteato da Destruição).* Belém: Grafisa.

——1979. "Protesto de seis mil pessoas contra violência em Xinguara." *O Liberal,* 23 October.

——1980. *Amazônia: No Rastro do Saque.* São Paulo: Hucitec.

——1985a. "Antes do sangue." *O Liberal,* 6 February.

——1985b. "Descarte fundiário." *O Liberal,* 7 February.

——1985c. "Um novo conflito," *O Liberal,* 14 May.

——1985d. "A Questão Kayapó." *O Liberal,* 15 May.

——1986. *Jari: Toda a Verdade sobre o Projeto de Ludwig.* São Paulo: Marco Zero.

——1986/1987. "O estado nacional: Padrastro da Amazônia." *Pará Desenvolvimento* 20/21:3–8.

——1987a. "Calha Norte: O projeto especial para a ocupação das fronteiras." *Povos Indígenas no Brasil— 85/86:*62–63.

——1987b. *Jornal Pessoal* 1(1) September.

——1988a. "Este é o país dos arranjos, Dr. Francelino." *Jornal Pessoal* 1(14) (March):6.

——1988b. "Os alvos na mira do ministro." *Jornal Pessoal* 1(17) (May):8.

——1988c. "Uma coincidência com final feliz." *Jornal Pessoal* 1(24)(October):6.

Pompermayer, Malorí José. 1979. "The State and the Frontier in Brazil: A Case Study of the Amazon." Ph.D. diss. Stanford University, Stanford.

——1984. "Strategies of private capital in the Brazilian Amazon." In Marianne Schmink and Charles H. Wood, eds., *Frontier Expansion in Amazonia,* 419–438. Gainesville: University of Florida Press.

Posey, Darrell A. 1979a. "Cisão dos Kayapó." *Revista da Atualidade Indígena* 3(16):52–58.

——1979b. "Pyka-Ttô-ti: Os Kayapó mostra a sua aldeia de orígen." *Revista da Atualidade Indígena* 3(15):50–57.

——1982. "The keepers of the forest." *New York Botanical Garden Magazine* 6(1):18–24.

References

———1983. "Indigenous ecological knowledge in the development of the Amazon." In Emilio Moran, ed., *The Dilemma of Amazonian Development* 225–257. Boulder: Westview.

———1987. "Contact before contact: Typology of post-Colombian interaction with northern Kayapó of the Amazon basin." *Revista do Museu Paraense Emílio Goeldi, Série Antropológica* 3(2)135–154.

———1989. "From war clubs to words." *NACLA Report on the Americas XXIII(1)* (May):13–18.

———1990. "The application of ethnobiology in the conservation of dwindling natural resources: Lost knowledge or options for survival of the planet." In Darrell A. Posey and William L. Overal, eds., *Ethnobiology: Implications and Applications*, 47–60. Belém: Museu Paraense Emílio Goeldi.

Posey, Darrell A., Elizabeth Elizabetsky, Anthony B. Anderson, M. Campos, A. de O. Rodrigues, and Guilherme M. de la Penha. 1987. *A Ciência dos Mebêngôkre: Alternativas Contra a Destruição*. Belém: Museu Paraense Emílio Goeldi.

Poulantzas, Nicos. 1973. *Political Power and Social Classes*. London: New Left Books.

Prado, Jr., Caio. 1971. *História Econômica do Brasil*. São Paulo: Editora Brasiliense.

Procópio Filho, A. 1984. "A miséria do colono e o ouro no Araguaia e Amazônia." In Gerôncio A. Rocha, ed. *Em Busca do Ouro: Garimpo e Garimpeiros no Brasil*, 121–144. Rio: Marco Zero.

PROMIX (Produtora de Minérios Xingu, S/A). 1973. "Relatório de pesquisa." Unpublished research report. Belém.

Ramos, Alcida R. 1984. "Frontier expansion and Indian peoples in the Brazilian Amazon." In Marianne Schmink and Charles H. Wood, eds., *Frontier Expansion in Amazonia*, 83–126. Gainesville: University of Florida Press.

Ramos, Carlos Romano. 1986. "O IUM como instrumento de política mineral." *Pará Desenvolvimento* 19:27–32.

Redenção e Silva, M. da. 1983. "Áreas com atividades de garimpagem." Paper presented at the seminar on "Oportunidades de Investimentos na Mineração", November.

Resistência, Ano V, No. 33, No. 45, No. 46; Ano VI, No. 55.

Ribeiro, Darcy. 1970. *Os Índios e a Civilização*. Rio de Janeiro: Civilização Brasileira.

Ricardo, Carlos Alberto. 1985. "Os Kayapó e os garimpos de ouro." *Povos Indígenas no Brasil 84*, Aconteceu Especial 15:115–119.

———1987. "Do lado debaixo do chão." *Povos Indígenas no Brasil - 85/86* Aconteceu Especial 17:44–46.

Ricardo, Carlos Alberto, and João Pacheco de Oliveira Filho. 1987. "Apresentação." In *Terras Indígenas no Brasil*, 1–5. São Paulo: CEDI.

Rich, Bruce M. 1985. "The multilateral development banks, environmental policy, and the United States." *Ecology Law Quarterly* 12:681–745.

Roche, Jean. 1959. *La colonisation allemande e le Rio Grande do Sul*. Paris: Université de Paris, Institute des Hautes Etudes.

Rodrigues, Lysias. 1945. *O Rio dos Tocantins*. Rio de Janeiro: Instituto Brasileiro de Geografia e Estatística.

Rodrigues, Osmarino Amâncio. 1990. "O segundo assassinato de Chico Mendes." *Cartas da Amazônia,* No. 1.

Rodrigues, Vera da Silva, and José Gomes da Silva. 1977. "Conflitos de terras no Brasil: Uma introdução ao estudo da violência no campo, período 1971–76." *Reforma Agrária* 7(1):3–24.

Roosevelt, Anna C. 1987. "Chiefdoms in the Amazon and Orinoco." In Robert D. Drennan and Carlos A. Uribe, eds., *Chiefdoms in the Americas,* 153–185. Lanham, MD: University Press of America.

Ross, Eric. 1978. "The evolution of the Amazon peasantry." *Journal of Latin American Studies* 10 (Nov.):193–218.

Sader, Regina. 1990. "Lutas e imaginário campones." *Tempo Social:* Revista Sociologia da Universidade de São Paulo 2(1):115–125.

Sahlins, Marshall. 1981. *Historical Metaphors and Mythical Realities: Structure in the Early History of the Sandwich Island Kingdom.* Ann Arbor: University of Michigan Press.

Sales, Herberto. 1955. *Garimpos de Bahia.* Rio de Janeiro: Ministério da Agricultura, Serviço de Informação Agrícola, Documentário de Vida Rural, No. 8.

Sá, Paulo César de, and Isabel Marques. 1987. "Projeto Albrás/Alunorte." In Francisco Rego Chaves Fernandes et al., *A Questão Mineral da Amazônia: Seis Ensaios Críticos,* 185–216. Brasília: MCT/CNPq.

Salomão, Elmer Prata. 1981. "Garimpos do Tapajós." *Ciências da Terra* 1 (Nov./Dec.):38–45.

———1982. "A força do garimpo." *Revista Brasileira de Tecnologia* 13(2) (April/May):13–20.

———1983. "O começo do fim de um conceito." *Ciências da Terra* 8:38–39.

———1984. "O ofício e a condição de garimpar." In Gerôncio A. Rocha, ed., *Em Busca do Ouro: Garimpos e Garimpeiros no Brasil,* 35–86. Rio: Marco Zero.

Sanders, Thomas G. 1973. "Colonization of the Transamazon Highway." *American Universities Field Staff, East-Coast South American Series,* Vol. 18(3).

Santana, Jerônimo. 1972. "A questão garimpeira de Rondônia." Discurso proferido na sessão de 13 de abril de 1972. Brasília: Departamento de Imprensa Nacional, Câmara dos Deputados.

Santana, Luís Ferreira. n. d. São Felix do Xingu: Sua História, 1888–1982. Unpublished. São Felix do Xingu.

Santos, Breno A. dos. 1981. *Amazônia: Potencial Mineral e Perspectivas de Desenvolvimento.* São Paulo: T. A. Queiroz.

———1987. "Carajás: Património nacional." In Francisco Rego Chaves Fernandes et al., *A Questão Mineral da Amazônia: Seis Ensaios Críticos,* 93–131. Brasília: MCT/CNPq.

Santos, Dalva Maria Vasconcelos dos. 1986. "Polamazônia: elementos para uma avaliação." *Pará Desenvolvimento* 18:7–9.

Santos, Roberto. 1978. *A Economia do Estado do Pará.* Belém: IDESP.

———1980. *História Econômica da Amazônia.* São Paulo: T. A. Queiroz.

———1984. "Law and social change: The problem of land in the Brazilian Amazon." In Marianne Schmink and Charles H. Wood, eds., *Frontier Expansion in Amazonia,* 439–462. Gainesville: University of Florida Press.

Santos Filho, José dos Reis. 1984. "GETAT - da regularização fundiária à prática de controle social." *Reforma Agrária* 14(3) (May/June):3–55.

References   *371*

Sawyer, Donald R. 1979. "Peasants and Capitalism on an Amazon Frontier." Ph.D. diss., Harvard University.

——1984. "Frontier expansion and retraction in Brazil." In Marianne Schmink and Charles H. Wood, eds., *Frontier Expansion in Amazonia*, 180–203. Gainesville: University of Florida Press.

Sawyer, Donald R., and Diana O. Sawyer. 1987. "Malaria on the Amazon frontier: Economic and social aspects of transmission and control." Research report, March. Belo Horizonte: CEDEPLAR.

Schiller, E. A. 1985. "Gold in Brazil." *Mining Magazine*, (October):313–319.

Schmink, Marianne. 1987. "The rationality of tropical forest destruction." In Julio C. Figueroa Colón, Frank H. Wadsworth and Susan Branham, eds., *Management of Forests in Tropical America: Prospects and Technologies*, 11–30. Río Piedras, Puerto Rico: USDA Forest Service.

——1982. "Land conflicts in Amazonia." *American Ethnologist* 9(2):341–357.

——1988. "Big business in the Amazon." In Julie S. Denslow and Christine Padoch, eds., *People of the Tropical Rain Forest*, 163–174. Berkeley and Los Angeles: University of California Press/Smithsonian Institution Traveling Exhibition Service.

Schmink, Marianne, and Charles H. Wood, eds. 1984. *Frontier Expansion in Amazonia*. Gainesville: University of Florida Press.

——1987. "The 'political ecology' of Amazonia." In Peter D. Little and Michael M. Horowitz, eds., *Lands at Risk in the Third World: Local Level Perspectives*, 38–57. Boulder: Westview.

Schuh, G. Edward, G. L. Moigne, Michael Cernea, and Robert J. A. Goodland. 1988. "Social and environmental impacts of dams: The World Bank experience." *Proceedings of the 6th International Congress on Large Dams*, San Francisco, 419–436.

Schwartzman, Stephan. 1986. *Bankrolling Disasters: International Development Banks and the Global Environment.* Washington, D.C.: Sierra Club.

——1989. "Deforestation and popular resistance in Acre: From local movement to global network." Paper presented at the American Anthropological Association meeting, Washington, D.C.

Scott, James. 1985. *Weapons of the Weak: Everyday Forms of Peasant Resistance.* New Haven: Yale University Press.

Schaeff, Gary W. 1990. "Igloos of Fire: Charcoal Production for Brazil's Programa Grande Carajás." Master's Thesis, University of Florida, Gainesville.

Silva, Fábio Carlos da. 1982. *A Frente Pioneira de Redenção: Origem e Desenvolvimento Capitalista numa área da Amazônia Oriental Brasileira.* Paper presented at the 9th meeting of PIPSA, Projeto de Intercâmbio Social na Agricultura, Agriculture in Amazon Group, Rio Branco, Acre, October.

Silva, Fábio Carlos da, and Léa Lobato de Carvalho e Oliveira. 1986. "A questão fundiária e a tensão social no meio rural paraense." *Pará Desenvolvimento 18*, 27 January:45–53.

Silva, José Graziano da. 1979. "A porteira já está fechando?" *Revista Ensaios de Opinião*, March, São Paulo.

Silva, José Graziano da, coord. 1978. *Estrutura Agrária e Produção de Subsistência na Agricultura Brasileira.* São Paulo: Hucitec.

Silva, Rogério da, M. de Souza, and C. Bezerra. 1988. *Contaminação por mercúrio nos garimpos Paraenses.* Belém: DNPM.

Simonsen, Roberto C. 1969. *História Econômica do Brasil, 1500–1820*. 6th edition. São Paulo: Companhia Editora Nacional.

Singer, Paul. 1982. "Neighborhood movements in São Paulo." In Helen Safa, ed., *Towards a Political Economy of Urbanization in Third World Countries*, 283–304. Delhi: Oxford University Press.

Sílvio, Costa Mattos, and Steven Lawrence Heim. 1978. "Projeto Mutuca, Pará: Relatório final de pesquisa." Unpublished research report. Goiânia: Minerasul, Mineração Serras do Sul.

Skocpol, Theda. 1979. *States and Social Revolutions: A Comparative Analysis of France, Russia, and China*. Cambridge: Cambridge University Press.

——1984. "Sociology's historical imagination." In Theda Skocpol, ed., *Vision and Method in Historical Sociology*, 1–21. Cambridge: Cambridge University Press.

Smith, Geri. 1989. "Space age shamans: The videotape." *Américas* 41(2):28–32.

Smith, Nigel. 1980/81. "Caimans, Capybaras, Otters, Manatees, and Man in Amazonia." *Biological Conservation* 19:177–187.

——1982. *Rainforest Corridors: The Transamazon Colonization Scheme*. Berkeley: University of California Press.

Soares, Glaucio A. D. 1978. "After the miracle." *Luso-Brazilian Review* 15(2):278–301.

Sondotécnica. 1974. "Plano de Desenvolvimento Integrado dos Vales dos Rios Xingu e Tapajós." Unpublished report.

Souza, Flávio Garcia de. 1979. "O agravamento da situação fundiária na Amazônia a partir da aprovação das exposições de motivos de No.s 5 e 6." Unpublished Manuscript, Rio de Janeiro.

Souza, Gerando Magela Cabral de, and José Maria do Régo. 1984. "Garimpo e cooperativismo mineiro no estado do Rio Grande do Norte." *Anais do XXXIII Congresso Brasileiro de Geologia*, 5081–5087.

Stefanini, Luiz de Lima. 1984. *A Questão Jusagrarista na Amazônia*. Belém: Edições CEJUP.

Steward, Julian, ed., 1946–50. *Handbook of South American Indians*. Washington, D.C.: Smithsonian Institution.

Steward, Julian, and Louise Faron. 1959. *Native Peoples of South America*. New York: McGraw Hill.

SUDAM (Superintendência para o Desenvolvimento da Amazônia). 1976. *Área de São Felix do Xingu-PA: Reconhecimento Pedológico*. Belém: SUDAM.

——1986. *I Plano de Desenvolvimento da Amazônia, Nova República, 1986–1989*, Projeto. April. Belém: SUDAM.

SUDAM/IBGE. 1988. *Levantamento da Alteração da Cobertura Vegetal Natural*. *Estado do Pará*. Belém: SUDAM.

Tardin, A. T., D. C. L. Lee, R. J. R. Santos, O. R. de Assis, M. P. dos Santos Barbosa, M. de Lourdes Moreira, M. T. Pereira, D. Silva, and C. P. dos Santos Filho. 1980. *Subprojeto Desmatamento, Convênio IBDF/CNPq-INPE 1979*. São José dos Campos, São Paulo: Instituto Nacional de Pesquisas Espaciais.

Taussig, Michael T. 1980. *The Devil and Commodity Fetishism in South America*. Chapel Hill: University of North Carolina Press.

Thompson, E. P. 1978. *The Poverty of Theory*. London: Merlin.

Tilly, Charles. 1978. *From Mobilization to Revolution*. Reading, MA: Addison-Wesley.

References   373

Treece, Dave. 1987. *Bound in Misery and Iron.* London: Survival International.
Trussell, James. 1975. "A re-estimation of the multiplying factors for the Brass technique for determining survivorship rates." *Population Studies* 29(1):97–108.
Turner, Frederick Jackson. 1921. *The Frontier in American History.* New York: Henry Holt.
Uhl, Christopher, and Robert Buschbacher. 1985. "A disturbing synergism between cattle ranch burning practices and selective tree harvesting in the eastern Amazon." *Biotropica* 17(4) (Dec.):265–268.
Umbuzeiro, Ubirajara Marques. n. d. *Altamira e Sua História.* Altamira: Gráfica Sagrada Família.
Vale, A. G., and E. R. Pereira. 1983. "Garimpos de ouro da região do Cumaru–PA." In Walter H. Schmaltz and Gerobal Guimarães, eds., *Garimpos do Brasil,* Avulsto No. 5. 199–236. Brasília: DNPM.
Veja, 10 September 1980.
Velho, Octávio Guilherme C. A. 1972. *Frentes de Expansão e Estrutura Agrária.* Rio: Zahar.
Verswijver, Gustaaf. 1978. "A história dos indios Kayapó." *Revista da Atualidade Indígena* 12:9–16.
Vidal, Lux. 1977. *Morte e Vida de uma Sociedade Indígena Brasileira.* São Paulo: Universidade de São Paulo/Hucitec.
——1981. "Pequeno guia prático de como invadir uma área indígena." In Dalmo de A. Dallari, Manuela C. da Cunha and Lux Vidal, eds., *A Questão da Terra Indígena.* Cadernos da Comissão Pró-Indio, No. 2, São Paulo: Global.
Vieira, Maria Antonieta da Costa. 1981. "Caçando o Destino (Um Estudo sobre a Luta de Resistência dos Posseiros do Sul do Pará)" Master's Thesis, Pontifica Universidade Católica, São Paulo.
Vosti, Stephen A. n. d. "Malaria among gold miners in southern Pará: Preliminary estimates of determinants and costs." Unpublished. Belo Horizonte: CEDE-PLAR.
Wagley, Charles. 1964. *Amazon Town: A Study of Man in the Tropics.* New York: Knopf.
——1985. "The Amazon caboclo" In Eugene P. Parker, ed., *The Amazon Caboclo: Historical and Contemporary Perspectives vii–xv.* Studies in Third World Societies Publication No. 32.
Weigel, Peter, and Charles R. Clement. 1981. "Relatório de viagem: Colônia Mata Geral, Conceição do Araguaia, Pará e arredores, GETAT em Marabá, PA e colaboração de outras entidades em Belém, 05 a 22 de julho de 1981." Unpublished. Manaus: Instituto Nacional de Pesquisas da Amazônia.
Weinstein, Barbara. 1983. *The Amazon Rubber Boom 1850–1920.* Stanford: Stanford University Press.
——1985. "Persistence of caboclo culture in the Amazon: The impact of the rubber trade, 1850–1920." *Studies in Third World Societies* 32:89–113.
Wesche, Rolf. 1985. "The transformation of rural caboclo society upon integration into Brazil's Amazonian frontier: A study of Itacoatiara." *Studies in Third World Societies* 32:115–142.
Willig, Cesar D. 1979. "Os garimpos e as empresas de mineração." *Mineração Metalúrgica* 52(409) (April):36–42.

References

Wilson, John F. 1985. *Ariquemes: Settlement and Class in a Brazilian Frontier Town.* Ph.D. diss., University of Florida, Gainesville.

Wolf, Eric R. 1982. *Europe and the People Without History.* Berkeley: University of California Press.

Wood, Charles H., and José Alberto Magno de Carvalho. 1988. *The Demography of Inequality in Brazil.* Cambridge: Cambridge University Press.

Wood, Charles H., and Marianne Schmink. 1978. "Blaming the victim: Small farmer production in an Amazon colonization project." *Studies in Third World Societies* 7:77–93.

World Bank. 1989. *Amazon Basin Malaria Control Project.* Staff Appraisal Report, Brazil. Washington, D.C.: The World Bank.

Wright, Eric Olin. 1979. *Class, Crisis, and the State.* London: Verso.

Wright, Robin M. 1987. "As guerras do ouro no Alto Rio Negro." *Povos Indígenas no Brasil - 85/86* Aconteceu Especial 17:85–88.

Yokomizo, Clando. 1989. *Incentivos financeiros e fiscais na pecuarização da Amazônia.* Brasília: IPEA/IPLAN Discussion paper no. 22.

Young, Frank, B. Edmonson, and N. Andes. 1983. "Community-level determinants of infant and child mortality in Peru." *Social Indicator Research* 12:65–81.

Zimmermann, Jörg. 1987. "Manaus importa alimentos e nas várzeas se produz fibras. Como explicar a contradição?" In Gerhard Kohlhepp and Achim Schrader, eds., *Homen e Natureza na Amazônia,* 207–219. Tübingen, Germany: Universität Tübingen.

INDEX

Abertura, see Political liberalization
AEA, see Association of Amazonian
Entrepreneurs
Aforamento: and Brazil nut extraction
in Marabá, 144; creation of, 63–64;
definition of, 63; legislation to
change, 65–66; and the Marabá
oligarchy, 153–54
Agrarian reform: abolishment of
MIRAD, 108; creation of Ministry
of Agrarian Reform (MIRAD), 106–
7; and escalation of rural violence,
107; the need for, 70–71; and the
New Republic, 96, 105–8; and the
1946 Constitution, 89n6; and the
1964 revolution, 61–64; in Pará,
107
Agricultural Colony Governor Aloysio
Chaves, creation of, 167
Aldeias: definition of, 38–39; effects
on Indians, 39; legislation
concerning, 40; see also Jesuits
Alves, Petrónio Dias, and the
discovery of gold in Pará, 234
Amazon Credit Bank, creation of, 48–
49, 59
Amazon Treaty for Cooperation and
Development, creation of, 121
Andrade Gutierrez Company:
constructing the PA-279, 290; and
educational program in São Felix do
Xingu, 333; history of, 195–96;
land purchase in southern Pará,
162–63; and the Tucumã
colonization project, 194–216; see
also Tucumã colonization project

Andrade, Ademir, and Rural Workers
Union election, 185
Araguaia War: history of, 4, 73; and
military populism, 73
Association of Amazonian
Entrepreneurs (AEA): and concern
for international meddling, 121–22;
and creation of, 77; and Nossa
Natureza, 123
Avelar, Bishop Estevio Cardoso, and
land conflicts, 153
Aviamento system: adapted to Brazil
nut collection, 46, 143–44, 258;
adapted to small scale mining, 52;
attempts to circumvent, 48;
disruption of during World War II,
56n51; factors that undermined, 50,
60; origins of, 43–45; in rubber
compared to mining, 52–53; in São
Felix do Xingu, 277, 281, 323–24,
325; in southern Pará, 141

Banner, Horace, and the Kayapó, 259
Barbalho, Jáder: 97; and abolishment
of INCRA, 107; and opposition to
Tucumã colonization project, 213,
215
Barbalho, Lucival, and Rural Workers
Union election, 185
Belém-Brasília Highway: and
Amazonia development, 49;
construction of, 10; effects in
southern Pará, 145–46; gold miners
barricading of, 230, 268
Belterra: construction of, 47; see also
Henry Ford

Bentes, Asdrubal, 106
Bessone, Leopoldo, and payment to
Andrade Gutierrez, 216
Bezerra, Haroldo: actions in Cuca,
242; actions in Serra Pelada, 229
BR-364 Highway, paving of, 115
Brasília, effects of moving the capital
inland, 10
Brazilian Institute for Renewable
Natural Resources and the
Environment (IBAMA), creation of,
122
Brazilian Mining Institute (IBRAM),
lobbying to mechanize Serra Pelada,
226, 228
Brazilian National Bishop's Council
(CNBB), 103
Brazil nut collection: and *aviamento*
system, 143–44, 258; and declining
production, 165n46; early history of
258; and economic diversification,
46; in Marabá and Conceição do
Araguaia, 140, 143; method of
collecting, 164n13; in São Felix do
Xingu, 278

Cabanagem revolt, 41–42
Caboclo: definition of, 8; meaning of,
55n35; and new forms of
extractivism, 1920–1960, 46;
origins of, 45–46; in São Felix do
Xingu, 280
Calha Norte, creation of, 96, 110–12
Camio, Father Aristides: actions in
Xinguara, 182; sentencing of, 183
CAPEMI, and Tucuruí hydroelectric
dam, 99
Carneiro, Oziel, 97
Carajás iron ore project: construction
of, 6; discovery of, 66
Catholic Church: actions in São Felix
do Xingu, 287–89; support of
peasants in southern Pará, 4, 102–3,
180–83; *see also* Jesuits
Cattle ranching: and contests over
land, 2; controversy over, 100
Caucho, in southern Pará, 142, 256
Cândido, and the founding of
Ourilândia, 206–7
CCPY, *see* Commission for the
Creation of a Yanomami Park

CEAT, *see* Special Coordinator for the
Araguaia-Tocantins
CEDI, *see* Ecumenical Center for
Documentation and Information
Change, social: contingent versus
patterned form of change, 345;
defined, 19–20; and relationship
between structure and action,
32n29
Chapeu de Couro: and the founding
of Xinguara, 168–69; murder of,
169, 188
Charcoal, production in Marabá, 99–
100, 128n13
Child mortality, *see* São Felix do
Xingu
Christian Base Communities: role of,
103; in São Felix do Xingu, 288; *see
also* Catholic Church
CIMI, *see* Missionary Indian Council
CNBB, *see* Brazilian National Bishop's
Council
Cold War: decline in the relevance of,
126; and military action in southern
Pará, 4; *see also* Developmentalism;
Ideology
Collor, Fernando: and nuclear
weapons in Amazonia, 131n45; and
the Yanomami, 120–21
Colonization projects, military, and
Calha Norte, 110; *see also* Crisis
colonization; Grupo Executivo de
Terras do Araguaia Tocantins
(GETAT)
Colonization projects, private (in
Pará), reasons for, 6; *see also*
Tucumã Colonization Project
Colonization projects, public (in Pará):
creation of 1–2; and crisis
colonization, 7, 172; criticisms of,
5, 76–77; state project in Xinguara,
167–69
Commission for the Creation of a
Yanomami Park (CCPY), creation of,
111
Companhia Vale do Rio Doce
(CVRD): 66; and environmental
program, Carajás, 99; and mining
research permits, 68
Conceição do Araguaia: history of,
140–57, 255, 259; and the PA-150,

2; and ranchers, 147–49; and the
rubber boom, 141–42; and social
conflict, 188
Concentration of landholdings: and
GETAT, 83, 130n40, 176–80; and
the history of frontiers, 11; in Pará,
127n4; and SUDAM fiscal
incentives, 97–98; and the Tucumã
colonization project, 199–200,
212–13; in Xinguara, 180, 191
Conceptual framework, definition of
13, 32n35
Conflict, see Contests
Constitutive aspects of social action:
definition of, 17, 349
Contests: and the analysis of social
change, 19–20; 24–25; competition
versus resistence, 14; and the
conceptual approach, 13–20;
conflict versus violence, 31n24; and
the constitutive aspects of social
action, 17
Contests over gold: in Cuca, 240–42;
during colonial period, 90n31; and
federal troops, 221; and Indians,
109, 131n48, 221, 233; on Kayapó
lands, 265–68; in Serra Pelada,
222–32; and similarities to land
conflicts, 86–87; in southern Pará,
tactics miners use in, 130n36; see
also Cuca gold field; Cumaru gold
field; Jabá gold field; Political
mobilization of miners; Serra Pelada
Contests over Indian lands: and Calha
Norte, 96, 110–11; and the
Catholic Church, 102–3; and early
history of the Kayapó, 254–55; and
ELETRONORTE's dam projects,
117–18; and gold miners, 7, 221,
232–33; and the Kayapó since
1945, 261–64; and legislation
concerning demarcation of Indian
lands, 108–10; and the military
worldview, 74–75; and the PA-150,
158; and the PA-279, 158–63; see
also Indian rights; Kayapó; Political
mobilization of Indians; Yanomami
Contests over land: causes of, 2;
dynamics of, 79–83; estimates of
workers killed in Pará, 187; federal
reaction to, 6–7; and the history of

frontiers in Brazil, 10–13; increase
in violence of, 186–90; and the
matrix of shaping influences, 9, 18–
20; and the PA-150, 152; and
perceived communist subversion, 4,
69; in São Felix do Xingu, 302–6;
and the shift in development
priorities, 78; and the state
colonization project in Xinguara,
167–72; in Xinguara area, 172–76;
see also Political mobilization of
peasants
Contests over timber: and effects on
land occupation and clearing, 157;
history in southern Pará, 154–58;
and intervillage rivalries among the
Kayapó, 264; in Xinguara area, 168;
in São Felix do Xingu, 292–94
CPT, see Pastoral Land Commission
Crisis colonization: and CEAT, 172;
definition and objectives of, 7, 349;
and GETAT, 81; see also
Colonization projects, public;
Grupo Executivo de Terras do
Araguaia Tocantins (GETAT)
Cuca gold field: as example of typical
garimpo, 220; and new technology,
221, 234–40; and the Tucumã
colonization project, 204, 207; see
also Contests over gold; Political
mobilization of miners
Cumaru gold field: as example of
typical garimpo, 220; history of,
232–34; and the Kayapó, 267–69;
and new technology, 221; see also
Contests over gold; Political
mobilization of miners
Curió: abilities of, 74; actions in
Cajueiro, 182–83; and the Araguaia
War, 73; and battle for Serra
Pelada, 225–32; and elections in
1982, 88, 104, 154, 225; and
organization of Serra Pelada, 223–
34; and Rural Workers Union
election in Xinguara, 186; and Serra
Pelada, 104, 223
CVRD, see Companhia Vale do Rio
Doce

Debt for nature swaps, definition of,
113, 132n59

Decree Law 1164; and federal takeover of state lands, 71–72; revocation of, 107, 189; and São Felix do Xingu, 286; and state colonization project in Xinguara, 169

Deforestation: and cattle ranching, 100; and the contest for resources, 26, 344; and criticism of development priorities, 8; degree of, 100–1, 129n20; and IBDF, 127n6, 134–35n84

Denis, General Bayma, 124

Departamento Nacional de Pesquisa Mineral (DNPM): and conflicts over mineral rights, 86–88; and regulation of mining activities, 67–69

Developmentalism: criticism of, 91n33; definition of, 5–6, 30n10, 39n9; and disdain for Indian rights, 74–75; and Getúlio Vargas, 47, 69; and Giovanni Queiroz, 150–51; joined to national security doctrine, 69; and perceived subversion, 6, 30n11; and preference for large projects, 347; see also Development priorities; Incentives to Amazonian development; Indian rights

Development priorities: and the change from public to private colonization, 191–92; change in, 5–6, 76–78, 351; continuities under New Republic, 126, 353; contradictions in, 2, 15, 61, 346–47; criticism of, 91n33; and environmental concerns, 8, 96–97; the need for new, 29; perspectives about, in São Felix do Xingu, 21; see also Developmentalism

Diet, see São Felix do Xingu

Directive 005, purpose of, 64

Directive 006, purpose of, 64–65

Disease: and child mortality in São Felix do Xingu, 335; and the division of villages, 258, 273n21; effects on Indian population in colonial Brazil, 39–40; effects on Indian population of road construction projects, 75; the Kayapó, 261; and the Maria Bonita

gold field, 274n53; mining and malaria, 101; see also Malaria;

DNPM, see Departamento Nacional de Pesquisa Mineral

DOCEGEO: and actions in São Felix do Xingu, 299–301; buying gold in Serra Pelada, 87

Ecological zoning of Amazonia, politics of, 101–2

Ecumenical Center for Documentation and Information (CEDI), creation of, 116

ELETRONORTE (Centrais Elétricas do Norte do Brasil): and the Kayapó Indians, 118, 271; and mining investments, 67; and negotiations with residents affected by Tucuruí, 104

Emancipation decree, effect on Indians, 75–76

Environmental concerns: and development discourse, 16; and development policy, 8; and green geopolitics, 121–25; and greenhouse effect, 113; growing popularity of, 96–97; history of, 132–33n61; and links to international lobbies, 16, 96–97; 112–14, 352; and perceived subversion, 6, 30n11; and World Bank and Inter-American Development Bank, 113–17

Environment and Indigenous Communities Protection Project (PMACI): creation of, 115; implementation of, 124

Environmental Defense Fund, role of, 114

Extractive reserves, creation of, 10, 117

Farias, Djalma, 183

Figueiredo, General: 80, 95; and the Tucumã colonization project, 197, 209

Filho, Jucá: attack on Indian rights, 109–10; and gold mining on Indian lands, 111; signing of Curió's bill, 230–31; veto of Curio's Serra

Marabá: and Brazil nut collection, 143–45, 164n13, 165n46; and highways, 2, 145–46, 151–54; history of, 140–57; initial study of, 20–22; and mining, 144–45, 221, 246, 268; as national security area, 4, 153; and the rubber boom, 141–42; *see also* Charcoal

Marabuto, Nelson, and the Kayapó, 268

Mata Geral: history of, 171–72; *see also* Crisis colonization; Grupo Executivo de Terras do Araguaia Tocantins (GETAT)

Matrix of shaping influences: definition of, 18–20; and the interpretation of change, 351; and new alliances, 97

Melo, Flaviano, 117

Melo, Sebastião José de Carvalho, *see* Marquis de Pombal

Mendes, Chico: biography of, 9; efforts to resist deforestation, 116–17; views of, 16, 133n67

Mercury, pollution by, 101, 129nn23–25, 247n6, 310

Military populism; consequences of, 92n58; and GETAT, 83, 95; origins of, 73; and Serra Pelada, 88, 95, 225; *see also* Crisis colonization

Miners: conflicts with mining companies, 7, 14, 294–301; ideologies of, 15; and lifestyle of, 221; and Mining Code of 1967, 67–68; *see also* Contests over gold; Political mobilization of miners

Mining boom, 1950–1964, 50–53

Mining Code of 1967: creation of, 61; and procedures to regulate companies and *garimpeiros*, 67

Mining fields (*garimpos*), closed versus open, 51, 83, 234–35

Mining, small scale: and absorption of rural labor by, 87, 94n87, 244; compared to traditional *aviamento* system, 52–53; effects on the town of São Felix do Xingu, 278, 310; history of, 51–53; social and economic effects of, 243–47; social relations of production in, 51–53; technological change in, 83–88,

93n72, 234–40; *see also* Contests over gold; Political mobilization of miners

Ministry of Agrarian Reform (MIRAD): abolishment of, 108; creation of, 106–7; and the Tucumã colonization project, 213–15; *see also* Agrarian reform

MIRAD, *see* Ministry of Agrarian Reform

Miranda, José Porfírio, role in the rubber boom, 257–58

Missionary Indian Council (CIMI): creation of, 103; investigation of, 122

Monteiro, Walcir, and São Felix do Xingu, 301

Moura, Sebastião Rodrigues de, *see* Curió

Municípios, creation of new, 49–50, 146, 281

National Council of Brazilian Bishops, and the Yanomami, 111

National Environmental Policy, creation of, 122

National Integration Plan, *see* Plano de Integração Nacional

National Radar Mapping Program, *see* RADAMBRASIL

National Security Council: and agrarian policy, 81; and Directives 005 and 006, 64; and GETAT, 7, 81–82; *see also* Grupo Executivo de Terras do Araguaia Tocantins

National Wildlife Federation, role of, 114

Natural Resources Defense Council, role of, 114

Nava, Ari, and the discovery of gold in Pará, 234–35

Neto, Delfim, view of the frontier, 166

Neves, Tancredo, 106

New Republic: and agrarian reform, 105–8, 352; and Calha Norte, 110–12; and contests in Amazonia, 96; and FUNAI, 131n49; and Indian policies, 108–10; and revocation of Decree Law #1, 107, 164; *see also* Political liberalization

Nossa Natureza: creation of, 122; objectives of, 123–24
Nunes, Alacid, politics of, 286

Oliveira, Iris de: 120; and land titles in Xinguara, 182
Operation Amazonia, creation of, 12, 59, 76; *see also* Incentives to Amazonian development
Ourilândia: founding of, 206–9; relationship with Tucumã, 207–9; and support of gold miners in Cuca, 242; *see also* Tucumã colonization project

PA-150: construction of, 2, 151; and new towns, 151–52
PA-279: and the Andrade Gutierrez Company, 162–63; anticipated effects of, 22–23; anticipation of in São Felix do Xingu, 284–86, 289–91; construction of, 21–22, 139–40, 166, 158–63; and migrants traveling, 276; precursors to, 142–43; and the Tucumã colonization project, 194, 198, 203–4, 206–7, 209
Padre Chico: actions in Xinguara, 182; sentencing of, 183
Paiakan, Chief, and contest for Kayapó lands, 262, 268–69, 271
Paiva, Francisco, founding of Ourilândia, 206–7
Passarinho, Jarbas, politics of, 286
Pastoral Land Commission (CPT): 102; and the death count in Tucumã, 215–16; and estimate of number of workers killed in Pará, 187; and land conflicts in southern Pará, 153
Patronage, effects of population growth on, 287
Pedra Preta mining site, battle over, 301
PIN, *see* Plano de Integração Nacional.
Placer miners, *see* Miners
Plan for the Valorization of the Amazon, creation of, 49
Plano de Integração Nacional (PIN):

and changing development priorities, 6, 8–10; creation of, 1, 70; criticism of, 70–71; and New Republic, 96; *see also* Colonization project, public
PMACI, *see* Environment and Indigenous Communities Protection Project
POLAMAZONIA: abolishment of 112; and roads in southern Pará, 159; creation of, 5, 78; and large projects, 98; and São Felix do Xingu, 284; and Tucumã colonization project, 203; *see also* Incentives to Amazonian development
Political liberalization: and criticisms of the Tucumã colonization project, 199, 212–13; and effect on contests in Amazonia, 9, 95, 102, 351
Political mobilization: basis of, 13; and the greening of the development discourse, 97; increasing sophistication of, 354; increasing visibility of, 104–5; and links to international environmental lobbies, 8, 96–97, 112–14, 125–26; and political liberalization, 95, 102; and role of communications network, 102; and role of nongovernmental organizations (NGOs), 114, 116, and social change, 350
Political mobilization of Indians: 8; and the Catholic Church, 103; and the Kayapó, 117–18, 261–72; in other countries, 130n32; *see also* Contests over Indian lands; Kayapó
Political mobilization of miners: 8; in Cuca, 240–42; and growing political power, 221–22; and the invasion of the Tucumã colonization project, 203–4; and the National Garimpeiro Union, 228; in Serra Pelada, 103–4, 225–32; *see also* Contests over gold
Political mobilization of peasants: 8; and the Catholic Church, 102–3; effects of mining boom on peasants, 87; and the invasion of the Tucumã colonization project, 211–12; in

Xinguara, 170–72; *see also* Contests over land
Political mobilization of residents affected by Tucuruí dam: 104; role of Catholic Church, 104
Political mobilization of rubber tappers, in Acre, 103, 116–17
POLONOROESTE: creation of, 78; history of, 114–17
Pombal, Marquis de: 39; policies of, 40–41
Pombo, Chief, and contest for Kayapó lands, 262, 265, 266
Portuguese exploration of Amazonia, 38
Posey, Darrell, and the Kayapó, 270
Posse: and landholdings in São Felix do Xingu, 320; and land legislation, 64; origins of, 42
Posseiros: definition of, 2; ideologies of, 15–16, 79–80; *see also* Contests over land; Political mobilization of peasants
Power, sources of, 14–18
Precolonial Amazonia, characteristics of, 37

Queiroz, Giovanni, and elections in Conceição do Araguaia, 150–51

RADAMBRASIL (National Radar Mapping Program): and mineral research in Amazonia, 66; and soil quality in southern Pará, 159
RDC, *see* Rubber Development Corporation
Redenção: and gold mining, 220–21, 232–33, 268; history of, 149–51; and the timber boom, 154–56, 292
Regatão (river trader): opposition to during rubber boom, 54n22; origins of, 41; role in rubber boom, 42–43; *see also* Rubber boom
Reis, Rangel: 75; visit to southern Pará, 150
Research design, description of, 20–28
Ribeiro, Antonio Marques, elected prefect of São Felix do Xingu, 281
Ribeiro, Darcy, and work with SPI, 260–61

Rio Branco gold field, history of, 265–67; *see also* Contests over gold; Political mobilization of miners
River trader, *see* Regatão
Rondônia: and malaria, 101; and public colonization, 5; and tin production, 51, 56n65, 85, 94n85–86
Rubber Credit Bank: abolishment of, 277; creation of, 48
Rubber Development Corporation (RDC), creation of, 48
Rubber extraction: collapse of, 45–46; economic effects of, 44–45; and the histories of Marabá and Conceição do Araguaia, 141–43; history of rubber boom, 42–43; and the history of São Felix do Xingu, 277–78; and migration to Amazonia, 44; production and marketing during rubber boom, 43–45; renewed demand during World War II, 259–60
Rubber plantations: in Brazil, 46–47; and the per-unit costs of production, 45, 54n30
Rubber tappers: during rubber boom, 43–45; effects of collapse of rubber trade on, 45–46; and environmental concerns, 16; *see also* Political mobilization of rubber tappers
Rural Democratic Union (UDR): actions in southern Pará, 188; creation of, 107
Rural Workers Union: and GETAT, 183–86; in São Felix do Xingu, 287

SAGRI, *see* Secretaria de Agricultura
Santa Tereza ranch, founding of, 147–48
Santana, Belmiro, and fishing cooperative in São Felix do Xingu, 292
Sarney, José: 105; and IBAMA, 122; and Indian lands, 109, 120; and North-South railroad, 132n55
São Felix do Xingu: agricultural production and employment in, 319–22; changes in food consumption in, 329–33; choice as research site, 21–24; conflicts

9; and attempts to keep migrants out, 203–4; compared to INCRA and GETAT projects, 194; comparison with Xinguara, 216; criticisms of, 197, 199, 212–15; demise of, 209–16; description of, 200–1; and the founding of Ourilândia, 206–9; gold miners invasion of, 203–4; impact of gold economy on, 205–6; INCRA handling of, 196–200; and land sales, 201–3; and the PA-279 road, 203; planning of, 194–95; and POLAMAZONIA, 203; reasons for, 195–96; Senate approval of, 196–200; and support of gold miners in Cuca, 242; *see also* Colonization projects, private

Tucuruí hydroelectric dam: construction of 6; criticism of, 98–99; resistence to, 104

U.S. Steel, and mineral rights in Amazonia, 66–67

UDR, *see* Rural Democratic Union

UNI, *see* Union of Indigenous Nations

Union of Indigenous Nations (UNI), creation of, 103

United Nations Conference on Environment and Development, 1992, decision to host in Brazil, 124–25

Urbanization, in São Felix do Xingu, 281–82

Val, Lanari do: and Cumaru gold field, 232–33; and land acquisition in southern Pará, 147–48

Vargas, Getúlio: industrialization policies of, 47; and meeting with rubber traders, 260

Vargas, Luis: and the founding of Redenção, 149–50; and support for Giovanni Queiroz, 150

Veiga, Colonel João Nobre da, 75

Vidal, Lux, and the route of the PA-279, 159–61

Vieira, Antonio, 38

Vieira, Ulysses, electoral campaign and colonization project, 167–68

Vigneau, Father Guillaume, and the Kayapó, 255

Vilanova, Friar Gil, and the Kayapó, 255

Violence, *see* Contests

Washington Accords: creation of, 48; effects in southern Pará, 259–60; *see also* Rubber extraction

World Bank, and Amazon development projects, 113–17

World War II: impact on rubber production, 47–48; and U.S.-Brazil alliance, 55–56n47

Yanomami Indians: and gold miners, 111, 119–20; health conditions of, 134n76; and land demarcation, 119–121; and land rights, 96; as security threat, 74, 111